THE LEGACY OF ARAB-ISLAM IN AFRICA

A Quest for Inter-religious Dialogue

RELATED TITLES PUBLISHED BY ONEWORLD

Speaking in God's Name: Islamic Law, Authority and Women, Khaled Abou El-Fadl,
   ISBN 1–85168–262–7
On Being a Muslim: Finding a Religious Path in the World Today, Farid Esack,
   ISBN 1–85168–146–9
Qur'ān, Liberation and Pluralism, Farid Esack, ISBN 1–85168–121–3
Revival and Reform in Islam, Fazlur Rahman, ISBN 1–85168–204–X

THE LEGACY OF ARAB-ISLAM IN AFRICA

A Quest for Inter-religious Dialogue

JOHN ALEMBILLAH AZUMAH

THE LEGACY OF ARAB-ISLAM IN AFRICA

A Oneworld book

First published by Oneworld Publications, 2001
Reprinted 2011, 2014, 2016, 2018, 2020, 2021

© John A. Azumah

All rights reserved.
Copyright under Berne Convention.
A CIP record for this title is available
from the British Library

ISBN: 978-1-85168-273-7
eISBN: 978-1-78074-685-2

Cover design by Design Deluxe
Typeset by LaserScript Limited, Mitcham, UK
Printed and bound in Great Britain by Clays Ltd, Elcograf S.p.A.

Oneworld Publications
10 Bloomsbury Street
London WC1B 3SR
England

Stay up to date with the latest books,
special offers, and exclusive content from
Oneworld with our newsletter

Sign up on our website
www.oneworld-publications.com

This Work is Dedicated to the memory of the tens of Millions of Africans who, in the name of God, were made to sacrifice their Lives, Freedom, Dignity, Heritage and History for no other reason than the content of their beliefs and colour of their skin; and to those of the present generation who are committed to an honest inter-faith dialogue and the promotion of peaceful and equal co-existence in the pluralistic African context.

CONTENTS

Acknowledgements	ix
Preface	xi

1. A GLANCE AT POST-COLONIAL ASSESSMENTS OF THE WESTERN-CHRISTIAN AND ARAB-ISLAMIC LEGACIES IN TROPICAL AFRICA — 1

Definition of the Problem	1
A Critique of Prevailing Approaches and Perceptions	7
Methodology, Outline and Sources	19

2. INDIGENOUS AFRICA AS A CULTIVATING GROUND FOR ARAB-ISLAM — 24

Introduction	24
The Introduction of Islam to Tropical Africa	24
The Indigenous African Environment and Conversion to Islam	33
Conclusion	61

3. MUSLIM JIHAD AND BLACK AFRICA — 63

Introduction	63
Sunni Muslim Doctrine of Jihad	64
Jihad: Theories and Campaigns in Africa	68
Interpreting the Jihad Tradition in Africa	80
Evaluating the Jihadists' *Shari'a* Rule	100
Conclusion	107

viii *The Legacy of Arab-Islam in Africa*

4. MUSLIM SLAVERY AND BLACK AFRICA — 109

Introduction	109
Slavery in Muslim Africa: Indigenous or Islamic Stimuli?	109
Classical Muslim Ideology of Enslavement	124
Muslim Slavery and the Slave Trade: The Arab-Oriental Dimension	141
Muslim Slavery and the Slave Trade: The African Dimension	147
The Various Roles of Slaves in Muslim Lands	156
The Condition of Slaves in Muslim Lands: Theory versus Practice	160
Conclusion	168

5. ENCOUNTERING THE ENCOUNTERS: ARAB-ISLAM AND BLACK AFRICAN EXPERIENCE — 170

Introduction	170
Truth, Dialogue and Confessional Loyalty	171
The Need to Rethink Arab-Islam in Light of the African Experience	180
The Arab Factor in Sunni Islamic Orthodoxy	216
Conclusion	228

6. CONCLUSION — 230

Bibliography	241
Index	257

ACKNOWLEDGEMENTS

I want, first, to thank God Almighty for granting me the grace, strength and good health of body, mind and spirit to undertake this research. Second, I would like to express my deepest gratitude to the following officers of the Presbyterian Church of Ghana: The Revd E.S. Mate-Kodjo (now retired Synod Clerk) and Revd Dr D.N.A. Kpobi, Inter-Church and Ecumenical Relations Secretary respectively for their individual interests and encouragement which made the study possible.

My profound gratitude also goes to the Ökumenisches Studienwerk in Bochum, Germany, for the generous scholarship offered me and my family for the duration of my Masters and Ph.D. programmes at the University of Birmingham between the periods of September 1993 and July 1998. There is no gainsaying that without their financial support this study would have been impossible. The disciplined and well-organized administration of the staff ensured that we received our monthly grant regularly and consistently. To all the staff, I say THANK YOU and GOD BLESS YOU ALL!

The Revd Dr David Thomas of the Centre for the Study of Islam and Christian–Muslim Relations, Selly Oak, Birmingham, who supervised this work as a doctoral thesis deserves thanks that words seem inadequate to convey. Dr Thomas was more of a senior brother than an academic supervisor to me during the course of the study. There is no doubt that his astute academic mind and the critical eye he cast over the work coupled with his uplifting compliments all helped in guiding, shaping and spurring me to this point. All I can say is THANK YOU, DAVID!

The warm fatherly guidance of Dr Sigvard von Sicard and Prof. Jorgen Nielsen (both of the Centre for the Study of Islam and Christian–Muslim

x *The Legacy of Arab-Islam in Africa*

Relations) has been of immense help to me during the course of my study. They both also took the time to read through the work and made valuable comments; those of Dr Sicard in relation to the East African situation have been especially helpful. In the same category is the Revd Dr David Marshall. David is a very good personal friend who made time to proofread the work in its doctoral thesis form making numerous useful and helpful grammatical corrections. God Bless you, David!

I cannot end this acknowledgement without mention of Prof. Humphrey Fisher of the School of Oriental and African Studies, London. Prof. Fisher read through some sections of the work as a doctoral thesis but more so as it was being revised for publication. In both cases, Fisher's critical comments and queries (most of which I accepted and some of which I resisted) have helped me a lot in reshaping the work to its present state. Dr Robert Shick, a colleague of mine at the Henry Martyn Institute, India, also read through the first four chapters of the book and made useful grammatical corrections. I also wish to express my sincere thanks to Mary Starkey, the copy editor, for her professionalism in carrying out her task on the manuscript, and to all the staff of Oneworld Publications. To all of you I say THANK YOU! Of course, I take full responsibility for the ideas expressed in this book and none of the above-mentioned persons should in any way be blamed for any shortcomings in this work.

Last but by no means least, My wife, Grace Asidbe, and children, Benjamin Asuguru, Nathaniel Apenada and Malemma Elizabeth also played a unique part in the successful completion of this work both as a doctoral thesis and in its present form as a book. Not least for the warmth and comfort they, and only they, could provide especially in times when the boredom and frustration of the research reared its ugly head. I want to thank you in our local language, *Mposia pamm!* The same goes to friends and relatives in Ghana, the UK (especially Dr Ida Glaser and Colin Chapman) and now India, many others too numerous to mention by name. Thanks and God Bless you all.

PREFACE

Since the second half of the twentieth century, inter-religious dialogue between people of different faith traditions, especially between Christians and Muslims, has gained much currency. Without denying the fact that dialogue still means different things to different people, inter-religious dialogue in general and Christian–Muslim dialogue in particular is seen as a move away from the mutual polemics, stereotyping and prejudices that have plagued and often been a source of numerous conflicts in past and present encounters between the two faith communities. The primary aim of dialogue therefore is to gain a better understanding of the Other and so do away with prejudices and stereotyping with the view of enhancing better relations and peaceful co-existence in a religiously pluralistic world.

Countless international, regional, national and local meetings, seminars, conferences, colloquia, etc., between people of different religious traditions and Christians and Muslims in particular with the view of promoting inter-religious dialogue have now become the order of our times. I have had the privilege of attending quite a few of these inter-religious conferences and gained a lot from them. One fact that is very apparent in all such inter-religious, especially Christian–Muslim, gatherings and discussions is that contemporary inter-religious relations are heavily coloured and most often revolve on the axis of various historical events. To use the words of a participant at one such Christian–Muslim consultation, 'history is very much the mistress of our lives. We must take history very seriously if we are to look to the future.'[1]

---

1. Joseph Hajjar, at a Christian–Muslim consultation organized by the World Council of Churches in Chambésy, Switzerland, in 1976. See *Christian Mission and Islamic Da'wah: Proceedings of the Chambésy Dialogue Consultation* (Leicester: Islamic Foundation, 1982), p. 97.

xii *The Legacy of Arab-Islam in Africa*

My own limited experience at Christian–Muslim dialogue consultations and conferences has led me to believe that history is more the mistress of contemporary Christian–Muslim relations than the Holy Scriptures of the respective communities, which are themselves heavily influenced and shaped by their own historical contexts. The call to take history seriously is therefore crucial if we are to understand, appreciate and better deal with contemporary inter-religious difficulties, tensions and conflicts. Taking history seriously will also help us learn the necessary lessons from the historical encounters in charting a path for better relations in the future. This means that the documentation and interpretation of what actually happened in the past is more than just an academic exercise. In a sense it is a sacred duty!

There is no gainsaying that most 'academic' and 'scientific' researches in the social sciences have been carried out either to serve specific ideological interests or used by successive generations to serve such purposes with far-reaching disastrous consequences for human life and dignity. As a child I remember a popular maxim that 'book no lie', i.e., written documents are infallible! The wisdom, or rather nonsense, of this maxim still holds sway in many societies. What is read, taught, heard or watched on televisions has mesmerizing effects in shaping lifestyles and relationships. Due to the impact of the media, it is very common nowadays to hear calls from civil and religious leaders for responsible journalism. It is high time though that these calls were extended to academics to exercise responsibility in their professions since the impact of their works taught in schools, colleges and read in university libraries have even far greater and lasting impact in shaping perceptions, attitudes and relationships between communities.

One of the greatest benefits of the post-colonial era with regard to inter-faith relations in general and Christian–Muslim relations in particular is the emergence and dominance of literature especially from the Western-Christian side aimed at presenting Islamic beliefs and Muslim history in a more positive and sympathetic light.[2] This has been accomplished mainly through the study of Islamic beliefs and Muslim history through Muslim sources. Bernard Lewis, one of the most outstanding Western scholars of Islam of the twentieth century, makes this submission in the following words: 'The scholarly student of Islam – especially if he is not a Muslim – studies Islam as a historical phenomenon, as a civilization with a long and distinguished record of achievement. The evidence he uses is that provided by Muslims – what they have said, written, and done in the course of the centuries.'[3]

---

2. I am aware that some scholars have demonized Western academic discourse on Islam ("Orientalism") and basically see not only nothing good in it but have in fact portrayed it as an attempt to undermine Islam and perpetuate Western dominance over the Muslim peoples. See for instance E. Said, *Orientalism* (New York: Vintage, 1979).

3. B. Lewis, *Islam and the West* (New York: Oxford University, 1993), p. 194 n. 1.

Preface xiii

The approach of studying Islam through Muslim evidence therefore became the standard academic norm, especially in post-colonial Western discourse. This approach is not only obviously reasonable, but crucial in light of past experience, especially medieval Western European approaches. However, the focus on Muslim evidence needs to be critical. All scholarly students and even more so non-Muslim students of Islam should resist the temptation of treating Muslim evidence as sacrosanct or representing the whole truth. There are two main reasons for the need for a critical approach quite apart from the fact that it is an essential part of every scholar's research. The first reason is that there is hardly any uniformity or consensus on most issues in Muslim sources. Muslims like all other groups have differed on many issues right from the very inception of Islam. This difference of opinions has to be acknowledged and respected by non-Muslim students.

The second reason why the Muslim evidence must be approached critically is that Muslims did not live and act out their history in isolation from non-Muslims. In fact, Islamic history from the very beginning has been the constant interaction between Muslim and non-Muslim groups. For instance, in the first three centuries of Muslim history in the Middle East and North Africa, Muslims lived, interacted and ruled over majority Christian communities. Similarly in India for a very long time Muslims constituted a minority ruling class over an overwhelming Hindu population. The same is true of sub-Saharan Africa where for nearly thirteen centuries Muslims lived with and acted out their history in the midst of overwhelming non-Muslim societies. In all these situations the Islamic past cannot be adequately understood and appreciated if our attention is focused solely on Muslim evidence. The non-Muslim evidence is just as essential in any such academic research.

Unfortunately in the study of the Islamic past in post-modern Western academic discourse non-Muslim scholars became preoccupied if not obsessed with Muslim evidence in the form of texts with little or no attempt either to acknowledge and respect the diversity of opinions within the Muslim sources themselves or to take the non-Muslim point of view into consideration. This procedure has distorted local histories with resultant negative consequences on Muslim relations with non-Muslims in many non-Western societies. Some individual scholars have, for various reasons, even gone beyond acknowledging the merits and achievements of the Islamic dispensation to romanticizing and idealizing the Islamic past.

Some of the reasons for this tendency, particularly in post-colonial Western discourse, may include the sense of inherited guilt about the colonial and missionary past. This past has since come under severe attack especially in Third World post-colonial discourse in general and Muslim discourse in particular. Another reason could be the general spiritual disillusionment in modern xiv *The Legacy of Arab-Islam in Africa*

Western society which has led and continues to lead many Westerners to Islam as an alternative. The temptation in such situations is to look for or invent something with which to judge the failings of Western society. Not a few Western Islamicists in the post-colonial era have ended up converting to Islam. Whatever the reasons and motives for this tendency, it is my conviction that the present idealization of Islamic traditions and history is just as detrimental to Christian–Muslim dialogue at local, national, regional and international levels as the past demonization.

It is right to insist that we should desist from using modern standards as measuring rods in passing judgements on past generations. But it is equally vital that we do not allow modern sensibilities to lead us into calling spades big spoons or covering up and denying what past generations took pride in. But unfortunately this is precisely what lies at the root of post-colonial Western liberal discourse on Islam. The bug of political correctness that has infected a large section of post-colonial Western society has in no small way vitiated a significant section of post-modern Western discourse on Islam. Hence in the study of Islam in the West, the dominant convention is that a critical approach is reserved for the Christian past but forbidden for the Muslim past. In this way some Western scholars have allowed memories and guilt of their own histories to affect their invaluable discourse of other histories which in turn has compromised inter-faith relations at various localities, as this work will show from the African context.

The focus on particular versions of the Muslim evidence with little or no regard to the diversity of Muslim opinions and the non-Muslim point of view is the approach that has dominated post-colonial discourse on Islam in sub-Saharan Africa. Commenting on the study of Islam in West Africa, David Robinson observes that the 'different Islamic realities – and their validity – have not been appreciated in the historical literature'. Robinson goes on to point out features that distort the appreciation of the variety of Islamic practice and belief in West Africa. 'First, the literature has been dominated by an *orientalist* approach, in which philological and theological training are paramount. The commentator typically knows Arabic in order to read the relevant indigenous literature [*sic*]. His task, as he moves from the center of the Islamic world to a periphery such as West Africa, is to discern and recount the spread of Islam and especially of Islamic orthodoxy, to the point where the peripheral region can be classed as a *Dar al-Islam* ("the Abode of Islam").'[4]

In Robinson's view, 'the orientalist bias' is further strengthened as the commentators limited themselves 'especially to the legitimating documents of

---

4. D. Robinson, 'An Approach to Islam in West African History', in K.W. Harrow (ed.), *Faces of Islam in African Literature* (Portsmouth: Heinemann Educational Books, 1991), pp. 107–8.

Preface xv

those who share their belief that the essential story is the progression of Islam and Islamic orthodoxy. The best case in point is the primary documentation created by the founders of the Sokoto Caliphate of Northern Nigeria and the secondary reinforcement created in the last thirty years by Islamicists on the basis of the primary material. The result is a very strong *received tradition* which makes it more difficult to reconstruct the history of religious practice in the late eighteenth and early nineteenth century Hausaland' (his emphasis).[5]

Thus we have a situation of Western scholarship not only constructing the history of Islam in West Africa from particular versions of the Muslim evidence, but even more crucially taking sides with their proponents in vilifying opposing Muslim and non-Muslim versions. On this procedure, Muslims in Africa are categorized into 'learned' and 'venal scholars', 'more orthodox' and 'less orthodox' with representatives of the militant jihad traditions lauded and placed above representatives of the pacifist and peaceful tradition. The net result is a romantic picture of the history of Islam avoiding and sometimes denying such issues as the jihadists' slaughter and massive enslavement of traditional African believers. On the basis of the distorted history, contemporary African Muslims in general and Islamic radicals in particular have come to regard and hanker for the militant jihadist tradition as the best representation of Islamic orthodoxy in Africa.

Most African Muslims have even gone a step further by blaming Africa's socio-political, economic and moral problems on Christian imperialism and recommend the adoption, if not imposition, of Arab-Islam as the solution. Muslim radicals have transmogrified these claims and perceptions into religio-political ideologies which, in effect, regard native Christians as agents of neo-colonialism, reject secularism on the basis that it is a product of the Christian West and hanker for the reintroduction of 'the glorious Islamic past', i.e. the militant jihadist tradition. As long as these romantic perceptions continue to hold sway the absolute and xenophobic claims of Muslim radicals would continue to gain currency at the popular level. The end result would not just be a predictable wave of Muslim–non-Muslim conflicts but serious intra-Muslim conflicts. This situation is already gaining ground in the Sudan, Nigeria and in lesser magnitudes in other parts of Africa.

The main thrust of this work is an exploration of the way forward for sustainable inter-faith dialogue in general and Muslim–non-Muslim dialogue in Africa in particular. In exploring the way forward for Muslim–non-Muslim dialogue in general and Muslim–Christian dialogue in particular, we realize that

---

5. Ibid., p. 108. After thus acknowledging the distortion of the history, Robinson goes on to submit that there is no alternative but to use the tools and concepts provided by the historical literature. In this connection he himself goes on to categorize West African Muslims into 'the more orthodox and the less orthodox' on the basis of the distorted historical evidence.

xvi *The Legacy of Arab-Islam in Africa*

the historical legacies of both the Islamic and Christian traditions continue to play an important, in fact crucial, role in contemporary inter-faith relations in Africa: crucial because contemporary African self-perception, is very much coloured and in most cases determined by these encounters.

What this work seeks to do is to challenge the romantic perception of a 'glorious Islamic past' by examining some important elements of that past from the non-Muslim African perspective. In chapter 1, I offer a brief survey of the uneven-handed treatment of the Western-Christian and Arab-Islamic legacies in post-colonial discourse. I then go on to re-examine critically certain key themes in the Arab-Islamic encounter with black Africa. These include the re-examination of the role of the indigenous African environment in conversions to Islam in chapter 2; the nineteenth-century jihad movements in West Africa (which have become the main source of inspiration and model examples for Muslims), the jihadists' attitude and policies towards traditional African believers and indigenous culture, the success or otherwise of jihadists' rule in chapter 3; and Muslim slavery, its religious and racial ideology, actual practice within and outside Africa and slave conditions in Muslim lands. This is done in chapter 4.

It is my sincere conviction that honestly confronting and examining the jihad tradition and Muslim slavery in Africa is not in conflict with the genuine desire for inter-faith dialogue. Rather, I share Bernard Lewis's concern that historians 'have a moral and professional obligation not to shirk the difficult issues and subjects that some people would place under a sort of taboo; not to submit to voluntary censorship, but to deal with these matters fairly, honestly, without apologetics, without polemic, and, of course, competently'. This is crucial because 'we live in a time when great efforts have been made, and continue to be made, to falsify the record of the past and to make history a tool of propaganda; when governments, religious movements, political parties, and sectional groups of every kind are busy rewriting history as they would wish it to have been, as they would like their followers to believe that it was'. For, 'those who are unwilling to confront the past will be unable to understand the present and unfit to face the future'.[6]

Hence, the critical re-examination of the 'negative' issues is an attempt not only to balance the hitherto one-sided version of the history but even more importantly to level the historical playing field for a more honest and sustainable interfaith dialogue and peaceful co-existence between Muslim and non-Muslim Africans. In this connection chapter 5 is an invitation and a challenge to all faith communities in general and Muslims in particular to reassess their inherited traditions critically. This 'critical-faithfulness', in my opinion, is vital for sustainable interfaith dialogue. Another inevitable consideration faith communities in Africa cannot afford to ignore is, not only an acknowledgement or

---

6. Lewis, *Islam and the West*, p. 130.

Preface xvii

'toleration', but *celebration* of plurality of belief systems that cut across family, ethnic and national boundaries. It is in this spirit that Africans across religious boundaries are invited to affirm and celebrate what unites them, i.e. our common historical, cultural and linguistic heritages, and eschew all forms of externally anchored racial and cultural chauvinism, be it from the West or Middle East.

1

A GLANCE AT POST-COLONIAL ASSESSMENTS OF THE WESTERN-CHRISTIAN AND ARAB-ISLAMIC LEGACIES IN TROPICAL AFRICA

DEFINITION OF THE PROBLEM

Encounters between black Africa and the Christian and Islamic civilizations and their corresponding legacies are crucial socio-religious and political loci for African self-perception. It is largely through the lenses of these encounters that the overwhelming majority of Africans now perceive themselves (as individuals, families, communities and nations), encounter one another and others and are perceived and encountered by others.

The main components of the socio-political and religious configuration of present-day sub-Saharan Africa are, first, the indigenous African traditions from which Africans encountered the incoming traditions of Islam and Christianity; second, the Arab-Islamic tradition in its varied orientations; and third, the Western-Christian traditions in their various denominational strands. Africans share these different, and most often competitive, religio-political traditions from the family, ethnic, to national levels.

Throughout sub-Saharan Africa, therefore, people in one way or another have to live and relate with others from different religious persuasions either as relatives, neighbours or fellow citizens. These relations and encounters have been, on the whole, peaceful and harmonious, but have in some instances during the post-colonial period been causes for concern. The raging civil war between the Arab-Islamic-dominated northern Sudan and the largely Christian/traditionalist southerners, the sporadic violence between different religious groups, mainly Christians and Muslims, in northern Nigeria, and a host of other inter/intra-religious conflicts throughout most of sub-Saharan Africa bear testimony to this unease.

2 *The Legacy of Arab-Islam in Africa*

Thus ordinary Africans, traditional authorities, political and religious leaders are now having to work for what they have hitherto taken for granted, i.e. peaceful and harmonious relations between people of different religious traditions. Certainly there are underlying socio-political and economic explanations for these conflicts. Our aim, however, is to examine the specifically religious factors and to explore possible ways of inter-religious dialogue among Africans. Working on the premise that present realities cannot be understood in isolation from past encounters, we considered a survey of post-colonial perceptions of Africa's encounters with the Arab-Islamic and Western-Christian dispensations.

Post-colonial assessments of Africa's encounters, engagement and exchanges with these two dominant religious civilizations and the resultant prevailing perceptions are, in my opinion, crucial for inter-religious dialogue in Africa. This is more so for African Muslim–Christian dialogue, and is crucial because contemporary African Muslim and Christian self-perception, directly and indirectly, derive from and are heavily influenced if not determined by these encounters and especially the way the legacies of the encounters are now perceived primarily by African Muslims and Christians and also by traditional and other faith communities.

The general post-colonial African elite opinion is that the African human, material and cultural heritage has been undermined and subverted by the Christian West through such encounters as the slave trade, missionary activities and colonialism. The Christian West's involvement in the slave trade, missionary activities and its attitudes towards indigenous Africans and their traditional heritages have been subjected to critical scrutiny, to put it mildly, by Africans (and Westerners) alike.[1] Western Christianity has been generally, and rightly (and one may add wrongly) viewed as a foreign, white, colonial, imperial and former slave-masters' religion. The logical conclusion of this is either to reject it outright or to adapt it to suit the cultural, historical and contemporary context of Africa.[2]

Consequently, scores of works by Christians, Muslims and African cultural revivalists have arisen aimed at addressing (and redressing the mishaps, if not

---

1. For a passionate African response to Western European attitudes towards African culture, see, O. p'Bitek, *African Religions in Western Scholarship* (Kampala: East African Literature Bureau, 1970). Of course a host of other literature abounds in this regard.
2. There are a number of examples of rejecting Christianity in the name of African identity. Within Africa itself, 'the Afrikania Movement' founded by a renegade Roman Catholic priest, Osofo Okomfo Kwabena Damuah, in the early 1980s, is one such example. See K. Bediako, *Christianity in Africa: The Renewal of a Non-Western Religion* (Edinburgh: Edinburgh University, 1995), pp. 17 ff. The Nation of Islam in America and, especially Britain, makes its appeal to the black community by portraying Christianity as a religion of the former slave-master that blacks must renounce to sever their links completely with the servile past.

mischief) this historical encounter through the African eyes. The main aim has been to vindicate, retrieve, reassert and celebrate African heritage and identity, whatever that means.[3] In line with this trend, Christian churches embarked upon what was called a 'theology of de-colonization' primarily to de-Westernize Christianity and reassert the 'self-hood of the Church in Africa'. Mission boards in Europe and America were seen as exercising religious imperialism just as their home governments exercised political imperialism. The All-Africa Conference of Churches (AACC) met in 1974 and passed a moratorium on all Western missionary assistance.[4]

The critical view of the Christian tradition in Africa characterizes post-colonial African Christian thought as primarily concerned with the appreciation, retrieval and reinstatement of the African heritage and identity.[5] In other words, the dominant trend in post-colonial African Christian thinking has been, on the one hand, to de-Westernize the Christian tradition and on the other to Africanize it as much as possible. This trend became variously characterized in post-colonial African-Christian thought as 'Africanization', 'indigenization', 'contextualization', 'translation' or 'inculturation', all with the aim of claiming a place for and asserting an African identity within mainstream Christian thinking.[6]

Liturgical manifestations of the same trend are represented in the 'African Independent Churches', i.e. indigenously initiated and led churches, which in their beliefs, worship and organizational structures give precedence to local materials over foreign ones.[7] In addition to these, there is also 'liberation theology', which has become the hallmark of black Christian thinking especially in North America and South Africa. This trend is aimed at confronting white supremacy from within the Christian tradition and seeking socio-political justice for oppressed blacks who have been victims of racial and cultural discrimination.

---

3. A.A. Mazrui, *The Africans: A Triple Heritage* (London: BBC, 1986), pp. 99 ff.
4. *Drumbeats from Kampala*, AACC Document (1963), pp. 32 ff. The moratorium never worked in practice, but the fact that it was passed shows the level of critical reappraisal and hostility African Christians adopted towards the relationship between Christianity and the West in Africa.
5. African Christian writers who have championed this trend include, J.O. Lucas, *The Religion of the Yorubas* (Lagos: CMS Bookshop, 1948); E. Bolaji-Idowu, *Oludumare: God in Yoruba Belief* (London: Longman, 1962); and J.S. Mbiti, *Concepts of God in Africa* (London: SPCK, 1982), among many others. Of course there have been voices condemning the appropriation of traditional elements into Christian practice, e.g. Byang H. Kato, *Theological Pitfalls in Africa* (Nairobi: Evangel Publishing House, 1975), but these remain marginal and in fact unpopular in post-colonial African-Christian thought.
6. In addition to a host of material on this issue, see articles in P. Turkson and F. Wijsen (eds.), *Inculturation: Abide by the Otherness of Africa and the Africans* (Kampen: Uitgeversmaatschappij J.H. Kok, 1994).
7. J.D.Y. Peel, *Aladura: A Religious Movement among the Yoruba* (London: Oxford University, 1968), pp. 114 ff.

4 *The Legacy of Arab-Islam in Africa*

In our opinion these assessments came about mainly due to the fact that the Western-Christian legacy has been examined from the Western, Christian and African (Christian and non-Christian) perspectives.

On the other hand, it appears the Arab-Islamic dispensation has been subjected to an entirely different methodological analysis, resulting in different and indeed contrary perceptions holding sway in post-colonial assessment of black African encounters with the Arab-Islamic tradition. These perceptions include claims that Islam, in contrast to Christianity, is an 'African religion' or has been more in tune with the African personality and heritage than its Western-Christian rival. This view had its most influential proponent in the person of E.W. Blyden, a celebrated nineteenth-century 'black spokesman'.[8] Blyden, an African-American missionary of the Presbyterian tradition, became, quite understandably, highly critical of the Christian tradition in Western European and American hands and how it was used to undermine and destroy African cultural heritage.

In Blyden's view, Western Christianity instilled servility, docility and dependence in the African in order to promote white domination. Looking at the psychological and physical effects of colonialism and the slave trade on the African psyche and personality, Blyden makes a strong point in his assessment of the effects of Western-Christian legacy in Africa and on Africans. This is more so when viewed against the background in which Blyden wrote, a time when colonialism, white supremacy and racial discrimination were at their peak and African self-esteem at its lowest ebb.

Blyden then goes on to contrast the effects of the Western-Christian legacy in Africa against that of the Arab-Islamic tradition. The effects of Arab-Islam upon the African, on the other hand, Blyden contended, inspired new 'spiritual feelings to which they had before been utter strangers' and 'strengthened and hastened certain tendencies to independence and self-reliance which were already at work'. Blyden contends further that:

> local institutions were not destroyed by the Arab influence introduced. They only assumed new forms, and adapted themselves to the new teachings. In all thriving Mohammedan communities, in West and Central Africa, it may be noticed that the Arab superstructure has been superimposed on a permanent indigenous substructure; so that what took place, when the Arab met the Negro in his own home, was a healthy amalgamation, and not an absorption or undue repression.[9]

A good number of Western and African (Muslim and Christian) scholars have made similar claims. Writing on the coincidences and similarities between Islam

---

8. E.W. Blyden, *Christianity, Islam and the Negro Race* (Edinburgh: Edinburgh University, 1967).
9. Ibid., pp. 11–12.

and traditional African cosmology, I.M. Lewis talks about 'the generous catholicity of Islam' towards traditional African values,[10] while Robin Horton, on his part, compares the 'catalytic role' of both Islam and Christianity in religious change in Africa and concludes that Islam allows 'the individual [African] to make his own particular selection from official doctrines', and, in contrast to Christianity, 'does not nag excessively at those who lie towards the pagan end of the continuum'.[11]

Ahmadou Hampâté Bâ, a renowned Malian-Muslim mystic, writes that 'en Afrique, l'Islam n'a pas plus de couleur que l'eau; c'est ce qui explique son succès: elle se colore aux teintes des terroirs et des pierres'.[12] In other words, in Africa, Islam, like water, has no colour of its own except that of the soil and stones it flows over. Ali Mazrui, a leading contemporary African-Muslim scholar, makes similar claims in comparison with Christianity: 'On the wider spectrum of comparison, it remains true that Islam has been more accommodating to indigenous African custom and traditions than European Christianity has been.'[13] Implicit in these claims are, that in Africa's encounters with the Arab-Islamic tradition the African and his/her traditional values fared better than in the encounters with Western Christianity.

Indeed, African-Christian ministers and scholars have not been immune to these claims. A good number hold the view that, in contrast to Christianity, which was 'imposed', Islam is 'organic', that mosques are 'indigenous' while churches are 'alien'.[14] An AACC report on its 1969 assembly in Abidjan observed that 'Islam is held [in Africa] to be an African religion, with almost no foreign missionaries, which tolerates African traditions'.[15] The report stated this almost as an indisputable fact and, like Hampâté Bâ, attributes Islam's appeal in Africa to this fact. The assembly stated this as a fact that should challenge the church in Africa into a 'search for cultural and liturgical forms through which we can express our Christian faith'.[16]

The African-Muslim elite in general, and a vociferous few in particular, have taken these claims to their logical conclusion, insisting that the solution to the ills of the Christian colonial and imperial legacy can be found in the Arab-Islamic dispensation. An influential contemporary Nigerian-Muslim scholar/activist, Shehu Umar Abdullahi, writing on Abdullahi Dan Fodio, brother of Uthman Dan Fodio and chief ideologue of the nineteenth-century northern

10. I.M. Lewis, 'Introduction', in I.M. Lewis (ed.), *Islam in Tropical Africa*, 2nd edn, (London: Hutchinson University Library, 1980), p. 74.
11. R. Horton, 'African Conversion', *Africa*, vol. 41, no. 2 (1971), p. 105.
12. V. Monteil, *L'Islam noir* (Paris: Éditions de Seuil, 1964), p. 41.
13. Mazrui, *Triple Heritage*, pp. 142–3.
14. See M. Echeruo, *Victorian Lagos* (London: n.p., 1977), pp. 80 ff.
15. *Engagement: The Second AACC Assembly – 'Abidjan 69'* (Nairobi: All-Africa Conference of Churches, 1970), p. 117.
16. Ibid.

6 The Legacy of Arab-Islam in Africa

Nigerian jihad movement, declared: 'The ideas of Shaikh 'Abdullahi Dan-Fodio, when translated into some Nigerian languages, can be instrumental in solving [Nigeria's] chronic political instability, economic aridity, social perturbance and juridical nonsense.[17] S.S. Nyang, a Gambian-Muslim scholar based in the United States, on his part observes that Islam has 'great prospects' in post-apartheid South Africa, 'more so with the young Africans who are born Christian and have learned belatedly that the racists in their country have appropriated the Bible to legitimize their racial rule'.[18] What Nyang is suggesting here is that, as a consequence of the evils of Christian apartheid, young South African Christians are going to become disillusioned with Christianity and start converting to Islam, which will provide them with answers and solutions. This is just a different way of saying that South Africans will soon have to turn to Islam to find solutions for the evils and woes of the Christian apartheid legacy.

At an Islamic conference in Abuja, Nigeria, in 1989, scores of African-Muslim scholars and activists decried Western cultural and ideological influences and in a resolution lamented Africa's predicament as 'the object of imperial plunder and serving as a theatre for Europeans to fight proxy wars' and 'of being a dumping ground for cultural and ideological ideas'. However, the participants resolved to 'encourage the teaching of Arabic ... as the lingua franca of the continent' and to 'struggle to re-instate the application of the Shari'a'.[19] In other words what the participants came out with from the Abuja conference, after having diagnosed the cause of Africa's illness as Christian imperialism, was a prescription in the form of Arab-Islam. Christian imperialism was the problem and an adoption, indeed enforcement, of Arab-Islam the solution!

These claims, as far as exploring possible ways for inter-religious dialogue among Africans is concerned, can be major obstacles. This is particularly so because, apart from the fact that some of the claims simply do not fit with the facts of the historical encounters, the absolute claims made in relation to the role of Arab-Islam in Africa's future effectively leave no room for dialogue. But what is even more important is that the claims made for the role of Arab-Islam in Africa's future are based on perceptions of its track record in Africa's past. Hence, it is our considered opinion that a critical reappraisal of prevailing perception of the Islamic past in Africa is crucial for any sustainable dialogue between Muslims and non-Muslim Africans in general and African Muslim–Christian dialogue in particular.

17. Shehu Umar Abdullahi, *On the Search for a Viable Political Culture: Reflections on the Political Thought of Shaikh 'Abdullāhi Dan-Fodio* (Kaduna: Commercial Printing Dept, 1984), p. 5. The title of the book speaks for itself.
18. S.S. Nyang, *Islam, Christianity, and African Identity* (Brattleboro: Amana, 1990), p. 46.
19. N. Alkali et al. (eds.), *Islam in Africa: Proceedings of the Islam in Africa Conference* (Ibadan: Spectrum, 1993), pp. 432–3.

A CRITIQUE OF PREVAILING APPROACHES AND PERCEPTIONS

Underlying the absolute claims made for Arab-Islam as the panacea for contemporary Africa's problems is the prevailing perception that in the past the Islamic tradition, as opposed to its Western-Christian rival, was more tolerant and accommodating to African values. Another perception is that Africans fared better under Islamic systems, most notably the jihadists' rule in nineteenth-century northern Nigeria, as compared to 'pagan' and Western-Christian systems, i.e. traditional African and Western colonial rules respectively. The Arab-Islamic past is seen as a golden age in Africa that is hankered for and must be rediscovered. Out of the 1989 Abuja conference, The Islam in Africa Organization was set up and part of the preamble to its charter speaks of the participants at the conference

> being determined to sustain the momentum of global Islamic resurgence and further encourage co-operation, understanding and the brotherhood of the Ummah; and desirous of forging a common front to unite the Ummah with the view of facing the common enemies – the imperialist and Zionist forces of domination and secularisation, illiteracy, poverty and degradation – *and to rediscover and reinstate Africa's glorious Islamic past.* (my emphasis)[20]

It must be said that the criticisms of Western-Christian legacy in Africa is, broadly speaking, valid. On the part of the Arab-Islamic legacy, as will be made clear in the course of this work, there can be no disputing the fact that African-Muslim practices are replete with indigenous African elements. However, what we are not sure of is whether the initiative can be attributed to the 'generosity' and 'flexibility' of Arab-Islam. And again can it be said that the amalgamation between Arab-Islamic and African elements was all 'healthy' and that there was no 'undue repression'? It is clear from the foregoing quotations that such claims are advanced with the aim 'to grant to Islam in Africa the capacity for tolerance and adaptation which [such scholars] refuse to a begrudged Christianity'.[21]

In other words the primary aim of discourses that speak of the Arab-Islamic tradition's 'flexibility' and 'generosity' towards African elements is to demonstrate how inflexible and uncompromising the Christian tradition has been. The bottom line of such arguments is to demonstrate that Arab-Islam, in contrast to Western Christianity, has not undermined the African heritage. These irresistible comparisons are clear from all the above quotations. The

---

20. J.O. Hunwick, 'Sub-Saharan Africa and the Wider World of Islam: Historical and Contemporary Perspectives', in D. Westerlund and E.E. Rosander (eds.), *African Islam and Islam in Africa: Encounters between Sufis and Islamists* (London: Hurst, 1997), p. 41.
21. L. Sanneh, 'The Domestication of Islam and Christianity in African Societies', *Journal of Religion in Africa*, vol. 11, no. 1 (1980), p. 1.

8 *The Legacy of Arab-Islam in Africa*

comparisons and their resultant impressions also contributed to the call by the Abidjan general assembly of the All-Africa Conference of Churches in its report for Christian churches to embark on a programme of de-Westernizing and Africanizing Christianity.

What is interesting, though, is that, beyond being used as a gauge against Christianity, the repeated references to the presence of indigenous elements in African Muslim practices has little if anything to do with an appreciation of the elements themselves. On the contrary, most African-Muslim scholars and activists who talk about rediscovering and reinstating the glorious Islamic past do not have any place for traditional values in Islam and regard indigenous African elements as one of the principal obstacles to their programme of Islamization. Ibraheem Sulaiman, a widely respected northern Nigerian-Muslim scholar/activist, describes indigenous customs as 'reprehensible and evil' and states elsewhere that: 'Indeed, Islam does not accept that people should have customs or traditions other than religious ones; for if Allah's way is a comprehensive way of life, what is there for custom and tradition?'[22] S.S. Nyang writes approvingly about the 'two processes of de-traditionalization and Islamization' during the jihad campaigns where 'successes of Muslims in many areas of the West Sudan led to the gradual destruction of the traditional cults and the emasculation of the old aristocracy'. Nyang then, in near disillusionment, draws attention to the European intervention at the time and wonders 'what would have happened had Europe's expansion into other areas of the world been delayed for a century or more'.[23] In other words Europe is blamed for interrupting and preventing Islam from accomplishing a noble task. Ali Mazrui on his part views trends of reviving indigenous African culture as 'a threat to Islam' comparable to secularism, albeit a lesser threat.[24]

Similarly, some Western observers tended to refer to the presence of indigenous African elements in African-Muslim practice in order to show how 'pure', 'original', 'normative' and 'orthodox' Islam has been 'mixed', 'corrupted' and 'contaminated' by African 'pagan' elements. Vincent Monteil, for instance, spoke of 'l'Islam noir' as 'la contamination religieuse' whereby 'fetish' and 'animist' African practices are combined with Islamic ones.[25]

H.J. Fisher, to take another example, propounds a three-stage model of conversion to Islam in Africa, which include, 'quarantine' and 'mixing' stages. 'In the quarantine stage', Fisher writes,

> the faith is represented by newcomers – traders, perhaps from North Africa, or refugees or clerics ... Orthodoxy is relatively secure because there are no

---

22. Ibraheem Sulaiman, *A Revolution in History: The Jihad of Usman Dan Fodio* (London and New York: G. Mansell, 1986), pp. 49 and 58.
23. Nyang, *African Identity*, p. 40.
24. Mazrui, *Triple Heritage*, p. 19.
25. Monteil, *L'Islam noir*, pp. 43–9.

converts, and thus no one to bring into the Muslim community heterodox beliefs and observances drawn from his or her non-Muslim past ... and sooner or later, as local people converted in increasing numbers, the stage of mixing succeeded, in which people combined the profession of Islam ... with many pagan survivals.[26]

Fisher's point is clear. African elements in Islam did not come about through a deliberate process of appreciation and appropriation on the part of, if you like, Muslim missionaries. In fact it was an unwelcome introduction of 'heterodox beliefs' into 'orthodox' Islam brought about by neophytes. Fisher's third stage of conversion is the 'reform stage' of the jihad movements during which time 'orthodoxy' is restored. Therefore, local converts to Islam in Africa carried their 'pagan survivals' into their new religion despite, and indeed in contravention of, 'orthodox' Islam.

It is this apparent fundamental incongruity that Muslim 'reformers' in Africa were quick to exploit and so swords of 'orthodoxy' were drawn during the jihad periods with the view of purging Islam of such aberrations. For 'the Islamic regime explicitly forbids, quite apart from refusing to recognize, involvement in African traditional religious customs. It consigns these customs to the sphere of unclean things. Doctrinally they qualify for jihad.'[27]

The eighteenth- and nineteenth-century jihad movements and the policies and attitudes of the jihadists towards traditional believers and indigenous African elements (as will be demonstrated in chapter 3) belie claims that Islam, or rather 'orthodox' Islam, is 'generous' towards old Africa. For the jihadists' programmes of Islamization have hitherto been depicted by key Western observers and the overwhelming majority of African Muslims as the nearest African Muslims ever came to expressing 'orthodox Islam'. And these jihadist policies of Islamization, as pointed out by H.J. Fisher,

> involved sometimes sharp and even cruel insistence upon proper standards, *and an equally sharp break with local traditions.* No one who has read of the stern law-enforcement of the theocracies – or, the eye-witness accounts of fatal floggings in Bornu, for violations of Ramadan, early in the nineteenth century – will ever think of that kind of Islam as coloured no more than water. It was dyed with blood.[28] (my emphasis)

Next, the attribution of 'flexibility' and 'generosity' to Islam is based on the unstated grounds that the incoming tradition of Islam was the main subject of the religious exchanges while the host indigenous traditions were mere passive

26. H.J. Fisher, 'Conversion Reconsidered: Some Historical Aspects of Religious Conversion in Black Africa', *Africa*, vol. 43, no. 2 (1973), p. 31.
27. Sanneh, 'Domestication of Islam and Christianity', p. 2.
28. H.J. Fisher, 'Conversion Reconsidered', p. 37. Fisher was responding to Ahmadou Hampâté Bâ's claim that Islam in Africa took the colour of the indigenous environment.

10 *The Legacy of Arab-Islam in Africa*

objects. Hence the use of such terms as 'flexibility', 'tolerance', 'accommodating' and 'generosity' to describe a dominant Islamic tradition in its relations with weak, accommodated and tolerated indigenous traditions. But this procedure is fundamentally flawed, for as we shall demonstrate in the next two chapters, the Arab-Islamic tradition was a tolerated and accommodated tradition under the traditional African environment and, more so, whenever and wherever the Muslim tradition got the upper hand, as under the regime of the jihadists, it was anything but tolerant to indigenous elements.

It should be pointed out that these impressions have come about largely because post-colonial discourse on Islam in Africa has been generally undertaken from the Muslim or if you like Arab-Islamic perspective. Little or no attention is paid to the host indigenous environment and its local religious traditions. This is particularly so in post-colonial discourse on the legacy of the jihad movements where the focus tended to be more on what, in theory, is supposed or claimed to be 'normative' Islam, as opposed to the dynamics of the exchanges that took place in practice.[29]

This procedure has been particularly unhelpful in that it has in no small way contributed to what has virtually become a set of self-justifying myths created on behalf of the Islamic tradition with the sole aim of chastising Western-Christian failures and mishaps. The chastisement is very necessary but we do not need to create myths for that purpose. These self-justifying myths in post-colonial discourses and interpretation of the Islamic past in Africa are most manifest in three main areas. The first concerns religious change as it relates to African conversion to Islam. As already pointed out above, on the issue of religious change, the Arab-Islamic tradition as opposed to Western-Christian tradition is widely credited with tolerance and generosity towards indigenous African values and traditions.

The second issue concerns the interpretation of the eighteenth- and nineteenth-century jihad movements in West Africa. Jihadists have been generally depicted as the best Islamic scholars and the jihad legacies as models of Islamic orthodoxy in tropical Africa. To use the words of one Western Islamicist, 'Islamic communities in West Africa can be divided between the more orthodox and the less orthodox, or between the more learned and the less learned', with the more 'orthodox' and more 'learned' referring to the jihadists.[30] The third issue is that of Muslim slavery, which in theory and in practice is

---

29. Those writing from other contexts take this situation more seriously. See N. Levtzion, *Muslims and Chiefs in West Africa: A Study of Islam in the Middle Volta Basin in the Pre-colonial Period* (Oxford: Clarendon, 1968); R. Launay, *Beyond the Stream: Islam and Society in a West African Town* (Berkeley: University of California, 1992); D.S. Gilliland, *African Religion Meets Islam: Religious Change in Northern Nigeria* (New York: University Press of America, 1986), among others.
30. Robinson, 'An Approach to Islam', p. 109.

directly linked to the jihad tradition and African conversion to Islam as a religious system. Here the myths range from denials of Muslim enslavement to rationalizing and claims that it was less brutal than the Western-Christian transatlantic dimension.

Taking the jihad tradition for example, Mervyn Hiskett's works on Dan Fodio's jihad movement of nineteenth-century northern Nigeria have had tremendous impact both within and without the confines of Nigeria. Hiskett, though, unashamedly states that the aim of his *magnum opus*, *The Sword of Truth*, is to describe 'Shehu Usuman dan Fodio's life and times as he, his contemporaries, and the generations that followed him saw them'. Hiskett goes on to state that 'I have tried, by avoiding gratuitous interpretations *simply to tell their story*' (my emphasis).[31] In other words Hiskett was more interested in being a loyal mouthpiece of Dan Fodio and his supporters than an objective critical scholar.

Hiskett, in following a tradition set by H.F.C. Smith and Murray Last in the 1960s, writes about and presents the jihad tradition as 'reform movements' aimed at bringing about the proper observances of Islam. No attempt whatsoever is made to give a detached analysis of the jihad movement, which many well-meaning Muslims at the time opposed and condemned. Indeed, Hiskett's *Sword of Truth* could not have been better written by Dan Fodio himself. Hiskett joins the jihadists in calling those Muslims who opposed it 'venal' or 'corrupt' scholars, and, as the title of his book indicates, regarded the jihadists' story as the 'truth'. What we have in the *Sword of Truth*, in effect, is not even the Muslim view, but a factional, albeit triumphant, Muslim view. The views of Muslims and non-Muslims who challenged the 'truth' of the jihadists and suffered the pain of the sword are simply ignored.

In what appears to be a complete academic U-turn and in near disillusionment nearly a quarter of a century after first writing *The Sword of Truth*, Hiskett, in a preface to the Second Edition of his book, acknowledges, if not apologizes for, giving a one-sided Muslim view of events in his book.[32] Hiskett admits that in the histories of the jihad movements hitherto written,

> the non-Muslim, 'pagan' point of view has been left largely untold. The brutality and intolerance of all 'jihad of the Sword', and especially that of the nineteenth-century western Sudan, has been veiled by an assumption of

31. M. Hiskett, *The Sword of Truth: The Life and Times of the Shehu Usuman Dan Fodio*, 2nd edn, (Evanston: Northwestern University, 1994), preface to first edition, p. xi. Hiskett's work is a culmination of a tradition started by H.F.C. Smith in post-colonial Nigeria. See J. Lawson, 'Nigerian Historiography and the Sokoto Jihads,' MA Dissertation, School of Oriental and African Studies, University of London, 1989), pp. 10–14. Murray Last continued with Smith's tradition in *The Sokoto Caliphate*, (London: Longmans, Green, 1967).

32. See his 'Preface to the 2nd edition', pp. vii–xviii. Because of the special nature of this preface, we shall henceforth single it out and refer to it as Hiskett, 'Preface'.

12 *The Legacy of Arab-Islam in Africa*

moral righteousness, based on the Muslim claim of divine revelation and a written law, that leaves no place for an approach from the point of view of the victims. The stark intransigence of this stance has not diminished over the generations.[33]

Hiskett goes on to add that 'inasmuch as the original edition of *The Sword of Truth*, in its desire to present the reformers' point of view, seems tacitly to accept and even approve such a stance, it surely falls short of true objectivity'.[34] Hiskett tries to redress the situation in his new preface. Thus, in his own words, he is attempting, in the new preface, 'to set such imbalances to rights by drawing on the 'downside' of the reform movement and the jihad to which it gave rise. It will also draw attention to the heritage of Muslim fundamentalist absolutism for which, as is now evident, these events have become a source of inspiration and an admired exemplar.'[35]

Uthman Dan Fodio has become, to many an African Muslim, a cult figure and a hero to be revered and emulated beyond the Nigerian and the West African context. An East African-Muslim intellectual referred to him as 'one of the greatest da'is [missionaries] in Africa'.[36] Very few Muslims dare criticize either his person or his role in the jihad he initiated in early nineteenth-century northern Nigeria. His legacy and those of other jihadists have generally been widely described in post-colonial Western discourse as the best representation of 'orthodox' Islam in tropical Africa, while Muslims generally see it as representing the 'glorious Islamic past' as referred to by The Islam in Africa Organization; in the preamble to its charter cited above. This is also evident from the African Muslim determination 'to re-instate the application of the Shari'a' in sub-Saharan Africa.[37]

Some may see Hiskett's acknowledgement and attempt to set the 'imbalances to rights' as too little too late. Nevertheless, its forthrightness, and the fact that it ensues from the pen of no less a figure than Hiskett, coupled with the fact that it has to do with the most acclaimed Islamic legacy in black Africa, shows the level of one-sided and near-propagandistic interpretations of the Islamic past in Africa. And as already alluded to, the jihadists' legacy has a far wider appeal within African Muslim circles beyond northern Nigeria. As for northern Nigeria, the recent implementation of *shari'a* rule in some northern states and the massive support from the Muslim masses show how naive it is to have perceived views expressed by Muslim 'fundamentalists' as no more than the froth of rhetoric.

33. Ibid., p. viii.
34. Ibid.
35. Ibid., p. ix.
36. Badru Kateregga, 'The Islamic Da'wah: How to Carry it to Christians', *al-Islam*, vol. 7, no. 2 (June 1983), p. 19.
37. Alkali et al. (ed.), *Islam in Africa*, pp. 432–3.

A Glance at Post-Colonial Assessments 13

Peter Clarke betrays such naivety in his observations on Islamic reform in northern Nigeria. Clarke thinks it important to distinguish between 'fundamentalist' and 'moderate' Muslims in Nigeria. He then goes on to accuse Nigerian Christians of exaggerating both the impact and radicalism of Muslim demands for the implementation of the *shari'a* in northern Nigerian states. Clarke writes:

> Many Christians who see the contemporary revitalisation of Islam in Nigeria as a threat and are not entirely confident it can be contained, are, however, inclined to exaggerate both its impact and the radicalism of its demands. *Many of these demands are neither new nor radical in themselves.* What is new ... is the context in which the demands are made and the means used to obtain these demands.[38] (my emphasis)

Unconscious of the irony in his argument, Clarke caricatures Nigerian-Christian concerns in the following words: 'To them we are addressing the resurgence of the old, militant Islam in a new guise determined to finish the work begun by the jihadist of the early nineteenth century by dipping the Koran in the Atlantic Ocean'.[39] So, on the one hand, Clarke does not think Muslim demands for the implementation of *shari'a* is new, and, on the other hand, he accuses Christians of exaggeration when they regard such demands as a resurgence of the jihadist brand of Islam. As pointed out above, Nigerian-Muslim activists who clamoured for the implementation of the *shari'a* have explicitly stated that they see the jihadist brand of Islam as a model.[40]

Indeed, Hiskett argues that the jihadist model appeals to contemporary African Muslims 'whether the Muslims involved came to Islam as a result of nineteenth century reformist ardor or were drawn in less spectacularly by slower influences during the colonial period'.[41] He then cautions against people who are always too keen to draw a sharp line between 'fundamentalist' and 'moderate' Muslims in that when it comes to Muslim attitudes to things non-Islamic or Muslim–non-Muslim relations the difference between 'fundamentalist' and 'moderate' Muslims in northern Nigeria (and one may even say not northern Nigeria alone) rest more in the intensity of their respective brands of rhetoric rather than profound differences in aims and aspirations. A critical reappraisal of the jihad movements is therefore particularly crucial in Muslim–non-Muslim dialogue in a multicultural and multireligious Africa,

> not only as concrete examples of shifting perceptions of Islam in the region, but also as indicating the likely consequences of modern Islamism because of

38. Peter Clarke, 'Islamic Reform in Contemporary Nigeria: Methods and Aims', *Third World Quarterly*, vol. 10, no. 2 (1988), p. 535.
39. Ibid., pp. 535–6.
40. Abdullahi, *Political Thought.*
41. Hiskett, 'Preface', p. ix.

14 The Legacy of Arab-Islam in Africa

the similarities in the orientation and objectives of the two phenomena. Like the previous *jihad*, modern Islamism is not only committed to an exclusive, legalistic, intolerant and militant conception of Islam as *sharia*, but also actively seeks to transform the state and society to bring them into conformity with that model.[42]

On the issue of Muslim slavery, the situation is even more disconcerting. Slavery as a form of wholesale humiliation of blacks is as real in African history as it is in contemporary black experience. Hence, since the beginning of the twentieth-century, slavery became quite understandably the concern, if not preoccupation, of numerous renowned academics (both blacks and whites) in any analysis of the black African encounter with the Christian West. This has resulted in volumes of scholarly research, novels and emotive films aimed at keeping alive the horrors of this dark side of the African encounters with the Christian West.

By contrast, despite the historical fact that the Arab-Islamic dimension of enslavement of blacks pre-dates and post-dates the Western-Christian dimension by centuries – right from the inception of Islam in the seventh century, well into the present day (as will be shown in chapter 4) – this dimension of black Africa's history is yet to be given parallel critical attention. This is despite the fact that, within the African context, the memory of eighteenth- and nineteenth-century Muslim slave raids and massive enslavement of traditional African communities, most of whom are now overwhelmingly Christian, is still alive and vivid in affected communities. Writing on the impact of the Fulani jihad on traditional peoples of the middle part of Nigeria, D.S. Gilliland notes that references to slave raids carried out by the Fulani remained 'a lingering issue among traditional people' and goes on to lament that 'so little reporting has been done on this dark side of Nigerian Islam'.[43]

For various reasons the Arab-Islamic dimension of the enslavement of Africans within the African context has been swept under the carpet and generally explained away by most Western Islamicists, treated by historians, sociologists, anthropologists and economists as an *African* rather than Muslim phenomenon, while Muslim scholars either deny the religious and Islamic motivation for Muslim slavery or in some cases deny Muslim involvement altogether. J.S. Trimingham, a stalwart in post-colonial discourse on Islam in Africa, throughout his invaluable works makes no more than incidental references to slaves, slavery, slave trade and slave raiding carried out by Muslims. Trimingham however points out in a footnote that slavery (within the Ethiopian context) 'is such an unfortunate [issue] that the writer has been careful to avoid overstressing the part played in it by Muslims, who were its chief agents'.[44]

---

42. A.A. An-Na'im, 'Islam and Human Rights in Sahelian Africa', in Westerlund and Rosander (eds.), *African Islam*, p. 83.
43. D.S. Gilliland, *African Religion Meets Islam*, p. 57.
44. J.S. Trimingham, *Islam in Ethiopia* (London: Oxford University, 1962), p. 142, n. 1.

A Glance at Post-Colonial Assessments 15

Trimingham's carefulness not to stress the Muslim involvement, despite the fact that they were the chief, but by no means the only, agents of the slave trade in most parts of Africa (as will be demonstrated in chapter 4), and that he could only state such a fact in a footnote, succinctly sums up post-colonial treatment on the subject of Muslim slavery. Most modern scholars (African and Western) who had the courage even to make incidental references to slavery within the Islamic context most often than not are quick to contrast its 'lesser' scale and 'lesser' cruelty with its transatlantic counterpart, almost always ending with the impression that Muslim slavery was mild and idyllic.

Mervyn Hiskett is another key Islamicist who not only shied away from discussing Muslim involvement in enslavement within the Sokoto caliphate, the largest slave-owning community in modern Africa, but in some cases has sought to downplay, if not deny it altogether. In his *Sword of Truth*, Hiskett makes no reference whatsoever to the massive raiding of neighbouring traditional African (and in some cases Muslim) communities, which became well-organized activities of the jihadists. On the contrary, he makes the bizarre suggestion that the jihadists were some sort of abolitionists in Hausaland.[45]

In another instance Hiskett claims that 'a tiny minority of the total Muslim population' actively practised slave raiding in West Africa and characteristically quickly contrasts 'the "chattel slavery" of the American trade, in which slaves were treated as if they were not human at all' with 'Islamic "domestic slavery", in which slaves were treated as members of the family'.[46] Meanwhile local sources belonging to the generation of the Muslim slavers depict Muslim raids and enslavement of 'pagans' in triumphalist tones. A Hausa praise song talks of one such notorious Muslim slaver of nineteenth-century Hausaland, Masaba, in the following terms:

> Mahamman Saba, Man of fine character, Chief who has no equal, Whoever discovers him will praise him Masaba ... Desirers of gowns and cowries, let them come, All is to be obtained here from Masaba, He who desires a slave girl or horses, let them speak, Let them come and obtain them here from Masaba ... Even if you go as far as Egypt, A chief like him you will not find, there is only Masaba, Burner of pagan villages, there and then, There is none like Masaba, the mighty Masaba.[47]

---

45. Hiskett, *The Sword of Truth*, pp. 77–9. This is based on the writings of jihad leaders in which they condemned the enslavement of Muslims. These condemnations were restatements of classical Muslim teaching on the categories of enslavables rather than attempts at abolition.

46. M. Hiskett, *The Development of Islam in West Africa* (London: Longman, 1984), p. 224.

47. M. Hiskett, 'Enslavement, Slavery and Attitudes Towards the Legally Enslavable in Hausa Islamic Literature', in J.R. Willis (ed.), *Slaves and Slavery in Muslim Africa*, vol. 1, (London: Frank Cass & Co. Ltd, 1985), p. 109. Right from the opening

16 *The Legacy of Arab-Islam in Africa*

Peter Clarke, in his *West Africa and Islam*, similarly makes no more than incidental references to 'slaves' with nothing to say on the massive Muslim slave raiding, slave-holdings and slave trade in the sub-region. Indeed, the terms 'slave' or 'slavery' are not in the index of the book. Meanwhile the same author in his book *West Africa and Christianity* has whole sections and critical references to the transatlantic dimension of the slave trade.[48] This is a very typical example of the uneven-handedness and blatant cover-ups in the subject of slavery in black African encounters with the Arab-Islamic tradition. As can be seen from the above, neither Hiskett nor Clarke can claim they did not know the practice was widespread and indeed endemic in Muslim societies, they simply chose to cover it up, thereby contributing to the self-righteous stance of contemporary radical African-Muslim activists.

Some well-placed African-Muslim scholars, on their part, colourfully document the cruel effects of Western-Christian slavery on black Africans, but say next to nothing about the Arab-Islamic dimension, sometimes even denying it altogether.[49] For instance Ali Mazrui writes that Anglo-Saxon 'racism certainly influenced slavery and the slave trade to a great extent, and converted Africans into commodities to be acquired and sold on the world market' leading to 'a substantial part of Africa's population dragged off, kicking and screaming, and shipped to the new plantations of the Americas'.[50] This again is true and well said.

Meanwhile, Mazrui went on to claim that even though Arabs were in contact with Africans, 'blackness was taken relatively for granted' and 'the primary criterion of differentiation between Arab and non-Arab [in Africa] is not skin colour'.[51] Thus Mazrui denies racial prejudice in Arab relations with blacks and, what is even more surprising, says nothing about Arab-Muslim enslavement of Africans both along the East African coast and in the Arab world. Mazrui's denial and silence is particularly surprising since he hails from East Africa, where Arab-Muslim enslavement of and racial prejudice towards Africans is a well-known fact.[52]

Ibraheem Sulaiman disingenuously characterizes the large slave farms that existed in the nineteenth-century Sokoto caliphate as 'agricultural colonies for the war captive'.[53] War captives indeed! To others, the negligible socio-political and religious impact of the black diaspora in the Middle East and North Africa

---

paragraph and throughout the article, Hiskett does not hide the uneasiness with which he is compiling material related to slavery in Hausaland. He ends up confining himself mainly to the pre-jihad Hausa, Habe, practice of slavery.

48. P.B. Clarke, *West Africa and Christianity* (London: Edward Arnold, 1986), pp. 7–11, 31–3, 43–5, 74–5, 233–4, etc.
49. Mazrui, *Triple Heritage*, pp. 102–13.
50. Ibid., p. 103.
51. Ibid., p. 105.
52. See F. Cooper, 'The Treatment of Slaves on the Kenya Coast in the 19th Century', in *Kenyan Historical Review*, vol. 1, part 1 (1973), pp. 87–108.
53. Sulaiman, *Revolution in History*, p. 111.

as compared to the Americas is proof that 'the trans-Saharan trade removed fewer Negroes than the Atlantic trade', and that its effect on the black African population 'was relatively minor'.[54] As far as some Arab Muslim scholars are concerned, the whole issue of Arab enslavement of Africans is a mischievous myth. One such scholar makes the following fantastic claim:

> I had the opportunity once to have a look into slave trade dealings in Zanzibar and to my great surprise I did not find a single Arab name in the list of the major financiers and traders which included hundreds of French, Indian and Portuguese names.[55]

Other scholars who have studied slavery in Muslim Africa have sought to portray it as African rather Muslim or Islamic. This is notwithstanding the facts that the contents of such works are full of traditional Muslim sources. The focus of the Fishers' book, *Slavery and Muslim Society in Africa*, based on the accounts of the nineteenth-century German physician Gustav Nachtigal, for instance, is one such interesting example. Despite the fact that the main focus of the Fishers' study is Muslim societies in Africa, the authors make it clear that the phenomenon presented in the book was not so much about Muslim slavery in Africa as it was about slavery as carried out by African Muslims.

The Fishers, in their own words, were presenting an 'independent African counterpart' of the transatlantic slave trade. The aim is apparent, to counteract and possibly silence the noise made by Africans on the transatlantic slave trade! The Fishers continued to reiterate that 'the book *amounts almost to an essay in the sociology of African Islam*, and may appeal to readers interested as much or more in the Islamic world as in the African' (my emphasis).[56] The point the Fishers are at pains to make in their introduction, never mind the content of the work itself, is that the phenomenon discussed in their work is *African* rather than *Muslim* or *Islamic*. Similarly, Suzanne Miers and Igor Kopytoff talk about 'slavery' (their quotation marks) in Muslim and traditional societies in Africa under the general theme of 'Slavery in Africa'.[57]

54. J.D. Fage, 'Slavery and the Slave Trade in the Context of West African History', *Journal of African History*, vol. 10 (1969), p. 399.
55. Abd Elrahman Abuzayd Ahmed, 'Comments', in K. El-Din Haseeb (ed.), *The Arabs and Africa* (London: Croom Helm, 1985), p. 79.
56. Allan G.B. Fisher and Humphrey J. Fisher, *Slavery and Muslim Society in Africa: The Institution in Saharan and Sudanic Africa and the Trans-Saharan Trade* (London: C. Hurst, 1970), p. 2. Of course the last part of the sentence which talks about the possible appeal of the book to those interested in the Islamic world is only a caveat that does not in any way diminish the fact that the Fishers want readers to see the slave system presented in their book as an *independent African* counterpart of the transatlantic slave system.
57. S. Miers and I. Kopytoff, 'Introduction', in S. Miers and I. Kopytoff (eds.), *Slavery in Africa: Historical and Anthropological Perspectives* (London: University of Wisconsin, 1977), pp. 3–85.

18 The Legacy of Arab-Islam in Africa

Of course, African Muslims are Africans, and so the 'African' rather than the 'Muslim' aspect these studies seek to highlight is legitimate as far as the historical and anthropological perspectives of slavery are concerned. But so are the ideological and religious, i.e. Islamic reference points. It will be made apparent later in this work that Muslim slavers, whether African, Arab, Persian or Turkish, were never ashamed of and indeed were proud of their common source for enslavement, namely, the Qur'an, Islamic traditions and Muslim jurisprudence, even if interpretations varied in time and space. All Muslims justified the institution and practice of slavery mainly along religious lines. Muslim slavery was therefore founded and regulated mainly on non-belief in Islam, *kufr*.

The underlying intention of this work is to draw attention to certain key historical trends and facts that have hitherto been de-emphasized if not ignored in Africa's encounters with the Arab-Islamic dispensation. Our aim is not to demonstrate how horrible and nasty the Islamic past in Africa has been, but rather to say that it was, as other systems of the time, not glorious. Our aim is therefore to challenge the monolithic construction of a 'glorious Islamic past' and the ensuing perceptions that hold sway in post-colonial Africa by drawing attention to the 'downsides' of the Islamic past. We shall then call for a critical engagement of both the Arab-Islamic and Western-Christian traditions in Africa for the sake of African inter-faith relations in general and Muslim–Christian relations in particular. This, we shall argue, can be best achieved when Africans across religious boundaries affirm and celebrate their common heritage.

Our motive in undertaking this critical approach towards these issues is rooted in the conviction that dialogue can only be conducted against realistic historical backgrounds. This is especially so because the Arab-Islamic tradition, like its Western-Christian rival, has not only come to stay in Africa, but has become an integral part of the African heritage. So is the future of Africa tied up with the Arab-Islamic Orient just as it is with the Christian Occident. Africa and the Arab-Islamic world cannot, therefore, afford to look meaningfully into their future relations without honestly confronting the dark sides of the historical encounters.

For, as honestly put by Samir M. Zoghby, within Arab Muslim relations with black Africa is 'an abscess', which, if not 'treated surgically' can lead to 'blood poisoning' or develop into 'gangrene'. However, Zoghby is under no illusions that treating it will probably leave 'an ugly scar and the memory of a throbbing pain'. It may also create 'awkward moments of embarrassment' and 'a numbing feeling'. But treat it we must, Zoghby insists, if we are 'to establish a dialogue' and 'look at the future fully aware of the past'.[58] We certainly share this conviction and, in fact, it is the main motivation in our task here.

---

58. S.M. Zoghby, 'Blacks and Arabs: Past and Present', *Current Bibliography on African Affairs*, vol. 3, no. 5 (May 1970), p. 5.

METHODOLOGY, OUTLINE AND SOURCES

As we have indicated and demonstrated above, there are two main difficulties that have beset post-colonial discourse on African encounters with Arab-Islamic civilization. These are, first of all, the irresistible comparisons with the Western-Christian dimension, and second, the fact that the encounters have been viewed mainly from the Muslim perspective. These approaches have, as we have indicated above (and will demonstrate in the rest of the work), led to the creation of myths of a glorious Islamic past that has to be rediscovered and reinstated.

Our approach in this work will, first of all, as much as possible, avoid undue comparisons between the Arab-Islamic and Western-Christian encounters. Our main focus will be the African encounters with the Arab-Islamic dispensation. This, in our view, is important because if a more realistic picture of the African encounters with the Arab-Islamic dispensation is to be painted, then it must be done in its own right not under the shadows of the Christian West. This does not mean that we will not occasionally draw attention to parallels or contrast from the encounters with the Christian West as and when we think it will help clarify or reinforce a particular point we are making.

Second, we are seeking to examine the African encounters with the Arab-Islamic dispensation from *an African perspective.* In contrast to the mistaken presentation of a factional Muslim view as 'an inside African perspective', we will present, in what can only be a preliminary attempt, the 'non-Muslim, "pagan" point of view', which has hitherto been left largely untold. Thus, contrary to the old procedure whereby traditional African values have been assessed from the lenses of the Arab-Islamic tradition, our approach is to reverse that procedure by examining Arab-Islam through the lenses of the traditional African and his/her cultural heritage. In our opinion, the non-Muslim perspective is vital not only for the sake of historical balance, but also for inter-religious dialogue in contemporary Africa.

The term 'Islam' as used in this work refers to historical Islam as it was perceived, lived and transmitted through the words and deeds of Muslims in their encounters with black Africa, rather than scriptural or text-based Islam. Thus, while we will, in some instances, refer to theoretical doctrinal and philosophical arguments relating to Muslim beliefs and practices, this will not be our primary concern. Also, the term 'Arab-Islam' is used in this context to highlight the Arab, and therefore non-African, origin and orientation of the Islamic religious tradition. For as Isma'il al-Faruqi, rightly described by Kenneth Cragg as 'vigorously representative of Islam',[59] observes, it was 'Arabism' that spread out of the Arabian Peninsula to other parts of the world, 'however

---

59. K. Cragg, *Troubled by Truth: Life Studies in Inter-faith Concern* (Edinburgh: Pentland, 1992), p. 127.

20 The Legacy of Arab-Islam in Africa

mastered and guided by Islam in every respect".[60] This is crucial, in our view, for a critical African reappraisal and appropriation of the Islamic tradition within a pluralistic African context.

The basic thrust of our work is an analysis of interpretations and the resultant perceptions mentioned above. It is not a historical and chronological narration of events. Hence even though we will definitely have to highlight some key aspects of the historical narrative to account for the analysis, we shall not concern ourselves with historical details. Rather, our focus will be on certain basic and fundamental themes that run through the encounters. These themes include, in chapter 2, the role of the *host* or *receiving* indigenous African environment in the processes and resultant configuration of the socio-religious exchanges during the encounters.

We will address this issue by looking at the nature of African conversion to Islam before the eighteenth- and nineteenth-century jihad movements and the European interlude. We will be seeking, in the main, to examine assumptions that indigenous African traditions were weak and passive objects of change. The two main points of focus will be the identities of Muslim groups in sub-Saharan Africa, and the traditional African understanding of religion and the socio-religious and political dynamics therein underlying the process and resultant configuration of the encounters.

The second theme, to be examined in chapter 3 is a continuation of the first, namely the jihadists' response or reaction to the first phase of the exchanges. Here our main aim will be an evaluation of post-colonial interpretations and presentations of the jihad movements. We will question, among other notions, the general perception that the jihad movements were 'reform movements' and therefore a largely if not wholly intra-Muslim conflict. We will assess the legacies of the jihad movements and the success or otherwise of their programmes. This will be done by highlighting some of the major jihad movements and the works of jihadists such as Uthman Dan Fodio and al-Hajj 'Umar Tal of the Senegambian region.

The third theme, investigated in chapter 4, concerns the issue of Muslim slavery. As we have indicated above, slavery, both in Muslim thought and practice, is inextricably linked to jihad. This is particularly so in the African encounters with Arab-Islam as will be demonstrated later in the chapter. While there have been some important studies relating to slavery in Muslim societies in Africa, on the whole very few have tried to locate it within its wider Islamic context by highlighting its religious and ideological underpinnings.[61] This will be our main concern in this chapter.

---

60. I. al-Faruqi, *On Arabism: 'Urubah and Religion: A Study of the Fundamental Ideas of Arabism and Islam as its Highest Moment of Consciousness* (Amsterdam: Djambatan NV, 1962), p. 204.

A Glance at Post-Colonial Assessments 21

In addition to highlighting the difference between Islamic-inspired slavery in Africa and indigenous African slavery, the main issues that we will seek to examine are conventional impressions regarding the theories and practices of slavery in Muslim societies. These include the disturbing silence, tinkering, rationalizations, justifications and blatant denials of the practice on the part of most Western Islamicists and modern Muslim apologists. In the same vein we will highlight the related issue of racial prejudice and discrimination against blacks in light-skinned Muslim sources and societies.

After thus confronting the past, chapter 5 will seek to prepare the ground for the future. Here the main thrust is to invite and challenge, first of all, the Arab Muslim world to acknowledge unequivocally the critical aspects of its historical past in relation to black Africa, as the Western-Christian world has being trying to do in recent times. This, we shall argue, is a necessary first step towards Afro–Arab dialogue. We shall further suggest that being critical of the actions of past generations of Muslims or the inherited traditions of Islam does not necessarily amount to scepticism or betrayal.

More importantly, we will invite Africans in general and African Muslims in particular to adopt a critical approach to the Islamic tradition, as is being done with the Christian tradition in Africa. This, we hope to demonstrate, will be in the best interests of Muslim–non-Muslim dialogue and peaceful co-existence within the pluralistic context of Africa. Finally, we shall address the Arab factor in Islamic religious expression as it affects rethinking Islam within the African context. Here questions will be raised about the place of the Arab factor in non-Arab-Muslim religious expression, on the one hand, and dialogue with indigenous African traditions, on the other.

Our attention on particular geographical areas or point of time in history at any given stage in our work will be determined by the particular theme under discussion. For instance, our discussion of the jihad movements will tend to be focused more on present-day West and Central Africa than East and Southern Africa. And even further, within that same context, much of our discussion will be on the jihad tradition of Uthman Dan Fodio and therefore present-day northern Nigeria. This is simply due to the fact that historically the jihad movements were concentrated around this part of the continent, while in terms of impact Dan Fodio's jihad stands out amongst all others. Generally speaking, however, our discussion will focus mostly on West Africa because again the

61. The works that have explicitly done this include Willis (ed.), *Slaves and Slavery*, E. Savage (ed.), *The Human Commodity: Perspectives on the Trans-Saharan Slave Trade*, (London: Frank Cass, 1992); P.E. Lovejoy (ed.), *The Ideology of Slavery in Africa* (London: Sage, 1981); P.E. Lovejoy, *Transformations in Slavery: A History of Slavery in Africa* (Cambridge: Cambridge University, 1983). There are a number of other important regional studies of Muslim slavery in Africa such as P.E. Lovejoy and J.S. Hogendorn, *Slow Death for Slavery: The Course of Abolition in Northern Nigeria, 1897–1936* (Cambridge: Cambridge University, 1993), among others.

22 The Legacy of Arab-Islam in Africa

demographic distribution of Islam in sub-Saharan Africa makes that inescapable.

From what has been said so far, it is clear that our sources as well as our approach will be interdisciplinary, including history, anthropology, sociology and religion. The bulk of the sources, though, are secondary in the form of published works, mainly in English. The main reason for this is our concern with post-colonial views and impressions. We will, nonetheless, make use of such works as those written by the jihadists, early Arab-Muslim and European historians, philosophers, geographers, travellers and observers (which might be deemed primary), albeit in translation. This is primarily due to the fact that the works of the jihadists and other early writers in the original languages are basically inaccessible partly because of language difficulties, but mainly due to the fact that these works are not published and therefore not readily accessible.

Now we are fully aware that some of the sources we shall refer to in this work will be seen by some as questionable because their authors have, for various reasons, been generally typecast in post-colonial Western discourse for expressing critical views on certain aspects of Islamic history and Muslim activities. So, a kind of 'academic canon' has been established on Islamic history in general and Islam in Africa in particular. Excluded from this 'canon' and relegated to the realm of 'academic heresy' are works written during European colonial rule and also those of the abolitionists. In fact, I was at one point warned by one of my professors to be careful in referring to J.S. Trimingham because his views have come under serious criticism.

But as we have just shown in this chapter, those who set themselves the task of 'correcting' the biased views of earlier writers have themselves been guilty of the sin of which they accused these early observers. So we will cite these works as and when we think necessary without any apologies whatsoever. We do this fully aware of the fact that the task we have set for ourselves here is likely to be viewed by some as a kind of academic heresy. We would rather that people challenge our conclusions or even contradict them on the basis of evidence and fact than what we see as sheer academic fundamentalism and intolerance so typical of post-modern Western liberal thought.

Another possible criticism is that it is not the business of a non-Muslim like myself to tell African Muslims what they ought or ought not to do with their religious heritage. Our response to such a charge is twofold. First of all, Islam addresses non-Muslims in its scriptures and has directly affected them in its history, so that they cannot afford to remain silent or indifferent to its discourse. In other words, both the universal claims of Islam and its course in history have directly impacted on non-Muslims so much so that its legacy cannot be claimed by Muslims alone. In fact any such claim from African Muslims would be as

A Glance at Post-Colonial Assessments 23

absurd as saying that African Muslims have no right to partake in discourses related to European colonialism because it is a 'Christian' affair.

Second, contemporary Islamic discourse addresses non-Muslims as well as Muslims and its course in the future is bound to affect them. This is more so in the face of Muslim insistence that Islam is not a private religious affair but a complete way of life covering such areas as political and legal spheres of public life that affect Muslims and non-Muslims alike. These claims are particularly important within the African multireligious and ethno-linguistic context where Muslims and non-Muslims are not only full-fledged nationals but belong to the same ethnic and linguistic groups and even family relations. In such a situation, the non-Muslim perspective of things Islamic is just as vital for inter-religious dialogue as Muslim perspective on things non-Islamic.

2

INDIGENOUS AFRICA AS A CULTIVATING GROUND FOR ARAB-ISLAM

INTRODUCTION

The main focus of this chapter is an analysis of the interaction between the Arab-Islamic tradition and the indigenous black African environment during the early phase of Islam in sub-Saharan Africa, that is, the interaction between the incoming Arab-Islamic tradition and the host indigenous African socio-religious and political environment before the eighteenth and nineteenth centuries. We shall examine this interaction by analysing some underlying currents of the history of Islam in Africa in order to show the dynamics involved in the conversion of Africans to Islam. This will involve the examination of the activities of early Muslim groups in their interaction with indigenous African communities.

These Muslim groups include traders and religious professionals known as 'holy men' and/or 'clerics', widely regarded as heralds of the Arab-Islamic dispensation in black Africa. We shall begin by briefly highlighting the activities of these heralds as far as they relate to the diffusion of Islam. We will then look at the status of these Muslim groups within the traditional black African environment and its implication for conversion to Islam. This will be done by highlighting the mechanisms that underlined the relationship, ensured the preservation of Arab-Islam, and facilitated and/or debilitated its diffusion within tropical Africa.

THE INTRODUCTION OF ISLAM TO TROPICAL AFRICA

Long before the advent of Islam in about 610 CE in Arabia, present-day north and north-east Africa had already been under considerable religious, military, political and commercial influence from such successive ancient powers as the Phoenicians, the Romans, the Vandals and Christian Byzantium. The Phoenicians are said to have been in direct touch with Africans south of the Sahara. Great cities such as Carthage, founded by the Phoenicians in about 814 BCE, and Alexandria, founded by Alexander the Great in 332 BCE, became centres of great civilizations.[1]

The first major Muslim impact in Africa followed the invasion by Arab-Muslim armies of Egypt in 638 CE. Plagued by sectarian rivalries between Byzantine and other Christian groups of North Africa regarded as 'heretics', Coptic Egypt offered little resistance, and capitulated in 644 CE to Arab-Muslim armies that then launched a series of campaigns to capture the rest of North Africa.

It was not, however, until the eleventh century that the Berbers (Imazighen) of present-day North Africa were subdued by the Arabs after many bloody feuds. An Arab governor of the time speaking about Berber resistance is reported to have said in exasperation that 'the conquest of Africa is impossible; scarcely has one Berber tribe been exterminated than another takes its place'.[2] Nonetheless Arab-Islamic civilization was destined to gain control over North Africa after that of Punic, Greek, Roman and Judaeo-Christian civilizations.

The tradition of militant Islamization was taken over by the Sanhaja ('veiled Berbers') who came under the influence of the Murābitūn (Almoravid) movement, founded by 'Abd Allah b. Yasin (d. 1059) early in the eleventh century. The movement employed Islam as a unifying tool for Sanhaja solidarity and conducted raids into the *sahil*, the 'shore' of the desert, which allegedly led to the conquest or rather weakening of ancient Ghana in 1076.[3]

To the southern and the north-eastern parts of the Sudan, this initial militant surge of invading Arab/Berber Muslim armies suffered serious setbacks at the hands of the African kingdoms of Makuria and Ethiopia. A Prophetic tradition was later adduced to the effect that the 'Abyssinians' (Ethiopians) should be left alone, and relations with northern Nubia normalized through an agreement known as the *baqt*, which allowed subjects of each side the right to travel and trade unhindered in the other's domains.[4] This agreement lasted for about seven centuries until the might of Mamluk Egypt finally overwhelmed Christian Nubia around 1371 CE, rendering the terms of the pact null and void.

1. J.K. Cooley, *Baal, Christ, and Muhammad: Religion and Revolution in North Africa* (New York: Holt, Rinehart & Winston, 1965), pp. 3–12.
2. E.W. Bovill, *The Golden Trade of the Moors* (New York: Oxford University, 1958), p. 57.
3. H.J. Fisher strongly disputes the Almoravid conquest of ancient Ghana from within Arabic sources that contain the information. See his review article, 'Early Arabic Sources and the Almoravid Conquest of Ghana', *Journal of African History*, vol. 23, no. 4 (1982), pp. 549–60.
4. Y.F. Hasan, 'The Penetration of Islam in the Eastern Sudan', in Lewis (ed.), *Islam in Tropical Africa*, pp. 113–15.

26 The Legacy of Arab-Islam in Africa

A huge cathedral in Dongola, Sudan, was converted into a mosque, signalling the beginning of the end of the long tradition of Christianity in North Africa and the Sudan. There ensued a series of sporadic raids into the region of sub-Saharan Africa, *bilād al-Sūdān*, mainly with the aim of acquiring slaves, with little or no intention to convert the indigenous people.

The Heralds of Arab-Islam in Tropical Africa

It is generally agreed among scholars that the introduction of Islam into black Africa was due to the activities of Muslim traders and religious experts. The trans-Saharan trade route that ran through tropical Africa, North Africa and the Mediterranean into Europe, and across the Red Sea into Arabia and the Middle East, long in existence before the advent of Islam, received a special 'Islamic stamp' and impetus after the Muslim conquest of North Africa and subsequent control of the trade routes.

The Berbers, after their subjugation by the Arabs, not only accepted Islam but a good number of them also took the mercantile profession of their Arab overlords, becoming principal Muslim traders among the Sonninke of ancient Ghana, as early as the eighth century. The Sonninke in turn introduced long-distance trade and Islam further south of the Sahara where they became variously known as Serakhulle in the Senegambian region and Marka in the middle Niger area.

A significant minority of the Malinke or Mande peoples of ancient Mali and Songhay took to long-distance trade, which resulted in their dispersion around the fourteenth century throughout the savannah zones of West Africa up to the fringes of the forest belt and the Gulf of Guinea. They became known as the Dafin in the Upper Black Volta; Dyula (which literally means trader) in the Upper Niger region; Yarse to the Moole–Dagbani-speaking peoples; and Wangara in Hausa/Yoruba lands. The Hausa and Yoruba picked up the mantle of Muslim long-distance trade and joined their Mande colleagues in the West African region.[5]

In the Horn and East African zone, Arab and Persian Muslim seafarers came via the Red Sea and the Indian Ocean and established a string of trading posts along the shores and the islands off the coast as early as the seventh century. These merchants tended, over the course of time, to settle more permanently, usually as local aristocracies, and took local women as concubines. The blending with local blood and culture produced Arab-Islamic-inspired cultures such as the Shirazi (Persian inspired), the Zeilawi (a blending of Arab, Somali and 'Afar elements) and the Swahili, a mixture of Arab and Bantu traits.[6]

---

5. N. Levtzion, 'Patterns of Islamization in West Africa', in N. Levtzion (ed.) *Conversion to Islam* (New York and London: Holmes & Meier, 1979), p. 208.

6. I.M. Lewis, 'Introduction', in Lewis (ed.) *Islam in Tropical Africa*, pp. 6–15.

Indigenous Africa as a Cultivating Ground for Arab-Islam 27

Arab and Swahili traders are said to have penetrated the interior of Zimbabwe by the tenth century. These had a boost in their commercial activities as a result of the high demand for slaves and ivory on the coast by the nineteenth century.[7] Here in East and Central Africa, African communities such as the 'Afar of Somalia, the Yao of Tanzania and Malawi and many other individual converts from the Nyamwezi and Ganda came into contact with Islam through the activities of early Arab and Swahili traders.

Muslim trading communities in their dispersion throughout tropical Africa always went with professional men of religion who, by virtue of their literacy in the Arabic script and expertise in Islamic law and rituals, acted as religious guides, prayer leaders, teachers and healers mainly for the community. The initial movement and dispersion of these religious professionals, therefore, was very much dependent on the travels and settlements of the Muslim trading communities, whose own dispersion and settlement (for reasons that will shortly become apparent) were dependent on political centres of influence.

Most of these experts were believed to have knowledge not only in the exoteric sciences of Islam (*'ilm al-zāhir*) which falls under Islamic law or *fiqh*, but also in the esoteric sciences (*'ilm al-bātin*), which comes under Islamic mysticism, *tasawwuf*. The *shurafā* (from the Arabic, *sharīf* – noble), who claimed descent from the Quraysh (Muhammad's tribe), were believed to have an inherited piety and holiness, which in turn conferred on them powers of healing, telling the future, interpreting dreams and effective intercessory prayers, *du'ā*. They became 'the most successful manufacturers of charms, and the most successful practitioners of Islamic divination and medicine' among the masses of West Africa.[8]

In the Horn and along the eastern coast of Africa immigrant Muslim divines established *jama'at* (semi-detached religious communities) that developed by offering prospects of stable livelihood to dispossessed peoples of servile origins and serving as sanctuaries for offenders fleeing from their own clans and families.[9] The Qadiriyya Sufi order founded by 'Abd al-Qādir al-Jilānī (1077–1166), is the oldest *tariqa* to be established in Harar in East Africa from Aden by one Abu Bakr ibn 'Abdallah al-'Aydarus (d. 1503).

Other *turuq* such as the Salihiyya, founded by Mohammad Salih of Arabia with a popular appeal within peasant circles in Somaliland, the Shadhiliyya, Husseiniyya, Ahmadiyya, and many others also made some impression.[10] In West Africa, the Kunta, under the celebrated leadership of one Sidi Ahmad al-Bakka'i (d. 1515), introduced the Qadiriyya *wird* where it was later

7. Ibid.
8. Hiskett, *Islam in West Africa*, pp. 54–5.
9. I.M. Lewis, *People of the Horn of Africa. Somali, Afar and Saho* (London: International African Institute, 1955), pp. 150 ff.
10. Lewis, 'Introduction', pp. 27–8.

28 The Legacy of Arab-Islam in Africa

popularized in the nineteenth-century under the leadership of Sidi al-Mukhtar al-Kabir al-Kunti (d. 1811).[11]

Tuareg Muslim religious professionals such as the Sanhaja *zawaya* (from the Arabic *zawiya*, literally meaning 'a corner' for religious activities) and other Mauritanian groups had a considerable influence in the Senegambian region of West Africa where they established Islamic *jama'at* in the villages.[12] Black African-Muslim divines in this category, popularly referred to in modern discourse as 'clerics' or 'marabouts',[13] had various local appellations. These include *mwalimu* in Swahili, *wadaad* in Somali, *malam* in Hausa, *karamoko* in Malinke, *alfa* in Songhay, *tcherno* in Tukulor, *modibo* in Fulani, *sereny/serigne* in Wolof, etc.

These appellations all carry the connotation of someone who is literate in the Arabic script. *Malam* and *mwalimu* are both from the Arabic *mu'allim*, which literally means 'teacher', while *karamoko* is from the Arabic *qara'a* which means 'to read', 'to be literate'. These indigenous Muslim religious professionals, both as individuals and organized communities, are well known throughout Muslim Africa as being the principal contributors to the spread of Islam through their provision of charms, amulets and prayers for various purposes.

The Jakhanke, a well-known organized group of this tradition, is said to have been founded by a twelfth-century Mande Muslim *'alim* (scholar) by the name al-Hajj Salim Suware.[14] The Jakhanke tradition is known to be a highly pacifist Muslim group responsible for inculcating a sense of aversion to militancy as a means of religious and political change into a wider section of West African Muslims, especially the Mande. They are chiefly associated with the pursuance of religious study, the production of charms and amulets, travel (sometimes for commercial purposes) and agricultural cultivation through which they made

---

11. A.A. Battran, 'The Kunta, Sidi al-Mukhtar al-Kunti, and the Office of Shaykh al-Tariqa al-Qadiriyya', in J.R. Willis (ed.), *Studies in West African Islamic History*, vol. 1, *The Cultivators of Islam* (London: Frank Cass, 1971) pp. 113 ff.
12. Hiskett, *Islam in West Africa*, pp. 47–55.
13. These terms have come to acquire such captious connotations in some circles that we have decided to minimize their unqualified usage. For instance the term 'cleric' means 'clergyman' as understood in the Christian Protestant tradition, while 'marabout' is a French corruption of *mrabet*, a Maghribi equivalent of *murabit*, which refers to a person living in a *ribat* (fortified monastery). However, the general use of the term 'cleric' is almost always an exclusive reference to black African-Muslim divines in contradistinction to Arab or North African Muslim divines, in most cases without any explanation whatsoever. Some scholars, however, make it explicit that the term 'cleric' refers to Muslim divines who share the worldview of black Africa and are therefore 'generally lesser scholars' than their counterparts who share the North African or Arab worldview, referred to as 'scholars'. See N. Levtzion, 'Sociopolitical Roles of Muslim Clerics and Scholars in West Africa', in E. Cohen et al. (eds.), *Comparative Social Dynamics: Essays in Honour of S. N. Eisenstadt* (Boulder: Westview, 1985), pp. 98 ff.
14. L. Sanneh, *The Jakhanke: The History of an Islamic Clerical People of the Senegambia* (London: International African Institute, 1979), pp. 13 ff.

Their most significant and enduring impact upon the wider indigenous non-Muslim communities.

Their contribution to the spread of Islam in West and Central Africa, especially among the Mande people groups, is well documented by Lamin Sanneh in the Jakhanke. It was not, however, until the nineteenth and twentieth centuries that organized Islamic mysticism, or Sufism, under indigenous African leadership made a considerable impact in the diffusion of Islam in tropical Africa. The Mouridiyya of Ahmad Bamba (d. 1927) and the Tijaniyya under Ibrahim Niass (d. 1975) in the Senegambia and most parts of West Africa are among the most influential groups.[15] In East Africa, indigenous holy men such as Ramiya (1856–1931) of present-day Tanzania and many others were those whose activities had a considerable impact on the indigenous people.[16]

There has been some discussion with regard to the respective roles played by Muslim traders and religious experts in the introduction of Islam in tropical Africa. There are those who think that the introduction of Islam was mainly the work of traders and trade, and those who take the view that trade played very little part in the introduction of Islam and that 'the missionaries of Islam in West Africa were clerics, not traders'.[17] With regard to the role of Muslim trading activities in the spread of Islam in tropical Africa, the following are the most important factors.

First, Muslim trade in tropical Africa developed in commercial networks essentially dependent on some common factors or interests such as kinship, common neighbourhood of origin or religious brotherhood. Trading alliances among the Dyula, for instance, developed largely along family or clan lines – *kabila*, marriage, study-mates or hājj-mates, i.e. those who performed the pilgrimage to Mecca in the same year.[18] These networks were bound together by these alliances. The trading units provided the beginner with his first capital or credit, and assured the established wholesaler of his outlets. Murray Last writes in this regard:

> Hausa trade is essentially dependent on networks. Growth depends on the number of trading friends, not on the cheapness of one's wares and the

15. Hiskett, *Islam in West Africa*, pp. 258–9.
16. F. Constantin, 'Charisma and the Crisis of Power in East Africa', in D.B.C. O'Brien and C. Coulon (eds.), *Charisma in African Islam* (Oxford: Clarendon Press, 1988), pp. 67–90.
17. N. Levtzion, 'Merchants vs. Scholars and Clerics in West Africa: Differential and Complementary Roles', in N. Levtzion and H.J. Fisher (eds.), *Rural and Urban Islam in West Africa* (Boulder: Lynne Rienner, 1987), pp. 21 ff; H. Ahmed, 'Clerics, Traders and Chiefs: A Historical study of Islam in Wallo (Ethiopia) with Special Reference to the Nineteenth Century' (Ph.D. thesis, University of Birmingham, 1985), pp. 145 ff.
18. I. Wilks, 'The Transmission of Islamic Learning in the Western Sudan', in J. Goody (ed.), *Literacy in Traditional Societies* (Cambridge: Cambridge University, 1968), p. 164.

30 The Legacy of Arab-Islam in Africa

number of new customers one can thus attract. 'Friends' are those to whom one gives goods on credit – in effect those to whom you can give capital.[19]

Thus one has to share one or more of the alliances, of which Islam was paramount, in order to engage successfully in long-distance trade. In fact, this writer knows a considerable number of relatives and friends in the upper regions of Ghana who converted to Islam in order to participate in long-distance cola-nut and cattle trade. Such long-distance ventures have therefore virtually become no-go areas for non-Muslims, not necessarily out of any deliberate effort on the part of Muslims to 'Islamize' and therefore monopolize it (even though deliberate monopolizing also cannot be ruled out completely), but due to the sheer intricacies of the networks.

Second, the lifestyles of Muslim merchants in the forms of dressing and the textiles they introduced into indigenous Africa impressed many Africans.[20] Imitation of Muslim ways of dressing, seen more as a higher level of social standing, gradually ended up in conversions. Hence, Islam in tropical Africa, as in Southeast Asia, developed almost entirely along the trade routes of central and western Sudan, and the coastal trading centres of East Africa.

In most areas of pre-European Africa, the distinction between Muslim and non-Muslim almost always corresponded to urban–rural or trader–peasant divide, which of course did not necessarily mean there were no rural peasant Muslims or urban non-Muslim dwellers. Nevertheless, the link was so strong that, for instance, in West Africa the term Dyula is synonymous to trader and Muslim, while in southern Ethiopia, the term *naggadi* (trader) became the universal term for 'Muslim'.[21]

The third area is that of the economic contributions of Muslim traders to the course of Islam. A local Muslim teacher in Ethiopia intimated that by financing the building of mosques, funding pilgrimages to Mecca, purchasing religious texts for the teachers, etc., traders were 'the patrons' of the propagation of Islam in Ethiopia.[22] As far as the Muslim divines are concerned, the main aim of their dispersion, as we have intimated above, was to act as guides and teachers to already existing Muslim communities.

19. M. Last, 'Some Economic Aspects of Conversion in Hausaland (Nigeria)', in Levtzion (ed.), *Conversion to Islam*, p. 140.
20. See Hiskett, *The Sword of Truth*, p. 48. Also K.L. Green, 'Dyula and Sonongui Roles in the Islamization of the Region of Kong', in Levtzion and Fisher (eds.), *Rural and Urban Islam*, p. 102.
21. Trimingham, *Islam in Ethiopia*, p. 140.
22. Ahmed, 'Clerics, Traders and Chiefs', pp. 151–2. Similarly, a Muslim teacher pointed out in Niger that the wealthy traders who supported the propagation of Islam were 'following the example of Siddiq Abubakar [first Khalīfah], a well-to-do person who provided material support to the Prophet for spreading Islam'. See E. Grégoire, 'Islam and the Identity of Merchants in Maradi (Niger)', in L. Brenner (ed.), *Muslim Identity and Social Change in Sub-Saharan Africa* (London: Hurst, 1993), pp. 107–9.

Indigenous Africa as a Cultivating Ground for Arab-Islam 31

The Dyula *karamoko*, in particular, saw themselves as guardians of the *sunnah* and regarded their leadership roles within the society as mainly concerned with *mu'aza*, social and moral guidance. It was in their principal role as guardians of the *sunna* that the *karamoko* helped in preserving 'intact the Islamic content of their culture' and through that exercised profound leadership influence upon the wider non-Muslim communities.[23]

The art of literacy in the largely non-literate indigenous African milieu gave Muslim divines special 'secular' roles as secretaries and recorders in traditional courts. Traditional Africans generally viewed literacy with a sense of reverent awe and mystery that made the religious arts of divination and the production of amulets and talismans by Muslim divines very desirable in the wider society at large and the traditional courts in particular. This 'literary magic', as Goody calls it, gave Muslim divines unique economic, socio-religious and political status within the communities.[24]

This was mainly due to their prayers and production of Islamic charms which were and still are regarded throughout tropical Africa as having special potency to heal, prevent sickness or assuage misfortune, to induce luck, ensure victory in wars, etc. Muslim arts of divination were particularly sought in times of war in order to know the propitious time to attack, prayers sought to win battles, war-coats and hats produced (stitched with leather saphies or silvered amulets of Qur'anic verses) to paralyse the enemy's hand, shiver his weapons and divert their courses.[25]

Writing on the crucial role of Muslim divinations, prayers, charms and amulets in times of war, a Muslim teacher wrote that 'actually, if you want to wage war and you do not find a *malam*, it is impossible for you to do so'.[26] These services are what mainly account for early Islamic influence on the traditional courts of the Western Sudan whence Muslims exerted their sphere of influence. Muslim influence in Ashanti and the Ashanti relationship with the northern kingdoms of Gonja, Dagomba, Nanumba and Mamprusi mainly centred around the fact that the kings of Ashanti valued the religious and ritual services of Muslims from the north in exchange for allowing Muslim traders access to gold and cola markets that were a preserve of Ashanti.[27]

In East Africa, to take another example, a nineteenth-century missionary gave an account of one Bana Osman, 'a Mohammedan of Zanzibar, who fills the office of king's physician, chief magician and court jester' and whose duty it was

---

23. Wilks, 'The Transmission of Islamic Learning', p. 193.
24. J. Goody, 'Restricted Literacy in Northern Ghana', in Goody (ed.), *Literacy in Traditional Societies*, pp. 208–14.
25. Goody, 'Restricted Literacy in Northern Ghana', pp. 202–3.
26. Levtzion, *Muslims and Chiefs in West Africa*, pp. 53–4.
27. See I. Wilks, 'The Position of Muslims in Metropolitan Ashanti in the Early Nineteenth Century', in Lewis (ed.), *Islam in Tropical Africa*, pp. 144 ff.

32 The Legacy of Arab-Islam in Africa

'to compose powerful talismans against Kisuma [presumably a rival], chief of Mafe'.[28] However, while the role played by the religious professionals was crucial in preserving the Islamic culture among existing Muslim communities, for reasons that will be made clear in the next section, the acquisition of these elements did not necessarily result in conversions of indigenous communities. As far as the vast majority were concerned, 'consulting a *karamogow* did not in any way mean conversion to Islam. It did represent the willingness to test the efficacy of Islamic specialists.'[29]

The main difficulty relating to attempts to distinguish the various roles played by Muslim traders and religious professionals in the diffusion of Islam in tropical Africa is that 'these two activities are often associated in Muslim communities and regularly combined in the same person'.[30] Muslim traders and religious men hardly saw their activities as mutually exclusive. As families, clans, ethnic and/or religious communities, Muslim traders and religious men saw their activities as complementary rather than competitive, as the former used their wealth to support the latter and the latter used their knowledge and influence in the interest of the former.[31]

What is even more important, perhaps, is that neither Muslim traders nor religious professionals at this stage considered themselves or their activities as 'missionary'. Conversions to Islam associated with their activities were by and large indirect and incidental. Mervyn Hiskett observes in relation to Arab and Swahili traders of East Africa that '[the] saving of souls was a by-product of the quest for gold, albeit an effective by-product'.[32] This observation, in a general sense, applies to the activities of both Muslim traders and religious professionals in tropical Africa.

The above analysis does not suggest that Islam lacked an intrinsic religious appeal. What it does, though, is to draw attention to the dynamics of the process of conversion in Africa in general and African conversion to Islam in particular.

28. J.S. Trimingham, *Islam in East Africa* (Oxford: Clarendon, 1964), p. 25.
29. Green, 'Islamization of Kong', pp. 103–5. The appeal of Sufism in nineteenth- and twentieth-century Africa has been partly attributed to socio-political and economic factors as well as to spiritual ones. See A.R. Mohammed, 'The Influence of the Niass Tijaniyya in the Niger–Benue Confluence Area of Nigeria', in Brenner (ed.), *Muslim Identity and Social Change*, pp. 117 ff. It should be added, though, that this situation is not in any way peculiar to Africa. It has been observed that Hindus in India patronize the religious services of Sufi teachers but do not become Muslims except in cases whereby the orders also had an economic and political appeal. See P. der Veer, 'Syncretism, Multiculturalism and the Discourse of Tolerance', in C. Stewart and R. Shaw (eds.), *Syncretism/Anti-Syncretism: The Politics of Religious Synthesis* (London: Routledge, 1994), pp. 206–8.
30. Lewis, 'Introduction', p. 20.
31. E.N. Saad, *Social History of Timbuktu: The Role of Muslim Scholars and Notables* (Cambridge: Cambridge University, 1983), p. 230.
32. M. Hiskett, *The Course of Islam in Africa* (Edinburgh: Edinburgh University, 1994), p. 157.

Indigenous Africa as a Cultivating Ground for Arab-Islam 33

In this connection, prevailing discourses on the issue have tended to focus on the role of the incoming tradition of Islam and that of Muslim agents with little or no attention given to the host indigenous African factor. The general theme in the discussion of conversion to Islam in Africa has been that the host traditional environment was a 'passive' partner while the incoming tradition of Islam 'brought the vital cohesive element' into the interaction.[33]

The traditional African socio-religious and political environment has therefore been treated as an *object* and hardly as a *subject* of conversion to Islam in Africa. The dynamics of basic and fundamental indigenous African conceptions of religion and other related factors and how these affected the process of religious change in the interaction between the incoming traditions of Islam (and Christianity) and the host indigenous traditions of Africa has not been taken into account. It is these basic and fundamental factors, and how they facilitated and/or debilitated the preservation and propagation of the incoming tradition of Arab-Islam, that we proceed to examine.

THE INDIGENOUS AFRICAN ENVIRONMENT AND CONVERSION TO ISLAM

Conversion to Islam in Africa: Some Observations

Since the nineteenth century the issue of religious change or 'conversion' in tropical Africa has received much attention from various scholars (both Western and African) of religion and social anthropology. The issues with which these scholars occupied themselves were the underlying factors for conversion or lack of conversion of black Africans to Christianity and Islam. Many theories emerged, as the discussion was in the main championed by Christian missionaries who tended to compare the expansion of Islam with Christianity. Their conviction of the spontaneous appeal of Christianity seems to have been shaken by the lack of mass conversions of Africans.

In their bid to explain the progress Islam had made on some communities at the time, the dominant theory, in the late nineteenth and early twentieth centuries, was that the African is by nature unable to grasp metaphysical issues. As such, being a sensual and materialistic religion, which required little or no intellectual sophistication, Islam suited the African's egocentric and less sophisticated mind.[34] People like Edward Blyden, widely acclaimed at the time as a sympathetic advocate of African identity and the Islamic tradition, wrote that Islam 'is no doubt better suited to the intellectual comprehension of a people steeped in ignorance and heathenism'.[35]

33. J.S. Trimingham, *The Influence of Islam upon Africa* (London: Longmans, Green, 1968), p. 44.
34. A.P. Atterbury, *Islam in Africa*, (New York: G.P. Putnam's Son, 1899), pp. 166–9.
35. Blyden, *Christianity, Islam and the Negro Race*, p. 45.

34 The Legacy of Arab-Islam in Africa

Other more recent theories with regard to religious change as specifically related to Islam in tropical Africa, include arguments that the representatives of Islam (in contrast to Christianity) were Africans themselves who made the Arab-Islamic tradition amenable to their compatriots. Not a few scholars have since tried to look for some similarities and coincidences between Islam and traditional African religious thought as possible explanations for African conversion to Islam.

Ali Mazrui, for instance, argues, among other things, that Islam is an African religion because 'indigenous Africans carried the banner of Islam' and that, unlike Christianity, Islam has a lot of similarities with the traditional African worldview, making it less difficult for Africans to convert to Islam.[36] A related argument to explain African conversion to Islam is that Islam is more tolerant, accommodating and flexible to traditional African socio-religious values. Writing extensively on the coincidences and similarities between Islam and traditional African cosmology, I.M. Lewis talks about 'the generous catholicity of Islam' towards traditional African values.[37]

In addition to some basic difficulties related to the theories of the African identity of the heralds of Islam in Africa and 'the generous catholicity of Islam' towards African values, which will be made apparent later in this chapter, there are two fundamental assumptions that have beset the discussion of conversion in tropical Africa with specific reference to Islam. The first is the focus on the incoming tradition of Islam (and Christianity) as the main if not sole determinant of conversion with little or no attention paid to the host traditional African environment.

This assumption is further based on another unstated related assumption that the host indigenous African traditions were always displaced by the incoming Islamic (or Christian) traditions whenever the two encountered each other. S.S. Nyang, for instance, speaks of the adoption of Islam in Africa as having 'displaced an indigenous belief system'.[38] We shall address these assumptions in later parts of this chapter and the next. However, suffice it to say now that these assumptions are in a sense rooted in the ancient competition between Islam and Christianity, a competition that in no small way contributed to the dismissive attitude towards the host indigenous traditions.

The only role given to the host indigenous traditions in this procedure is that of passive recipients and objects of change, with little or no resilience in the face of alien traditions. As cogently stated by Lamin Sanneh, though, the past procedure upon which

> Islam has achieved the double victory of successful conversion and of
> generosity towards African values [is] a contradictory state of affairs that

36. Mazrui, *Triple Heritage*, pp. 136–43.
37. Lewis, 'Introduction', p. 74.
38. Nyang, *African Identity*, pp. 25, 47–53.

Indigenous Africa as a Cultivating Ground for Arab-Islam 35

clearly discredits that procedure. The imputing to Islam of a wide degree of flexibility in its interaction with African societies completes the process by robbing traditional societies of a crucial element of their heritage; [namely] the tradition of 'enclavement' (which accords protection and guarantee to stranger and non-kin groups) on the one hand, and on the other the inclusive and tenacious nature of local religions.[39]

It is this tradition of 'enclavement' and the 'inclusive and tenacious' nature of the indigenous environment that we now proceed to highlight in order to examine the relationship between early Muslim communities and indigenous African societies to show how the relations not only facilitated and/or debilitated conversion to Islam before the jihad and colonial periods but also determined the direction and content of the socio-religious exchanges.

The second assumption is that the issue of conversion or religious change in tropical Africa in the discussion of most scholars has almost always been centred around the coming into awareness of a 'proper' conception of the Supreme Being. In other words conversion of Africans to the so-called monotheistic religions of Islam and Christianity is always seen as Africans coming to a 'proper', if not first-time awareness of and relationship with the Supreme Being. Tied up with this assumption is the conception of the Supreme Being as a philosophical concept expressed in a set of doctrines or creeds subject to elaboration in epistemological terms.

Hence people like Emil Ludwig were surprised as to how the 'untutored' African could conceive God, 'a philosophical concept which savages are incapable of framing'.[40] Many leading African scholars such as E. Bolaji-Idowu and J.S. Mbiti have endeavoured to demonstrate that before Islam or Christianity emerged in Africa, Africans knew God and related to 'Him' in their own ways.[41] A famous Akan proverb that states that 'nobody teaches a child about God' is often cited to underline the pervasive and almost intuitive awareness of the Supreme Being by Africans. The assumption that conversion in Africa is a coming into awareness of the Supreme Being has in no small way vitiated many discussions on the issue, as we shall shortly demonstrate.

The association of African conversion with the coming into awareness of the Supreme Being is particularly evident in the debate on religious change in tropical Africa between Robin Horton and H.J. Fisher.[42] Horton's thesis is particularly intriguing in that in his discussion he does not assume traditional

39. Sanneh, 'Domestication of Islam and Christianity', p. 6.
40. E.W. Smith (ed.), *African Ideas of God: A Symposium* (London: Edinburgh House, 1950), p. 1.
41. E. Bolaji-Idowu, *Oludumare;* Mbiti, *Concepts of God in Africa.*
42. See Horton, 'African Conversion'; Fisher, 'Conversion Reconsidered; R. Horton, 'On the Rationality of Conversion', part I, *Africa*, vol. 45, no. 3 (1975); part II, *Africa*, vol. 45, no. 4 (1975); H.J. Fisher, 'The Juggernaut's Apologia: Conversion to Islam in Black Africa', *Africa*, vol. 55, no. 2 (1985).

36 The Legacy of Arab-Islam in Africa

Africa as a passive object of religious change but an active subject of the process. Horton argues on the basis of a 'two-tier structure' of what he calls the 'basic' African cosmology made up of the world of the lesser spirits, which underpin events of the local community, i.e. the 'microcosm', and the world of the Supreme Being that underpins events in the world at large, the 'macrocosm'.[43]

On this basis Horton suggests that the belief in the Supreme Being ('conversion') in tropical Africa came about as a result of the development of traditional African religious thought under the stimulation of developments such as long-distance trade etc. which were brought about by the advent of Islam and Christianity but which were not in themselves expressions of the missionary concern of either faith.

The role played by Islam and Christianity in this process, Horton argues, is that of 'catalysts', 'stimulators', 'accelerators' 'of changes which were "in the air" anyway'.[44] As far as Horton is concerned, the indigenous African environment was the principal determining factor in the process and resulting configuration of the changes.

However, apart from obvious difficulties in this thesis pointed out by numerous critics, such as the mechanical fashion in which it assumes religious conversion in Africa to have taken place, his arguments are nevertheless based on the assumption that conversion or religious change is a belief in or coming to awareness of the Supreme Being. Belief in the Supreme Being is no doubt the doctrinal cornerstone of the so-called monotheistic religions of Islam and Christianity. This is even more so with Islam where numerous Prophetic traditions and doctrinal expositions declare that the mere confession of the unity of God, *tawhid*, is enough to make one a Muslim in, at least, the technical sense of conversion.[45]

However, as will be made apparent as we proceed, the dynamics of conversion to Islam (and Christianity) in Africa (and one would suppose other parts of the world) involved (and still involve) more than the profession of a belief in the Supreme Being. What is even more curious about Horton's hypothesis is that while insistent, and rightly so, in attributing an active role to the indigenous environment, he attributes 'generosity' and 'flexibility' to the incoming accommodated tradition of Islam rather than the host and dominant indigenous environment.[46]

H.J. Fisher on his part focuses on the incoming missionary traditions of Islam and Christianity as the principal determining factors of religious conversion in Africa. Fisher points out that Horton has exaggerated the

43. Horton, 'Rationality of Conversion', part I, p. 220.
44. Horton, 'African Conversion', pp. 102–4.
45. Goldziher, *Muslim Studies*, vol. 1, *(Muhammedanische Studien)*, ed. S.M. Stern (London: George Allen & Unwin, 1967), pp. 46–8.
46. Horton, 'African Conversion', p. 105.

potential of traditional religious thought and underrated the role played by missionary Islam and Christianity in bringing about religious change in Africa. Fisher rightly points out that Horton's mechanical theory does not explain why in many areas in Africa what Horton calls the 'microcosm' still holds sway, even though these areas have been in contact with long-distance trade and the nation/state system for a considerable length of time.

Fisher goes on to discount Horton's thesis on the grounds that 'for progress to be carried over from one leap forward to the next, literacy is necessary',[47] albeit without any explanation as to why and how this is so.

The implication of Fisher's argument is that since indigenous African traditions were non-literate, they could not develop a belief in the Supreme Being independent of missionary Islam and Christianity. This is strongly implied in his cogent and valid criticism of Horton's thesis where he emphasizes the necessity of literacy in bringing about the development of the idea of the Supreme Being. Again, implicit in Fisher's argument on the role of literacy is the idea of the Supreme Being as a 'philosophical' concept, which the non-literate or 'untutored' African traditions cannot develop independently of the literate traditions of Islam and Christianity. Meanwhile, Fisher does not tell us how literacy has contributed in bringing about the development of the idea of the Supreme Being in either Christianity or Islam. Rather, he argues about the role literacy has played and continues to play in the preservation of what he calls 'the proper standards of the faith' from being corrupted by local elements.[48]

It is important to remember, also, that the conception of religion in general, and the idea of the Supreme Being in particular, in epistemological or literary terms is hardly sustainable when talking about the African understanding of religion in general and conversion to both Islam and Christianity in particular, as we shall demonstrate in the next section. Indeed, as G.C. Oosthuizen has observed, 'belief in Africa is not an epistemological issue . . . it is more a question of trust, more a matter of relationships than of propositions of logical arguments which predominates'.[49]

Another point raised by Fisher on the importance of literacy is that non-literate traditions are less resilient in a pluralistic situation. In other words, the non-literate host indigenous African worldviews stood little or no chance when they came into contact with the literate Muslim (and Christian) traditions. According to Fisher, the orally transmitted African religions do not offer their adherents a framework within which to enter into a 'creative and resilient

47. Fisher, 'Conversion Reconsidered', p. 29.
48. Ibid., pp. 34 ff.
49. G.C. Oosthuizen, 'Traditional Religion in Contemporary South Africa', in J.K. Olupona (ed.), *African Traditional Religions in Contemporary Society* (New York: International Religious Foundation, 1991), p. 40.

38 The Legacy of Arab-Islam in Africa

pluralism'.[50] The implication here is that, in the encounter between indigenous African believers and the Muslim (or Christian) traditions, the former stood little chance of survival or were predisposed to indiscriminate borrowings, which does not even qualify to be termed syncretistic.

The unformulated nature of the exchanges on the part of the indigenous traditions is the reason Fisher offers elsewhere for referring to the process as 'mixing' rather than syncretism, 'which suggests rather more of a formulated, conscious combination of religions'.[51] The openness of indigenous traditions is what underlies Fisher's point here. However, he regards such openness as a sign of weakness and fragility rather than strength and resilience, as most African scholars have done. For example, K.A. Opoku is of the opinion that

> Contrary to the impression that the spread of other religions in Africa is due to the palpably clear 'weakness' of the host religion, it may be affirmed that the ability to accept truth outside of one's own immediate environment and tradition is a sign of strength and maturity rather than its lamentable opposite.[52]

It is the interaction between the host indigenous traditions and the incoming tradition of Islam as it relates to conversion to the latter that we now proceed to examine.

Muslims under Indigenous Patronage: Implications for Conversion

As can be seen from the first part of this chapter, it was mainly in the diaspora that Muslim communities in tropical Africa, whether traders or 'clerics', retained a distinctive Islamic culture. The practice of Islam at this stage was found amongst itinerant rather than settled communities, and settled Muslim communities saw mobility as a way of strengthening their religious vocation. This is indicated by Lamin Sanneh, who writes: In the religious circles the practice of retreat (khalwa) and the theme of mobility (safar) share a common history and a common purpose, which is to revitalize the religious spirit and set it in critical contrast to the alleged natural corruption of settled living.'[53] Sanneh goes on to refer to medieval Sufi manuals in which 'being separated from one's native land, from friends and familiar things' and facing the challenges involved

50. H.J. Fisher, 'Many Deep Baptisms: Reflections on Religious, Chiefly Muslim, Conversion in Black Africa', *Bulletin of the School of Oriental and African Studies*, vol. 57, part I (1994), p. 74.
51. Fisher, 'Conversion Reconsidered', p. 38.
52. K.A. Opoku, 'African Traditional Religion: An Enduring Heritage', in J.K. Olupona and S.S. Nyang (eds.), *Religious Plurality in Africa* (Berlin: Mouton de Gruyter, 1993), p. 68.
53. L. Sanneh, 'Tcherno Aliou, the Walī of Goumba: Islam, Colonialism and the Rural Factor in Futa Jallon, 1867–1912', in Levtzion and Fisher (eds.), *Rural and Urban Islam*, pp. 95–6.

Indigenous Africa as a Cultivating Ground for Arab-Islam 39

in a foreign land are as desirable and effective as *nawāfil* (supererogatory devotions), fasting and praying.[54] This, of course, does not imply that Muslim groups in tropical Africa were deliberately dispersed to preserve and strengthen their faith. Rather, it is to emphasize the state of Islam and the identities of Muslim communities throughout most parts of black Africa at this stage.

The general status of Muslim communities throughout most parts of Africa is that as dispersed communities they always found themselves not only as minorities in the midst of an overwhelming non-Muslim majority, but also as non-kin groups (strangers) in an indigenous environment. The first time a Muslim minority found itself in this situation (if we are to believe Muslim traditions) goes back to the time of the Prophet of Islam when he advised over eighty male adults and their families of his followers to seek asylum in Abyssinia (Ethiopia) in 615 CE, i.e. the first *hijra* (migration or flight) in Islam.[55]

This was, according to the traditions, to escape persecution from the Quraysh of Mecca. Muhammad advised his followers to seek protection in Ethiopia on account that 'it is a friendly country', and one of the female refugees who later became a wife of Muhammad is reported to have said: 'When we reached Abyssinia the Negus [the king] gave us a kind reception. We safely practised our religion, and we worshipped God, and suffered no wrong in word or deed.'[56] In other words, black Africa provided a safe haven for persecuted Muslims, thereby making a vital contribution to the preservation of nascent Arab-Islam.

Many writers who refer to this tradition always speak of 'Christian Abyssinia' in a bid to stress the 'Christian' aspect of Ethiopia at the time. The 'Christian' aspect of Ethiopian heritage at the time was no doubt an important contributory factor in motivating the Prophet of Islam to advise his persecuted followers to seek asylum there. Having said that, it is our suggestion, indeed contention, that the goodwill and hospitality accorded persecuted nascent Islam is attributable to the indigenous African tradition of enclavement, on the one hand, and the inclusiveness of the indigenous environment, on the other.

Even though we do not dispute the profound impact of the Christian tradition on Ethiopia at the time, so indigenized were and still are its ritual practices that it was declared a 'heathen land' by European missionaries who went out to 'convert' it in the eighteenth and nineteenth centuries.[57] In suggesting that the tolerance and accommodation accorded nascent Islam is attributable to the inherent inclusiveness of the indigenous environment, we do

---

54. Ibid.
55. A. Guillaume, *The Life of Muhammad: A Translation of Ibn Ishāq's Sirat Rasul Allāh*, (London: Oxford University, 1955), pp. 146 ff.
56. Ibid., pp. 146 and 150.
57. J. McManners (ed.), *The Oxford History of Christianity* (Oxford: Oxford University, 1993), chapter 13, *passim*.

40 The Legacy of Arab-Islam in Africa

not necessarily imply or suggest that Christianity is inherently intolerant. The historical fact, though, is that Christendom, especially Western Christianity in power, has been anything but tolerant.

The indigenous African tradition of enclavement formed the basis of a 'client–patron' and 'stranger–host' relationship between dispersed Muslim communities and their largely traditional host communities throughout most of black Africa. The tradition derives from a general custom whereby the first settlers on a land enter into a 'steward–owner' relationship with the earth god/dess or spirit. The earth god/dess is believed to be the owner of the land, including all natural objects such as trees, minerals, rocks, etc. on it, while the first settlers become the 'stewards' of the land.

Writing on traditional Birom and Kilba beliefs on land ownership in northern Nigeria, Lisa Rasmussen observes that land is considered as a 'sacred trust, a gift from the community (or ancestors), and land rights originated from sanctified ancestors or gods'.[58] In most cases, while as 'stewards' first settlers can sell natural objects such as trees of economic value or minerals, they cannot sell the land.[59]

First settlers reserve the right of land 'custodianship' and all later settlers are expected to settle and cultivate the land as guests of the first settlers. The first settlers then act as host or patrons to later settlers who are almost always regarded as 'strangers'. Patronage to non-kin groups was a traditional African requirement, which in turn assured the survival of and safeguarded the interest of non-kin or 'stranger' groups in general.

As has been intimated in the preceding section, Muslim groups settled in tropical Africa not as a result of any military conquest but largely if not solely as dispersed professionals, i.e. traders, artisans, pastoralists and religious professionals. These communities did not disperse as whole ethnic or tribal units but as individuals and only occasionally as family units. The first priority of these dispersed Muslim minorities was, therefore, to guarantee their lives and wares, a guarantee they could not afford by themselves for obvious reasons. Muslim traders in particular needed protection from banditry, safe passage through potentially hostile lands, and patronage for the promotion of their business interests.

Traditional rulers among the more centralized societies and kingdoms, and influential families and individuals among the less centralized communities, by and large provided this patronage under the tradition of enclavement. This

---

58. L. Rasmussen, *Religion and Property in Northern Nigeria: Socio-economic Development and Islamic and Christian Influence in Northern Nigeria, with Special Reference to the Rights and Views of Property among the Birom and Kilba* (Copenhagen: Academic, 1990), p. 100.

59. K.A. Busia, *The Position of the Chief in the Modern Political System of Ashanti* (London: Oxford University, 1951), pp. 50 ff.

Indigenous Africa as a Cultivating Ground for Arab-Islam 41

explains why, as we intimated in the first part of this chapter, dispersed Muslim groups across tropical Africa tended to settle around areas of political authority. It is from these settlements that the concept of *zongo*, strangers' quarters, emerged in most parts of East and West Africa. Some of these 'stranger-quarters' developed into big cities like Mombasa in Kenya, Bobo-Dioulasso in Burkina Faso and a host of other smaller towns.

Early Arab and Persian Muslim traders in East Africa sought patronage and protection from indigenous rulers amongst the Sofali, Beja, Ganda, Nyamwezi and Yao. According to T.O. Beidelman, Arab traders 'appear to have found the larger and more effective political systems of the Nyamwezi and the central lakes region to be admirably organized' for their trading activities.[60] Similarly, P.J.A. Rigby, writing on the Gogo people of Tanzania, describes the trade routes that passed through Ugogo as 'considered hostile by all travellers', and observes that 'relations between the Muslim traders and the Gogo were mainly concerned with the right of passage through Ugogo and the provision of supplies for the caravans'.[61]

Other observers writing as late as 1860 about Arab traders in the interior enclaves of East Africa appeared amazed that 'the Arabs now depend for existence there [Nyamweziland] not upon prestige, but sufferance, in consideration of mutual commercial advantages.'[62] In the same way, founders of Muslim religious settlements, *jama'at*, in Somaliland were initially 'adopted' into the various clans and tribes by means of clientele, having to accept the 'inferior status of a client, bound to observe the obligations of a tribesman and subservient to chiefs and elders'.[63]

The principle of patronage was also widespread in the western Sudan. As early as the mid-eleventh century, Muslim groups in ancient Ghana lived in separate quarters – like the *zongos* of modern Ghana – under the auspices of the traditional ruler. One such ruler 'was praised for his love of justice and generosity towards the Muslims... He had a mosque near his court where Muslims prayed when they called upon him.'[64] This tradition continued among such African kingdoms as Bornu, Jolof, Mandinka, Bambara, Moosi, Hausa, Mamprusi, Dagomba, Gonja, Ashanti, etc.

A traditional elder of the Birom tribe of northern Nigeria relayed the following typical example of how strangers, and in this case dispersed Hausa Muslim traders, were received through the tradition of enclavement:

A few Hausa men came to the chief and asked him for a place to live ... The chief led them to a certain place where, he said, they could build their houses.

60. Quoted in P.J.A. Rigby, 'Sociological Factors in the Contact of the Gogo of Central Tanzania with Islam', in Lewis (ed.), *Islam in Tropical Africa*, p. 269.
61. Ibid., pp. 269–70.
62. Trimingham, *Islam in East Africa*, p. 24.
63. I. M. Lewis, *Peoples of the Horn of Africa*, pp. 149–50.
64. Al-Bakri, cited in Levtzion, 'Islamization in West Africa', p. 208.

42 The Legacy of Arab-Islam in Africa

But first the *sarkin tsafi* [traditional land priest] performed a ritual of purification in the ground and it was declared that from that time forward no Birom should live on this 'foreign land' or even plant a farm on it.[65]

The traditional mechanism of enclavement allowed non-kin Muslim communities and other artisans and their religious professionals to acquire land for settlement and to transact their activities relatively peacefully within largely indigenous traditional societies. In what is now modern-day Gambia, Mandingo rulers played host to 'stranger' groups like the Fulani (in their various dialect groups), the Wolof, the Dyula and the Serakhulle.[66] Alien and non-kin groups were generally received and in most cases allowed to live in fairly autonomous settlements as long as they recognized the traditional authority and posed no threat to it.

Muslim communities for their part accepted the system and lived, traded and practised their religion relatively peacefully among the overwhelming non-Muslim host indigenous communities. Muslim settlements in most parts of black Africa, therefore, in the words of J.S. Trimingham, represented 'islands of Islam in a sea of paganism'.[67] Some scholars have suggested that the patronage given to Muslim communities by traditional rulers amounted to reducing the former to the status of *dhimmī*, protected minorities, and therefore was a contravention of the *shari'a*, which does not permit Muslims to live as *dhimmīs* under a non-Islamic system.[68]

Leaving aside the fact that this theory is advanced to justify the jihad movements, the meaning of *dhimmī* in the old African context needs some qualification since the concept is alien to traditional Africa. If by *dhimmīs* what is meant is that Muslim groups were protected minorities as the literal meaning of the word stands, then there can be hardly any dispute of its applicability in the African context. For, as we have stated above, Muslims were at this stage, by and large, non-kin minorities who sought patronage and protection from already settled majority indigenous communities.

However, if by *dhimmīs* it is meant that Muslim communities were regarded as a sort of second-class citizen with specific discriminatory regulations aimed at them, as some spokesmen of the jihadists' tradition would have us believe,[69] then the suggestion is part of post-jihad apologia to justify eighteenth- and nineteenth-century Muslim militancy mainly in western Sudan. Contrary to

---

65. Gilliland, *African Religion Meets Islam*, pp. 62–3.
66. C.A. Quinn, *Mandingo Kingdoms of the Senegambia: Traditionalism, Islam, and European Expansion* (London: Longman, 1972), pp. 17–28.
67. Trimingham, *Influence of Islam*, p. 39.
68. J. R. Willis, 'Jihād Fī Sabīl Allāh – its Doctrinal Basis in Islam and Some Aspects of its Evolution in Nineteenth-Century West Africa', *Journal of African History*, vol. 8, no. 3 (1967), p. 398.
69. Sulaiman, *Revolution in History*, p. vii.

Indigenous Africa as a Cultivating Ground for Arab-Islam 43

claims that Muslim minorities were oppressed and discriminated against, J.S. Trimingham makes a lucid observation of the traditional system with regard to the status of subjects within the body politic of traditional Africa as follows: 'In the same way, as each individual had his status in the family defined according to age, sex, and filiation, so in the state each lineage had its hereditary status and role according to occupation.'[70]

In other words, non-kin Muslim groups, who were invariably regarded as of a different lineage from the wider indigenous communities, had their status and heritage safeguarded under the body politic of traditional Africa. In this way Arab-Islam was preserved under the traditional system. Apart from the fact that within the traditional system different lineage groups (including Muslim) had their 'rightful' places, early Muslim communities were by and large accorded a specially favoured status not shared even by the masses of the indigenous society. Muslim groups were generally regarded as second only to the ruling classes throughout most of traditional black Africa.

This had to do with the fact that literary expertise of the Muslim divines 'became invested with a supernatural power, particularly where writing is primarily a religious activity'.[71] This special technological enterprise, i.e. writing: the alphabet, pens, ink, paper, earned Muslim religious men high esteem and reverence in the wider society. The traders, on the other hand, were welcomed and held in high esteem because of their wares such as salt, cloth, etc. In addition to this, traditional African respect and homage to religious objects and personalities as sacred were extended to Muslims and their lives were regarded in most traditional societies as inviolable.

Early European visitors were generally amazed at the way non-kin Muslim minority groups enjoyed peaceful and prosperous status within indigenous communities despite their numerical vulnerability. Writing about the status of the Dyula in the midst of traditional Bambara society, a nineteenth-century European visitor was astonished that the Bambara, 'owing to their superiority of numbers [could] molest them [the Dyula] if they choose, yet they refrain from doing so, and go to their villages to sell them the superfluous produce of their harvest.'[72]

Similarly, J. Dupuis, the British consul to Ashanti in 1818, wrote that the Ashanti population venerated Muslims in Kumasi as 'demi-gods, and look for an increase of wealth in proportion as they compete in tendering respect and offers of service to their visitors'. Dupuis even claims that throughout a journey the Muslim 'seldom disburses a miskal of gold or cowrees (the value of ten shillings) but, on the contrary, is frequently a gainer by the generosity of princes, and his

70. J.S. Trimingham, *A History of Islam in West Africa* (Oxford: Oxford University, 1962), pp. 34–5.
71. Goody, 'Restricted Literacy in Northern Ghana', p. 230.
72. Trimingham, *A History of Islam in West Africa*, p. 187.

44 The Legacy of Arab-Islam in Africa

daily wants are moreover liberally supplied at their expenses, and oftentimes with unbounded hospitality'.[73]

From the above examples, it can be said that if Muslims were protected minorities (*dhimmis*) at all, as they certainly were in the literal sense of the word, then they were, by and large, favoured rather than oppressed minorities. Having said that, one has to guard against romanticizing or overstating the inherent hospitality of the indigenous environment towards non-kin groups in general and Muslim minorities in particular. To give the impression that indigenous hospitality was slavishly accorded to Muslim groups regardless can be misleading. A related romanticism that needs to be guarded against is the impression that Muslim groups were accorded a favourable protected-minority status because of the spontaneous appeal of their unique Islamic identity.

Sulayman Nyang falls into this trap of romanticism when he claims that indigenous people welcomed Muslim groups because the former were 'very impressed by the religious devotion of the merchants who most likely stopped their business transactions to engage in the prescribed five daily prayers'.[74] Real and significant as the inherent inclusiveness and openness of the indigenous environment and the socio-religious esteem for Muslim groups were in the relationship, overstating one or the other risks losing sight of the crucial art of pragmatism which was the watchword on both sides.

It is said, for instance, that Nana Osei Kwame, King of Ashanti (1777–1804), was dethroned because of what the elders saw as his unguarded enthusiasm towards the Muslim tradition, which was viewed as a potential threat to the traditional system.[75] Starting from about the sixteenth century, the Moosi, to take another example, had the Yarse (a Mande Muslim trading group) settled in separate communities throughout the kingdom and had *imams* at their courts who had significant influence over the rulers. The flirtation of the Moosi rulers with the Islamic tradition ranged from using the services of Muslim divines to conversion to Islam.

The tension of striking a balance between the traditional system and the Islamic tradition remained evident, as one Moosi ruler is said to have sent away his heir apparent for 'being too favourable to Islam' and deposed a sub-chief for the same reason. So delicate was the relationship that even the most devoted Muslim Moosi ruler, Moro-Naba Kutu, sent most of his sons to Qur'anic schools except his first-born, the heir apparent.[76] Muslims also had their own dilemmas, which culminated in the jihad movements of the eighteenth and nineteenth centuries, as will become apparent in chapter 3. It is the ramifications of the relationship as they relate to the preservation and propagation of Islam that we now proceed to highlight.

73. Wilks, 'Muslims in Metropolitan Ashanti', pp. 148 and 153.
74. Nyang, *African Identity*, pp. 36–7.
75. Wilks, 'Muslims in Metropolitan Ashanti', pp. 160–1.
76. Levtzion, *Muslims and Chiefs in West Africa*, p. 168.

THE SOCIO-RELIGIOUS DYNAMICS

The implications of the status of non-kin Muslim minorities in the midst of overwhelming non-Muslim societies were profound and complicated for both parties. Muslim minorities, on their part, were caught between the desire to preserve their identity and status, which, thanks to Islam, distinguished them from the majority indigenous communities they lived with, and the universal missionary imperatives of sharing Islam with the wider community. The apprehension that minority Muslim groups had of losing their distinctive identity, which Islam accorded them, was not just theoretical and unfounded but real.

There have been instances in some parts of northern Ghana and Togo, whereby Muslim groups underwent a cultural assimilation, losing their distinctive Islamic identity and turning their praying-grounds into shrines where sacrifices were made to invoke the aid of the 'Muslim god'.[77] In an apparent self-protectionist endeavour therefore Islam among early dispersed Muslim communities (Arab, Swahili, Moor, Dyula, Fulani, Hausa, etc.) in tropical Africa was jealously guarded as a divinely sanctioned social and cultural entity that was not to be opened to or shared with others.

Among the Dyula Islam was a Dyula way of life! As observed, 'the question "are you Muslim?" was always translated "are you Dyula?"'.[78] Thus, the distinction between Muslim and non-Muslim corresponded to that of the divide between Dyula and non-Dyula. This made it difficult both for the Dyula Muslim to share Islam with the non-Dyula and for the non-Dyula to adopt Islam.

An early colonial administrator in Korhogo in the Ivory Coast relates the following anecdote, which reflects the lack of interest in sharing the Islamic tradition among the Dyula. The anecdote has it that once a traditional chief converted to Islam and began to practise the faith with all the enthusiasm of a neophyte. The chief's zeal ironically caused some embarrassment to the local Muslim divines. When an epidemic broke out, the Muslim divines reportedly told the chief:

> Do not be astonished if the village is subjected to Allah's wrath. He has done well by putting everyone in his place. You have transgressed His orders, and have abandoned the faith of your fathers, whom God manifestly commanded to drink palm wine, to eat unclean meat, and to worship only stones, mountains, and trees.[79]

In East Africa, Arab, Persian, Shirazi, Swahili and Asian-Muslim groups developed an even greater sense of social distancing from their traditional

77. Ibid., pp. 144–5.
78. Green, 'Islamization of Kong', p. 106.
79. Launay, *Beyond the Stream*, p. 57.

46 The Legacy of Arab-Islam in Africa

African neighbours. This had more to do with racial and cultural chauvinism towards the indigenous people than a purely minority syndrome as in the case of the Dyula in West Africa. Here Islam came to be closely identified with perceived Arab superiority on the coast and regarded as an *ustaarabu*, i.e. civilization, whereas the indigenous people living in the hinterland were referred to as *washenzi* (savages). In Tanzania in particular, Muslim traders were specifically known as *valungwana* (civilized people) and people had to become Muslim in order to become *valungwana*.[80]

To share Islam with the *washenzi* under such circumstances risked compromising the status of Muslims. Thus the Ibadis are said to have encouraged their African slaves to follow the Shafi'i legal tradition in order to preserve Ibadiyya as a tribal religion of the waManga.[81] Indigenous people who nevertheless converted to Islam were, therefore, by and large treated by immigrant Muslim groups as second-class Muslims. Religious leadership such as the office of the *imam* became the preserve of immigrant Muslims over indigenous converts to Islam irrespective of the level of religious education, a situation very reminiscent of the way early Arab-Muslims regarded non-Arab-Muslims (*mawālī*).[82]

As a result, right up to the twentieth century, and in some cases the present day, Arabs and Swahilis would not assume a subordinate religious role to, say, a Yao Muslim in East Africa, or the Moorish before a Wolof in Senegal, a Hausa/Fulani before a Yoruba in Nigeria or a Dyula/Hausa before a Moosi, Dagomba, Senufo, Akan, etc., in the Middle Volta Basin. In all those cases immigrant Muslims are the automatic prayer leaders more by virtue of their ethnic origins than the level of their religious knowledge.

The same is true of the Ahmadiyya Movement, founded by Ghulam Ahmad of Qadian in India during the latter part of the nineteenth century, introduced into Ghana in 1921 whence it spread to other parts of Africa. Despite its professed missionary zeal, for a very long time Pakistanis monopolized the leadership ranks of the movement in Africa. This monopoly assumed ideological complications during the nationalistic fervour that gripped the continent at the end of European colonial rule.

Ghanaian Ahmadis presented a memorandum to the then head of the Qadiani faction, Mirza Nasir Ahmad, during a visit to Ghana in 1970 in which they expressed the indigenous Ghanaian grievance in the following words: 'Since Ahmadiyyat is looked upon though wrongly in this country as a foreign religious

---

80. C.K. Omari, 'Christian–Muslim Relations in Tanzania: The Socio-political Dimension', *Bulletin on Islam and Christian–Muslim Relations in Africa*, vol. 2, no. 2 (April 1984), p. 7.
81. Trimingham, *Islam in East Africa*, p. 81.
82. B. Lewis, *Race and Slavery in the Middle East: An Historical Enquiry* (New York: Oxford University, 1990), pp. 37–8.

Indigenous Africa as a Cultivating Ground for Arab-Islam 47

organisation, manned only by foreigners, we humbly suggest that this wrong notion be removed by allowing greater participation in the local religious administration by Ghanaians.'[83]

Affiliation to Sufi orders was also premised along family and kinship lines. Ahmad al-Bakka'i al-Kunti of the Kunta condemned one Muhammad Aqiq of Kel al-Suq *zawaya* of betrayal 'for having chosen the Sudanis in preference to the whites – the Fulanis in preference to the people of al-Suq',[84] because the latter left the Qadiriyya, which presumably was regarded as the order of the whites, to join the Tijaniyya order (of the blacks) of al-Hajj 'Umar Tal. In Nigeria it is known that the Tijaniyya order is strongly patronized by the Hausa while the Qadiriyya has largely remained the preserve of the Fulani.

These developments meant that particular communities already competing against each other on different grounds further demarcated themselves by joining rival Islamic persuasions, thereby further complicating the issue of religious conversion. The strong communal and ethnic bonds as they relate to Islam, and the notion of the Muslim *umma* has been commented upon by J.S. Trimingham, who observed that 'the change brought about by Islam [and Christianity for that matter] in this respect should not be exaggerated, the old bases of community remain paramount and the ideal of the unity of believers a superimposed linkage'.[85]

The Dyula in particular seem to have recognized the inherent contradiction between the universal claims of Islam and their apparent tribalization and quarantining of the religion. They developed a curious doctrine to the effect that all just men – including non-Muslims – could be admitted to Islam after death and saved eventually in a sort of purgatory called the Tabakoroni.[86] But this compounded rather than alleviated their dilemma. For the Dyula of Korhogo ironically referred to their Senufo neighbours collectively as *banmana*, 'refusers' or those who refused Islam,[87] even though they themselves were anything but keen to convert the non-Dyula.

The label 'refusers', though, reveals two other dilemmas on the part of traditional people. First of all, like the village chief mentioned above, there were those indigenous people who admired Islam and aspired after full conversion but were literally made to feel uncomfortable and awkward by the attitude of the minority Muslim groups. The second dilemma had to do with converting to Islam, which, in the eyes of indigenous communities, was an aspect of the way of

---

83. A.K. Atta-Wenchie, 'Ahmadiyya Movement in Ghana', (BA dissertation, University of Cape Coast, 1986), p. 32.
84. J.R. Willis, *In the Path of Allah: The Passion of Al-Hajj 'Umar: An Essay into the Nature of Charisma in Islam* (London: Frank Cass, 1989), p. 203.
85. Trimingham, *Influence of Islam*, p. 85.
86. Y. Person, 'Samori and Islam', in Willis (ed.), *The Cultivators of Islam*, p. 261.
87. Launay, *Beyond the Stream*, p. 55.

48 The Legacy of Arab-Islam in Africa

life of a non-kin group, and entailed the implied but real risk of losing one's own identity. Thus, these became 'refusers'.

The dilemmas on the part of the indigenous communities with regard to conversion to Islam had to do mainly with the traditional African understanding of 'religion' whence ensues their perceptions of 'Muslim' and 'Islam'. This is reflected in the way indigenous people referred to Muslim settlements as *zongos* (strangers' quarters) in the towns or by the ethnic name of the group such as Yarsin (Yarse settlement), Moosin (Moosi settlement), Wangarasin (Wangara settlement), etc. in some parts of northern Ghana. Muslim groups were, therefore, identified by their ethnicity followed by their profession, which in most cases was trade rather than their religion, Islam. Their identity as 'Muslims' was hardly prominent, and where it did appear it always served more as an adjective than a proper noun.

A court official of the paramount chief of the Moosi insisted in an interview that 'les Yarse [a Muslim merchant community] font le salam, mais ils ne sont pas des croyants; ils sont commerçants et voyageurs'.[88] In other words, the Yarse perform prayers, but they are not believers, they are traders and travellers! The official's 'confusion' here reveals something of the traditional African understanding of religion, namely that religion is not and cannot be institutionalized. Talking about the traditional African understanding of religion, R.E.S. Tanner makes the following perceptive observation:

> African languages have no equivalent for the western word 'religion' or indeed 'ritual' so in order to consider the religions of Christianity and Islam, they have to start using an alien and imported word. Similarly the practitioners of African traditional religions do not look upon their religious beliefs and practices as a distinct set of activities separated from economic or other ones, nor are they defined as the religions of Yoruba, Zulu or Kamba peoples as if they were national churches. An old traditionalist on being asked his religion would reply 'I am a Zulu' or whatever.[89]

Consequently, even though Africans are pervasively religious one cannot talk of 'religion' *per se* in traditional African terms. In other words one can talk of 'religiosity' but not 'religion' if the former is seen as the awareness and quest for metaphysical phenomena while the latter is seen in terms of a codified and institutionalized set of doctrines and ritual practices. The African way of life in every aspect is immersed in 'religion', so much so that to ask him/her what is religion is like asking: who are you? As a Chinese proverb has it, 'If you want a definition of water, do not ask a fish.' The only definition of 'religion' to the African, therefore, is that it is indefinable; because 'the religion of Africa does not

---

88. Levtzion, 'Merchants vs. Scholars and Clerics', pp. 21–3.
89. R.E.S. Tanner, 'African Traditional Religions and their Reactions to Other Faiths', *Studia Missionalia*, vol. 42 (1993), p. 378.

live in the pages of books on "world religions", rather it lives in the hearts and lives' of people.[90]

As far as the traditional African is concerned, kinship rather than 'religion' is what distinguishes one community from another. Muslim groups were seen as any other lineage or clan, with their own culture of which Islam was just a part of the whole. Islam as a way of life or system of beliefs and practices was therefore conceived by the wider non-Muslim community in relation to particular ethnic groups. It was hardly seen as an institutionalized universal system of beliefs and practices meant for everyone to *belong*.[91] In traditional African thought, therefore, one can speak of religious figures like prieststesses rather than 'religious communities'.

The term 'Muslim' (in all its variations in the vernaculars) was used to refer to Muslim religious divines in the same sense as traditional priests and priestesses rather than whole communities. In fact, within Muslim groups like the Dyula and the Wolof, the stricter observances of Islamic rituals such as the liturgical prayers, fasting, etc., were regarded by the ordinary members of the community as binding only on the religious professional class. Thus, while 'the distinction between Muslim and non-Muslim corresponded to that between Dyula and non-Dyula; among the Dyula in turn, only the *mory* (Dyula variant for "Muslim" used to refer to religious scholars) were obligated in principle to follow the strictures of Islamic law diligently'.[92]

This religious 'laxity' on the part of the majority of ordinary African-Muslims (and Christians) reveals the African perception of religion as specialized but not institutionalized. This perception regards the priest/ess as those under obligation, in addition to the general observances of the community, to observe the minutest details associated with a particular cult or god/dess because of his/her special role.

The implications of the traditional African understanding of religion are twofold. First of all, it raised a serious barrier for indigenous conversion to Islam. For in a sense, since there are no 'religious' boundaries in traditional thought, there was, in effect, nothing to cross over or convert from. 'Religion' is therefore non-missionary. Also, since Islam was seen by the traditional indigenous person in relation to particular non-kin ethnic groups, the implication was that to become Muslim amounted to changing one's ethnicity. As J.S. Mbiti puts it, 'a

90. Opoku, 'African Traditional Religion', p. 68.
91. A well-known incident in this connection is reported of the amazement and bemusement of a traditional chief of Ghana, Akropong, at white missionary zeal and demands of 'conversions' of his people to Christianity. The chief is reported to have told the missionaries to produce one black Christian to convince him that Christianity was for blacks. As far as the chief was concerned, Christianity was a white man's affair.
92. Launay, *Beyond the Stream*, p. 55; See also Levtzion, 'Merchants vs. Scholars and Clerics', p. 22.

50 The Legacy of Arab-Islam in Africa

person cannot be converted from one tribal religion to another: he has to be born in the particular society in order to participate in the entire religious life of the people'.[93]

In this regard an indigenous Tiv of northern Nigeria observed: 'Anyone who does *salla* (*salāt*) is considered a Hausa man, he is no longer accepted as a Tiv. Why then should anyone wish to do it?'[94] This is because as far as the Tiv are concerned, Islam is an aspect of Hausa way of life. Contrary, therefore, to claims that Islamization was easy and conversion less of a problem to Africans because Muslim agents were Africans, the 'non-kinness' of the African-Muslim groups became a barrier to the adoption of Islam by the wider indigenous communities.

Because 'religion' has no defined boundaries the whole question of 'religious conversion' of individuals *per se* did not arise, and where it did, it was perceived both by the Muslim group and the wider community in terms other than religious. Among the Wolof in West Africa, it is reported that a person of noble origin converted to Islam at the risk of losing his right of inheritance and marriage within the nobility, while in East Africa conversion within some communities was seen as becoming a Swahili, which also warranted losing one's claim of inheritance and land tenure.[95] In fact, as will be made clear in chapter 3, sudden and mass conversions to Islam in northern Nigeria evoked a sense of unease, apprehension and hostility from the Hausa ruling elite.[96]

One ruler, Nafata (1794–1801), literally imposed a ban on Hausa conversion to Islam, or rather a particular version of Islam as espoused by the preacher turned jihadist Uthman Dan Fodio (d. 1817), and asked all male converts to revert to the traditions of their fathers. Nafata viewed the wearing of turbans and veils ('Fulani nomadic dresses' in that context) as a challenge to the system he represented, and banned their use. These measures, taken to safeguard the traditional Hausa way of life, were in turn seen by Dan Fodio as religious intolerance and persecution of the Muslim religion, leading to confrontation and jihad.

The second implication of the African understanding of 'religion' as non-institutionalized and a non-codified system of beliefs and practices is that people could appropriate religious arts, rituals and other services without necessarily being 'members' of or having to 'convert' to the particular tradition. In other words, there is an implicit openness and inclusiveness in traditional African religiosity that permits the appropriation and exchanges of ideas and rituals at the individual and communal level without one having to change one's 'religion'.

---

93. J.S. Mbiti, *African Religions and Philosophy*, 2nd edn (Oxford: Heinemann, 1989), p. 101.
94. Gilliland, *African Religion Meets Islam*, p. 63.
95. L.G. Colvin, 'The Shaykh's Men: Religion and Power in Senegambian Islam', in Levtzion and Fisher (eds.), *Rural and Urban Islam*, p. 57.
96. Hiskett, *The Sword of Truth*, p. 48.

As J.S. Mbiti puts it, 'as with material culture, religious ideas and activities are exchanged when people come into contact with one another... this exchange of ideas is spontaneous, and is probably more noticeable in practical matters like rain-making, combating magic and witchcraft and dealing with misfortunes'.[97] Thus, while one could not participate as a 'member' of a religious system – since there is nothing like a 'religious' system anyway – one could be a 'client' or customer to any religious services.

'Conversion' in the traditional African understanding of religion was therefore more a matter of the freedom of appropriating religious rituals, arts and services for personal or communal use than the crossing over of persons from one 'religion' to another. Thus, ironically, the strength and appeal of Islam manifested in the high demand for Islamic religious elements was equally the main debilitating factor in the adoption of Islam as an institutionalized system or way of life. It is within this context that our earlier intimation that Muslim religious arts of divination, charms and amulets were, and still in most cases remain, at best indirect means of conversion to Islam should be understood.

The spread of Islam as an institutionalized system of beliefs and practices or as 'a way of life' was not, therefore, only neutralized by the traditional African perception of religion, but where Islam was adopted it meant a blending with, rather than a complete break away from, indigenous practices. Consequently, African Muslim and Christian groups and individuals throughout the continent continue, after centuries of conversion, to combine their traditional cultural and religious customs with Arab-Islamic and Western-Christian ones.[98]

The eclectic religious cosmology of traditional Africa and the consequent 'inclusive religiosity' of Africans, meant that most African Muslims could go for Christian religious arts and services and vice versa or continue to dabble in traditional African religious elements.[99] This eclectic perception of religion was bound to pose a serious challenge to Islam and Christianity with their abrupt and exclusive doctrinal claims. Over the years African Christian and Muslim 'puritans' have expressed concern and open hostility to this phenomenon, describing the 'inclusive religiosity' as 'nominalism', lack of faith or incomplete conversion, descriptions that reveal a lack of appreciation of African religiosity.

Indeed, as far as the so-called nominal Muslims and Christians are concerned, trying and experimenting with other traditions is an expression of deep religiosity. To use the words of A.A. Berinyuu, 'it is not a question of lack of faith, or unconversion; it is a question of who can do what and when'.[100]

---

97. Mbiti, *African Religions and Philosophy*, p. 101.
98. Lewis, 'Introduction', pp. 45–75; Trimingham, *Influence of Islam*, pp. 34 ff.
99. Abraham A. Berinyuu: 'The Encounter of Western Christianity and Civilization, and Islam on Ghanaian Culture: Implications for the Ministry of Pastoral Care and Counseling', *Africa Theological Journal*, vol. 17, no. 2 (1988), pp. 140–7.
100. Ibid., p. 147.

52 The Legacy of Arab-Islam in Africa

The query might be raised as to what then happens to 'truth'. The traditional African's response to such a query is that truth, in so far as it relates to religious matters, is functional. Religious truth is not a set of doctrinal or creedal statements meant to be logically argued and proven.

The resultant configuration of the interaction between black African heritage and its Arab-Islamic counterpart within the eclectic traditional African religious environment has been described in rather derogatory and unfavourable terms by different observers. In general, contemporary Western observers refer to it as 'African Islam', 'l'Islam noir', 'popular Islam', 'mixed Islam', etc., in contra-distinction to what these writers perceive as 'orthodox Islam', 'normative Islam' or 'pure Islam'.[101] We shall examine the notion of 'pure', 'orthodox' or 'normative' Islam and what precisely is meant by 'religious contamination' in chapter 5.

However, the point to be noted here is that one of the main reasons advanced to justify military jihad as a religious duty in black Africa by its advocates was this same notion of 'contaminating' Islam with traditional African religious and customary elements, as will be elaborated in chapter 3. In other words, the eighteenth- and nineteenth-century jihad movements of West Africa were a direct response or reaction to the African tradition of 'inclusive religiosity' which the jihadists regarded as a threat to 'orthodox' and 'pure' Islam.

A curious aspect of the 'inclusive religiosity' of indigenous Africa that has fascinated some observers in relation to conversion to Islam has to do with situations in which non-Muslims are said to pledge unborn children to be born as Muslims. This normally happens in cases when a woman has her children persistently dying soon after birth, or barrenness. In some cases the misfortune could be ill health. Among the Moosi of Burkina Faso for example, the misfortunes relating to childbirth among non-Muslim women may be treated by divinatory diagnosis that the would-be children are refusing to be or are prevented from birth or survival except as Muslims.[102] In this case the remedy is for the would-be child to be born 'Muslim'.

Among the Giriama of Kenya, to take another example, people suffering from some chronic illness may be diagnosed as having been possessed by Muslim spirits for which the cure is, once again, conversion to Islam. In fact, these practices are very common among the Kusasi of north-eastern Ghana and other Moole–Dagbani people groups of the Middle Volta Basin of West Africa. The fascination here, in the context of Muslim (and Christian) competitive triumphalism and expansionism, is the way in which traditional religions apparently conspire against their own interest.

---

101. See Monteil, *L'Islam noir,* pp. 41–9; Fisher, 'Conversion Reconsidered', p. 31; Levtzion, 'Islamization in West Africa', pp. 215 ff.
102. E.P. Skinner, 'Islam in Mossi Society', in Lewis (ed.), *Islam in Tropical Africa,* p. 183.

First of all, the question that needs to be addressed is the rationale behind the phenomenon as far as the people involved are concerned. In other words, why do traditional African people pledge unborn children to be born as 'Muslims'? The first point to bear in mind is that the practice no doubt ensues from the inherent openness and 'inclusive religiosity' in indigenous traditions, which encourages experimentation with all religious phenomena, as discussed above. This religious eclecticism, as alluded to above, does not mean competition and therefore superiority and inferiority on the part of any tradition.[103] It is a question of which particular spirit, god, medium, cult or tradition is associated with what functions.

The second point is that the practice was an age-old custom within such societies long before the Muslim presence and is still widespread amongst the Kusasi and other people groups of north-eastern Ghana. Here unborn children are pledged to particular deities, the most famous known as *goonab*, in northern Togo. Such children, when born, are taken to the god and made to observe certain dietary and other restrictions. The pledging of unborn children to the 'Muslim Deity', therefore, is done alongside those of other African divinities and cults. The same is true of ill health, especially mental or psychiatric disorders.

The third point is that these misfortunes are understood as having various causes, among which are the following. First, when a woman experiences the death of her children soon after birth, for instance, the belief is that the necessary enquiries and provision for the child's sojourn in this world have not been adequately carried out. For example, all children are believed to come with their destinies, which include special 'vocations'. Thus, some children may be born to serve specific deities, in which case the deity must be identified and the necessary provision in terms of sacrifices and items needed for the vocation such as special uniforms, made in advance. Without these, it is believed the child will 'return' (die) soon after it 'arrives' (is born). In addition, the child is made to observe dietary and other restrictions as it relates to the deity in question. Hence, when a diviner indicates that a soon-to-be-born child is destined to be 'Muslim', a belief that must have been influenced by the Muslim presence, then alms will be offered to a Muslim religious divine, and then upon birth the child is given a 'Muslim name' and circumcised; a Muslim prayer circle is erected in the compound and the child is made to observe Islamic dietary restrictions.[104]

Second, when in such misfortunes as infant mortality the sex of the children happens to be the same two or three consecutive times, the belief is that it is the same child who keeps coming and going because of a struggle between the living

---

103. Levtzion talks of Islam making its appeal 'in *competition* with the African traditional religions, proving its *superiority* as a source of blessings' (emphasis added). See 'Islamization in West Africa', p. 210.

104. Skinner, 'Islam in Mossi Society', pp. 183–4.

54 *The Legacy of Arab-Islam in Africa*

and ancestral worlds for the child's custody. Some of the ways to outwit the ancestral world include pledging the child to a strange deity, thereby spiritually 'excommunicating' the unborn child out of the kin group, which includes the ancestral world. The Kusasi call this *zamba'an*, which means 'pegging'. Thus in actual fact 'pledging' could be slightly misleading. This 'excommunication' or 'pegging' is believed to discourage or prevent the ancestors from coming for the child, since he/she is no longer kin.

Another way is to give the child a horrible name at birth, such as Ayamdaog for males and Ayampoak for females, meaning male and female slave respectively amongst the Kusasi.[105] Yet another way is to disfigure or disguise the child by giving it particular facial marks. In all these the belief is to make the child less attractive or recognizable by the ancestral spirits. In cases where children are 'pegged' to the 'Muslim deity', they are simply given names like Amor (Muslim), Ayarig or Asimiig, denoting Yarse and Fulani (both Muslim groups) respectively.

The main point that needs to be borne in mind here is that 'pegging' unborn children to the 'Muslim deity' or 'converting' to Islam to avert a misfortune is just one of many remedies in non-Muslim African societies.[106] Even more significantly, instances of actual conversion to Islam to remedy a misfortune are as rare as they are curious. Rarely do such individuals, especially children, grow up as practising Muslims beyond having the 'Muslim name'. The fact that any one such child may be called 'Muhammad' does not mean they share the Muslim faith in reality just as those who are called Ayarig or Asimiig do not belong to the Yarse or Fulani ethnic group in reality.

Speaking from experience of what pertains amongst the Moole–Dagbani people groups (of which the Moosi are a part) in general and the Kusasi in particular, whose traditions, customs and worldviews the writer knows and shares, in actual practice most if not all children 'pegged' to the Muslim god grow up in the traditions of their non-Muslim parents. This is mainly because of the non-Muslim environment in which such children are brought up. Therefore to speak of the practice as an 'effective … technique for gaining converts to Islam'[107] is misleading.

'Conversion' to Islam (and Christianity) in tropical Africa is therefore ambiguous, not only because of the very subjective nature of conversion itself, but because of how religion is perceived in traditional African terms. Conversion was not a simple matter of people coming to a 'better' or 'fuller' awareness and experience of the Supreme Being systematically set out in doctrinal or creedal formulae. Lamin Sanneh makes this point well:

105. For the importance and meaning of African names, see Mbiti, *African Religions and Philosophy*, p. 115.
106. For the various traditional methods see, ibid., pp. 162–7.
107. Skinner, 'Islam in Mossi Society', p. 184.

Conversion or resistance to belief is not, at least initially, a matter of verbal debate but of social custom and convention expressed in such things as dietary and sartorial habits, ritual taboos, and ethnic and residential identity. Even in the doctrine of tawhīd, of prescribed belief in the divine unity, is transmitted within the indigenous mythological code of belief in the supernatural and the ethical system based on it, rather than by philosophical disputation, as in Avicenna's or al-Ghazālī's treatises.[108]

J.S. Trimingham's observations about conversion to Christianity in particular and religious change in general within the West African context are very instructive. After acknowledging that direct evangelistic work has had little impact in the conversion of masses of people to Christianity throughout its whole history, Trimingham was struck by the fact that spiritual motives played little part in religious change in West Africa. He declares:

> Most people join Christianity (and Islam) from what we call secondary motives. It seems to be a fact that religions have little chance of spreading upon their own merit. Freedom of choice is rarely involved in change of religion. Conversions in general take place, not because of new insight into reality, but are determined by factors over which most people have no control.[109]

These factors are the socio-political considerations in conversion within traditional African society and this needs to be taken into account. This is particularly important in talking about conversion to Islam in Africa because we are dealing with religious changes and exchanges that took place largely within politically structured systems, i.e. the centralized societies in which dispersed Muslim communities sought and were generally given patronage. For as rightly observed by David Owusu-Ansah, 'the decision to allow or control the "peaceful" process of conversion [to Islam and Christianity] in a centralised African kingdom was a political one and needs to be given that proper treatment'.[110] It is this socio-political dimension of religious change that we now proceed to examine.

THE SOCIO-POLITICAL DYNAMICS

The trickiest aspect of the stranger–host, client–patron relationship between Muslim and non-Muslim indigenous communities was in the socio-political arena. This has to do with the traditional system of land tenure briefly

108. L. Sanneh, *The Crown and the Turban: Muslims and West African Pluralism* (Boulder and Oxford: Westview, 1997), p. 27.
109. J.S. Trimingham, *Islam in West Africa: A Report of a Survey Undertaken in 1952* (London: Wyman & Sons, 1953), pp. 37–8.
110. D. Owusu-Ansah, 'Islamization Reconsidered: An Examination of Asante Responses to Muslim Influence in the Nineteenth Century', *Asian and African Studies*, vol. 21, no. 2 (1987), p. 163.

56 *The Legacy of Arab-Islam in Africa*

referred to above, which is inextricably linked to the office of the chief in more centralized societies as opposed to autochthonous or less centralized societies. The chief holds the land in trust for the community and must always come from a recognized royal lineage, i.e. the first settlers. He is, therefore, not just a political head but successor to the ancestors and representative of both the living and the 'living dead' (J.S. Mbiti's term for ancestors).

As such 'an African ruler is not to his people merely a person who can enforce his will on them. He is the axis of their political relations, the symbol of their unity and exclusiveness, and the embodiment of their essential values. His credentials are mystical and are derived from antiquity.'[111] Rulers drew their political authority from this system and were therefore obliged to maintain the traditional order with its religious and ritual paraphernalia. As K.A. Busia put it,

> no one could be an adequate chief [in Ashanti] who did not perform the ritual functions of his office. ... It is as successors of the ancestors that they are venerated and their authority respected, and they could not keep the office without maintaining contact with the ancestors through the traditional rituals.[112]

There are some implications associated with the traditional land tenure. First of all, it meant that non-kin Muslim communities like all other non-kin groups were given usufructuary rights to settle and cultivate but not to own and sell land. In this regard, it has been pointed out that in Senegambia the term 'Sonninke' came to be identified with the aristocratic class of landowners and rulers, and the term 'marabout' came to be associated with the 'Muslim stranger' who had no land ownership rights.[113] This is due to the fact that, as Lisa Rasmussen summarizes within the context of northern Nigeria, traditional attitudes toward land ownership are as follows:

> 1. Rights in land were vested *in* the community. 2. Rights in occupancy depended upon residence *within* the community. 3. The community, represented by the chief, exercised the control, occupation and use of land. 4. Land could not be alienated by sale but only transferred through inheritance, gift or temporary loan.[114]

Even in areas where Muslims wrested political power by dint of arms from the traditional rulers in Senegambia, Mervyn Hiskett observes that the issue of land

---

111. M. Fortes and E.E. Evans-Pritchard, *African Political Systems* (London: Oxford University, 1940), p. 16.
112. Busia, *The Position of the Chief*, p. 38.
113. C.A. Quinn, 'Mandingo States in the 19th Century', in C.T. Hodge (ed.), *Papers on the Manding* (Bloomington: Indiana University, 1971), p. 215.
114. Rasmussen, *Religion and Property in Northern Nigeria*, p. 100.

Indigenous Africa as a Cultivating Ground for Arab-Islam 57

ownership changing from being traditional to *shari'a* based was largely theoretical, for 'the traditional owners were left in possession provided they co-operated with the Islamic state'.[115]

In Somalia a Muslim religious leader is reported to have said: 'The land is not ours, and if the Shidle [host tribe] desire, they can take it away because they have only adopted us'.[116] Chiefs, sub-chiefs and elders of the host indigenous communities have the right to sell natural objects of economic value on the land and to collect land taxes; 'stranger' groups are not allowed under any circumstance to do any of these.[117] A traditional Ashanti man informed K.A. Busia in 1946 thus: 'The plantains and cocoyams you plant are yours. The land is the chief's. You cannot sell the land. You may mortgage your kola. Only the stool [i.e. the chief and his elders] can sell land ... When a stranger buys land, he buys the surface; that is, the right to use it.'[118]

The second and most crucial implication of the traditional system is that non-kin groups could not become chiefs. Even though Muslims enjoyed special favours from the ruling classes, they, like all other non-kin groups, were allowed to act as leaders of their own communities and to represent them at the traditional court. Their leadership within their communities related to such matters as business affairs, contract signatories and inheritance. As subjects, Muslim groups shared the civic responsibilities of all subjects in general and non-kin groups in particular towards the system, i.e. to render services and pay levies in cash and kind to the traditional courts. To use the words of the traditional Ashanti man once again:

> In the old days everyone who lived on your land was your subject, and so he accompanied you and fought in your wars ... Every year the chief claims money from him, if he has cocoa. If he has no cocoa, he provides a sheep for the stool.[119]

Tariffs, known as *sayhalé* in Bambara and *hongo* in some parts of East Africa, were levied on Muslim traders as transit fees, and the land tax known as *jangali* in Hausaland and *lew* in some parts of Senegambia, were levied on non-kin settler communities (including Muslim).[120]

115. Hiskett, *Islam in West Africa*, pp. 144–5.
116. Lewis, *People of the Horn of Africa*, pp. 149–50.
117. In parts of the Senegambia and northern Ghana where colonial rulers imposed Muslim chiefs over the autochthonous communities or gave land out to non-kin Muslim groups, these new rulers and leaders never assumed certain roles like collecting found treasure-troves or land taxes, which was left to the traditional land priest, known as the *dugu-tigi* or *boroom-lew* and *tengdaan* respectively.
118. Busia, *The Position of the Chief*, p. 50.
119. Ibid. In most cases, the chief also reserved the right to certain portions of animals killed in hunting or during family and clan sacrifices and celebrations. Ibid., p. 51; Quinn, 'Mandingo States', p. 210.
120. Quinn, 'Mandingo States', p. 210.

58 The Legacy of Arab-Islam in Africa

In most cases, however, Muslims were generally exempted from active participation in war and throughout tropical Africa were always distinguished from the warrior group, who were almost always the ruling class. This was the case in the 'marabout–Sonninke' divide of the Senegambia and Dyula–Sonongui divide of Kong in present-day Ivory Coast. The Sonongui are said to have 'recognized the right of the Dyula to refrain from fighting on religious grounds'.[121] Similarly, it is reported that in northern Ghana during a civil war in Salaga in the nineteenth century, militant Hausa Muslims offered to join one faction only to be ordered home by the chief because 'fighting was the business of chiefs, not of Muslims'.[122]

Related to the Muslim–warrior-ruling-class divide is the 'separation' between religion (din), on the one hand, and politics (dawla) seen as worldly and secular (dunya), on the other, as incompatible by some Muslim groups. Philip Curtin has suggested that this stance fitted the interest of minority Muslim groups in Africa who used 'religious prestige to buy a degree of autonomy from secular control' building up a reputation for neutrality in times of war.[123] Lamin Sanneh on his part maintains that the repudiation of war and political neutrality was an ideological rather than strategic position within the Jakhanke communities thanks to the teachings of al-Hajj Salim Suware.[124]

It should be said, though, that the emphasis on a 'principled' and 'consistent political neutrality' of the Jakhanke implies that the Jakhanke were in a position to take political power but declined on (matters of) principle. Although some individual Muslims did decline offers of political offices, in the light of the status of Muslim groups as non-kin minorities delineated so far, such an emphasis risks losing sight of the various traditional mechanisms that were in effect employed to keep non-kin and alien groups out of the political arena, as we shall shortly demonstrate.

Also, the emphasis on Jakhanke pacifism as a consistent ideological principle fails to explain why leading members of the tradition initiated and took part in military jihad during the nineteenth century, albeit for a limited time.[125] This is not to suggest that all Muslims were potential usurpers. What we are saying is that room should be left for pragmatism and indeed opportunism on both sides

---

121. Green, 'Islamization of Kong', pp. 110–12.
122. Levtzion, *Muslims and Chiefs in West Africa*, p. 44. Muslims, through their prayers, divinations, amulets, etc., were nevertheless often intimately involved in the war effort.
123. P. Curtin, 'Jihad in West Africa: Early Phases and Inter-Relations in Mauritania and Senegal', *Journal of African History*, vol. 12, no. 1 (1971), pp. 13–14.
124. L. Sanneh, 'The Origins of Clericalism in West African Islam', *Journal of African History*, vol. 17, no. 1 (1976), pp. 62 ff.
125. Sanneh, *The Jakhanke*, pp. 77–86. The fact that Jakhanke war leaders faced opposition from within the community does not make much difference since all their non-Jakhanke counterparts faced similar oppositions on similar grounds.

Indigenous Africa as a Cultivating Ground for Arab-Islam 59

when talking about the relations between non-kin Muslim minorities living under the patronage of overwhelming indigenous non-Muslim communities. Otherwise the different dilemmas and tensions faced by both parties in the relations can easily be overlooked.

Muslim relations to and influence in traditional courts was, nevertheless, institutionalized, and in some cases quite significant. In Gonjaland of northern Ghana, officiating Muslim divines reminded chiefs during enskinment ceremonies that 'Mallams were to the chief as his wives'.[126] This proverbial statement has a double-edged meaning. First, it confirms the favoured position accorded Muslim divines within the traditional system. Mallams should be treated by the chief as his 'wives'.

A particular group of Muslims in Gonjaland, called the Dogtes, shared the chief's food, came before him without prostrating or removing footwear and could sit on the royal skin, privileges not enjoyed by sub-chiefs or the chief's sons. It also reminded the chief of his responsibility towards the Muslim, to provide him with such material things as he would his wives. This included being gentle and considerate and not harsh with Muslims.

The second meaning is a reminder to the Muslim that he is a 'wife' and not a 'son' who should rival the chief for his office. Like all wives in the traditional sense, Muslims were expected to take the back seat and exert their influence from there. This principle was applied throughout most of tropical Africa in different ways and as the English adage has it, 'behind every successful man there is a woman', so it can be said, 'behind every successful traditional ruler in Africa there was a Muslim'.

This arrangement, while ensuring the protection and indeed favoured position of Muslims in general, as non-kin members of the wider society, effectively circumscribed Muslim direct participation in political affairs, or so traditional rulers thought. But, as alluded to above, Muslim influence on rulers and the traditional courts was more than apparent. European travellers to late nineteenth- and early twentieth-century present-day Burkina Faso, for example, talk of the influence *imams* had on chiefs. In one particular case, one traveller remarked that, 'as a counsellor of the chief, the imam is overtly acknowledged as the second official in the village, but in reality he often commanded it'.[127]

There were two ways in which Muslims could become chiefs. One was through the conversion of a regent or heir apparent, and the other through marriage from the royal line, especially in matrilineal societies where the offspring could be eligible for the office of chief. These did happen (especially among the Beja), but in such cases the chiefs then had to strike a balance

---

126. Levtzion, *Muslims and Chiefs in West Africa*, p. 58, n. 2.
127. Ibid., p. 171.

60 The Legacy of Arab-Islam in Africa

between the demands of Islam and those of the indigenous system, a difficult balance that, almost always, tilted in favour of the latter.[128]

The implication of the monopoly of political power through the office of the chief, coupled with the eclectic nature of traditional religious thought, meant that the indigenous environment enjoyed the privilege of being in a position to select those aspects of the Arab-Islamic dispensation it found useful. In the selection, 'elements alien to the local genius were rejected and those adopted were moulded into conformity'.[129] The discriminatory and selective borrowing was most manifest in the fact that throughout most of tropical Africa, the wider indigenous non-Muslim communities in general and the ruling classes in particular, while very enthusiastic about the ritual content of Islam, showed little if any interest in its legal and political content.

In other words, the socio-political and legal prescriptions of Islam were regarded as incompatible with and detrimental to the indigenous systems. Thus it could be said that 'traditional African cultures have intrinsic resources of adaptability and discernment, that they can take from Islam (or from Christianity) what agrees with their values, rejecting or radically modifying other elements that conflict'.[130]

Some rulers, like those of Ashanti, employed the services of Muslims in their courts but hardly adopted 'Muslim names' or performed the *salāt*. Others, like those of Mali, Songhay, Hausa, Bornu, Bambara, Dagomba, etc., adopted Muslim names, ways of dressing, and performed the *salāt* but were less keen on its legal and political content. Related to this is that since, generally speaking, rulers hardly sought to espouse Islam as a state policy, the vast majority of the wider indigenous societies remained non-Muslim.

This was due to the conception of rulership or dominion in traditional African political thought. As J.S. Trimingham perceptively points out, dominion in traditional African political thought is 'a reverse of an imperium if by that is meant a dominium which seeks to extend its form of civilization over diverse societies'. The ruler, Trimingham observed, 'was not interested in dominating territory as such, but in relationship with social groups upon whom he could draw to provide levies in time of war, servants for his court, and cultivators to keep his granaries full'.[131]

Hence, contrary to claims that the non-literate traditions of Africa cannot enter into 'a creative and resilient pluralism', they have proven to have an in-built mechanism that fostered the adoption of Islam by individual lineages, even the powerful ruling classes, 'without affecting the rest of society'.[132] David Owusu-

---

128. Ibid., pp. 168–72.
129. Trimingham, *Influence of Islam*, pp. 41–2.
130. Sanneh, *The Crown and the Turban*, p. 22.
131. Trimingham, *A History of Islam in West Africa*, p. 35.
132. Ibid., p. 34.

Ansah, in analysing the Ashanti attitude to Islam, also concluded that even though Islamic charms and amulets were sought and deeply desired for war purposes, 'the Asante rulers clearly saw that a strong Muslim presence, if not selectively controlled, was incompatible with the preservation of the traditional culture upon which their power rested; [because] Islamization calls for adjustments in local culture, changes that are likely to affect the structure of political power'.[133]

The tradition of enclavement made possible by the socio-religious and political inclusiveness of the indigenous environment on the one hand ensured the preservation and cultivation of Arab-Islam in tropical Africa, while on the other hand the pragmatic and discerning attitudes towards the appropriation of Islamic elements ensured that traditional values were not surrendered in the process. Consequently, as in the seventeenth century – after about seven centuries of Islam in tropical Africa – the Islamic dispensation remained a class religion of the mercantile bourgeois and religious elite, and an additional royal cult in centralized African societies.

It is this situation that J.S. Trimingham referred to as the 'stagnation' of Islam in tropical Africa.[134] In stating this fact, we are by no means suggesting that Islam made little or no impact whatsoever on African societies. Islam definitely did make an indelible impact, both on Muslim and non-Muslim African communities in their socio-religious and political lives and institutions. This is an incontrovertible fact well attested at times with exaggerations, in many post-colonial writings on Islam in Africa.[135] The point we are making here, though, is that it was mainly as accommodated, tolerated and favoured guests within indigenous Africa that Muslims exerted their influence and made their contributions. So in a sense the exchanges and influences were mutual.

CONCLUSION

We have tried to establish three basic points in this chapter. First, we have shown that Islam was introduced into tropical Africa not by an invading army, as happened in other parts of the Muslim world, but by dispersed Muslim professionals, i.e. traders and religious divines. We have intimated that neither of these groups of Muslims were 'missionaries' and that conversion associated with their activities were in the main indirect and as such by-products, albeit effective by-products. The second point we sought to highlight is that Muslim groups were, generally speaking, non-kin groups under non-Muslim African patronage.

133. Owusu-Ansah, 'Islamization Reconsidered', pp. 162–63.
134. Trimingham, *A History of Islam in West Africa*, pp. 141 ff.
135. See Trimingham, *Influence of Islam*; Lewis (ed.), *Islam in Tropical Africa*; Nyang, *African Identity*; and many others.

62 *The Legacy of Arab-Islam in Africa*

Our main aim in highlighting the non-kinness of the largely dispersed Muslim groups in their relations with the indigenous traditional communities in tropical Africa is to bring out the pragmatic accommodation and preservation of Arab-Islam within the traditional African environment. In this regard, our conclusion is that 'traditional religions were on the whole favourably disposed towards the presence of Muslims – and Christians for that matter – in their midst',[136] without prejudicing their own interest. Thus we sought to challenge impressions that the 'non-literate' indigenous traditions were weak and passive objects of change determined by the 'literate tradition' of Islam.

Indeed, after describing African culture as a 'passive factor', J.S. Trimingham went on to admit that 'when assimilation took place between African and Islamic institutions, the basic institution into which the other was assimilated might be either, but was generally the African'.[137] Trimingham even went further to state that 'it is incorrect to talk about the adaptation of Islam to Africans'. African Muslims, Trimingham explains, 'did not so much adapt Islam, a legalistic religion, as secure the acceptance of certain Islamic customs in such a way that the customary framework of society remained intact'.[138]

We also demonstrated that the eclectic and open nature of traditional African religious thought was by no means evasive and syncretistic and that it fostered a 'creative and resilient pluralism'. Thus the traditional order fostered the preservation and indeed propagation of Arab-Islam without prejudice to its own value systems. This state of affairs, as far as some Muslims were concerned, meant that the preaching jihad (*jihad al-qawl*) was an ineffective method of propagating Islam in Africa. Hence jihad of the sword (*jihad bi'l-sayf*) had to be resorted to. This is the subject of the next chapter.

136. Sanneh, *The Crown and the Turban*, p. 20.
137. Trimingham, *Influence of Islam*, p. 44.
138. Ibid.

3

MUSLIM JIHAD AND
BLACK AFRICA

INTRODUCTION

In the preceding chapter we examined the development of Arab-Islam under indigenous black African patronage and the dynamics of religious changes and exchanges that took place. We established how non-Muslim indigenous communities hosted non-kin Muslim groups and how the traditional environment acted as a safe haven for minority Muslim groups and a cultivating ground for the preservation and propagation of the Arab-Islamic tradition. Among the things established previously is the fact that Africans appropriated Islamic religious sciences, although even chiefs who adopted Arab names, performed their prayers and went on hajj remained cautious if not suspicious of the legal and political content of Islam. On the whole the indigenous order held sway.

Lamenting over the marginal position of Islam in Ashanti, an exasperated Muslim leader, Muhammad al-Ghamba (d. 1826), made the following statement revealing the frustration of Muslim inability to overthrow the old indigenous order. Al-Ghamba starts by bemoaning the lack of help from other Muslim communities up-country as a result of which, he declares, 'believers are checked in their efforts to propagate God's worship by dint of arms'. Had there been any such help, 'every nation down to the sea coast itself, would have been converted to the service of Allah, long ere this, and the Koran would have been known throughout Africa; whereas now the idolators are strong in the south'.[1]

The Kumasi 'alim's frustration was apparently fuelled by the fact that some Muslim groups in other parts of the sub-region had succeeded in invoking the doctrine of jihad to overthrow the indigenous system. One such jihad movement

---

1. Wilks, 'Muslims in Metropolitan Ashanti', pp. 151–2.

64 *The Legacy of Arab-Islam in Africa*

was that of Uthman Dan Fodio (d. 1817) of nineteenth-century present-day northern Nigeria, which will be discussed later in this section. Writing on Dan Fodio's jihad Umar Abdullahi states that Abdullahi Dan Fodio (d. 1828) – Uthman Dan Fodio's brother and chief ideologue of the northern Nigerian jihad tradition – was 'disappointed by the first peaceful method of changing the old order' and 'found he was duty bound' to overthrow 'the said old order intellectually and militarily'.[2]

In other words, some Muslims became increasingly convinced that military jihad was the only alternative means if Islam was to triumph over the old indigenous order, as peaceful exchanges had failed. Our intention in this section is to examine the key trends of military jihad mainly as a Muslim religious duty and a response or reaction to the indigenous African environment and its values during the eighteenth and nineteenth centuries.

Our main aim here is, first of all, to highlight the classical Muslim doctrine of jihad in Sunni Islam. We shall endeavour to focus mainly on those aspects of the doctrine that are relevant to the African situation. This background is crucial in our estimation not only because it will throw some light on the doctrinal basis of the campaigns in black Africa but also because of the enigmatic nature of the doctrine in contemporary times.

Second, we will trace and highlight the historical background to the theory of military jihad within the sub-Saharan African context. Third, we will briefly highlight some jihad movements that took place in sub-Saharan Africa in an attempt to analyse the socio-religious and political dynamics underlying the campaigns. Fourth, we will examine the jihadists' attitude towards indigenous African believers and their customs. This we shall endeavour to do by critically analysing the main reasons or causes of the jihad movements as advanced by the activists themselves. The alternative programme the jihadists sought to enforce will then be examined, followed by a brief evaluation of the jihad tradition in tropical Africa.

SUNNI MUSLIM DOCTRINE OF JIHAD

The definition of jihad has become something of an enigma since the beginning of the twentieth century due to various factors. These include the fact that, first, the term 'jihad' has a rather wide range of meanings and lends itself to differing interpretations and emphasis. Second, Muslim sources such as the Qur'an and *sunna* are themselves not immediately clear on the subject. Third, early and modern intra/anti-Muslim polemics and apologetics have added to the enigma.

Jihad is the Arabic verbal noun derived from the verb *jahada*, which means 'strain', 'exertion', 'endeavour', etc., on behalf or for the sake of something. Jihad is translated by E.W. Lane as 'the using, or exerting one's utmost power, efforts, endeavours, or ability, in contending with an object of disapprobation ...

2. Abdullahi, *Political Thought*, p. 39.

Muslim Jihad and Black Africa 65

namely a visible enemy, the devil, and one's self'. Lane goes on to point out that jihad came to be used by Muslims to signify fighting or waging war against 'unbelievers and the like' as a religious duty.[3]

Muslims of the mystical Sufi tradition and other modern Muslim apologists tend to emphasize the esoteric meaning of the term by insisting that jihad against one's sinful inclinations (*jihad bi al-nafs*) is the greater jihad while military jihad against non-Muslims is the lesser jihad. This is claimed to be based on a saying of Muhammad on his return from a military expedition to the effect that 'We are returning from the "lesser jihad" to "the greatest jihad".' This claim is countered in another Prophetic tradition which says 'whosoever among you sees anything blameworthy shall alter it with his hand [jihad of the sword, *jihad bi al-sayf*]; if he cannot do this, he shall do it with the tongue [preaching jihad, *jihad al-qawl*]; if he cannot do this, he shall do it at heart [jihad against one's sinful inclinations, *jihad bi al-nafs*]; this is the least that religion demands'.[4]

Qur'anic stipulations on the subject itself range from verses that enjoin Muslims to be tolerant towards non-Muslims to those that permit Muslims to fight and slay 'unbelievers' who persecute them, to verses that instruct Muslims to make war upon non-Muslims 'wherever ye find them' until or unless 'they repent and establish worship and pay the poor dues', in what has come to be known as the 'sword verse'.[5] Classical Muslim thought tried to reconcile these apparently conflicting texts through the doctrine of *naskh* (abrogation),[6] by which the generality of classical Muslim thought maintains that Qur'anic verses which sanction all-out warfare against non-Muslims recited during the latter years of Muhammad's life in Madina overrule those that stipulate peaceful and pacifist co-existence recited during the earlier years of Muhammad's mission in Mecca. As a result, 'the sword verse' is said to have abrogated a large number of verses in the latter category.[7]

The legal interpretation of jihad in mainstream Sunni jurisprudence is 'fighting the unbelievers by striking them, taking their property, demolishing

3. E.W. Lane, *An Arabic–English Lexicon*, part 2 (London: Williams & Norgate, 1865), p. 473.
4. Ref. Muslim, *Sahih*, vol. 1, p. 50. cited in J.R. Willis, 'Jihād fī Sabīl Allāh', p. 399. It can be seen from these traditions that the categorizations are likely to be a reflection of early intra-Muslim sectarian controversies.
5. Sura 9: 5. All Qur'anic quotations are based on M.M. Pickthall, *The Meaning of the Glorious Qur'ān: An Explanatory Translation* (London: Ta-Ha, 1930).
6. The doctrine of abrogation stipulates that in an instance where earlier recited Qur'anic verses are at variance with later ones on a particular subject the latter abrogates the former and renders its injunctions null and void. *Naskh* was developed on the basis of Sura 2: 106 which states: 'Such of our revelations as We abrogate or cause to be forgotten, we bring (in place) one better or the like thereof. Knowest thou not that Allah is Able to do all things?'
7. Anwar-ul-Haqq, *Abrogation in the Koran*, 1st edn., (Bihar: n.p., 1926), pp. 5 ff.

66 The Legacy of Arab-Islam in Africa

their places of worship, smashing their idols and the like'.[8] Ever since, the term jihad, when used without qualification, has always meant the fighting of non-Muslims for the sake of Islam or in the service of Allah (*fī sabīl Allah*). Two main categories of non-Muslims are identified in relation to jihad, i.e. outright 'unbelievers' (*kuffār*) such as adherents of primal religions, and 'People of the book', *ahl al-kitāb*, which includes Christians, Jews and Zoroastrians.

With regard to the *kuffār*, traditional Sunni jurists (with the exception of Malik ibn Anas) agree they have three options when a jihad is declared on them; conversion to Islam, enslavement or death. Malik left the fate of the *kuffār* to the discretion of the Muslim conqueror, *emir*, who is at liberty to kill, enslave or exact taxes from them.[9] It will become clear, as we proceed, how African advocates of jihad invoked the classical rulings on the fate of the *kuffār* in relation to traditional African believers. As far as the *ahl al-kitāb* (Jews, Christians and Zoroastrians) are concerned, they have the option of conversion to Islam or subjugation under Islamic rule as 'protected minorities' (*dhimmī*).

Wars between different groups of Muslims were never regarded as jihad, at least according to the theory of general Sunni doctrine, even though many such wars were branded as such. There is even hesitation in referring to the struggle against renegade groups in Islam as jihad.[10] The *khawārij* ('seceders'), largely of Persian origin, who emerged against the background of early intra-Muslim political schism in about 661 CE, became known, among other things, for their reactionary and militant puritanism. The *khawārij* declared all other Muslims who did not subscribe to their view as 'unbelievers'.

In contrast to the Sunni position, which was at this stage identified with the political interest of the Quraysh (Muhammad's tribe), the *khawārij* held that the commission of major sins renders a Muslim, especially the ruler, an unbeliever who becomes a legitimate target of jihad. The *khawārij* instituted jihad as the sixth pillar of Islam and became a source of constant insurrections against the Khilāfah on account of what they saw as 'un-Islamic' practices of the rulers.[11] They were ruthlessly suppressed but by no means exterminated and most of their thought survived in North Africa, Oman in eastern Arabia and East Africa where they persist in the more moderate modern form of the Ibadiyya.[12]

8. R. Peters, *Islam and Colonialism – The Doctrine of Jihad in Modern History* (Paris and New York: Mouton, 1979), p. 10.
9. See Averroes' chapter on jihad in *Bidāyat al-Mujtahid*, in R. Peters (trans. and ed.), *Jihad in Medieval and Modern Islam*, (Leiden: E.J. Brill, 1977), pp. 21–3. A tradition of Muhammad is reported which excludes the Abyssinians and the Turks from the group of non-Muslims who are to be fought in a jihad. (Ibid). In practice, though, Muslim rulers after conquest, for economic considerations, have always preferred taxes to converting or killing the *kuffār*.
10. E. Tyan, 'Djihad', *Encyclopaedia of Islam*, new edn, (Leiden: E.J. Brill, 1960), vol. 2, p. 538.
11. I. Goldziher, *Introduction to Islamic Theology and Law*, trans. Andras and Ruth Hamori (Princeton: Princeton University, 1981), pp. 170–4.

Muslim Jihad and Black Africa 67

The mainstream Islamic doctrine of jihad (like most other dogmas) was largely formulated against the background of intra-Muslim political squabbling and in direct response to *khawārij* challenges. The Sunni position maintained that no Muslim becomes an unbeliever on account of sin. Ruling as to when a Muslim becomes an unbeliever was declared a divine prerogative suspended until the day of judgement. This position, known as the *murji'a* (from *irjā'*, postponement), was developed to the effect that the murder of a fellow Muslim is highly reprehensible.

Mainline Sunni Islam goes on to stipulate that the ruler or *imam* had the sole prerogative of declaring a legitimate jihad and called for total obedience to the ruler and/or the *imam* under every circumstance. A Prophetic tradition was found to buttress this position: 'Obey whoever is put in authority over you, even if he be a crop-nosed Ethiopian slave.'[13] This political quietism was however more theory than practice. In fact the emphasis on political quietism only serves as a reflection of the tensions that characterized Muslim rule as it did other medieval political systems. Nevertheless, the principle was quite clear and it is important to bear the Sunni and *khawārij* stances in mind, for they will be instructive when we come to examine the position of the West African jihadists and their fellow Muslim opponents.

The Sunni doctrine of jihad is embedded in the traditional Muslim juridical division of the world into *Dar al-Islam,* the House of Islam, in which Islamic government and law prevailed, and *Dar al-Harb,* the House of War, where 'infidel' rulers remain in power. Certain territories were regarded as falling into an intermediate category between the House of Islam and House of War. These are variously designated as *Dar al-Sulkh,* the House of Truce, or *Dar al-Ahd,* the House of Pact or Covenant. These territories were normally in a tributary or subordinate relationship to the House of Islam whose governments made a commitment to guarantee safe passage and/or temporary residence for Muslims. Between the House of Islam on the one side, and the Houses of War and Pact or Covenant on the other, there is a morally necessary, legally and religiously obligatory state of war – that can only be interrupted, at Muslim expediency, by a truce of limited duration but not by a peace treaty – until the final and inevitable triumph of Islam over non-Islam.

This is because Islam is not just a religion but 'a revolutionary ideology and programme which seeks to alter the social order and rebuild it in conformity with its own tenets and ideals'.[14] Permanent Muslim residence in non-Muslim territory is discouraged and in most cases strongly condemned on the basis of Qur'an 4: 97–100 with the support of a number of *hadiths*. The only option for

12. G.L. Della Vida, 'Kharidjites', *Encyclopaedia of Islam*, new edn, vol. 4, pp. 1074–7.
13. Goldziher, *Islamic Theology and Law*, pp. 69–74 and 171, n.e.
14. S. Abu 'Ala Mawdūdī, *Jihad in Islam*, 3rd edn (Lahore: Islamic Publications, 1980), p. 5.

68   The Legacy of Arab-Islam in Africa

Muslims with a conscience and the means living in *Dar al-Harb* is *hijrah* (migration), in keeping with the Prophetic example (*uswa khasana*), to prepare for military jihad against such a system. Jihad is, therefore, a necessary religious duty to which a Muslim dedicates himself in the service of God. The final jihad will be waged by the *mahdi*, the expected 'divinely guided one' who will come at the end of time to establish Islam conclusively.[15]

There is no consensus as to the actual understanding of jihad amongst contemporary modern Muslim scholars. There are those who hold the view that jihad is permitted only in 'self-defence' and was never meant or used as a means to spread Islam. They emphasize the Qur'anic verse that 'there is no compulsion in religion' (Sura 2: 256), the esoteric meaning of the term as a spiritual and moral struggle, and present the wars fought by the Prophet of Islam in seventh-century Arabia as provoked and therefore defensive.

Mahmud Shaltut, former rector of al-Azhar University in Cairo, writing on jihad, argues that the message of Islam 'is a simple and easy one', containing no elements opposed to human nature, and speaks for itself enough to 'require any further means to enlist adherents'.[16] Shaltut concludes, from his own interpretations of the verses of fighting in the Qur'an, that 'there is not a single verse in the Koran which could support the opinion that the aim of fighting in Islam is conversion'.[17] But there are those Muslim scholars and activists who, however, regard such interpretations as false and insist that 'the aim of fighting in Islam is raising God's word on earth, both by attacking and by defence', because 'Islam was spread by the sword' and there should be no apologies whatsoever for that.[18]

JIHAD: THEORIES AND CAMPAIGNS IN AFRICA

As has been intimated in the previous chapter, the introduction of Islam in tropical Africa, unlike North Africa, was mainly through the activities of Muslim merchants and religious experts. There have, nevertheless, been instances where

15. The idea of the *mahdi* is an extra-Qur'anic one which developed in Islam on account of a tradition attributed to Muhammad in which he predicted the gradual decay of Islam as well as its ultimate redemption at the end of time. The *mahdi* is believed by some Sunnis to be an ordinary man and a descendant of Muhammad. Thus, the title is applied to 'Ali in contradistinction to the three other *khulafa*, and as an honorific title to the Umayyad *khulafa*. Other Sunni sources identify the *mahdi* with Jesus, 'Isa (*al-Masih al-Muhtadi*) who is expected to come at the end of time, destroy the Anti Christ, *dajjal*, and establish Islam. See. D.B. Macdonald, 'Al-Mahdi', in *Encyclopaedia of Islam* (Leiden: E.J. Brill, 1936), vol. 3, pp. 112–15.
16. Shaykh Mahmud Shaltut, 'The Koran and Fighting', in Peters (ed.), *Jihad in Islam*, pp. 61–2; see also M.C. Ali, *A Critical Exposition of the Popular 'Jihad', Showing that all Wars of Muhammad were Defensive; and that Aggressive War, or Compulsory Conversion, is not Allowed in the Koran* (Delhi: Idarah-I Adabiyat-I Delli, 1884).
17. Shaltut, 'The Koran and Fighting', p. 79.
18. 'Abd al-Salām Faraj, quoted in Peters (ed.), *Jihad in Islam*, p. 165.

Muslim Jihad and Black Africa 69

war and raids were waged against traditional believers in the name of jihad. Militant Islamization was carried out by the Sanhaja, who were inspired by the Murābitūn (Almoravid) movement, founded by 'Abd Allah b. Yasin (d. 1059) early in the eleventh century.

The Murābitūn conducted raids into the *sahil*, the 'shore' of the desert, in the eleventh century. According to Ibn Khaldun, the Sanhaja 'triumphed over the Sudanis, plundered their territories, imposed tribute and poll tax, and forced many of them to join Islam'.[19] The Sanhaja Almoravid dynasties were overthrown by the Muwāhhidun (loosely translated 'Unitarians') of the Znaga. The Mansas (rulers) of Mali regarded themselves as Muslims and one of the most celebrated rulers, Mansa Mūsā (1312–37), is said to have performed an ostentatious pilgrimage to Mecca in 1324–5.[20] Mali's rulers conducted raids and fought wars but they had not the remotest idea of Islamization as an intended objective, nor are the wars described as jihad.

The seeds of militant Islamization in the form of jihad in the heart of tropical Africa found its socio-political seedbed when Songhay eclipsed Mali in the mid-fifteenth century. Sonni Ali, regarded as the founder of the Songhay empire, certainly regarded himself as a Muslim, and indeed did observe the Muslim prayers, fasted and gave alms. Sonni Ali, however, found himself in the dilemma of most African rulers of the time who tried to keep an uneasy balance between the traditional order to which they owed their authority and the comprehensive applications of Arab-Islam. In the words of Lamin Sanneh:

> The dilemma of Sonni Ali under such circumstances is a classic one: he had adopted the religion, observed its tenets in a haphazard fashion, and encouraged its propagation under official direction. Yet he perceived that Islam in its irreducible Arabic scaffolding raised the spectre of being a state within a state.[21]

Sonni Ali did not seek to impose Islam as a state policy. He is said to have been harsh in his treatment of the largely Sanhaja Muslim divines of Timbuktu, apparently because he regarded them as sympathizers of the Tuareg whom he had conquered. Muhammad Ture, a general and governor (*farma*) in the Sonni's administration in 1493, eventually overthrew Ali's dynasty.

Askiya Muhammad, as he came to be known, was a 'Sonninke' and not a native Songhay, which meant that he had no legitimate claim to the throne. In an apparent attempt to depart from Ali's legacy, Askiya Muhammad from the outset of his rule espoused Islam as a state policy and adopted a process

---

19. Ibn Khaldun, *The Muqaddimah: An Introduction to History*, vol. 1, trans. F. Rosenthal, (London: Routledge & Kegan Paul, 1958), pp. 109–10.
20. Ibid., pp. 67–8.
21. L. Sanneh, *Translating the Message: The Missionary Impact on Culture* (Maryknoll: Orbis, 1989), p. 225.

70 The Legacy of Arab-Islam in Africa

of appeasement towards the Muslim divines of Timbuktu. Having no legitimate claim to the throne, Askiya Muhammad could not count on the indigenous community for support and had to seek this from the largely immigrant Muslim community. Askiya Muhammad's policy, according to J.O. Hunwick,

> was to take advantage of Islam as a positive factor in government, using the Muslim establishment to give his rule popular legitimacy. To this end he not only paid flattering attention to the Muslim scholars of Timbuktu in particular, receiving them on terms of intimacy and even visiting them in Timbuktu, but also showed special respect to returning pilgrims and to visiting sharifs.[22]

The Askiya's example was to be re-enacted in the western and central Sudan some three centuries later with the largely immigrant Muslim rising up in arms against the non-Muslim indigenous population; these uprisings proved successful in some areas leading to the takeover of the reins of power in the name of Islam.

Abd al-Karim al-Maghīlī and the Concept of Jihad in Africa

Askiya undertook a pilgrimage to Mecca and is said to have received an insignia from the khalīfah in Cairo who appointed him as an emir to rule 'the lands of Takrur'. It was, however, due to his admiration for returning pilgrims and sharīfs that Askiya Muhammad came into contact with Abd al-Karim al-Maghīlī (d. 1505), a Tunisian jurist, who was to become the authoritative proponent of jihad in tropical Africa. Al-Maghīlī is well known in North African sources as a militant activist whose anti-Jewish pogroms led to the massacre of Jews in Tuwāt and Gurāra in the late fifteenth century.

The Jews were an economically influential dhimmi, and al-Maghīlī launched a campaign to have them pay the jizya, which, in his view, is 'intended to enforce degradation and humility upon them in their manner of speech and action, their entire condition until they come under tramp of the foot of every Muslim man and Muslim woman, free-born or slave'. The best way of achieving this humiliation was by denouncing their religion and 'forcing them to conceal it and bury its teachings'.[23] Al-Maghīlī declared the Jews chief enemies of Muhammad and Islam and proclaimed that 'to kill a single Jew is more rewarding than waging a war in the land of polytheists'.[24]

---

22. J.O. Hunwick (ed. and trans.), Shari'a in Songhay: The Replies of Al-Maghīlī to the Questions of Askia Al-Hājj Muhammad (New York: Oxford University, 1985), p. 27.
23. Hassan Ibrahim Gwarzo, 'The Life and Teachings of al-Maghīlī, with Particular Reference to the Saharan Jewish Community' (Ph.D. Thesis, University of London, 1972), pp. 145–6.
24. Ibid., p. 156.

Muslim Jihad and Black Africa 71

Al-Maghīlī was mainly against *muwālāt*, (maintaining friendly relations with non-Muslims, in this case Jews). In one of his numerous treatises he cites a host of Qur'anic verses and traditions to the effect that 'every true believer must be severe against the unbelievers', for 'it is one of the signs of love for the Prophet ... that we should hate those who are hated by God or the Prophet and become hostile to those who are enemies of God and the Prophet'.[25] All those Muslims who associated with non-Muslims in general, and Jews and Christians in particular, are unbelievers by association, because 'it is only a person who has no religion, sense and integrity that will bring an unbeliever near to himself or his family or put some of his wealth in his hands'.[26]

Al-Maghīlī's views and militancy did not go down well with the leading *'ulama* and rulers of the time, and he became increasingly regarded as an unwelcome troublemaker intent on usurping power in the region. He found himself less of a hero in Tuwāt than he had imagined and decided to move further down into the *bilād al-Sūdān* where he was to be canonized as a pious, authoritative *'alim* and reformer imbued with *baraka*, whose name in a *silsila* (traditional 'Muslim curriculum vitae') became very desirable.

Al-Maghīlī set out for Kano in present-day northern Nigeria (with whose ruler, Muhammad Rumfa, he was already corresponding) and then finally to Gao in about 1502 where he came into contact with Askiya Muhammad. Askiya Muhammad had apparently inquired from al-Maghīlī about issues relating to government, scholars and state, *tajdīd* or religious reform and theories of jihad.[27] Askiya Muhammad wanted assurance that his overthrow of Sonni Ali, a professing Muslim ruler, was in consonance with Islamic teachings.

With regard to the local *'ulama*, some of whom seemingly condemned the Askiya's action, the Askiya alleged that they 'understand no Arabic except a little of the speech of the Arabs of their towns, in an incorrect and corrupted fashion'.[28] Al-Maghīlī then ruled that these were 'venal scholars' who 'falsely devour people's wealth and debar folk from God's way'. The Askiya should have nothing to do with them and 'jihad against them and their supporters is more worthy than any other jihad'.[29]

Al-Maghīlī went on to hint at what was to become a central motivational factor to later African jihad movements, the traditional Muslim belief in a *mujāddid* (regenerator or reformer) expected at the beginning of every century to call erring Muslims back onto the right path. This millenarian figure, in al-Maghīlī's words, 'will be an odd man out' because of the truth he would stand for, as opposed to his contemporaries.[30]

25. Ibid., p. 139.
26. Ibid., p. 127.
27. Hunwick, *Shari'a in Songhay*, pp. 60 ff.
28. Ibid., pp. 60–1.
29. Ibid., p. 64.

72 The Legacy of Arab-Islam in Africa

On the question of the Askiya's overthrow of Sonni Ali, al-Maghīlī, referring to Sura 2: 26–7, assured him that Ali and all his supporters 'are no doubt among the most unjust oppressors and miscreants, who cut asunder what God has ordained to be joined and commit mischief in the earth'. So the Askiya's jihad 'against them and his seizing of power from their hands is one of the most worthy and important of jihads'.[31] The Muslim jurist arrived at this ruling by employing the doctrine of *takfīr* (anathematizing fellow believers).

Three categories of unbelievers, in whose case a jihad was legitimate, were identified by al-Maghīlī,. First are outright unbelievers, like Christians, Jews, Magians and 'those like them who inherited outright unbelief from their fathers'. Second are Muslim apostates (*murtadd*), while in the third group is the person who claims to be Muslim 'and whom we adjudge to be an unbeliever because he has committed an outward action such as none but an unbeliever would'.[32] This was again a potent ruling that was to be employed and followed to its logical conclusion in nineteenth-century West Africa.

With regards to government, al-Maghīlī ruled that in the case of an 'ungoverned' land (*bilād sā'iba*), a land where Muslims live under non-Muslim rule, such Muslims should be summoned to pay homage or *bay'a* to a lawful *emīr*, and if they refuse a jihad should be declared against that land. Similarly, a land whose ruler can be proven to be oppressive and has 'declared unlawful taxes to be lawful' is a legitimate target of jihad, 'more fitting and more pressing' than a jihad against outright unbelievers. Fighting and killing such rulers and their supporters is not reprehensible, 'even if they pray and fast and pay *zakāt* and perform the pilgrimage'.[33]

Al-Maghīlī urged an end to such practices as Muslim divination, astrology, numerology and the production of charms and amulets, commercial malpractice, non-observance of the seclusion of women from men and the proper dressing of women. In other words al-Maghīlī called not only for jihad to extend the sway of *Dar al-Islam*, but also for the strictest implementation of the *shari'a*, an end he saw jihad as a legitimate and noble means of attaining.

Throughout his 'replies', al-Maghīlī useds jihad in connection with 'corrective' or 'reformist' activity (*tajdīd*). As rightly pointed out by Hunwick, 'there is an unspoken assumption that the Askia as an *amīr* governing a portion of the Islamic *umma* would carry out the statutory jihad against *dār al-harb*.[34] Al-Maghīlī's preoccupation with legitimizing fighting and killing of fellow

---

30. Ibid. pp. 66–7. H.I. Gwarzo strongly opines that al-Maghīlī's description of the *mujāddid* was in veiled reference to himself bearing in mind his own experience in North Africa: see 'The Life and Teachings', pp. 227–35.
31. Hunwick, *Shari'a in Songhay*, p. 72.
32. Ibid., pp. 73–4.
33. Ibid., pp. 80–3.
34. Ibid., p. 128.

Muslim Jihad and Black Africa 73

Muslims should not be taken to mean he was not interested in fighting non-Muslims to spread Islam. Al-Maghīlī did not need to spend time elaborating on such a fundamental and non-disputable issue. The essence of his exposition of 'corrective' jihad, nevertheless, is in three important ways at variance with the mainstream Sunni position and in consonance with the *khawārij* position highlighted above.

These are: al-Maghīlī's doctrine of *takfīr* which declared fellow Muslims as 'unbelievers' on account of their deeds; his sanction of fighting and killing other Muslims as jihad; and his legitimization of jihad against Muslim rulers because of 'oppression'. Mervyn Hiskett describes al-Maghīlī's teaching as 'essentially those of Maliki fundamentalism'.[35] It is not surprising that al-Maghīlī could have been influenced by *khawārij* ideas for, as pointed out above, remnants of this sect survived in North Africa. Even though this remains to be proven it is nevertheless suggestive. J.O. Hunwick suggests that al-Maghīlī intended various types of jihad for various types of *kufr* and that a distinction should be drawn between 'jihad of the hand' or 'bloodless jihad' and jihad of the sword.[36]

Hunwick's suggestion, though, is possibly too subtle. Nowhere in the text is it immediately or even remotely apparent that al-Maghīlī's use of jihad is meant to be understood otherwise than as jihad of the sword. Indeed, those jihadists like Uthman Dan Fodio and the rest who were to quote him three centuries later as an authority on the legitimacy of jihad against fellow Muslims within the African context did not make any such distinctions.

Be that as it may, Askiya Muhammad is known to have conducted numerous expeditions, one of which – the campaign against the Moosi in 1498/9 – has been singled out and explicitly referred to in local Muslim sources as 'the only (proper) jihad undertaken in the way of Allah' in the Western Sudan.[37] As to what extent Askiya Muhammad saw himself as the *mujāddid* of the tenth century of the *hijra* is not clear. What is clear, however, is that local Muslim sources record that he was the eleventh and last *mujāddid* whose reign would be followed by that of the *mahdi* and the subsequent end of the world.[38]

Despite legendary praises of the Askiya in local Muslim sources, it is known that his programme of reforms was largely cosmetic and did not go beyond the

---

35. Hiskett, *The Sword of Truth*, p. 120.
36. Hunwick, *Shari'a in Songhay*, pp. 128–30. The position of the *zindiq* (pl. *zanādiqa*), from the Persian *zand* ('free thinking' regarded as 'heresy') used to refer to converts from Zoroastrianism and Manichaism to Islam, was somewhat ambiguous. The *zanādiqa*, considered as untrustworthy, were apparently not automatically included in this tolerant position. Maliki and Hanbali traditions legitimize their murder while scholars of the Shafi'i and Hanafi traditions remain divergent. A.J. Wensinck, *The Muslim Creed: Its Genesis and Historical Development* (London: Frank Cass, 1965), pp. 30–1.
37. Trimingham, *A History of Islam in West Africa*, p. 97.
38. Willis, 'Jihād fī Sabīl Allāh', p. 402.

74 The Legacy of Arab-Islam in Africa

centres of authority. In fact, little attempt was made by the Askiya and his successors to reform his administration in line with *shari'a* requirements or the actual practice of other Muslim countries. He 'maintained and even enlarged the Songhay system of titles and offices which he inherited from Sonni Ali'; traditional practices continued at the court and people appearing before him had to prostrate themselves and cover their heads with dust.[39]

Askiya Muhammad, therefore, sought al-Maghīlī's views in order to legitimize his rule but paid lip-service to his militant and prescriptive ideas. These had to wait for three centuries to be turned into potent formulae for Muslim campaigns in West Africa. It is these campaigns we now proceed to examine.

Jihad Campaigns in Africa

The wave of military jihad in tropical Africa appeared in its major form in southern Mauritania in the seventeenth century. This was initiated by a certain Imam Nasir al-Din (d. 1674), of the Sanhaja clan of the Berbers.[40] Nasir directed his jihad at the imperial Arab ruling elite of present-day Mauritania. The jihad lasted four years (1673–7) and soon spread from southern Mauritania into the present-day Senegambian region, mainly directed at traditional African peasant communities in areas such as Walo, Futa Toro and Cayor.

Many of the Muslim clerical communities, *zawaya*, refused to support Nasir al-Din's course, while his supporters portrayed him as the *mujāddid*. Nevertheless Nasir's actions broke the tradition of Muslim religious pacifism and served as an immediate precursor for a number of Muslim divines who 'had preached Islam and, notwithstanding the fact that their religious pre-eminence had been acknowledged, had wished to further dominate the local Wolof people'.[41] As a direct result, a series of Muslim Fulbe and Tukulor campaigns ensued throughout the eighteenth century against the Wolof, the Jallonke and Deniake dynasties during the early part of the eighteenth century.[42]

Most of the campaigns ravaged the region and plunged the area into wide-scale pillage and enslavement of hitherto prosperous traditional African communities. The campaigns were, however, largely unsuccessful in establishing

39. J.O. Hunwick, 'Religion and State in the Songhay Empire, 1464–1591', in Lewis (ed.) *Islam in Tropical Africa*, pp. 134–8. Comparing the rule of Askiya Muhammad and that of Sonni Ali, A.W. Pardo concluded that 'Askia was the continuation in many important respects of Sonni Ali' and that the difference between them 'centred rather around personality and the use of religion'. See A.W. Pardo, 'The Songhay Empire under Sonni Ali and Askia Muhammad', in D.F. McCall and N.R. Bennett (eds.), *Aspects of West African Islam* (Boston: African Studies Centre, 1971), pp. 56–8.
40. T.H. Norris, 'Znaga Islam during the Seventeenth and Eighteenth Century', *Bulletin of the School of Oriental and African Studies*, vol. 32 (1969), pp. 496–526.
41. Ibid., p. 501–13.
42. Trimingham, *A History of Islam in West Africa*, pp. 160 ff.

Muslim Jihad and Black Africa 75

any meaningful and effective Islamic rule despite the resultant numerous almamates, the Fulani equivalent of sultanate. The campaigns also failed in converting people in any meaningful numbers to Islam. On the contrary, it filled the rulers of the region with suspicion and sometimes open antagonism towards the Muslim clerical elite and 'drove traditional rulers further away from Islam than they had ever been in the preceding century'.[43]

By the late eighteenth and early nineteenth centuries a Fulbe cleric, Uthman Dan Fodio (d. 1817) launched a jihad in Hausaland in present-day northern Nigeria. Dan Fodio, like most of his contemporaries, gained much influence through patronage from the Hausa ruling class of Gobir. He apparently taught royal members and was the tutor of Yunfa, the ruler of Gobir in the early 1800s. He became something of a kingmaker, and his support for Yunfa is said to have won the latter the throne of Gobir in 1801.[44] As we pointed out in the previous chapter, Muslim clerics exerted a lot of influence at traditional courts, albeit from the background, and Dan Fodio's influence is a typical example of the situation across sub-Saharan Africa at the time.

This royal patronage provided Dan Fodio with some sort of immunity and enhanced his prestige to enable him to undertake preaching tours within the Hausa kingdoms, during which he attracted a considerable number of followers. He was moderate and criticized certain contemporary scholars (including his own teacher) who held on to austere conservatism. The turning point in Dan Fodio's life apparently came during a series of visions he claimed to have had. In one such vision (in 1794) he claimed to have met with the Prophet of Islam and 'Abd al-Qādir al-Jilānī, founder of the Qadiriyya Sufi order. In the alleged vision, 'Abd al-Qādir dressed and enturbaned him as 'Imam of the saints', then girded him with the 'sword of truth' (*sayf al-haqq*) to unsheathe against 'the enemies of God'.[45]

These alleged visions apparently made Dan Fodio conceive of himself as the *mujāddid* of the century whose coming heralded the appearance of the *mahdi*. His preaching brought about the wearing of turbans and veils by Muslim men and women respectively, a practice he had earlier condemned others for advocating. The adoption of 'non-Hausa lifestyles' by an increasing number of Hausa people caused some amount of consternation among the Hausa ruling class. Nafata, then ruler of Gobir (1794–1801), introduced laws banning all public preaching except that undertaken by Dan Fodio himself and ordered a stop to the conversion of sons whose parents were themselves non-Muslims. All such converts were ordered to revert to the traditions of their fathers. The edict also banned the wearing of turbans and veils.

43. Hiskett, *Islam in West Africa*, p. 144.
44. Hiskett, *The Sword of Truth*, p. 49.
45. Ibid., pp. 42–9 and 63–6. Most of the material that follows on Dan Fodio's jihad is taken from this book.

76 The Legacy of Arab-Islam in Africa

Nafata was succeeded in 1801 by Yunfa, a former student of Dan Fodio, and relations between the new chief and Dan Fodio proved more difficult. The latter then undertook what he regarded as *hijra* (in line with Muhammad's flight from Mecca to Medina in 622 CE) to a village called Gudu in 1804.[46] Dan Fodio's withdrawal, in the words of a modern Nigerian Muslim scholar, 'was to bring the Muslim community to the threshold of jihad ... He [Dan Fodio] also envisaged the jihad which would follow almost immediately.'[47] So, sensing danger, Yunfa launched an attack on Dan Fodio and his community but the attack was repulsed and the army of Gobir defeated. This was to be the beginning of a series of Fulbe military campaigns against the Hausa and other people groups in the area.

Yunfa sent messages to other Hausa rulers of Katsina, Kano, Zegzeg, Dawra and Ahir, warning them that he had neglected a small fire in his country until it had spread beyond his power to control. Having failed to extinguish it, it had now burnt him. 'Let each beware lest a like calamity befall his town also.'[48] But this was too late. Sokoto was established as the seat of the caliphate, as it came to be known, and Fulani adventurers visited Dan Fodio from different parts of the region to receive blessed flags to enable them to undertake local military campaigns in their localities.

The Sokoto jihad was opposed by leading Muslim scholars at Yandoto in northern Nigeria. The town was attacked and defeated by the jihadists. The campaigns came under severe doctrinal criticism from other leading Muslim scholars of the time, especially Muhammad al-Amin al-Kanimi, a highly respected *'alim* of early nineteenth-century Bornu, where Fulani subjects under the inspiration of Dan Fodio's jihad started hostilities against local rulers. Dan Fodio made an early retirement from political life, divided the empire between his son Muhammad Bello and his brother Abdullahi Dan Fodio and died in 1817.

The flame of Muslim Fulani campaigns and raids on indigenous communities in areas of modern-day northern Nigeria, parts of southern Niger and north-western Cameroon in the name of God was carried on by his flag bearers and their successors until the British intervention in 1904. These campaigns resulted in the formation of a large number of separate, often hostile, states loosely acknowledging the titular suzerainty of the ruler of Sokoto.

One of many post-jihad Muslim Fulani apologia attributed to Dan Fodio cites works of past authorities to the effect that Sudan meant land of 'infidels' and that the few Muslims who lived and traded with these 'enemies' were committing a 'disgraceful' and 'reprehensible' act.[49] It goes on to quote at length

46. Ibid., pp. 70–4.
47. Sulaiman, *Revolution in History*, p. 114.
48. Trimingham, *A History of Islam in West Africa*, p. 199.
49. H.R. Palmer, 'An Early Fulani Conception of Islam', *Journal of the African Society*, vol. 13 (1913–14), pp. 408, 411–14.

Muslim Jihad and Black Africa 77

a work of a celebrated fifteenth-century Timbuktu *'alim*, Ahmad Baba, and declares that Islam in Hausaland was widespread 'among other than kings. The kings are unbelievers and nothing else!' It then makes the following declaration: 'The government of a country is the government of its king without question. If the king is a Muslim, his land is Muslim, if he is an unbeliever, his land is a land of unbelievers.'[50]

In other words, the status of a land being *Dār al-Islam* or *Dār al-Harb* depended not on the beliefs of the majority of the subjects but on that of the ruler. Dan Fodio in another work approvingly quotes from al-Maghīlī thus:

> It is not right for you [the sultan] to leave a sinner in his sins when you can save him from them by chiding, or imprecation, or binding him in prison, or beating, or by crucifixion and death, or by banishment, or by confiscation of his house, or by other chastisement imposed by the sharia.[51]

In yet another post-jihad apologia,[52] Dan Fodio decried, among other things, the traditional Hausa system of succession by hereditary right and the prevalence of traditional customs in the courts. He also accused the Hausa rulers of friendly relations with and the failure to undertake jihad against neighbouring traditional believers. Other charges against the Hausa rulers included corruption, the imposition of non-canonical taxes, recruiting Muslims into armies, and the enslavement of Fulani people who, in Dan Fodio's view, were Muslim.

Dan Fodio demanded the enforcement of the *hijāb*, the *hudūd* (lashing, amputation, stoning and death prescribed in Islamic law for various crimes such as adultery, theft, drinking alcohol, etc.), strict adherence to the observance of Islamic commercial laws, and a stop to the practice of drumming, singing and dancing, adjudged as satanic innovation, *bid'a shaytaniyya*.[53] Al-Maghīlī's doctrine of *takfīr* and *kufr* were employed by Dan Fodio to declare fellow Muslims unbelievers 'based on what they do or say'. Thus al-Maghīlī's influence upon Dan Fodio, in the words of Louis Brenner, 'was significant, indeed central, for questions of *takfīr* and *kufr* as they related to jihad and to social and political relationships in the caliphate'.[54]

In an exchange of polemical correspondences, al-Kanimi intimated that, serious and reprehensible as some of the allegations against the Hausa were, they were in no way peculiar to the sub-region. He pointed out that such practices

---

50. Ibid., pp. 53–4.
51. Uthman Ibn Fudi, *Bayān Wujūb al-Hijrah 'Ala 'l-'Ibad*, ed. and trans. F.H. El Masri (Oxford: Oxford University, 1978), pp. 185–6.
52. M. Hiskett, 'Kitab al-Farq: A Work on the Habe Kingdoms attributed to "Uthman Dan Fodio"', *Bulletin of the School of Oriental and African Studies*, vol. 23 (1960), pp. 558 ff.
53. Ibid., pp. 566–70.
54. L. Brenner, 'Muslim Thought in Eighteenth-century West Africa: The Case of Shaykh Uthman b. Fudi', in N. Levtzion and J.D. Voll (eds.), *Eighteenth-century Renewal and Reform in Islam* (New York: Syracuse University, 1987), pp. 51–4.

78 The Legacy of Arab-Islam in Africa

could be found throughout other parts of the Muslim world and insisted that they did 'not render a person an unbeliever so long as his faith remains unbroken, even in disobedience (*ma'asi*)'. Furthermore, al-Kanimi maintained that it was impossible, in a war situation, to differentiate a Muslim from a non-Muslim, and under such circumstances 'the abandonment of the unbeliever is more acceptable than the killing of a Muslim'.[55] In other words, al-Kanimi was restating the mainline Sunni *murji'ah* position delineated above, namely that the ruling as to when a Muslim becomes an unbeliever and qualifies for jihad or to be killed is in the hands of God.

Another major jihad after that of Dan Fodio was the jihad of al-Hajj 'Umar Tal (d. 1864),[56] a Tukulor of Futa Toro in the Senegambian region. Al-Hajj 'Umar performed the *hājj* in 1828, where he came under the influence of Muhammad al-Ghani Abu Talib, the Tijani *khalīfah* for the Hijaz, who allegedly appointed him as a *khalīfah* of the Tijaniyah order for the western Sudan. Upon his return in 1832 al-Hajj 'Umar spent some time in Sokoto and married the daughter of Muhammad Bello, son and successor of Dan Fodio. 'Umar proceeded to Futa Jallon where he established a *jamā'a* of Tijani persuasion at Diaguku, attracting an increasing number of followers.

Like those of Dan Fodio, 'Umar's preaching successes raised a sense of apprehension and suspicion from the Muslim Almami of Futa Jallon, leading to the withdrawal of the latter and his *jamā'a* in 1851 into a territory under non-Muslim African rule called Dinguiray. Here 'Umar began to prepare his *jama'a* militarily by instituting a standing army and purchasing large quantities of arms and armaments. These acts alarmed the traditional ruler of the area who launched what looked like a panic attack on the *jama'a*, presenting al-Hajj 'Umar with the immediate context, or rather pretext, for his jihad.

Al-Hajj 'Umar claimed to have had a vision in which 'Allah informed me that I was authorised to undertake the jihad, and He repeated it three times'.[57] The jihad was launched in 1852 with the principal aim of conquering and converting the largely autochthonous non-Muslim people of the region to Islam. 'Umar's main targets were the Mandinka state of Tamba and the Bambara courts of Karta and Segu.[58] His forces achieved some spectacular successes until they suffered a severe setback at the hands of French forces at Médine. At Segu 'Umar's forces also came into confrontation with the almamate of Massina instituted through jihad by one of Dan Fodio's vassals, Ahmad Lobbo, otherwise known as Ahmad of Massina.

---

55. L. Brenner, 'Muhammad al-Amin al-Kanimi and Religion and Politics in Bornu', in Willis (ed.), *The Cultivators of Islam*, p. 168.
56. Much of the following information on al-Hajj 'Umar's jihad is from Willis, *In the Path of Allah*; and D. Robinson, *The Holy War of Umar Tal. The Western Sudan in the Mid-nineteenth Century* (London: Oxford University, 1985).
57. Willis, *In the Path of Allah*, p. 412.
58. Robinson, *The Holy War of Umar Tal*, chapters 7 and 9.

Muslim Jihad and Black Africa 79

This Muslim–Muslim confrontation sparked off a doctrinal debate, which assumed a Qadiri–Tijani nature because of the Qadiri leanings of Ahmad Lobbo and his mentor Ahmad al-Bakka'i al-Kunti. Ahmad al-Bakka'i strongly condemned claims that 'Umar was the *mujāddid*, *mahdi* and a reincarnation of Jesus, claims that persisted long after his death among his followers.[59] On the legitimacy and wisdom of 'Umar's jihad, al-Bakka'i wrote:

> I am fully aware of the merits of jihad, but jihad leads to *mulk* [worldly authority] and *mulk* leads to tyranny [*zulm*]. Our present condition as it is, is more suitable to us than indulgence in jihad, and more assuring to us for not having indulged in unlawful things which jihad would entail.[60]

Al-Bakka'i went on to outline the classical Muslim understanding of jihad:

> Jihad is to be strictly limited to fighting of infidels. If you contend otherwise, bring me an evidence from the *Qur'an* and the sunna to prove your assertion. It is the tyrant Muslims who are to be fought in order that the *shari'a* become established. And even this type of fighting has to be executed at the behest of the *Imam al-Muslimin* ... On the other hand, such fighting cannot be recognised as jihad. And the person who dies in the participation in such activity will not receive the honors of a martyr in jihad.[61]

Al-Hajj 'Umar on his part accused the Massina Muslim authorities of not only failing to embark upon jihad against the 'infidel' indigenous communities but of befriending 'the enemies of Allah, the enemies of all the Muslims – our enemies, his enemies and the enemies of his forefathers'.[62] This controversy, like that between al-Kanimi and the Sokoto rulers, ended inconclusively. However, al-Bakka'i made a significant military contribution towards the eventual demise of al-Hajj 'Umar and his political programme by sponsoring a rebellion which led to the death of 'Umar in 1864 and the subsequent withering of his conquered territory.

Another jihad of the period worth mentioning was that initiated by Samori Turè.[63] Samori's jihad is of particular interest, in that, unlike most of the other main jihadists, he was of the Mande and not Fulbe tribe. Samori was, unlike Dan Fodio and al-Hajj 'Umar, a soldier by profession and non-literate. He launched his campaigns in 1870 in the region of present-day Guinea and the Ivory Coast and claimed to be fighting for the Muslim cause ostensibly to protect Muslim trade from 'pagan' taxes. This attracted a section of the Muslim trading communities into his jihad. Samori attacked and ransacked both Muslim and non-Muslim communities in the region until the French halted him in about 1898.

59. Willis, 'Jihād fī Sabīl Allāh", pp. 404–5.
60. Willis, *In the Path of Allah*, p. 199.
61. Ibid., pp. 203–4.
62. Ibid., p. 186.
63. For information on Samori's jihad, we are relying mainly on Person, 'Samori and Islam', pp. 259–77.

80 *The Legacy of Arab-Islam in Africa*

As with most of the other jihadists, however, a significant proportion of the Muslim leadership opposed his campaigns because 'they were too firmly established, on too good terms with their [largely indigenous] neighbours and made too good a living from trade to wish to upset the system'.[64] His defeat was a big relief to both Muslim and non-Muslim societies. A Muslim appreciation for the defeat of Samori by the French and the stability and security it brought is contained in an address from the 'Muslims of Korhogo to the people of Mecca' written during the 1914 to 1918 war. It reads in part:

> Whoever does not wish to see the French in our colony [Ivory Coast] is also held in contempt by us Muslims, since our prosperity depends entirely on the arrival of these latter in our colonies. It is moreover thanks to the French that we are spared the ravages and pillages of Samori, slavery, and wars between one village and another. At present, we are free, we can live, work in peace, and perform our prayers in tranquillity.[65]

Yves Person and most other Western observers seek to downplay the religious nature of Samori's campaigns by referring to the fact that the French 'attributed his followers' courage not to any determination to conquer in the name of Islam or to defend the faith, but to their belief in and awe of their leader'.[66] This argument, in our view, is rather shallow because if one were to judge the 'religiosity' of the other jihad movements by looking at the motives of the fighters, then one could easily end up with similar conclusions.

As M.G. Smith comments on the nature of the jihad tradition in general and that of Dan Fodio in particular, 'where religious scruples obstruct effective political action, the jihad will normally fail'.[67] In other words, non-religious mundane considerations contributed to the success of the jihad movements. Nevertheless, the extra-religious dimension does not in any way negate the underlying source of inspiration for the jihad movements, namely Islamic religious considerations. The secular and mundane were as important as and indeed inseparable from the religious. In any case, had Samori been literate or had his cause any systematic ideologues like those of Dan Fodio and al-Hajj 'Umar, his story could hardly have been any different.

INTERPRETING THE JIHAD TRADITION IN AFRICA

Interpretation of the jihad legacies in sub-Saharan Africa has, for various reasons, been fraught with difficulties. The reasons for these include, as we have suggested above, the very broad nature of the doctrine of jihad itself. But even

64. Ibid., pp. 263–7.
65. Launay, *Beyond the Stream*, pp. 59–60.
66. Person, 'Samori and Islam', p. 259.
67. M.G. Smith, 'The Jihad of Shehu Dan Fodio: Some Problems', in Lewis (ed.), *Islam in Tropical Africa*, p. 224.

Muslim Jihad and Black Africa 81

more importantly, interpretation of the jihad legacy in present-day West Africa has been heavily vitiated by the politicization of the subject. As perceptively pointed out by Julie Lawson, 'the writing of Northern Nigerian history has been a politicised activity from the outset: from the histories written by the jihadists through to those of the colonialists, the de-colonialists, and so on up to the Islamists and Marxists of the 1980s'.[68]

Most of the jihadists' writings were undertaken during or after their campaigns, and, as we have already pointed out above, were in response to criticism from their fellow religionists who questioned and condemned their actions. These writings are therefore, in a very large measure, post-jihad apologia representing the jihadists' version of the story. The writings of the jihadists therefore sought to portray the systems they overthrew as 'pagan', 'un-Islamic', unjust and evil. The colonialists' version, written during British conquest and colonial rule in northern Nigeria (between 1904 and 1960), also in an apparent attempt to justify their imperial motives, dismissed religion as a pretext for Fulani nationalism, and described a decaying, backward and bankrupt system overthrown by the British.

Then followed the interpretations of the de-colonialists, who sought to challenge and dismiss the colonialists' representations. The de-colonialists' trend, championed and dominated by H.F.C. Smith, in its attempt to reverse the colonialist stereotype, focused their attention rather uncritically on the works of the jihadists, believing their approach to be from 'the inside African perspective' as opposed to the external conquerors' perspective of the colonialists. Louis Brenner and Murray Last rather lamely point out in conversation with Julie Lawson that research on the history of jihad movements was restricted because there was 'considerable pressure from the authorities who, after all controlled access to both the resources that could be spent on education and frequently to the sources themselves: in the form of documents and permission to conduct oral research'.[69]

So here we have a clear admission that much of the discourses that came to dominate the history of the jihad movements in particular and Islam in West Africa in general was not only exclusively constructed from the jihadists' and therefore Muslim sources, but selected and controlled sources at that. This serious academic limitation was only belatedly acknowledged after the one-sided, selective, romantic picture had been painted and taken root. In fact, fieldwork carried out by de-colonialists was in the main at the palaces of local Muslim rulers. Murray Last's chief oral informant was the vizier of Sokoto at the time, al-Hajj Junaidu. Mervyn Hiskett on his part talks of having received 'much help and kindness from the Madaki, Malam Alhaji Ahmad (in Kano); and in

68. Lawson, 'Nigerian Historiography', p. 2.
69. Ibid., p. 14.

82 The Legacy of Arab-Islam in Africa

Sokoto from the Waziri, Malam Alhaji Junaidu'.[70] It is clear from the above that despite the belated claims of 'control' of sources, the 'much help and kindness' lavished on these scholars played an important part in compromising their academic objectivity. Perhaps scholars should take note of an Arab proverb which states that 'the worst of scholars is the one who visits princes and the best of princes is he who visits scholars'.

The end result of this uncritical and politicized approach 'was that the Caliphate and the C19th was presented as a monolithic construction: one hundred years of good, progressive Islamic government', thereby distorting the historical picture in favour of the jihad movements.[71] The romantic and one-sided approach of the de-colonialists has since dominated and influenced a greater part of post-colonial Muslim and Western discourse on Islam in tropical Africa in general and the histories of the jihad movements in particular. In fact, these interpretations of the jihad movements in no small way helped in shaping the political landscape of post-independence Nigeria.[72]

Contemporary Muslim activists such as Ibraheem Sulaiman and Umar Abdullahi emerged in the 1980s and succeeded in transmogrifying the monolithic and romantic version into claims about the Islamic destinies of Africa in general and Nigeria in particular. Their main aim is to rediscover and re-establish the jihadist version of Islam. Also in the 1970s and early 1980s attempts were made by the Hausa Muslim victims of the Fulani jihad to question the monolithic and romantic version of the jihad legacy. The main aim of this trend is to restore the hitherto vilified Hausa system that was overthrown by the Fulani jihadists. Their central argument is that, contrary to claims by the jihadists and their admirers, the Hausa were good Muslims before the Fulani intervention.[73] But, as pointed our by Hiskett, these somewhat unconventional interpretations of the jihad tradition have had little impact, if any, on Nigerian Muslims.[74]

Notwithstanding the above historiographies, an important feature of the jihad tradition in the western and central Sudan is, first of all, that they were uprisings of non-kin 'stranger' Muslim communities against the indigenous overwhelmingly non-Muslim host communities. This, as far as we are concerned, is the critical dividing line in the jihad movements. There is no evidence that the status of Islam in pre-jihad Hausaland, for instance, was in any way different from what pertained in other parts of the sub-region. Namely that, as outlined in the preceding chapter, Islam was largely the religion of migrant communities and a royal cult for traditional rulers in the midst of overwhelming indigenous traditional African peasant communities.

70. Hiskett, *The Sword of Truth*, p. xxvi.
71. Lawson, 'Nigerian Historiography', p. 14.
72. Ibid.
73. See ibid. for a brilliant analysis of these trends.
74. Hiskett, 'Preface', p. xv.

Muslim Jihad and Black Africa 83

In fact, Trimingham makes this point very explicitly on the state of Islam in pre-jihad Hausaland. He writes that 'Islam was only practised by foreign communities settled in the towns and a few even of the rulers made a profession of Islam'.[75] The relative ease with which the non-kin Fulani conquered Hausaland, for instance, is largely explained, as Trimingham informs us, by the ravages of Gobir and perpetual hostilities between the Hausa states.[76]

The hostility between non-kin migrant Muslim communities and the indigenous host communities was further exacerbated by the mutually conflicting interest of the largely nomadic Muslim Fulani, for instance, and the largely peasant non-Muslim indigenous communities. The opposition between migrant Muslim and indigenous communities was, however, always tied up with other bonds and alignments, such as kinship, ethnic identity, differing understanding of Islam amongst Muslims, political resentments and loyalties, calculations of personal and collective advantages, communal solidarities and antagonisms, etc.

The fact, nevertheless, remains that the jihad movements were almost entirely initiated and led by Fulbe and Tukulor Muslim divines (except that of Samori Turè) against other ethnic communities and their supporters. This led some observers such as J.S. Trimingham to opine that the preaching of the jihad movements was carried out in such a way that it almost 'became a racial as well as religious war' behind which lay 'a class struggle between the Torodbe clerical class and the ruling classes'.[77] These assessments are true to a large extent, when viewed against the background of what has been said in the preceding chapter on the rising influence of the Muslim divines in tropical Africa and their controlled involvement in socio-political affairs.

However, the pan-Fulani theory, be it in terms of race or religion, has a number of shortcomings. This is especially so with regard to the conflicting allegiances and interests that ran through all the jihad movements between and among supporters and opponents alike. First, the thesis of pan-Fulani nationalism fails to take into account that 'the Yandoto ulama who opposed the jihad had some prominent Fulani leaders and here neither religious nor ethnic affinity convinced them to join the jihad'.[78] This meant intra-Fulani feuds between those of Dan Fodio's own clan, on the one hand, and the Fulani of Western Katsina, on the other.[79]

---

75. Trimingham, *A History of Islam in West Africa*, p. 153.
76. Ibid.
77. Ibid., pp. 161–2.
78. Yusufu Abba, 'The 1804 Jihad in Hausaland as a Revolution', in Y.B. Usman (ed.), *Studies in the History of the Sokoto Caliphate: The Sokoto Seminar Papers* (Zaria, Nigeria: Ahmadu Bello University, 1979), p. 27.
79. Ibid.

84 *The Legacy of Arab-Islam in Africa*

The second factor that makes the pan-Fulani theory weak is the support of the jihad movements by non-Fulani who surely had interests other than Fulani nationalism. Nevertheless, the leadership of the new dynasties remained exclusively in the hands of the Fulani, who regarded membership of the new orders more in tribal than religious terms. They 'despised the non-Fulani, even if they are learned, pious or *mujāhidūn*'.[80] So also was the socio-political and religious content of the jihadists' programme 'une culture Arabo-Peule'.[81] In other words, the conquered people groups would have seen the jihad movements as nothing short of Fulani imperialism.

As can be deduced from the foregoing, the second key feature of the jihad movements is that they were carried out solely by African-Muslim groups as a religious duty. It was not an external Muslim force like Arabs or Berbers coming down to wage jihad and convert black Africans. And as indicated above, the jihad campaigns during the latter part of the nineteenth and earlier parts of the twentieth centuries were mostly halted by European forces who were out to stop the slave trade and create an atmosphere conducive for their own political and commercial interests.

Most of the jihad leaders like al-Hajj 'Umar, Samori Turé and others in their campaigns came into direct confrontation with the French and British. In this connection, the jihad movements became an African (Muslim) confrontation with foreign European (non-Muslim) powers. This situation has led some observers to opine that the jihad campaigns are indicative of Islam, unlike Christianity, instilling in the African a sense of 'superior manliness' and an affirmation of 'the harder warrior values of Africa' by offering Africans the word and the sword for defence against external forces as opposed to the servile, docile and 'feminine virtues of Christianity'.[82]

Writing on 'the impact of Jihad on Senegambian Society', an African-Muslim observer makes the same assertion in the following words:

> It goes without saying that such a national consciousness was never obvious amongst the African tribes before the spread of Islam. It was this natural consciousness that helped to rally West African Muslims to fight against colonial forces which led eventually to some national independence during the 1950s and 1960s. This view is supported by the very fact that Alhaji Omar

---

80. Muhammad Bello's comments in Last, *The Sokoto Caliphate*, p. 59. A legend about al-Hajj 'Umar has him declare that he was inspired in his mission by reading the life of Muhammad and recognising the similarities between the Fulani and the Arabs: 'the idea flashed upon me that I could become the Muhammad of the Soudan, and combine the Foulas into a great nation' as Muhammad did with the Arabs. Willis, *In the Path of Allah*, p. 150.

81. M. Dia, *Islam et civilisation Negro-Africaines* (Dakar: Les Nouvelles Editions Africaines, 1980), p. 64.

82. Blyden, *Christianity, Islam and the Negro Race*, pp. 12–13; Ali A. Mazrui, *The African Condition: A Political Diagnosis* (London: Heinemann Educational Books, 1980), p. 52.

Al-Futi was the first African Muslim leader to clash with the European colonial forces. The banner of his resistance to foreign domination was carried on by other Muslim leaders in various parts of the region.[83]

In other words, the jihad campaigns, in the view of these observers, were African nationalist movements against European invasion. In this regard another African-Muslim scholar described the European intervention and the subsequent halting of the jihad campaigns as a 'tragic experience' and a 'European blunder' in Africa.[84] The association of the jihad tradition with African nationalism, on the one hand, and European intervention in halting it with imperialism, on the other, are, however, simplistic. In the next section we shall examine the expressed views and implemented policies of the jihadists towards indigenous Africans and things African.

While our aim is not to discuss the relationship between European and Muslim interests in Africa, assertions that European intervention was 'tragic' and a 'blunder' can only be taken as representing the views of the inheritors of the jihad legacy. It is a well-established fact that Islam made more progress in tropical Africa during the relatively brief colonial period than it did in its previous twelve centuries.[85] And so the European intervention, with all its shortcomings and controls, could not have been altogether 'tragic'. This is even more so for Muslims and non-Muslims who suffered the brunt of the jihad campaigns and for whom the jihad movements were the worst of tragedies, and not just blunders. An old Hausa Muslim lady, Baba of Kano, recounting the British intervention in northern Nigeria had this to say:

> We Habe wanted them to come, it was the Fulani who did not like it. When the Europeans came the Habe saw that if you worked for them they paid you for it, they didn't say, like the Fulani, 'Commoner, give me this! Commoner, bring me that!' Yes, the Habe wanted them; they saw no harm in them.[86]

As the statement makes clear, as far as the conquered, exploited and oppressed non-Fulani Muslims and non-Muslims were and still are concerned, the European intervention was regarded as God-sent. This was especially so for the vast non-Muslim indigenous communities who became the main target of Muslim slave raiding, plunder and slaughter during the jihad period. The jihad was and may still be regarded and cherished as 'manly' within some Muslim circles, but as far as the peasant indigenous African and his/her socio-religious and political values were concerned, it was not just 'une colonisation

---

83. Omar Jah, 'The Impact of Jihad on the Senegambian Society', in Alkali et al. (eds.), *Islam in Africa*, pp. 185–6.
84. Nyang, *African Identity*, p. 40.
85. Hiskett, *Islam in West Africa*, pp. 281 ff; C.N. Ubah, 'Colonial Administration and the Spread of Islam in Northern Nigeria', *Muslim Word*, vol. 81, no. 2 (1991), pp. 133–48.
86. M.F. Smith, *Baba of Karo: A Woman of the Muslim Hausa* (London: Faber & Faber, 1954), p. 64.

86 The Legacy of Arab-Islam in Africa

peule',[87] but physical and cultural brutalization in the name of God. Julie Lawson is therefore right in pointing out that the 'African' and monolithic interpretations of the jihad movements are 'political histories concerned with events rather than structures, and the elite rather than the people'.[88]

The third, and perhaps most important, feature of the jihad tradition in tropical Africa is that the jihadists all claimed to be 'reformists' aimed at 'purifying' Islam from indigenous 'pagan' accretions. In fact this is the official Muslim view particularly with regard to the jihad of Uthman Dan Fodio. Dan Fodio, in the words of Ahmadu Bello, 'declared a Holy War against the polluters of the faith' starting with the chief of Gobir, 'one of the worst offenders, in whose territory he was living'.[89] This view is paramount in all post-jihad Muslim apologia attributed to Dan Fodio and his immediate successors, modern Muslim sympathizers and admirers of the jihad tradition, plus a host of post-colonial Western observers.

Leaders of the jihad tradition have, therefore, been widely acclaimed as champions of 'orthodox', 'normative' and 'pure' Islam as opposed to their Muslim opponents who represented 'mixed', 'compromised' and 'heterodox' Islam. They have also been perceived as more learned in Islam than their contemporaries, if not the best in the history of Islam in tropical Africa.[90] The issue of 'pure', 'normative' or 'orthodox' Islam as opposed to 'mixed', 'popular' or 'contaminated' Islam will be specifically addressed in chapter 5. What is to be noted here, though, is that the 'reformist' theory of the jihad movements has some inherent difficulties.

First of all, if there is anything like Sunni Islamic orthodoxy, then there is an apparent doctrinal difficulty in maintaining that the jihadists' campaigns were aimed at 'reforming' Islam while at the same time referring to these campaigns as jihad. Al-Bakka'i certainly had the weight of mainstream Islamic thinking on his side when he pointed out that even though it is legitimate to fight to enforce the *shari'a*, such fighting cannot technically, be dubbed a jihad. This was a feature of *khawārij* thought, as observed earlier in this chapter.[91] In fact, Mervyn Hiskett, who describes al-Maghīlī's views as 'Maliki fundamentalism', points out that Dan Fodio owed many of his reformist ideas to the former, quoting 'extensively from his writings and refers constantly to his opinions'.[92]

Al-Maghīlī's influence on Dan Fodio's thought and actions included such crucial areas as the position of the Muslim sinner. The former's ruling against

---

87. Dia, *Islam et civilisation*, p. 64.
88. Lawson, 'Nigerian Historiography', p. 13.
89. A. Bello, *My Life* (Cambridge: Cambridge University, 1962), p. 10.
90. Levtzion, 'Islamization in West Africa', pp. 207–16; Fisher, 'Conversion Reconsidered', pp. 31 ff; Robinson, 'An Approach to Islam', pp. 109 ff.
91. See Tyan, 'Djihad', p. 538.
92. Hiskett, *The Sword of Truth*, p. 121.

Sonni Ali and his supporters and his legitimizing of jihad against them became the standard model for Dan Fodio and other West African jihadists. These rulings, though, were passed without any fixed definitions for sin and unbelief and were therefore clearly subjective. It is precisely because of the risks of this subjectivity that mainline Sunni Islam, in the face of early *khawārij* fundamentalism, opted for 'postponement' (*murji'a*), leaving the judgement in such matters to God. The impact of al-Maghīlī's ruling made it possible to regard any professing Muslim as an unbeliever and thus a fit victim for jihad – a convenient state of affairs for those who wished to usurp power from fellow Muslim rulers by dint of arms.

Thus by anathematizing his fellow Muslims as unbelievers, one can say, as far as established mainline Sunni position on this subject is concerned, Dan Fodio's teachings and actions were just as 'fundamentalist' if not 'heterodox' as his inspirer, al-Maghīlī. In addition, granted that there was 'corruption' of belief in nineteenth-century Hausaland and that there was a need for a 'revolution' to purge Islam and restore 'orthodoxy' by way of enforcing the *shari'a*, again, mainline Sunni Muslim teaching does not sanction such an action as jihad. For, to quote al-Bakka'i once more,

> Jihad is to be strictly limited to fighting of infidels ... It is the tyrant Muslims who are to be fought in order that the *shari'a* become established ... And, such fighting cannot be recognised as jihad. And the person who dies in the participation in such activity will not receive the honors of a martyr in jihad.[93]

So if the jihadists were 'reformers', as their Western and Muslim apologists would have us believe, then their actions do not qualify to be called jihad. *Tajdīd* (reform) and jihad cannot be one and the same thing as far as our understanding of mainline Sunni Islamic thought is concerned. Dan Fodio and his colleagues were therefore either reformers or jihadists, they could not have been both! It is in these grey areas of doctrinal controversies that non-Muslim observers have to exercise academic sobriety and integrity, and abstain from getting involved in these purely intra-Muslim matters. It is academically unsound for a non-Muslim to depict the jihadists as representatives of 'orthodoxy', by implication subscribing to the idea that all other well-meaning Muslims who opposed their teaching and actions were ignorant charlatans and venal compromisers.[94]

Upon what objective basis can an outsider make such categorizations? Nehemiah Levtzion, who categorizes African Muslims into 'true Muslims', 'unqualified Muslims' and 'not complete Muslims', admits that it is upon 'the standards set by the *'ulamā'* that he defines what he called 'normative Islam'.[95]

93. Willis, *In the Path of Allah*, pp. 203–4.
94. See Hiskett, *The Sword of Truth*, pp. 128–30.
95. Levtzion, 'Islamization in West Africa', p. 215.

88 The Legacy of Arab-Islam in Africa

The term 'ulama' though, is used loosely as if it applied to a coherent group of religious professionals. And by declaring the jihadists to be representatives of Islamic 'orthodoxy' in Africa, we are by implication suggesting that all the other eminent Muslim scholars who took exception of the jihadists' view are representatives of 'heterodoxy'. As pointed out above, both the jihadists and their Muslim opponents had Islamic reference points. Indeed, as noted by Fahzlur Rahman, there has hardly being a consensus among Muslim 'ulama' on any given subject not even on the doctrine of consensus, *ijmā*', itself.[96]

There is no doubt that the history of the jihad movements, especially in the discourses of the de-colonialists, is the verdict of the victors built upon the ashes of the evidence of the vanquished. Indeed, not only were research sources controlled by local authorities in post-colonial times, but in their bid to exterminate all traces of the conquered, the Fulani conquerors of northern Nigeria – and in all probability other areas in which the jihad tradition had successes, even if temporarily – right from the outset of their campaigns encouraged and 'purposely destroyed' local chronicles and historical documents.[97] History is replete with examples to show that but for the fact that the jihadists emerged victorious in their campaigns, they would probably have gone down in history as a rebellious band of renegades (like the *khawārij*) who tried to usurp power through 'un-Islamic' means.

The point we are making here is that claims that the jihadists are the best representatives of Islamic 'orthodoxy' in sub-Saharan Africa are unsustainable, especially when advanced or echoed by outside observers. If by 'orthodoxy' we mean the views of the victors over against those of the vanquished (for that is what, in actual fact, 'orthodoxy' in both Islam and Christianity means), then the claim is valid. But if 'orthodoxy' is taken to mean 'truth' and 'purity' or even faithful adherence to established tradition, then the claims are difficult to sustain, to put it mildly. As outsiders, it is important to acknowledge the views that Muslims express about their co-religionists but it is even more important to present those views without appropriating terminologies and vocabularies of the protagonists as if they were our own.

Third, and perhaps more importantly, the view that the eighteenth- and nineteenth-century jihad movements were 'reformist' has sometimes left the impression that the conflicts were largely, if not entirely, an intra-Muslim affair. As we have made clear in numerous instances above, there is no doubt

96. F. Rahman, *Islam*, 2nd edn. (Chicago: University of Chicago, 1979), pp. 72–8 and 262. Similarly, I.M. Lewis has noted very cogently that 'Islam is not the "religion of the book" but, rather, the "religion of the books", a package of written compendia'. Lewis, *Religion in Context: Cults and Charisma* (Cambridge: Cambridge University, 1986), p. 107.

97. F.L. Shaw (Lady Lugard), *A Tropical Dependency: An Outline of the Ancient History of the Western Soudan with an Account of the Modern Settlement of Northern Nigeria* (London: James Nisbet, 1905), p. 236.

Muslim Jihad and Black Africa 89

that the jihad campaigns had an intra-Muslim dimension. These include the confrontations between Dan Fodio and the Yandoto Muslim 'ulama', al-Hajj 'Umar and the Massina Muslim community and Samori and the Muslim communities of northeastern Ivory Coast. It was this intra-Muslim dimension that exercised the jihadists and their fellow Muslim protagonists into writing the treatises that have since attracted and indeed distracted the attention of most observers.

The intra-Muslim dimension notwithstanding, the main goal of the jihadists has been succinctly expressed by Muhammad Bello in the following words: 'May God help us to pluck up the tents of the heathen from our lands, and set up the tents of the law'.[98] Indeed, it was in the attacks and destruction of traditional non-Muslim communities that lay the strength and appeal of the jihad movements. As already pointed out above, the jihadists' cardinal charges against their fellow Muslim protagonists (Sokoto jihadists against al-Kanimi and 'Umar against al-Bakka'i) was that they failed to carry out jihad against surrounding traditional African believers.

'Umar's main initial aim, as observed above, was therefore to attack and convert the autochthonous non-Muslim people groups of Mandinka and Bambara. 'Umar wrote to his Massina Muslim opponents that 'everyone of us should fight the infidels nearest to him; we should become one hand against the enemies of Allah, our enemies – the enemies of our ancestors'.[99] This he did with spectacular results and won wide acclaim from West and North African Muslims. David Robinson, who has researched and written extensively on the jihad campaigns of 'Umar Tal and many others in the region, is of no doubt that 'the highest priority for the militant Muslim leader was the destruction of paganism, and especially those ruling dynasties who had gone against the tide of West African history by establishing "pagan" states and priesthoods in the eighteenth and nineteenth centuries'.

Robinson goes on to sum up 'Umar's main objective and achievements during the early phase of his jihad in the following words:

> Umar took as his special obligation the destruction of the Mandinka state of Tamba, and the Bambara courts of Karta and Segu, which served as a stigma on the body of West African Islam. Much of the excitement among West and North African Muslims at the conquest of Segu in 1861 stemmed from the destruction of this capital of 'paganism', and much of the respect Umar's son Amadu enjoyed during his reign in the late nineteenth century stemmed from the fact that he had built a capital of Islam on the cinders of the 'pagan' center. Sokoto, the capital of militant Islam in the Central Sudan, was a new city, which began as a military camp. Segu, the capital of militant Islam in the Western

98. Hiskett, *The Sword of Truth*, p. 96.
99. Willis, *In the Path of Allah*, p. 176.

90 The Legacy of Arab-Islam in Africa

Sudan, was a transformed 'pagan' site, whose national shrines had been publicly destroyed and where new Islamic palaces had been constructed.[100]

The situation in the central sudan was no different, even if Uthman Dan Fodio started his jihad against the Muslim ruling class of Gobir. First of all, to paint the Hausa–Fulani confrontations as an intra-Muslim affair is to give the impression that the Hausa were overwhelmingly if not entirely Muslim. That the pre-jihad Hausa were overwhelmingly traditional believers is supported by facts on the ground. As we have already observed above, a few of the Hausa ruling class subscribed to Islam but the overwhelming majority of the population remained attached to their traditional religious beliefs. In fact, in some cases traditional and Muslim rulers alternated in many Hausa states.

In Zaria, for instance, Jatau (1782–1802) is known to have been a Muslim, but his son, Makau, who succeeded him was a practising traditional believer and upon succession demolished the mosque his father had built. It was after the conquest of Zaria by a jihadist expedition in 1804 that the conversion of the people started. The overthrown ruling class took refuge among the Gwari where it is well known that, at least, the first refugee chiefs continued with their traditional religious practices.[101] Heinrich Barth, described by Hiskett as an 'uncommitted observer', visited the region from 1850 to 1854 and in his observations noted that 'it is evident that the larger portion of the population all over Hausa, especially that of the country towns and villages, remained addicted to paganism till the fanatic zeal of their conquerors, the Fulbe, forced them to profess Islam, at least publicly'.[102] Apart from traditional Hausa who were converted by dint of arms of the jihadists, other traditional Hausa groups who were conquered by the Fulani but treated as tribute-paying cultivators, the Maguzawa, constituted more than half the total Hausa population at time of British intervention in 1904. And as late as the early 1950s there were 'still large blocks of animists between Sokoto and Katsina'.[103] All these confirm that the vast majority of pre-jihad Hausas whom the jihadists fought and subjugated were traditional believers and so the jihad was far from an intra-Muslim conflict.

Second, the intra-Muslim theory arises from the fact that most discussion on the jihad of Uthman Dan Fodio and his successors tended to be focused mainly if not exclusively on the Hausa–Fulani wars. This has largely excluded the vast numbers of neighbouring non-Hausa people groups who were entirely traditional African believers on whom the jihad fell much more heavily. These included the Bura and Pabir people of Bornu province as well as the Batonubu

---

100. Robinson, 'An Approach to Islam', p. 115. See also chapters 7 and 9 of Robinson, *The Holy War of Umar Tal.*
101. Trimingham, *History of Islam in West Africa*, p. 153.
102. H. Barth, *Travels and Discoveries in North and Central Africa*, 2nd edn, (London: Longmans, Green, 1857), vol. 2, p. 118.
103. Trimingham, *Report of Survey*, p. 7.

Muslim Jihad and Black Africa 91

and the Zugwe who had professing Muslim chiefs while the population remained almost exclusively traditional believers,[104] and other areas such as Bauchi, Gombe, Katagum, Missau and Jamaari on the plateau; plus Keffi, Nasarawa, Lafia, Doma and Keana in the Benue area.

Adamawa emirate, which was founded by one Modibbo Adama who received a blessed flag from Dan Fodio in 1806 and launched his jihad in 1809, was carved out of traditional people groups in the region. Non-Muslim indigenous people groups who were the principal victims of Adama's campaigns included the Fali, Mufu, Daba, Mundang, Vere, Chamba, Namchi, Doni, Longuda, Marghi, Mumuye, Kilba, Bata, Mambilla, etc. Local Muslim chronicles affirm this fact by stating that Adama, as opposed to many of his contemporaries, conducted his jihad against 'pagan' tribes 'for the faith, not to capture slaves and fill his harems'.[105] Heinrich Barth in his account talks of how incessant Muslim Fulani and Tuareg campaigns reduced former populous, stable and prosperous non-Muslim communities to a condition of utmost misery and insecurity.[106]

The many emirates that were formed throughout present-day northern Nigeria were carved out of areas previously inhabited by traditional African communities. Abdullahi Dan Fodio, brother of Uthman Dan Fodio, undertook a series of campaigns against non-Hausa traditional people groups like the Gurma and the Debe, in Tanda, Fas, Jarma, San Balgo, Jarori and Nupeland. He succeeded in conquering these areas and founded that part of the caliphate purely on 'pagan' land.[107] The emirs of Zaria and Kontagora are also known to have laid waste vast areas of land previously inhabited by indigenous African communities. The once-great traditional Gwari tribe were the chief victims in the founding of Kontagora as a Muslim town.

Writing on 'The Relationship Between the Sokoto Caliphate and the Non-Muslim Peoples of the Middle Benue Region', T. Makar states his main purpose as an assessment of 'how successfully the Sokoto Caliphate Emirs (whose territory lay close or had a common frontier with the non-Muslim people) were able to fulfil one of their most important religious duties, i.e. jihad in the Benue area, as contained in their letters of appointment'.[108] Makar then goes on to outline the campaigns undertaken by different emirs against various indigenous non-Muslim communities and concludes that 'the relationship between the Emirates and the non-Muslim peoples was characterized by wars which were partly to extend the political influence of the individual rulers (emirs)'.[109]

104. Ibid., pp. 8–9.
105. R. Cornevin, 'Fulbe', in *Encyclopaedia of Islam*, 2nd edn., vol. 2, p. 942.
106. Barth, *Travels*, vol. 4, chapter 59.
107. Abdullahi, *Political Thought*, pp. 24–7.
108. T. Makar, 'The Relationship between the Sokoto Caliphate and the Non-Muslim Peoples of the Middle Benue Region', in Usman (ed.), *History of the Sokoto Caliphate*, p. 450.
109. Ibid., p. 456.

92 The Legacy of Arab-Islam in Africa

The waging of holy war against traditional African communities was always explicitly stated in the appointment letters of emirs, and the jihad movements subjected traditional African communities to unimaginable brutality. In some instances, the brutality inflicted upon traditional communities is relayed with some chilling details. The following example is reported on the terror inflicted on the indigenous Montagnard people groups by Hamman Yaji, a particularly ruthless Muslim jihadist (1912–27) of a small territory, Madagali, in north-eastern Adamawa state of Nigeria.

> On one raid Hamman Yaji's soldiers cut off the heads of the dead pagans in front of [the palace], threw them into a hole in the ground, set them alight and cooked their food over the flames. Another time they forced the wives of the dead men to come forward and collect their husbands' heads in a calabash ... One witness told me how he had seen children have a coil of wire hammered through their ears and jaws by the soldiers, while another related how, when Hamman Yaji learned of the great significance attached to the Sakur [a sub-clan of Montagnard] burial rites, he ordered his troops to cut up the bodies of the dead so that they could not be given a decent burial.[110]

The people groups of the Middle Belt of Nigeria remained traditional believers despite or rather because of incessant Hausa–Fulani Muslim raids in the name of jihad. These militant campaigns against traditional people groups continued well into the late 1950s, especially in the Middle Belt of Nigeria where campaigns were conducted against the Kilba people and others, with the British colonial administration turning a blind eye on the raids.[111] It is these Muslim campaigns against traditional African communities in the sub-region that S.S. Nyang refers to approvingly as 'two processes of de-traditionalization and Islamization' where 'successes of Muslims in many areas of the West Sudan led to the gradual destruction of the traditional cults and the emasculation of the old aristocracy'.[112]

In fact Dan Fodio, right from the beginning of his 'reform' movement, considered military jihad against the vast numbers of traditional communities in the region to be a top priority. In his *Kitab al-Farq*, Dan Fodio states the obligations of a Muslim ruler, in contrast to 'pagan' rulers, as stripping of 'evil things' and introducing reforms into religious and temporal affairs. He goes on to declare: 'and an example of stripping evil things from religious and temporal affairs is that every governor of a province should strive to fortify strongholds

---

110. J.H. Vaughan and Anthony H.M. Kirk-Greene, *The Diary of Hamman Yaji: A Chronicle of a West African Muslim Ruler* (Bloomington: Indiana University, 1995), pp. 13–14. Hamman Yaji, who is remembered locally as a particularly brutal tyrant, in his diary prides himself for enslaving more than 2000 people, killing numerous others and plundering the Montagnard people.

111. Rasmussen, *Religion and Property in Northern Nigeria*, pp. 41–2.

112. Nyang, *African Identity*, p. 40.

Muslim Jihad and Black Africa 93

and wage holy war against the unbelievers, and the war makers and the oppressors and forbid every disapproved thing'.[113] The 'unbelievers', i.e. traditional African believers, are here deliberately distinguished from enemy Muslim and/or non-Muslim states ('war makers') and oppressive Muslim rulers.

The 'reform' the jihadist sought to bring about was not therefore merely getting rid of un-Islamic practices and elements or to 'purify' Islam and restore 'orthodoxy', but even more so to inject fresh dynamism into the propagation of the religion in the sub-region, which, as we have shown in preceding discussions, had remained the religion of stranger communities and an aristocratic cult. This new dynamism was the invocation of holy war against traditional African believers, sanctioned by the Qur'an and mainline Muslim teaching. The 'reformist' programme of the jihadists was therefore not simply a question of Muslims washing their dirty linen in public, but involved tackling the root cause of the dirt, i.e. the traditional African socio-religious and political symbols and structures, and their custodians and practitioners.

Both the jihadists and their Muslim opponents had little disagreement on embarking upon jihad against traditional African believers. For this reason Muslim scholars who opposed the jihad were careful to argue their case along lines other than the intrinsic value of the traditional African as a good 'pagan' who should be left to hold on to his/her religious beliefs. The abiding principle of the opposition to the jihad by such leading Muslim scholars of the time as al-Kanimi was that 'the abandonment of the unbeliever is more acceptable than the killing of a Muslim'.[114] The issue here is the spilling of fellow Muslim blood. Indeed, al-Kanimi referred to ordinary traditional Africans in Bornu as *kawalib* (dogs) who may be spared as potential source of booty.[115]

Al-Bakka'i, on his part, had no doubt that 'jihad is to be strictly limited to fighting infidels', i.e. traditional African believers.[116] Likewise, contemporary Nigerian Muslim scholars who question the assumptions and allegations of the jihadists against the pre-jihad Hausa do not

> take a dispassionate view of, let alone laud, the non-Muslim past. Indeed, for the most part they reject it with the same vigour as the protagonists of the reform movement ... Their argument is not just that the pre-jihad Hausa were commendable pagans forced into Islam by tyrannous Muslim jihadists

113. Hiskett, 'Kitab al-Farq', pp. 569–70.
114. Brenner, 'Religion and Politics in Bornu', p. 168.
115. Abdullahi Mahadi, 'The Aftermath of the Jihad in Central Sudan as a Major Factor in the Volume of the Trans-Saharan Slave Trade in the Nineteenth Century', in Savage (ed.), *The Human Commodity*, p. 115. This term, *kawalib* in Arabic, is still used by Arab Sudanese to refer to some Nuba tribes of the Sudan. See *Facing Genocide: The Nuba of Sudan* (London: African Rights, 1995), p. 11.
116. Willis, *In the Path of Allah*, p. 203.

94 *The Legacy of Arab-Islam in Africa*

(which may well be the view of non-Muslim students of the events of the nineteenth century), but rather that these Hausas were good Muslims long before the jihad was unnecessarily and unjustly inflicted upon them.[117]

It is clear from the above that while the jihad movement no doubt involved Muslim–Muslim conflicts, throughout the eighteenth, nineteenth and first half of the twentieth centuries traditional African believers were the principal targets and victims of the jihadists. The strenuous attempts by some Western scholars to portray the jihad movements as 'reform movements' can only be attributed to what we may call the bug of post-modernism, which in its discourse on Islam seeks to deny or avoid everything critical in order to avoid giving the impression that Islam was ever spread by dint of arms. This type of scholarship, in our estimation, is just as detrimental to sustainable inter-faith dialogue as the past procedure on which Islam was depicted as a religion of violence that was spread only by the sword.

If one contends that eighteenth- and nineteenth-century jihad campaigns were an intra-Muslim affair, one obvious question that begs an answer is whence then did the jihadists acquire their slaves in such large numbers that northern Nigeria for instance could be described as 'one of the largest slave societies in modern history'?[118] Traditional believers would have certainly constituted an overwhelming proportion of the slave population. And we cannot say slave raids were excesses or abuses of the jihad movements, for as we shall go on to demonstrate in the next section (and later in the next chapter), views and policies expressed by the jihadists towards traditional African believers and things traditional, were deeply rooted in their understanding of things essentially Islamic and un-Islamic.

Jihadists Views and Policies Towards Traditional Africa

The jihadist views and policies towards traditional African believers and things indigenously African were in many ways informed by the believer–unbeliever, Muslim–non-Muslim and Islam–non-Islam dichotomy in the Qur'an and Muslim traditions. These were further embellished by the views of Muslim jurists and theologians on what relations should and should not exist between the believer and unbeliever, Muslim and non-Muslim and Islam and non-Islam.[119] Echoing traditional Muslim teaching on the subject, eighteenth- and nineteenth-century African jihadists were basically of the view that 'unbelievers'

---

117. Hiskett, 'Preface', p. xv.
118. Lovejoy and Hogendorn, *Slow Death for Slavery*, p. xiii.
119. See D. Marshall, *God, Muhammad and the Unbelievers: A Qur'anic Study* (London: Curzon, 1999) for a perceptive discussion on the Qur'an and Muhammad's attitude towards non-muslims.

Muslim Jihad and Black Africa 95

(who in their particular context were traditional African believers) were essentially enemies of Muslims. They should not rule over Muslims, they should be fought, killed, enslaved or subjugated by Muslims.

In their mission, the jihadists portrayed the traditional African with whom Muslims had lived for centuries as a representative of *kufr* and as such an 'enemy' of God, Muhammad, Islam and Muslims. To use the words of 'Umar once more, traditional African believers were 'the enemies of Allah, the enemies of all the Muslims – our enemies, his enemies and the enemies of his forefathers'.[120] Used countless number of times throughout the writings of the ideologues of the jihad tradition, the term 'enemy' is employed as a general ideological term for non-Muslims who in their particular context were traditional African believers. Thus, the traditional African was an 'enemy' of God, Muhammad and Muslims by virtue of the content of his/her beliefs, customs and practices and therefore a legitimate target of jihad.

In the opinion of the jihadists and their contemporary Muslim admirers, therefore, the very existence of the non-Muslim in general and the traditional African believer in particular is a smear on the dignity of Islam and a potential threat to the interests of Muslims. In his *Bayān Wujūb*, Dan Fodio, after quoting a number of Qur'anic verses, *hadiths* and works of past scholars, called upon Muslims to emigrate from the land of 'unbelievers' to the 'land of Islam' that they 'may attain paradise and be companions of [their] ancestor Abraham, and [their] Prophet Muhammad'.[121] In a similar vein he declared that 'there should be no friendship, counsel, or living together between an unbeliever and a believer' even if they are blood relations. On the contrary, believers 'must bear ill-will towards them [traditional believers] and fight them on account of the faith'.[122]

After citing relevant Qur'anic texts, *hadiths* and works of past scholars concerning the fact that 'unbelievers' are to be fought, killed and their property, children and women seized as booty, Dan Fodio ruled, 'My view is that the unbelievers of the Sudan [traditional African believers] should be treated like the rest of the unbelievers in all respects'.[123] The only legitimate relation with traditional believers, in the view of the jihadists, is at best to subjugate and treat them with contempt or at worst kill or enslave them. Uthman Dan Fodio's grandson, Sa'idu Dan Bello, wrote, 'Let us thank God, the Lord of the office, the Unique/The King who shows no mercy to the unbeliever', and goes on to add, 'a man who has no knowledge [of Islam], he is a mere creature of the bush/He can have no wish to live among men'.[124]

---

120. Ibid., p. 186.
121. Ibn Fudi, *Bayān Wujūb*, p. 52.
122. Ibid., pp. 58–9.
123. Ibid., pp. 86–7.
124. Hiskett, *The Sword of Truth*, p. 166.

96 The Legacy of Arab-Islam in Africa

Traditional believers, in the view of the jihadist, had no right to rule over Muslims. Muslims should not live under the authority of non-Muslims. Rulership is the divine right of Muslims over non-Muslims and wherever the former find themselves living under the rule of the latter, they must emigrate, prepare and launch a jihad against the non-Muslim system. Thus central to the jihadist twin mission of 'de-traditionalization and Islamization' was their passionate struggle to wrest political power from those they considered 'infidel' rulers. The following is Dan Fodio's ruling on the issue:

> And that flight (*al-hijra*) from the land of the heathen is obligatory by assent ... And that by assent the status of a town is the status of its ruler: if he be Muslim, the town belongs to Islam; but if he be heathen the town is a town of heathendom from which flight is obligatory. And that to make war upon the heathen king who will not say 'There is no God but Allah' is obligatory by assent, and that to take the government from him is obligatory by assent. And that to make war upon the heathen king who does not say 'There is no God but Allah' on account of the custom of his town (*bi-sabalbi 'urfi 'l-baladi*), and who makes no profession of Islam, is (also) obligatory by assent.[125]

The status of a land depended on the 'Muslimness' of its ruler whose religious status in turn depended on the judgement of the jihadists. Thus, if the ruler is indicted of *kufr*, the land becomes a legitimate target of jihad irrespective of the religious make-up of the subjects. On the other hand, a Muslim ruler presiding over a land with 'pagan' subjects could also be indicted of *kufr* by association. Al-Hajj 'Umar accused Ahmad ibn Ahmad of Massina of tolerating 'pagan' subjects alongside Muslim subjects and referring to them as 'his pagans' and 'his Muslims'.[126]

The jihadists had no doubt that in order to carry out the mission of Islam, as they perceived it, political power was vital. In fact, Umar Abdullahi explicitly states that 'the Sokoto jihād Movement was not principally designed to re-enforce the spiritual aspects of Islam, but rather its politico-social aspects'.[127] This view appears to be grounded in the traditional Muslim maxim that there is no separation between religion and politics. Hence the launching of jihad against traditional African communities in West Africa from the seventeenth right through to the first half of the twentieth century with the view of 'emasculating the old aristocracies'.

Similarly, the jihadists viewed the indigenous African socio-political and religious values, customs, systems and structures as un-Islamic and therefore sources of 'contamination' of Islam. Thus, in the words of 'Umar, 'wherever they went, their central theme was one and their target was one; that is the total

---

125. A.D.H. Bivar, 'The Wathiqat ahl al-Sudan: A Manifesto of the Fulani Jihad', *Journal of African History*, vol. 2, no. 2 (1961), pp. 239–40.
126. Willis, *In the Path of Allah*, p. 169.
127. Abdullahi, *Political Thought*, p. 23.

destruction of all customs and traditions that were in conflict with the Sharia'.[128] In other words, in northern Nigeria the jihad of Dan Fodio was primarily concerned with exterminating traces of traditional African religious, social and political values from Islam.

Dan Fodio quoted Muslim authorities to support his view that African arts in the form of singing, drumming and dancing are forbidden in Islam and declared everything of the 'ignorant' *'ajam* as *bid'a*.[129] One of the many accusations levelled against Hausa rulers by Dan Fodio was 'they will not abandon the custom which they found their forebears practising, even though it is evil'.[130] The people of Nioro in Bambaraland and many others in the Senegambian region were, in the words of J.R. Willis, 'caused to sacrifice the memorials of their cultural past to the mercilessness of al-Hajj 'Umar'.[131]

So in their twin mission of 'de-traditionalization and Islamization' the jihadists made the old aristocracies their chief targets and, in effect, demanded immediate and unconditional cultural, political and socio-religious surrender. In the words of Dan Fodio, 'it is incumbent upon the Commander of the Believers ... to follow the habits of the Muslims in their governments, and to avoid the habits of the unbelievers in their governments'.[132] The traditional principles of accommodation and compromise that enhanced mutual acceptance and in fact celebration of diversity as demonstrated in the preceding chapter – and from which the jihadists themselves rose to prominence – was thrown overboard and an exclusivist and intolerant system imposed. To quote Mervyn Hiskett, 'the reformers' society was a closed one in the sense that it deliberately excluded non-Muslims, except as slaves or as tribute-paying subjects to the Islamic state.'[133] A whole set of limitations and discriminatory restrictions in traditional Muslim jurisprudence aimed at non-Muslim subjects of a Muslim-ruled state were employed by the new rulers which, in effect, relegated non-Muslim subjects to, at best, the status of second-class citizens and, at worst, sub-humanity.

Traditional African believers were not only disenfranchised, but where they were tolerated they stood very little chance, if any, of obtaining justice at Muslim courts. It has been reported that a Muslim ruler of nineteenth-century northern Nigeria once declared that 'from now on I shall allow no more uncircumcised

128. Abdullahi, *Political Thought*, p. 30.
129. Ibn Fudi, *Bayān Wujūb*, p. 90. The term *'ajam* is a derogatory term originally used to refer to non-Arabs but later adopted by some Muslim groups to anathematize their non-Muslim neighbours. In Dan Fodio's case the term was used in reference to the Hausa.
130. Hiskett, 'Kitab al-Farq', p. 569.
131. Willis, *In the Path of Allah*, p. 145.
132. Hiskett, 'Kitab al-Farq', pp. 566–9.
133. Hiskett, *The Sword of Truth*, p. 166.

98 The Legacy of Arab-Islam in Africa

people in the courtyard of my palace'.[134] In other words, one must circumcise, i.e. become Muslim, in order to seek justice under the new system. It can therefore be said that the jihadists, all with an impeccable African pedigree, were avowedly anti-African.

The main motivation for the jihadists' anti-Africanness was their zeal for a prescriptive Islam. All the jihadists called for or claimed to stand for the full enforcement of the *shari'a*. They were not happy with the superimposition of Islamic religious norms upon traditional African socio-political structures. Neither were they content with Muslims living and practising their faith freely under non-Islamic rule. Indeed, they regarded the political and legal content of Islam as equally important, if not more so. They regarded the *shari'a* as divine law, which must be enforced in all its totality. Dan Fodio charged Hausa rulers for disregarding the application of the laws of God:

> One of the ways of their governments is to change the laws of God, and an example of that is that the shari'a decrees that the adulterer shall be flogged if he is not married, and stoned [to death] if he is married, and that the thief shall have his hand cut off, and that he who kills a person deliberately shall be killed, or if the killing was unintentional, shall be ordered to pay the blood money, which shall be divided among the heirs of the slain man. The Shari'a also decrees that one who destroys one of the limbs of the body, a similar limb of his shall be destroyed. And for wounding it lays down retaliation in far as retaliation is possible, and compensation where retaliation is not possible.[135]

This seventh-century Arab penal code was to replace traditional Hausa court practice. Dan Fodio urged jihadist rulers to see to the scrupulous enforcement of the *shari'a* for 'most of the people are ignorant of the Shari'a, and it is obligatory that there should be, in every mosque and quarter in the town, a *faqīh* teaching the people their religion'.[136] In the words of Umar Abdullahi, Abdullāhi Dan Fodio, whom he describes as 'the intellectual schemer' and 'military strategist' of the Sokoto jihad movement, 'has harped in his works on the imperativeness of strict imitation of the companions of the prophet especially the rightly guided khulafā and the worthy ancestors'.[137]

The Arab factor in Islam, i.e. Arabization, was crucial and central in the jihadists' conception of 'pure' Islam. Dan Fodio and his followers called for the ban of African forms of entertainment (music) and popularized poetry; they anathematized local languages like Hausa as *'ajami*, profane, and eulogized Arabic as the language of God; they promoted Arab and nomadic ways of

---

134. C.F. Molla, 'Some Aspects of Islam in Africa – South of the Sahara', *International Review of Missions*, vol. 56 (1967), p. 463.

135. Hiskett, 'Kitab al-Farq', p. 568.

136. Dan Fodio, cited in Ismā'il A. B. Balogun (ed. and trans.), *The Life and Works of 'Uthmān Dan Fodio* (Lagos: Islamic Publication Bureau, 1975), pp. 74–5.

137. Abdullahi, *Political Thought*, p. 58.

dressing (wearing of the veil by women and turban by men) as against traditional Hausa forms. The jihadists not only venerated Arabic language and culture but deeply longed to be part of it.

Abdullahi Dan Fodio laments his non-Arab descent and confesses his inferior status thus: 'a poor slave, ignorant, drowning in a sea of sin, confused in a sea of fantasy. Humble, *speaking Arabic incorrectly, non-Arab in tribe*.'[138] Where the jihadists had to write in the vernacular, i.e. in such popular literature as poetry, it served only 'as an embellishment on the Arabic motif', which they regarded as the pre-eminent standard of the religious and political life for Muslims.[139] In other words 'reform Islam [in Africa] pressed for a choice between the old and the new, and although there were gaps, the pressure was towards the "orient" in terms of orientation toward Mecca and Medina'.[140]

On the whole, the jihad tradition of eighteenth- and nineteenth-century Africa aimed at 'the sacralization of the Arabic cultural milieu with which Islamic mission is properly identified'.[141] The jihadists were therefore just as thorough in their Islamization and Arabization as they were in their de-traditionalization. This included vilifying and demonizing traditional believers as 'enemies' of God and Islam, claiming Muslim rule over non-Muslims as a divine right, type-casting African traditions and values as evil and satanic while upholding Islam in its seventh-century Arab cultural scaffoldings as the model. It was this thorough Islamization and Arabization that the jihadists not only sought for themselves but also upheld as the uncompromising model of Muslim religious orientation in the sub-region.

If the views and policies of the jihadists towards traditional African believers were to be espoused by, say Western-Christian missionaries or any group in our present day and age, they would be rightly branded religious fascism. If the campaign against traditional believers were to be carried out in any part of the world today it would be viewed as religious cleansing and the massacres that went with it would be first-class genocide. Cultural genocide and religious imperialism would have been the appropriate terms for their programmes of Islamization and Arabization had it been undertaken by any other group. But alas, this was not the case; it was Africans mercilessly enforcing Arab ways of life upon fellow Africans in the name of God! Even more so is the fact that these were carried out by a community of people who thought that their case was made in heaven and should not be questioned.

---

138. 'Abdallāh B. Fūdī, *Tazyīn al-Waraqāt*, ed. and trans. M. Hiskett (Ibadan: Ibadan University, 1963), p. 97.
139. L. Sanneh, 'Translatability in Islam and Christianity in Africa: A Thematic Approach', in T.D. Blakely et al. (eds.), *Religion in Africa: Experience and Expression* (London: James Currey, 1994), p. 36.
140. Sanneh, *Translating the Message*, p. 229.
141. Ibid., p. 225.

100 *The Legacy of Arab-Islam in Africa*

What is worrying, though, is that the anti-African, anti-non-Muslim and anti-non-Islam attitudes of the jihadists, plus their desire to follow the Arab model, far from diminishing, is still alive in varying degrees in contemporary African-Muslim thought. The absolute claims of the jihadists in the eighteenth- and nineteenth-centuries have remained the source of inspiration and exemplar model for the overwhelming majority of present-day African Muslims, even if only a few radical but nevertheless influential ones like Ibraheem Sulaiman, Umar Abdullahi and Mahmud Gumi are those who publicly articulate these views. We shall explore the various attempts of contemporary Muslims to re-enact the jihadist model of *shari'a* rule in chapter 5.

It should be pointed out, though, that this attraction persists largely due to the myths created in post-colonial discourse on the history of the jihadist rule, especially that of the Sokoto caliphate of nineteenth-century northern Nigeria, to the effect that *shari'a* rule of the jihadists brought about stable and progressive governments as compared to the traditional order that was overthrown; and that 'the Islamic revolution' did away with injustice and established social justice unparalleled and unknown in the history of Africa. These myths are certainly the source of the nostalgia for the past and uninformed imitation of Arab governance. It is the myths that seek to present the jihadist rule as the golden epoch of Islam in Africa that we now proceed to examine.

EVALUATING THE JIHADISTS' SHARI'A RULE

Most post-colonial Muslim and Western assessments of the eighteenth- and nineteenth-century jihadist rule in parts of present-day West and Central Africa have sought to paint a romantic and idealistic picture of the jihadists' achievements, implicitly and explicitly suggesting that the lofty ideas set out in the jihadists' manifestos were achieved in practice. These are mainly in the area of the jihadists' views of an Islamic state, an Islamic government and Islamic legal systems. Murray Last in this regard wrote: 'Throughout the [nineteenth] century the ideals, and to a large extent the practice, of Sokoto did not change. This was achieved because the Caliph and his court upheld the traditions of the Shaikh.'[142]

Ibraheem Sulaiman, on his part, makes the same assertion in an even more confident tone. He writes: 'We can ask the historians: has there ever been more successful, more integrated, more disciplined states and governments in Africa, and on our own very soil [Nigeria], than the Islamic states and the Islamic governments?'[143] The problem with these assessments however, is that they are not only based on the 'histories of the victors but their programmes and

---

142. Last, *The Sokoto Caliphate*, p. 235.
143. I. Sulaiman, 'The "Moment of Truth" in Nigeria: Truth is that you can Build Nothing on "the Debris of Western Imperialism"', *Impact International* (13–26 April 1984), p. 10.

Muslim Jihad and Black Africa 101

manifestos and to take them at face value is like taking a party political broadcast as evidence of success in government'.[144] Some of those like Sulaiman and other Muslim activists who laud the jihadist *shari'a* are not only uncritical but 'frequently untrue' omitting 'anything contentious or difficult' thereby degenerating into 'propaganda'.[145]

There is certainly no question that the socio-political, judicial and intellectual legacies of the jihadists have left an indelible imprint on Islam and Muslim identity in areas with a long and sustained jihad tradition as northern Nigeria.[146] Muslim religious and political awareness and self-assertion in most parts of Africa, in addition to contemporary global and local factors, are directly and indirectly inspired by the jihad tradition. As far as Islamization is concerned, the jihadists' contribution is equally apparent. This is evidenced from the demographic distribution of Islam in sub-Saharan Africa in general and West Africa in particular.

There is no doubt that Islam is more visible and entrenched in West Africa than East, Central and Southern Africa, and, as is demonstrably clear from the preceding discussion, West Africa felt the impact of military jihad more than any other part of sub-Saharan Africa. Within West Africa itself, Islam is much more manifest in areas with successful jihad traditions like present-day northern Nigeria, Niger, Mali, Senegal, Gambia, Guinea, northern Chad, etc., while it is less so in areas like Ghana, Togo, Benin, Sierra Leone, Ivory Coast and Burkina Faso. In other words the demographic distribution of Islam in sub-Saharan Africa suggests a correlation with the jihad tradition.

Although Lamin Sanneh has argued that the role of the jihad tradition should not be overestimated in the diffusion of Islam in tropical Africa to the neglect of the less-dramatic peaceful diffusion, he himself admits elsewhere that, 'work done in Ghana and evidence gathered from Sierra Leone, to mention a couple of examples, suggests that Islam does not possess the momentum the reformers and the Western scholars they carried along claimed for it'.[147] The point here is that indigenous traditions in areas with minimal or no successful jihad campaigns have proved they can hold Islam at bay. For a possible explanation for the comparative success of Islam in the aforementioned areas, therefore, the jihad tradition is certainly a strong contributory factor. This is mainly due to the fact that the militant Muslim campaigns,

> though ephemeral, in some ways prepared the ground for the spread of Islam, for by their massacres and slave-raiding, accompanied by the destruction of

144. Lawson, 'Nigerian Historiography', p. 14.
145. Ibid., p. 37.
146. See Hiskett, *The Sword of Truth*, pp. 152–65.
147. Sanneh, 'Domestication of Islam and Christianity', p. 6. Sanneh is responding to assertions that the spread of Islam resulted in the displacement of indigenous traditions.

102 The Legacy of Arab-Islam in Africa

symbols, statuettes, masks, and ancestor houses, they broke up the old religio-social structure of many peoples; whilst on the positive side nominal attachment to Islam often led under peaceful conditions to permanent islamization.[148]

The dislocations brought about by the jihad campaigns on traditional communities, among other factors, contributed to the consolidation of Islam in those areas during the more stable and peaceful times of European colonial rule, which coincided with the rise of Sufism and its tremendous appeal to disinherited people groups.[149] Also in areas where the jihad tradition achieved a measure of success, the commoners were for the first time moving towards Islam, not only because of greater coercion but because 'only by becoming Muslims could they again become recognised members of the system'.[150]

In some cases, the contempt with which traditional believers were regarded and treated by Muslim communities put psychological pressures on people to convert to Islam in northern Nigeria. Traditional believers had no way of ascending the social ladder under Muslim governance. A Hausa proverb has it that 'farming is the "pagan's" sole occupation'. To be a non-Muslim was therefore a big hindrance in one's socio-political and economic advancement. Even under British colonial administration, besides the ruling class all native officials were Muslims and only Muslims were chosen to fill vacant positions in Native Authorities.[151] So it was only by converting to Islam that traditional communities could gain a modicum of recognition and hopefully find their way into occupations other than farming.

Muslim enslavement of traditional African believers during the wake of jihad movements is one single factor that accounts for large-scale conversion to Islam in eighteenth- and nineteenth-century Western and Central Sudan. This fact will be made clear in the next chapter as we produce census figures showing percentages of people of servile origins in Muslim areas. Slaves gradually and generally took up the religion of their masters because it is only by becoming Muslim that they could serve their Muslim masters better in observing the relevant dietary and other socio-religious rites.[152] The mass enslavement of traditional African believers by African, Arab, Turkish and other Muslim societies (as will become apparent in the next chapter) makes the institution of slavery the one factor that accounts for the introduction to Islam of vast numbers of Africans who otherwise would not have come into contact with the religion.

148. Trimingham, *A History of Islam in West Africa*, p. 165.
149. Hiskett, *Islam in West Africa*, p. 281.
150. Levtzion, 'Islamization in West Africa', p. 215.
151. Trimingham, *Report of Survey*, p. 20.
152. N. Levtzion, 'Slavery and Islamization in Africa: A Comparative Study', in Willis, (ed.), *Slaves and Slavery*, p. 191.

At the initial stages 'conversions' related to the above factors were nominal. There were vast numbers of ordinary people in Sokoto for instance who called themselves Muslims but hardly performed the daily liturgical prayers. Muhammad Bello identified ten groups of people in nineteenth-century Sokoto with only one group described as 'real Muslims'. The vast majority, according to Bello, hardly observed their prayers.[153] Similarly, instead of producing Muslim rulers with the promotion of Islam as their top priority, the jihad movements, with a few exceptions, brought in its wake a new band of rulers who had interests other than Islamization. Most of the emirs were more interested in raiding and brutalizing neighbouring traditional communities than in seeking to convert them to Islam.[154]

The jihad campaigns therefore engendered violence and antipathy in non-Muslim areas and in some cases became stumbling blocks to the conversion of indigenous people. Among the vast majority of the people groups of the Middle Belt of Nigeria, there emerged and still exist a strong anti-Hausa/Fulani and anti-Islam feeling because of memories of Muslim slave-raiding activities in the area. Among the Longuda, for instance, so strong is the feeling that fellow Longuda who are Muslim are scorned because Islam is seen a mark of slave descent. They would say 'I am not a slave that I should do the *salāt*'.[155] In some areas, especially French-administered West African territories, after the jihad campaigns were halted by colonial forces people reverted in large numbers to their traditional African beliefs.[156]

On the question of 'reform' and getting rid of un-Islamic elements from Muslim religious practice, the success of jihadist rule in this regard too was not decisive. Shrines were indeed attacked and destroyed and indigenous customs demonized as 'satanic', but the sword of 'orthodoxy' could not get rid of them altogether. Muslim practices point to the fact that traditional religious elements persist. These include the *bori*, a Hausa spirit possession cult, the *homtu* or *homturu*, *hirsi*, *dando*, seasonal ceremonies of the Wodaabe Fulani of northern Nigeria, and a host of others.[157] Singing, drumming and dancing, all condemned by the jihadists, continued, and in fact had to be reinstated by Dan Fodio, albeit under special circumstances.[158]

Also, although Dan Fodio in his earlier writings declared that it is incumbent upon Muslim rulers to 'avoid the habits of the unbelievers in their government',[159] the old habits never died easily. Most taxes that were condemned

---

153. Muhammad Bello in Last, *The Sokoto Caliphate*, p. 59.
154. Makar, 'Sokoto Caliphate and the Non-Muslim Peoples', pp. 456–7.
155. Gilliland, *African Religion Meets Islam*, pp. 57–64.
156. Person, 'Samori and Islam', p. 275.
157. Lewis, 'Introduction', pp. 45 ff.
158. Ibn Fudi, *Bayān Wujūb*, p. 29.
159. Hiskett, 'Kitab al-Farq', p. 566.

104 The Legacy of Arab-Islam in Africa

by the jihadists as un-Islamic were retained and new ones even introduced. For instance, taxes that were levied by Hausa rulers and condemned by Uthman Dan Fodio, such as the cattle tax known as *jangali*, were retained in addition to new ones that were introduced.[160] The wearing of silk, gold, silver and other forms of traditional Hausa royal regalia, all of which were strongly condemned by Dan Fodio in his earlier manifestos, remained the order of the day. Similarly the temptation to make use of traditional Hausa titles condemned by Dan Fodio could not be resisted. Mervyn Hiskett writes: 'These prohibitions were clearly never taken very seriously, as many of the titles became accepted into the new hierarchy and have persisted to the present day. Indeed it does not appear that they were observed even by the generation immediately following the Shehu.'[161]

Dan Fodio also condemned the traditional Hausa system of hereditary succession as follows: 'One of the ways of their government is succession to the emirate by hereditary right and by force to the exclusion of consultation (*shūrā*)'.[162] Meanwhile, Dan Fodio himself paved the way for his son Muhammad Bello to succeed him as the sultan of Sokoto. Throughout the caliphate, accession to the office of emir in the emirates remained the preserve of descendants of the original flag-bearers.[163] On the whole, therefore, 'the change of ruling dynasties did not alter the system of administration, based on historical tradition and Islamic culture'.[164] The emergent political and administrative system merely changed from those of ephemeral Muslim–Hausa dynasties to those of ephemeral Muslim–Fulani dynasties.

The enslavement of free people, i.e. Muslims, continued and indeed escalated throughout the nineteenth century, despite the fact that it constituted one of the emotive charges levelled against the old Hausa ruling class by Dan Fodio in his works. Baba of Kano talks of continued indiscriminate raids of her people (the Hausa) and the enslavement of her relatives, irrespective of the fact that they were Muslims.[165] Corruption, materialism, extortion, oppression and abuse of power became commonplace. A Fulfulde proverb bears witness to the degenerative effect of the jihad movements thus: 'The cleric (*tyeerno*) begets a chief (*lamido*), the chief begets an infidel (*kefero*).'[166]

This trend of degeneration, pillage and devastation perpetuated by most of the new Muslim–Fulani leadership, coupled with the European presence, was

160. H.A.S. Johnson, *The Fulani Empire of Sokoto* (London: Oxford University, 1967), pp. 172–4.
161. Hiskett, 'Kitab al-Farq', p. 576.
162. Ibid., p. 567.
163. Abdullahi, *Political Thought*, pp. 63–4.
164. S.J. Hogben and A.H.M. Kirk-Greene, *The Emirates of Northern Nigeria: A Preliminary Survey of their Historical Traditions* (London: Oxford University, 1966), p. 122.
165. Smith, *Baba of Karo*, pp. 67 ff. See also Abdullahi, *Political Thought*, p. 23.
166. Trimingham, *A History of Islam in West Africa*, p. 161.

Muslim Jihad and Black Africa 105

interpreted by Muslims in the Senegambian and Niger Bend region of West Africa as signs of the end times. Most of them migrated eastwards into the Niger–Chad region in anticipation of the appearance of the *mahdi*.[167] So disappointing were the realities of jihadist *shari'a* rule, judged against their own ideals, that four years after the Sokoto jihad was launched, Abdullahi Dan Fodio became disillusioned and momentarily abandoned the cause. In a poem, Abdullahi lamented thus:

> When my (sincere) friends died, our goals were lost, I was left behind in the midst of liars who claimed that which they did not do, pursued their whims, and chased rapacity in preference to what was obligatory on them ... devouring [people's wealth], self gratification, booty and bribery, enjoyment of lutes, flutes and the beating of drums. They have also sold free persons into slavery in the market, some of them appear as judges but are wolves in the garb of foxes.[168]

In another poem Abdullahi Dan Fodio makes an almost identical indictment thus: 'I am now left in the midst of liars and hypocrites who say one thing and do entirely another ... people whose preoccupation is attainment of political power for the procurement of sensual comfort through concubines, flutists, gorgeous clothing and brisk horses.'[169]

In fact Mervyn Hiskett could not but admit that the Fulani administration tended to slip back to the old Hausa norms, but then quickly went on to suggest that 'an important aspect of the reformers' achievement' is the critical way the society tends to react to such backsliding.[170] In other words it is thanks to the legacy of the jihad movements that critical voices always emerge to challenge and call people back to the proper observance of Islamic practices. That might be the case but this does not still deny the fact that the rule of the jihadists was a far cry from the glorious past being claimed for it.

As far as the judicial system is concerned, the jihadists certainly made the idea of the *shari'a* very popular in theory, but it was quite another matter in practice. Judging from the words of such pivotal personalities of the jihad tradition as Abdullahi Dan Fodio and contemporary admirers of the jihadist model, one is inclined to suggest that while the jihadists definitely had lofty ideas regarding the *shari'a*, the application and implementation appear to have been doomed right from the start. According to Umar Abdullahi, it was the question of the application (or otherwise) of the *shari'a* that caused Abdullahi Dan Fodio's frustration and disillusionment with the vast majority of his contemporaries (including Uthman Dan Fodio) and was the main source of his disagreement with them. In Umar Abdullahi's words:

167. S. Biobaku and M. al-Hajj, 'The Sudanese Mahdiyya and the Niger–Chad Region', in Lewis (ed.), *Islam in Tropical Africa*, p. 230.
168. Abdullahi, *Political Thought*, p. 23.
169. Ibid., p. 61.
170. Hiskett, *The Sword of Truth*, p. 154.

106 The Legacy of Arab-Islam in Africa

The principal goal of the Shari'ah is, among others, to make people honest, temperate, disciplined, sincere and decent by way of imitating the deeds of the companions especially the rightly guided Khulafā and the worthy ancestors. But within four years of the initial successful establishment of the Khalifal administration, some Mujāhidūn betrayed the aims and ideals of the jihad.[171]

Most jihadist rulers were just as guilty of changing the laws of God, a charge Dan Fodio levelled against pre-jihad Hausa rulers. Describing the degenerative and dysfunctional effect of the *shari'a* in twentieth-century Sokoto in graphic and sombre detail, F.L. Shaw recounts that the tyranny and judicial abuses in the system were only tempered by the weakness or moderation of individual rulers. She writes about *alkalis* (local Muslim judges) being either disregarded by local rulers, over-ruled by emirs 'or worse still subjected to the authority of the emir's favourite slaves, who decreed to their enemies inhuman punishments of their own invention'.[172]

Some of these inventions included the tearing out of nails with red-hot pincers, pounding of limbs one by one in a mortar while the victims were still alive, and for important offenders to be built alive gradually into town walls, until the head was finally walled up. A good number of the walls of Hausa towns, according to Shaw, are known locally and called by the names of the victims whose corpses they contain. Impalement and mutilation were the lesser penalties for less-grievous offences.[173]

Mervyn Hiskett argues that the fact that the British recognized and retained the *shari'a* courts as part of their policy of indirect rule in northern Nigeria 'is evidence of their importance' and therefore a success story of the jihad tradition.[174] This argument, though, is not entirely convincing. The British sanctioned the Islamic judicial system in northern Nigeria and other parts of Africa *not* because the system was unique and therefore of special importance, but as part of the Native Authority Ordinance which recognized 'the native law and custom prevailing in an area'.[175] This policy applied to non-Muslim judicial systems as it did to the *shari'a* courts of Muslims. Moreover, the recognition of the British does not necessarily mean the application and implementation of the *shari'a* was up to the standard claimed in the jihadists' manifestos.

From the preceding discussion, some interesting features emerge about the thought pattern of Dan Fodio that we wish to point out. In the first phase, we have Dan Fodio the teacher as a moderate, criticizing those who held austere and

171. Abdullahi, *Political Thought*, p. 61.
172. Shaw, *Tropical Dependency*, p. 401.
173. Ibid. During the post-independence era, some local Muslim scholars attacked the jihadist Fulani rule on the grounds that 'the end of colonial interregnum meant the restoration of repression and inequality'. See Lawson, 'Nigerian Historiography', p. 16.
174. Hiskett, *The Sword of Truth*, p. 154.
175. J.N.D. Anderson, *Islamic Law in Africa*, 2nd edn (London: Frank Cass, 1978), pp. 3 and 174.

Muslim Jihad and Black Africa 107

prescriptive views of Islam, including his own teacher. He criticized certain Fulbe *'ulama'* for making knowledge of the *kabbe* (a translation and adaptation of classical Islamic texts and commentaries in Fulfulde) the measuring rod of being a good Muslim. Dan Fodio advocated *taqlīd* (unquestioning imitation of the local *'ulama'*) for ordinary Muslims.[176] In other words, Dan Fodio the teacher was, as in the nature of all good teachers, understanding and less severe with ordinary Muslims.

In the second phase we have Dan Fodio the preacher in opposition (to the Hausa establishment) who then became idealistic and espoused monolithic, exclusivist, puritanical, intolerant and even militant Islam. He succeeded in declaring other Muslims 'unbelievers' for failing to perceive things the way he perceived them, and launched a militant movement to overthrow the old system and tried to implement his religio-political manifestos. Throughout this period, Dan Fodio saw things as either black or white. In the third phase we have Dan Fodio in power, who appears to have become more pragmatic and realistic and began to tone down, reinstating things he had hitherto condemned and falling back on some of the policies of the former regime.

It is this evolution in Dan Fodio's thought pattern that F.H. El-Masri sees, and he claims Dan Fodio 'lacked the power of critical analysis in his approach to problems'.[177] But rather than seeing this as lacking the power of critical analysis, when we look at Dan Fodio in the different roles we have just outlined above, the stances he took in fulfilling them can be seen as consistent and nothing out of the ordinary. For we know good teachers are considerate; good preachers are supposed to be the conscience of states and therefore have to be critical wherever the need arises; opposition leaders are idealistic and think they have all the answers; while those in power know only too well how crucial the art of pragmatism is. It is only when all these roles are confused and combined together (as they were in Dan Fodio) that contradictions and inconsistencies become inevitable.

CONCLUSION

In this chapter we have taken the analysis of the interaction between Arab-Islam and black Africa forward by looking at military jihad, which in the view of some Muslim groups was the only way to overthrow and completely overhaul the indigenous host environment. Despite the ambiguous nature of the doctrine of jihad, as far as the African jihadists were concerned, 'the move was not at all new. It is, in point of fact, profoundly rooted in the Islamic tradition.'[178] There was equally no doubt about the purpose of jihad, namely, 'exalting and promoting

176. Brenner, 'Muslim Thought', pp. 45–6, 50.
177. Ibid., p. 31.
178. Abdullahi, *Political Thought*, p. 5.

108 The Legacy of Arab-Islam in Africa

Islam for the benefit of humanity in general'.[179] In seeking to exalt and promote Islam, the jihadists had to subdue the traditional African environment, its people and worldview by dint of arms. Traditional Africans and their socio-religious and political symbols and structures therefore became the principal targets of the jihadists.

In their task, the jihadists had the twin programme of 'de-traditionalization and Islamization', the latter part of which involved the imposition of Islam in its seventh-century Arab cultural scaffoldings. On de-traditionalization, despite the untold suffering and irrecoverable blows meted out to indigenous African religious practitioners, symbols and socio-political institutions, the jihadists did not succeed in destroying the intrinsic appeal of some socio-religious African values and rituals. On Islamization they achieved a measure of success in that their campaigns helped in no small way in moving Islam from the periphery to the centre stage of the African experience in jihad-affected parts of sub-Saharan Africa. The realities on the ground show, however, that the jihadists' *shari'a* rule was far from successful and that on the whole jihadist rule tended to slip back into the old systems they overthrew.

179. Ibid., p. 63.

4

MUSLIM SLAVERY AND
BLACK AFRICA

INTRODUCTION

As we pointed out in chapter 1, even though there have been some studies on Muslim slavery very few have tried to locate slavery in African-Muslim societies within its wider Islamic context, and even fewer have made a distinction between African-Muslim and indigenous African-slavery. That is what this chapter seeks to do. To put the whole discussion in context, we will start by examining the underlying stimuli for slavery within African-Muslim societies. Our aim is to demonstrate that slavery in Muslim Africa was not necessarily an indigenous African practice that underwent internal transformations but had deep and independent roots in the Islamic tradition.

We will then go on to examine traditional Muslim ideology relating to the enslavement of black Africans and the related enigma of racial prejudice in light-skin Muslim sources and societies. The actual practice of Muslim enslavement of blacks, first outside black Africa and then within it, will be detailed. This will be followed by an examination of the condition of slaves in Muslim societies. Finally, we will briefly highlight Muslim attitudes towards the abolition of slavery. In all these we will seek to examine the assumptions and myths created over the years that claim that Muslim enslavement was less devastating and less cruel than, say, its transatlantic counterpart.

SLAVERY IN MUSLIM AFRICA: INDIGENOUS OR ISLAMIC STIMULI?

The discussion of the enslavement of Africans over the years, especially the transatlantic dimension, as one would expect, is fraught with controversies. One

110 The Legacy of Arab-Islam in Africa

major persistent controversy is whether slavery existed in Africa prior to the Christian-West and Arab-Islamic interludes, and if it did, whether it explains, if not justifies, the traffic of Africans across the Atlantic into Christian Europe and the Americas, and across the Sahara, Red Sea and Indian Ocean into Muslim North Africa, the Middle East, Turkey and India.

One school of thought that argued that slavery was an age-old and deep-seated practice in Africa, with Africans enslaving one another long before Europeans ever appeared on the scene between the fifteenth and nineteenth centuries, apparently originated with European slavers who were making a bid to exonerate themselves of their role in the transatlantic slave trade.[1] What those claims sought to do was to explain, if not justify, the mass enslavement of Africans by Westerners on the grounds that it was the practice of African self-enslavement that brought others onto the scene to take part.

This line of thinking still persists in more subtle forms. In an acclaimed recent book, Hugh Thomas highlights slavery in Africa and the role of Africans who were 'neither bullied nor threatened' into capturing and supplying their own kind as slaves to Europeans.[2] Some scholars, in response to such innuendoes, are known to have taken the other extreme end of the argument. In this regard there are those who, while not entirely denying the existence of slavery in pre-European Africa, have insisted that 'the forms of slavery and subjection present in Africa in the nineteenth and twentieth centuries and considered indigenous to that continent were in reality engendered by the Atlantic slave trade'.[3] In other words, all forms of slavery in nineteenth-century Africa were a direct result of external European demand.

Then there are some who, in response to these assertions, question any suggestion that the transformations of slavery in Africa could have had anything to do with external factors. Suzanne Miers and Igor Kopytoff opine that to see the transformations of slavery in Africa as a 'response to outside stimuli is to deprive the African past of internal economic dynamism, inventiveness, entrepreneurship, and, above all, of its fundamental cultural concepts of rights-in-persons'.[4] In other words, the transformations of slavery in Africa, including the large-scale raiding of the eighteenth and nineteenth centuries could, or rather would, have arisen with or without any external stimulus such as European or Arab-Muslim activities.

---

1. W. Rodney, 'African Slavery and Other Forms of Social Oppression on the Upper Guinea Coast in the Context of the Atlantic Slave-Trade', *Journal of African History*, vol. 7, no. 3 (1966); Fage, 'Slavery and the Slave Trade', p. 393.
2. H. Thomas, *The Slave Trade; The History of the Atlantic Slave Trade: 1440–1870* (New York: Simon & Schuster, 1997), p. 793.
3. Rodney, 'African Slavery', p. 443; D. Fage also shares this view: 'Slavery and the Slave Trade'.
4. S. Miers and I. Kopytoff, 'Introduction', in Miers and Kopytoff (eds.), *Slavery in Africa*, p. 67.

Both these positions are hardly sustainable. First of all, the argument that all forms of slavery that existed in nineteenth-century Africa were a direct result of the transatlantic slave trade seems to deny the historical fact that slavery in most parts of Muslim Africa, such as the savannah belt of West Africa and the East African coast, had little if anything to do with the Atlantic trade. The generalization of 'slavery in Africa' confuses slavery in Muslim Africa and that of traditional African societies. The thesis of Miers and Kopytoff, on the other hand, falls into the same trap. They have outlined slavery in both Muslim and non-Muslim Africa under the general theme of 'African slavery'. But as we shall shortly argue, slavery as practised by African-Muslim communities was not necessarily the same as slavery in traditional African societies.

Apart from the generalizations both theses have fallen victim of, the views expressed by Miers and Kopytoff have two basic difficulties. First of all, by 'rights-in-persons', they claim that slavery in Africa was just another process like marriage or adoption, whereby outsiders were incorporated into a kin group in exchange for wealth. But to compare wives or adopted persons in Africa with slaves is a gross misrepresentation of these institutions in indigenous Africa, to say the least, and an undeserved deferential treatment of slavery. Second, that African slavery could or would have escalated with or without external stimulus is at best an intellectual speculation that can only be consigned to the realms of the big 'ifs' of history. The question not answered by such speculations, though, is why the ancient slave systems of Europe and Asia did not escalate to the extent their African counterpart did.

Similar claims and innuendoes have been advanced in relation to the oldest, most systematized and unparalleled form of enslaving Africans, i.e. the Arab-Islamic dimension of slavery. Claims that slavery was deep rooted and widespread in pre-Islamic Africa and that Africans actively enslaved and traded their own kind long before the introduction of Islam into Africa have been advanced in a bid to explain, excuse and justify Arab-Muslim involvement in the enslavement of Africans. In this regard, the Fishers, writing on slavery in Muslim Africa, caution thus:

> The fact that the institution of slavery, in one form or another, had deep roots in many parts of Africa long before Islam became a significant social influence there, and that even in regions which were thoroughly islamized there were many pre-Islamic survivals, demonstrates how misleading it would be to suggest a hard-and-fast distinction between Muslim and traditional slavery'.[5]

The Fishers do not provide evidence for their claim that slavery had 'deep roots in many parts' of pre-Islamic Africa. Fadel Abdallah, who sets out to 'defend Islam' against 'self-righteous criticism' by Western scholars, on his part quotes

5. Fisher and Fisher, *Slavery and Muslim Society in Africa*, p. 7.

112 The Legacy of Arab-Islam in Africa

the above statement of the Fishers and counsels that, 'for a discussion of slavery within the context of Islam in Africa, there is always the difficulty of determining how much arises from the original Islamic teachings and how much from local African custom'. Abdallah goes on to assert that 'Africans were active [slave] trade agents both at the individual level and at the official level' before the introduction of Islam in the seventh century.[6]

Again no evidence whatsoever is provided to back the claim that Africans were 'active' slave-trading agents before the introduction of Islam. Abdallah all the same lets out the underlying motive of such assertions thus: 'Suppose that the institution of slavery did not exist in Africa before the presence of Islam, was it then possible for Islam to impose and enforce slavery upon the African society? The answer to this question is a categorical "no".'[7] What Abdallah is suggesting here is that Islam could not and did not introduce any new ideas into any society, not least Africa. Of course, this is an absurd suggestion, for Islam did introduce new ideas into the African worldview, including the age-old practice of slavery, as will be made clear shortly.

To begin with, there can be no questioning the reality of active and indeed crucial participation and complicity, and, therefore, responsibility in the part that Africans played as suppliers of the human commodity to the Western-Christian and Arab-Islamic worlds. This is a hard historical fact that Africans have to confront and address. Denying this fact is in no one's interest, not least the African. The African role in slavery within the Arab-Islamic dimension, which is our primary concern here, will be made clear in the course of this chapter. At the same time it is strange, to say the least, to attempt to explain and justify the part played by people who regarded themselves as 'believers' with a higher level of civilization out to 'convert' and 'civilize' 'pagan' and 'barbaric' Africans on the pretext that slavery had 'deep roots' in African societies.

It has to be said that it is more than probable that slavery existed in Africa long before the emergence of both the Arab-Islamic and Western-Christian interludes. Slavery in one form or another has been in existence from time immemorial. It existed in all the ancient civilizations of Asia, the Middle East, Europe and pre-Columbian America.[8] That ancient African civilizations such as Egypt and other societies shared this general human phenomenon cannot therefore be denied. With regards to ancient sub-Saharan Africa, it is known

---

6. F. Abdallah, 'Islam, Slavery, and Racism: The Use of Strategy in the Pursuit of Human Rights,' *The American Journal of Islamic Social Sciences*, vol. 4, no. 1 (1987), p. 45.
7. Ibid., p. 46.
8. A.H.M. Jones, 'Slavery in the Ancient World,' in M.I. Finley (ed.), *Slavery in Classical Antiquity: Views and Controversies* (Cambridge and New York: Heffer/Barnes and Noble, 1968), pp. 1–15; see J. Vogt, *Ancient Slavery and the Ideal of Man*, trans. Thomas Wiedemann (Oxford: Basil Blackwell, 1974), pp. 1–25.

Muslim Slavery and Black Africa 113

from literary and legal sources of private landlords that some wealthy and powerful individuals had slaves.[9]

Studies on the nature of ancient slavery in general (Africa included) reveal that – with the exception of the large-scale use of slaves in such civilizations as Greece, Rome and Egypt – slaves were generally owned by a few powerful and wealthy individuals in all classical and pre-classical societies.[10] It was never an institutionalized system. Under such circumstances, and in the absence of hard historical evidence, claims that slavery was 'deep rooted' in ancient Africa and that Africans actively traded other Africans in pre-Islamic times are exaggerations if not mere assertions to assuage Western-Christian and Arab-Islamic guilt and responsibility.

The scanty allusions to slavery in ancient Africa and surmises from more detailed studies of slavery in pre-European non-Muslim African societies suggest that slavery in classical and pre-classical African societies, allowing for differences in detail, shared most of the characteristics of domestic slavery in other ancient societies as those mentioned above (possible abuses here and there included). Studies on slavery in such non-Muslim African societies as the Sena of Mozambique, the Batsawana of Botswana, the Kerebe of Tanzania, the Imbangala of Angola, Igbo of Nigeria and the Sherbro of Sierra Leone all reveal this trend.[11] These characteristics include the fact that a few individuals, mainly the ruling elite of the more organized and powerful kingdoms within the pre-European non-Muslim African context, owned slaves more as conspicuous examples of wealth and authority than as a labour force.

In line with domestic slavery in other ancient societies, within the less specialized economies of non-Muslim Africa, 'slaves could add to the size of the population ... but performed virtually the same functions as lineage members', and therefore 'did not form a distinct stratum or class apart'.[12] Hence slavery in traditional African societies has been described as one of many types of dependency and '*incidental to the structure of society* and the functioning of the economy' (my emphasis).[13] We agree with P.E. Lovejoy that 'if we mean by "slave" people who were kidnapped, seized in war, or condemned to be sold as a result of crime or in compensation for crime, then slaves there were. Structurally, however, slavery was marginal.'[14]

First of all, to say slavery is a type of dependency in traditional Africa is different from suggesting that slaves in traditional African societies were 'quasi-

---

9. Jones, 'Slavery in the Ancient World', p. 11.
10. Ibid., pp. 3–11; Vogt, *Ancient Slavery*, p. 4.
11. See Miers and Kopytoff (eds.), *Slavery in Africa*.
12. Lovejoy, *Transformations in Slavery*, p. 13; Miers and Kopytoff, 'Introduction,' p. 5. For a comparison with ancient Greece see Vogt, *Ancient Slavery*, pp. 7–9.
13. Lovejoy, *Transformations in Slavery*, p. 9.
14. Lovejoy, *Transformations in Slavery*, p. 20.

114 *The Legacy of Arab-Islam in Africa*

kinsmen' and kinsmen 'quasi-slaves' as suggested by Miers and Kopytoff.[15] They are of the opinion that slaves in Africa stood 'in the continuum of marginality whose progressive reduction led in the direction of quasi kinship and, finally, kinship'.[16] In other words, according to the position taken by Miers and Kopytoff, slavery in traditional Africa was a *process* rather than a *status*. Hence they use 'slaves' and 'slavery' in inverted commas throughout. Apart from the mistaken assumption that all, or at least most, slaves eventually became kin, by referring to slaves as quasi-kin is like referring to a child as a 'quasi-adult' because he/she is an adult in the making.

Second, to say slavery was a type of dependency does not necessarily imply that slavery in these societies was benign. Indeed, slaves within certain traditional African societies were in some cases killed for sacrificial purposes or buried along with nobles.[17] But even under these circumstances slaves did not suffer this fate necessarily because of their slave status, even though some abuses in later times cannot be denied. In some African societies slaves were, for instance, buried along with nobles just as were other relatives such as wives, children, etc., in line with the belief in ancestors and the need for dependants in both the living and ancestral worlds.

Another important feature of slavery in pre-European non-Muslim Africa (with the exception of those areas, such as Bambara in West Africa and Nyamwezi in East Africa, that shared borders with or were in some form of relation to neighbouring or powerful Muslim states and people) is that there is hardly any known evidence of raids with the specific aim of acquiring slaves. In this regard an Ashanti ruler is reported to have said 'I cannot make war to catch slaves in the bush like a thief. My ancestors never did so.'[18] Slaves were mainly captives of war, augmented through sale, mainly though not exclusively of criminals, and victims of insolvency.

These forms of slavery differed from the institutionalized and specialized systems that pertained in the Christian West (and in the Muslim world as will be demonstrated shortly), where slaves were 'used extensively in production, the monopoly of political power, and domestic servitude (including sexual services)'.[19] The latter situation, as pointed out by P.E. Lovejoy, 'required a regular supply of slaves, either through trade or enslavement or both, and the number of slaves in society became significant enough to affect its organization',[20]

---

15. Miers and Kopytoff, 'Introduction', pp. 22–4.
16. Ibid., p. 24.
17. Lovejoy, *Transformations in Slavery*, p. 15.
18. I. Wilks, *Asante in the Nineteenth Century: The Structure and Evolution of a Political Order* (London: Cambridge University, 1975), p. 176. The same opinion is said to have been expressed by the ruler of Dahomey: Fage, 'Slavery and the Slave Trade', p. 402.
19. Lovejoy, *Transformations in Slavery*, p. 9.
20. Ibid.

Muslim Slavery and Black Africa 115

and even more importantly were backed by a systematic religious ideology. There is therefore no evidence that the practice of slavery in ancient Africa was any more deep rooted or widespread than it was in other ancient European, Middle Eastern and Asian societies.

Concerning the sale or purchase of slaves from Africa, literary and archaeological evidence shows that while the trans-Saharan trade flourished during the time of ancient Greece and Carthage, slaves were hardly among the commodities exchanged with Africans. Only after Rome replaced Carthage in 202 BCE, were a few black slaves found in North Africa; a single epigram indicates the import of an individual slave of sub-Saharan origin.[21] While these bits of evidence reinforce the point that slavery in one form or another probably existed in Africa and that blacks were enslaved, the evidence in itself suggests that the traffic of Africans as slaves at the time was incidental and unusual.

The Greek *Periplus*, written probably around the early second century CE, gives an indication that the export of African slaves had by then become a major business. Arabs are said to have been exporting 'the better sort of slaves to Egypt in increasing numbers' from Somaliland.[22] While the exact role played by Africans themselves in this trade is not immediately clear, the localized nature of the escalation still makes it unusual within the wider African context, thereby suggesting direct and/or indirect external Arab agency as the possible stimulus. What is more, this information does not tell us about the nature of slavery in ancient Africa.

However, between the fifteenth and nineteenth centuries slavery in non-Muslim areas along the West and Central African coast was significantly transformed from a structurally marginal feature of society into an institutionalized and well-organized economic venture leading to an increase in the capture and sale of slaves.[23] Those transformed societies were those who were in direct contact with European trade. Herein lies the crux of the matter. The question therefore is how do we explain the apparent transformations of slavery in those parts of non-Muslim Africa during this particular period? This could not have been a mere coincidence due to internal African 'economic dynamism, inventiveness and entrepreneurship'.

21. R.C.C. Law, 'The Garamantes and Trans-Saharan Enterprise in Classical Times', *Journal of African History*, vol. 8, no. 2 (1967), p. 196. Also Bovill, *The Golden Trade*, pp. 46–7.
22. R.W. Beachey, *A Collection of Documents on the Slave Trade of Eastern Africa* (London: Rex Collings, 1976), p. 1.
23. Indeed, this is the underlying thesis of Lovejoy's book *Transformations in Slavery*. It should also be borne in mind that Africans enslaved and battered people from other weaker tribes who were *not* their own kind as Western European racially obsessed discourses tend to suggest. Blacks did not therefore enslave or batter each other any more than Whites or Asians did to one another once upon a time.

116 The Legacy of Arab-Islam in Africa

If the Ashanti ruler's claim quoted above is anything to go by (and unless there is evidence to the contrary) such transformations are mainly if not solely explained by the impact of European trade. European trade included the supply of guns and gunpowder to their African trading-partner communities and states, which in turn exacerbated prevailing precarious situations. These brought in their wake wars and their attendant instability, insecurity and famine (all potential sources of slaves), coupled with the insatiable demand for slaves for the New World.

Commenting on the transformation of slavery among the Igbo of Nigeria, V.C. Uchendu writes: 'there is good evidence that when slavery became a profitable business, as a result of the demand for slaves in the New World, the incidence of warfare and slave raids increase'.[24] In other words, European demand determined African supply. After all, is it not a basic economic principle that demand determines supply and not the other way round? European demand for the human commodity not only increased African supply but it influenced the use to which slaves were put in powerful African kingdoms such as Ashanti, transforming slavery from a marginal feature of society into an elaborate institution.

That the large-scale African supply and usage of slaves was a direct result of external involvement is supported by the fact that in the drive to abolish slavery and the slave trade the main targets were European and Arab ships in the Atlantic and Indian Oceans and caravans across the Sahara rather than traders in the thickets of Ashanti or Dahomey.[25] Generally speaking, the abolition of slavery in non-Muslim Africa involved the negotiation of anti-slavery treaties with the colonial powers,[26] and when the abolitionists managed to stop or drastically reduce the external European and Arab-Muslim outlets, slavery in non-Muslim African societies, unlike Muslim societies (as will become apparent later in this chapter), withered away and died a natural death.

Surely a 'deep-rooted and widespread' practice could not have died out so quickly to the extent that mere mention of the subject became a taboo in non-Muslim African communities.[27] Hence, between the extreme positions that slavery in Africa was a result of an external stimulus, i.e. transatlantic trade on the one hand, and the view that the transformations of slavery from isolated domestic use to institutional plantation slavery was due to internal dynamics on the other, therefore, lies the more thoughtful view that though slavery existed in Africa long before European trade, the latter was the main contributory factor to

---

24. V.C. Uchendu, 'Slaves and Slavery in Igboland, Nigeria', in Miers and Kopytoff (eds.), *Slavery in Africa*, p. 125. Many of the articles on slavery in non-Muslim African communities in this book make similar points.
25. Thomas, *The Atlantic Slave Trade*, pp. 590–627.
26. Lovejoy, *Transformations in Slavery*, p. 248.
27. Levtzion, 'Slavery and Islamization', p. 193.

Muslim Slavery and Black Africa 117

the dramatic transformations of the practice in some non-Muslim African societies, mainly those that were in contact with this activity. P.E. Lovejoy points out that: 'One important result of European trade ... was the consolidation of a distinctively non-Muslim form of slavery. Slavery [in some non-Muslim African societies] underwent a transformation from a marginal feature of society to an important institution.'[28]

With regard to most parts of Muslim Africa, however, long before Europeans ever appeared on the scene slavery was a well-organized and institutionalized system. These include such Muslim states and dynasties as Sokoto, Bornu, Wadai, Dar Fur, Sennar and Futa Jallon, all in West and Central Sudan, while in East Africa slavery and the slave trade was virtually an Arab-Muslim monopoly, with the Yao and Nyamwezi as active middlemen and suppliers. It is this dimension of slavery in Muslim Africa that most scholars have studied as part of 'African slavery' as pointed out in chapter 1. The question that we seek to address briefly here is to what extent the practice of enslavement in Muslim Africa was indigenous and to what extent it was not and therefore Islamic.

The most fundamental difference that sets slavery in Muslim Africa apart from non-Muslim Africa can be found in the justification of the practice. Muslims right across ethnic, racial and geographical boundaries, like the Christian West, had a systematic religious and racist justification for enslavement. As we shall demonstrate in the next section, the main justification of slavery in classical Muslim thought, borne out in practice by generations of Muslims, is non-belief in Islam, *kufr*. The basis for Arab-Islamic ideology of enslavement includes, of course, the Qur'an, Prophetic traditions, the legal codes according to the various *madhāhib* such as the Maliki in West Africa, and a corpus of literary works written and commented upon by eminent Muslims from the heartland of the Muslim world.[29]

This is not to say that Muslim ideology on enslavement, or for that matter any other issue, was uniformly understood and applied by Muslims down the ages. The haphazard application of Islamic prescriptions on slavery by African Muslims, though, was in no way unique, and should not be seen as a basis for regarding African-Muslim slavery as non-Islamic. It shall be demonstrated in this chapter that while African Muslims exploited slavery to satisfy mundane economic needs, they also, in line with traditional Muslim thought, sincerely regarded it as an Islamic response to the problem of *kufr*. The raids, slaughter,

---

28. Lovejoy, *Transformations in Slavery*, p. 19. J.F. Searing, *West African Slavery and Atlantic Commerce: The Senegal River Valley, 1700–1860* (Cambridge: Cambridge University, 1993), shows that the growth of the Atlantic trade stimulated the development of slavery within West Africa.

29. See Fisher and Fisher, *Slavery and Muslim Society in Africa*, pp. 5–6; see also, Willis (ed.), *Slaves and Slavery*, vol. 1: *Islam and the Ideology of Enslavement*.

118 *The Legacy of Arab-Islam in Africa*

kidnapping, trade and enslavement of millions of traditional African believers by African Muslim societies, as we shall shortly outline, were basically viewed as a religious duty.

Concerning the ideological and religious basis of Muslim slavery in general and enslavement in Muslim Africa in particular, there are those who maintain that slavery was a deeply rooted pre-Islamic practice independent of and, indeed, antithetical to the teachings of Islam. Muslim, African and non-African slavers alike were therefore either ignorant or wrong in their understanding of Islamic teaching. Fadel Abdallah for instance claims that 'everything in Islam in relation to slavery was intended to eliminate an existing, disagreeable, and deep-rooted institution' and insists throughout his article that slavery persisted in Muslim society because of 'deviation from Islam'.[30] That is an internal Muslim debate. However, notwithstanding variations in applications, to claim that slavery is a 'disagreeable' institution in Islam begs the question, which Islam?

As far as the evidence available to us is concerned, Muslim slavery (including that of African Muslims) had a single source, i.e. Arab-Islam as those generations of Muslims perceived, practised and lived it. Hence, slavery as perceived and practised by African Muslims had more in common with their Muslim counterparts in other parts of the Muslim world than it had with their traditional African compatriots. Slavery in Muslim Africa is therefore not a good example of 'an independent African counterpart' of the transatlantic dimension.[31] It is Muslim slavery in Africa and *not* African-Muslim slavery. For, as honestly acknowledged by a few individual Muslims, in bringing Islam to black Africa, Arabs 'introduced a new meaning to the concept of slavery',[32] as they did to many other institutions and practices.

Surely, there are those who have maintained that Africans had the tendency to corrupt 'pure' Islamic teachings, and so would suspect that slavery in African Muslim societies must have been 'corrupted' with 'pagan survivals'. H.J. Fisher, for example, is not immune from this, and it is in this connection that the Fishers' caution against making a hard-and-fast distinction between slavery in Muslim and non-Muslim Africa should be understood. Nevertheless, the caution is not completely without merit. For instance, it has to be borne in mind that some of the uses for slaves (for example as domestic menials) cut across cultural, geographical, ideological and religious boundaries. So does the whole status of slaves. Slaves are slaves irrespective of whether they are under a Muslim or traditional African master.

However, in addition to the ideological basis for Muslim slavery, there are important characteristics that distinguish slavery in traditional African societies

---

30. Abdallah, 'Islam, Slavery, and Racism,' p. 46.
31. Fisher and Fisher, *Slavery and Muslim Society in Africa*, p. 2.
32. Zoghby, 'Blacks and Arabs: Past and Present', p. 9.

from the institutionalized model of Muslim slavery. Indeed the Fishers themselves, after cautioning against making hard-and-fast distinctions, went on to submit that 'the general pattern of slavery in the Muslim countries of tropical Africa ... *can fairly easily be recognized as different from that in areas unaffected by Islam*' (my emphasis).[33] This is precisely the point we are seeking to draw attention to and to underscore. The differences include the institutionalization of slavery, the scale of slave concentration and the uses of slaves in administration, as sexual objects and in large-scale production ventures, as was the case within such Islamic-inspired dynasties mentioned above long before the European interlude.

Regarding slave concentration, for instance, the Fishers, who based their study of slavery in Africa on the accounts of Gustav Nachtigal (a German physician who explored various parts of the interior of Africa between 1869 and 1874), submitted that in contrast to his numerous references to the number of slaves in Muslim societies, there was 'next to nothing to be said about the number of slaves held by pagan masters' in his accounts.[34] This does not, of course, mean that such non-Muslim African societies did not own slaves. Neither are we suggesting that the lack of such evidence is proof that slavery did not exist in pre-Islamic Africa.

What it does mean, though, is that for Nachtigal – with such a keen interest in slavery as manifested throughout his accounts – not to have said anything about slavery in non-Muslim areas (as he did extensively with regard to Muslim areas, notwithstanding how little his contact with non-Muslim people was as compared to Muslim communities) suggests that the practice was, at least, less obvious. Thus our suggestion above, that there are good and tangible reasons why slavery in African-Muslim societies cannot be regarded as 'African', at least without significant qualifications.

Slave raiding and slave trading, which were virtually unknown in pre-European African non-Muslim societies, were a common practice in Muslim societies. The long tradition of Muslim slave raids and slave trade in West Africa intensified during the period of the jihad movements. If one is to speak of slavery as a deep-rooted and widespread practice in African societies, it was in Muslim rather than non-Muslim societies. This is evident from colonial anti-slavery policies in Africa. European colonial powers everywhere recognized that, unlike 'pagan' societies, slavery was at the heart of the religious, cultural and economic lives of Muslim societies and that it had to be tackled with all the sensitivity and expediency it deserved. A British colonial officer captured the spirit of European anti-slavery policies in African Muslim societies in the early twentieth century when he commented:

33. Fisher and Fisher, *Slavery and Muslim Society in Africa*, p. 7.
34. Ibid., p. 14. For the accounts, see Gustav Nachtigal, *Sahara and Sudan*, vols. 2, 3 and 4, English trans. by A.G.B. and H.J. Fisher (London: Hurst, 1987).

120 *The Legacy of Arab-Islam in Africa*

Not only is the holding of slaves legal, by religion and long usage, in these territories, but the sudden discontinuance of the system would produce an enormous dislocation of all social conditions; the owner, who is dependent on his slaves for the cultivation of his estates and for every form of his wealth, would be impoverished by their loss; and the slaves themselves, though not immediately, would to a great extent fall into idle habits and bring about a general economic loss.[35]

F.L. Shaw, wife of Lord Lugard (colonial high commissioner of northern Nigeria), argued for a gradual rather than sudden enforcement of abolition in twentieth-century northern Nigeria in the following words:

The fact has to be faced by the administrator in Mohammedan Africa, that the abolition of slavery is not a straightforward task of beneficence. It carries with it grave and undeniable disadvantages to the slaves as well as to their owners, and the objections urged against it by the local rulers and employers are not by any means without foundation.[36]

William Wallace, acting as high commissioner of northern Nigeria, on his part wrote: 'I am in complete touch and sympathy with the semi-civilised [Muslim] peoples of the Hausa States and I can assure you most positively that if a policy of wholesale liberation of domestic slaves is pursued it will mean the ruin of this protectorate at no distant date.'[37] As a result, slave raiding and trading were banned, but the legal status of slavery in Muslim territories, as opposed to 'pagan' territories, was recognized and, indeed, sanctioned under colonial law on religious, economic and social grounds. In Zanzibar; for instance, the British, in recognition of Muslim and 'native' customary laws, ruled that non-Muslims could not legally own slaves but that a Muslim could, upon appeal to Muslim law.[38]

'Particularly striking' distinctions in slave concentration and the socio-economic and religious importance of slavery between the Muslim Maraka and their traditional Bambara cousins in the Senegambia have also been noted.[39] The Maraka and Bambara example is particularly important, not least because both spoke the same language, lived in the same ecological zone and shared the same social formation. The differences in slave concentration and socio-economic and religious importance between traditional Bambara and their Muslim cousins typifies the difference between traditional African societies and their Muslim counterparts in general. Indeed, regarding slave concentration and the institutionalization of slavery on the whole, Muslim states and communities

35. Lovejoy and Hogendorn, *Slow Death for Slavery,* p. 68.
36. Shaw, *Tropical Dependency,* p. 460.
37. Lovejoy and Hogendorn, *Slow Death for Slavery,* p. 73.
38. Fisher and Fisher, *Slavery and Muslim Society in Africa,* p. 17.
39. R.L. Roberts, *Warriors, Merchants, and Slaves: The State and the Economy in the Middle Niger Valley, 1700–1914,* (Stanford: Stanford University, 1987), pp. 121 ff.

Muslim Slavery and Black Africa 121

in Africa have an unrivalled record throughout Africa as compared to their traditional counterparts.

Studies on slavery in such non-Muslim states as Ashanti, Dahomey, Oyo, Bambara, the Kong, etc., between the sixteenth and nineteenth centuries (the factor of European trade notwithstanding) show that internal slave holdings in these areas were far less than such Muslim areas as Sokoto, Bornu, Wadai, Dar Fur, Sennar, Futa Jallon etc.[40] Unlike traditional kingdoms, slave raiding was an organized state enterprise in virtually all the Muslim domains mentioned above. Indigenous peasant African societies were sources of slaves for Muslim and European slavers and their African political and trading allies rather than slave owners. Hence those within the savannah areas of West Africa have been described as 'more a source of slaves [for neighbouring Muslim states], than employers of slaves'.[41]

How then are the distinguishable patterns of slavery in African-Muslim societies noted above as compared to their non-Muslim counterparts to be explained? Many factors such as sociological, economic and historical ones can, and have been, adduced to account for slavery in African-Muslim societies as they have been in other slave-owning societies. Important and crucial as these factors are, however, the underlying factors of systematic religious and racist ideologies substantially affected slavery in Muslim Africa and explain its distinguishing characteristics. Any denial or minimizing of the religious and, hence, Arab-Islamic motivation and stimulus for slavery in African-Muslim societies is to deny something African Muslims stood, fought and died for, namely that slavery was an important part of their religious life.

Our contention, therefore, is that slavery in African-Muslim societies underwent significant transformations, first of all as a direct result of contacts with the Arab-Islamic world and the insatiable demand for slaves by those Muslim states and communities. In addition to this, like the transformation of slavery in non-Muslim African societies that were in contact with European trade, non-Muslim African states that shared borders with Muslim kingdoms or had some form of relations either as tributary or subordinate states to Muslim governments developed a more institutionalized slave system, not on the same level with their Muslim neighbours, but in many significant ways different from other traditional African communities.

Examples of these non-Muslim African states and communities include the traditional Segu Bambara state and numerous other Sudanese tribes of West Africa and the Yao and Nyamwezi of East Africa.[42] These non-Muslim African societies embarked on slave raiding and slave trading mainly with their Muslim

---

40. Ibid., pp. 66 ff.
41. Lovejoy, *Transformations in Slavery*, p. 218.
42. Roberts, *Warriors, Merchants, and Slaves*, pp. 121 ff.

122 The Legacy of Arab-Islam in Africa

neighbours, middlemen or overlords, first as an economic venture but then also to pay tribute to their Muslim overlords. These developments in non-Muslim African society consequently transformed slavery from incidental enslavement of individuals into extensive employment of slave labour in local industries. Hence stronger non-Muslim tribes started raiding weaker tribes to sell to Muslim slavers, employ in local economies or pay tribute to Muslim overlords.

The earliest example of non-Muslim states paying tribute in the form of slaves to Muslim overlords is contained in the *baqt* signed in the seventh century between Arab-Muslim rulers of Egypt and Nubia, which involved the payment of 360 slaves a year by Nubia to their Muslim overlords.[43] This agreement lasted and the tribute was paid on a fairly regular basis up to the thirteenth century. The practice of non-Muslim people paying tribute in the form of slaves to Muslim overlords was adopted and duplicated by Muslim rulers in Africa, especially during the jihadists' rule in Western Sudan in the nineteenth and twentieth centuries.[44] So both the commercial and political links and ties between Muslims and non-Muslim states transformed slavery in non-Muslim African societies by way of introducing slave raids and slave trade hitherto unknown in the histories of those non-Muslim societies.

Our second contention is that the Arab-Islamic stimulus was, however, in other crucial ways different from that of the Christian West. While there was hardly any internalization of European attitudes to slavery and its ideology in Africa, African-Muslim societies adopted the Arab-Islamic ideological basis of enslavement. African converts to Islam imbibed and internalized the religious motivation and justification of enslavement along with many other Islamic teachings. The Arab-Islamic ideology of enslavement became the main stimulus and reference point for the institution of slavery in African-Muslim communities. As far as we are concerned, this is the fundamental distinguishing feature of African-Muslim slavery from that of their non-Muslim counterparts. This will become abundantly clear as we proceed to outline slavery in African-Muslim societies.

Some people may accuse us of a fundamental logical flaw in our presentation, given that we have argued in chapter 2 that the host indigenous African societies and their worldview had a profound influence on the Muslim guests, and yet want to exempt the institution and practice of slavery from that influence. First of all any such accusation along these lines will be a gross misrepresentation of what we have intimated in chapter 2. We never said or even implied that the influence was one way only. If anything at all, it is the spokespersons of Arab-Islam who have sought to paint a picture of a one-way

---

43. Hasan, 'The Penetration of Islam', pp. 113–15.
44. It is known that during the first half of the fourteenth century, traditional communities of Kana paid an annual tribute of 200 slaves to the Muslim ruler, Tsamia. See M. Hiskett, 'Enslavement, Slavery and Atitudes towards the Legally Enslavable in Hausa Islamic Literature', in Willis (ed.), *Slaves and Slavery*, vol. 1, p. 107.

Muslim Slavery and Black Africa 123

influence, with the 'literate traditions' of Islam having the initiative and upper hand over 'non-literate traditions' of indigenous Africa. As far as we are concerned, the borrowings, exchanges and influences were mutual.

Second, accusations of 'logical flaws' presume that everything, including historical events, followed and must be fitted into a certain mechanical process and therefore must come out with a 'logical' result. That is certainly a false assumption, especially when we are dealing with encounters and exchanges such as those that took place between host traditions in general (not only African traditions) and the incoming traditions of Islam and Christianity. Third, traditional African societies influenced their Muslim guests with what they had within the framework of the indigenous worldview. And as we have argued above, slavery as an institution backed by a systematic ideology (religious or otherwise) is alien to pre-Islamic and pre-Western African societies. So surely traditional communities could not have influenced their Muslim guests on things they never had or knew of in the first place.

It should be added here that what we have argued and established with regards to the Islamic stimulus for the transformation of slavery from a marginal social phenomena to a wide-scale institutionalized practice does not pertain only to African societies. Similar observations have been made on the transformation of slavery in Turkish society. Robert Brunschvig writes:

> Throughout the whole of Islamic history, down to the nineteenth century, slavery has always been an institution tenacious of life and deeply rooted in custom. The Turks, who were to come to the relief of the Arabs in the victorious struggle against Christianity, seem to have practiced it but little in their primitive nomadic state: after providing for so long their unwilling quota, through kidnapping or purchase, to the slave class of the Muslim world, they became themselves supporters of the institution in an ever-increasing degree, as they adopted Islam and the sedentary way of life.[45]

This is precisely what we are saying about the Islamic stimulus for the transformation of slavery in African societies. First, that Africans seem to have practised slavery but little in their pre-Islamic state; second, that African societies who were themselves victims of Arab-Muslim enslavement, became the principal supporters and agents of the institution in an ever-increasing degree as they got into alliances with their Muslim neighbours and/or overlords, and more so as they adopted Islam completely or even nominally. We shall now proceed to demonstrate that slavery has always been an institution tenacious of life and deeply rooted in Muslim thought and way of life right from the Islamic heartlands of Arabia down to Muslim Africa by giving an overview of Islamic justification of enslavement and the Muslim practice of slavery from the Islamic heartlands to Muslim Africa.

45. R. Brunschvig, 'Abd', in *Encyclopaedia of Islam*, new edn, vol. 1, p. 31.

124 *The Legacy of Arab-Islam in Africa*

CLASSICAL MUSLIM IDEOLOGY OF ENSLAVEMENT

In pre-Islamic times, slavery was well known in the whole of the Mediterranean region and the Arabian Peninsula. Slaves were mainly captured during wars. This pre-Islamic practice, like many others, is accepted in classical Muslim traditions as a matter of course. In the Qur'an, the periphrasis 'those whom your right hand possess' is used more frequently to refer to slaves than *'abid*, plural of *'abd*, the Arabic term for slave. In the language of the Qur'an, slaves are a legitimate property for Muslims. The Qur'an accepts and endorses the basic inequality between master and slave as part of the divinely established order and uses this inequality as a metaphor to depict the difference between God and His creation. In Sura 16: 75, the Qur'an castigates Meccan polytheism in the following words:

> Allah coineth a similitude: (on the one hand) a (mere) chattel slave, who hath control of nothing, and (on the other hand) one on whom We have bestowed a fair provision from Us, and he spendeth thereof secretly and openly. Are they equal? Praise be to Allah! But most of them know not.[46]

The pre-Islamic Arab practice of using female slaves as prostitutes is condemned by the Qur'an, which instead sanctions the institution of concubinage, which permits a Muslim male to have lawful conjugal relations with an unrestricted number of his female slaves. Any Muslim who cannot afford to marry a free Muslim woman may take his female slave as a wife. The Qur'an urges, without actually commanding, kindness to slaves as a meritorious act of piety. In the same way it recommends, without requiring, their liberation by purchase or manumission, to which the legal alms of *zakat* may be devoted, or by the slaves buying their own freedom.

In the event of a Muslim wilfully breaking the fast during Ramadan, committing unintentional homicide or perjury, the Qur'an prescribes, among other things, the freeing of a Muslim slave as expiation.[47] The *hadith* generally follow the Qur'anic pattern in accepting slavery, urging kindness and recommending manumission as acts of piety. Slavery as a practice is therefore not condemned in either the Qur'an or *hadith*. If anything at all the practice is endorsed with modifications and stipulations aimed at regulating and mitigating possible abuses. But these are only the theories and pious stipulations, which do not in any way suggest a reflection of what actually took place in practice, as some people would have us believe.

---

46. Other texts include Suras 16: 71 and 30: 28.
47. On the use of female slaves as concubines and wives, see Suras 24: 33; 23:6; 4: 25; on kindness and manumission, see Suras 4: 36; 2: 177; 90: 13; on the freeing of slaves as religious and legal expiation, see Suras 4: 92; 5: 89 and 58: 3.

Non-Belief in Islam as Justification for Muslim Slavery

The traditional Muslim ideology of slavery is closely linked to the doctrine of military jihad. Just as jihad is directed against non-belief in Islam, *kufr,* so the 'unbelievers', *kuffār* captured in a jihad are the legally and religiously enslavable in Muslim society. The Qur'an in this regard admonishes Muslims thus: 'When you meet the unbelievers [in a jihad], smite their necks, then, when you have made wide slaughter among them, tie fast the bonds [of slavery]'. The victorious Muslim ruler could then choose either to free his captives out of generosity (presumably after their conversion to Islam), or in exchange for a ransom.[48]

The choice of freeing captives or exchanging them for ransom did not, of course, rule out the possession of captives as slaves. In fact, both in theory and practice, enslavement of captives was the general norm, while the freeing and exchange of captives remained important exceptions. Taking exception to Muslim apologists such as M.C. Ali who insist that 'it is a false accusation against the Koran that it allows enslavement of the captives of war',[49] H. Ghoraba accepts the Qur'anic position and offers his own explanation.

In Ghoraba's view, Islam allowed prisoners of war to be enslaved because Muslims had to fight people who enslaved them when captured. 'If Islam had refused to allow Muslims the right claimed by their enemies', writes Ghoraba, 'it would have put the Muslims at an unfair disadvantage in their wars. Hence it is logical and just that Islam gave the ruler of the Muslims the right to act in the same manner as their enemies.'[50] Here we have the modern apologetic and traditional views succinctly summed up by these two Muslim scholars.

There are therefore two main sources of slaves in Islam: capture in jihad or birth to slave parents. The latter means one inherits the servile status of one's slave ancestors until or unless one is manumitted through one of the above-mentioned processes. So once captured and enslaved, conversion to Islam offers no escape route for a slave or a slave's offspring. *Fiqh,* traditional Muslim law, recognizes purchase as a third legitimate source of acquiring slaves. In practice, however, raiding (*ghazw*) and kidnapping by Muslim individuals and communities became popular sources of slaves.

Since legitimate jihad is only permitted against non-Muslims, and jihad is the main lawful source of slaves, only non-Muslims, especially *mushrikūn* (idolaters) can be enslaved by Muslims. A medieval Muslim jurist, 'Abd al-'Azīz ibn Ahmad al-Bukhārī (d. 1330), sums up the traditional Muslim justification of enslavement thus: 'Servitude is a vestige of obstinacy in refusing to believe in

---

48. Sura 47: 4.
49. Ali, *Exposition of the Popular 'Jihad',* p. 193.
50. H. Ghoraba, 'Islam and Slavery', *The Islamic Quarterly,* vol. 2, no. 3 (1955), p. 158.

126 *The Legacy of Arab-Islam in Africa*

the One God (*kufr*), and this in the eyes of the law is death itself.'[51] Hence, in traditional Muslim law, as J.R. Willis points out,

> slavery becomes a simile for the heathen condition – a symbolic representation of the very antithesis of Islam. And if a slave is hewn out of the simile of his heathenness, it is submission to Islam which hones the possibilities for redemption. Thus, non-belief is the signal cause of possession – the underlining principle for the existence of slavery in Islam.[52]

In line with this notion, traditional Muslim jurisprudence sanctions the enslavement of Jews and Christians but, rather curiously, excludes non-Muslim Arabs from the category of the enslavable.[53]

There is also a general consensus in traditional Muslim jurisprudence that women and children are not to be killed in a jihad but rather taken and divided as booty (*ghanīmah*) among the victors as slaves. Al-Maghīlī's admonition in this regard, pre-echoed in all the legal texts, reads as follows: 'Make jihād against the infidels, kill their men, make captive their women and children, seize their wealth.'[54] By sanctioning the enslavement of women and children as booty alongside livestock and other movable properties, traditional Islamic thought regards slavery as the means, on the one hand, of dealing with the antithesis of Islam, *kufr*, and, on the other hand, of compensating for Muslim losses in jihad as well as a motivation for jihad.

In theory, no Muslim is permitted under traditional Muslim law to enslave a fellow Muslim. This was hardly the case in practice, though, both in Muslim Africa and in the heartland of the Islamic world.[55] If one converts to Islam after being captured in a jihad or purchased, that does nor change one's fate nor that of one's offspring. A fifteenth-century Islamic legal edict reads:

> If it is proven that a slave was originally an unbeliever of one kind or another – unless he is of Quraysh [Muhammad's clan] – and if on the other hand it is not proven that he adopted Islam when he was in his own country and a free agent, then once his captors have laid hands on him after conquest and

51. Quoted in P.G. Forand, 'The Relation of the Slave and the Client, to the Master or Patron in Medieval Islam', *International Journal of Middle East Studies*, vol. 2 (1971), p. 61.
52. J.R. Willis, 'Jihad and the Ideology of Enslavement in Islam', in Willis (ed.), *Slaves and Slavery*, vol. 1, p. 4.
53. See the chapter on jihad from Averroes, in Peters (trans. and ed.), *Jihad in Islam*, pp. 31–2; also R. Brunschvig, 'Abd', p. 26.
54. Willis, 'The Ideology of Enslavement', p. 22.
55. In 1153 CE the Oghuz Turks of Balkh, who were themselves Muslims, laid waste to Khorasan and reduced many Muslims from Tus and Nishapur to slavery. Similarly, Muslim khans of Iran enslaved fellow Muslims of Gilan in the early fourteenth century, while Sunni lawyers in Ottoman Turkey and Central Asia declared it legal to enslave Shi'is in the sixteenth century. See I. Petrushevsky, *Islam in Iran*, trans. Hubert Evans, (London: Athlone, 1985), p. 158–9.

Muslim Slavery and Black Africa 127

victory, it is lawful for them to sell or buy him, without hindrance. The profession of the monotheistic creed by these slaves does not prevent the continuance of their status as slaves.[56]

In other words the status of slavery is permanent. E.W. Blyden was, therefore, ill informed, both in theory and in practice, when he asserted that in Islam 'the slave who becomes a Mohammedan is free'.[57]

Black Africa, considered the bastion of 'unbelief', became a major source of slaves for Muslim lands such as North Africa, the Middle East, Turkey and South Asia, starting as early as the seventh century. As will be pointed out in the following pages, within black Africa itself, Muslims, through the waging of jihad, raiding (*ghazw*), kidnapping and purchase, reduced millions of traditional African believers into slavery on account of their non-belief in Islam.

Ahmad Baba (1556–1627), a celebrated Muslim *'alim* of Timbuktu, wrote an important treatise popularly known as the *Mi'raj*, in which he spelt out the non-Muslim people in the Western Sudan against whom legitimate jihad could be undertaken and who could be enslaved.[58] In his treatise, which became a standard reference for the categories of the enslavable in the western Sudan, Ahmad Baba declared that 'the reason for slavery [in Islam] is non-belief', and went on to rule that:

> Those who come to you from the following clans: the Mossi, the Gurma, the Busa, the Yorko, the Kutukul, the Yoruba, Tanbughu [Dogon of the Hills], the Bobo are considered non-believers who still adhere to non-belief until now; also Kunbay, except a few from Hanbar and Da'ananka [Denianke], although their Islam is weak. You are allowed to own all these without questioning. This is the ruling about these clans, and Allah, the Highest, knows and judges.[59]

Muslims, like their Western-Christian counterparts centuries later, regarded the enslavement of black Africans as a blessing in disguise to the victims. Black slaves, it was believed, were fortunate in that they were spared the 'barbarities' of their own kind and even more so because they were destined to be introduced to the religion and 'civilized' values of Islam. In a famous, albeit 'weak' *hadith* the Prophet of Islam is alleged to have said:

56. A fifteenth-century legal Muslim ruling translated from *Kitāb al-Mi'yār al-Mughrib*, by Ahmad al-Wansharisi, in Lewis, *Race and Slavery*, p. 148.
57. Blyden, *Christianity, Islam and the Negro Race*, pp. 15–16. It must, however, be pointed out that a slave under non-Muslim control who flees into *Dar al-Islam* is a free man provided, of course, he becomes a Muslim as soon he crosses over. See Willis, 'The Ideology of Enslavement', p. 21.
58. B. Barbour and M. Jacobs, 'The Mi'raj: A Legal Treatise on Slavery by Ahmad Baba', in Willis (ed.), *Slaves and Slavery*, pp. 125 ff.
59. Ibid., p. 137.

128 The Legacy of Arab-Islam in Africa

Will you not ask me why I laugh? I have seen people of my community who are dragged to paradise against their will. They asked, 'O Prophet of God, who are they?' He said, 'They are the non-Arab people whom the warriors in the Holy War have captured and made to enter Islam.'[60]

The same notion is portrayed in a Persian tale where Muslim traders took advantage of the hospitality of an African ruler, abducted him and sold him into slavery. The ruler was then taken to Basra in Iraq, converted to Islam in the process, then managed to escape some years later back to Africa. Then, the tale continues, these same traders happened to come back to the same place only to meet the same man in power. The ruler, instead of raging with revenge towards his abductors, pardoned and thanked them for making it possible for him to be introduced to the religion and values of Islam. In the ruler's own alleged words:

I am glad and satisfied with the grace which God has accorded me and mine, instructing us in the precepts of Islam, the true faith, in the usage of prayer, fasting, and pilgrimage, and in the knowledge of what is forbidden and what is allowed; none other in the land of the zindjs has received such favor. And if I pardon you, it was because you were the first cause of the purity of my faith.[61]

It was with this incredible notion that slavery was a blessing in disguise for the victims, especially black African victims, that millions of black Africans were reduced to slavery by various Muslim communities, within and without the continent, in the past fourteen centuries of Islamic history.

Colour and Race in the Muslim Ideology of Slavery

Another crucial feature of the classical Muslim ideology of enslavement is that blacks became legitimate slaves by virtue of the colour of their skin. The justification of the early Muslim equation of blackness with servitude was found in the Genesis story popularly called 'the curse of Ham', one of Noah's sons. The biblical version describes how Noah got drunk and lay uncovered inside his tent. His younger son, Ham, saw his father's nakedness and informed his two elder brothers, Shem and Japheth. These two laid a garment over their shoulders and walked backwards into the tent and covered their father. Noah woke up and upon hearing what happened, cursed the descendants of Ham's son, Canaan, to be slaves of the descendants of Shem and Japheth.[62]

---

60. B. Lewis, *Islam from the Prophet Muhammad to the Capture of Constantinople*, vol. 2, *Religion and Society* (New York: Macmillan, 1974), p. 211.
61. 'A Ship's Captain's Tale', translated from Buzurg ibn Shahriyar, *Kitāb ʿAjaʾib al-Hind*. In G.W. Irwin, *Africans Abroad: A Documentary History of the Black Diaspora in Asia, Latin America, and the Caribbean during the Age of Slavery* (New York: Columbia University, 1977), pp. 110–15.
62. Genesis 9: 18–27.

Muslim Slavery and Black Africa 129

The biblical curse of servitude (not blackness) fell on the youngest son of Ham, Canaan, and not his other sons, including Kush (who was later projected in Judaeo-Christian traditions as the ancestor of blacks). Apparently transmitted to Muslims by Jews, Christians and converts from Judaism and Christianity, the story found its way into early Muslim-Arab historiography and ethnology.[63] All the Muslim-Arab versions portray Arabs as descendants of Shem, and blacks (sometimes including Copts and Berbers and the Sindh of India) as descendants of Ham, with most assigning the Turks and Slavs to Japheth. In the Muslim-Arab versions, blacks are condemned to be slaves and menials, Arabs are blessed to be prophets and nobles, while Turks and Slavs are destined to be kings and tyrants.[64]

In early and medieval Muslim sources, the link between Ham and blacks was fully forged and blackness became a simile for the servile condition, a clear departure from the Judaeo-Christian version of the myth. Al-Tabari, the great Muslim historian, cited not less than six Prophetic traditions to support the Arab-Muslim version of the descendants and fates of the three sons of Noah. One such tradition reads:

> Ham begat all those who are black and curly-haired, while Japheth begat all those who are full-faced with small eyes, and Shem begat everyone who is handsome of face with beautiful hair. Noah prayed that the hair of Ham's descendants would not grow beyond their ears, and that wherever his descendants met the children of Shem, the latter would enslave them.[65]

On his part Ibn Qutaybah (828–89) wrote that 'Ham, son of Noah, was light-skinned and handsome. Then God Most High changed his complexion and that of his progeny [into black] because of the curse [invoked by] his father'.[66] Thus the biblical curse that originally fell on the youngest son of Ham (Canaan), in Arab-Muslim versions of the myth, falls on Ham himself, whose descendants are cursed not only with servitude but in addition with the change of their colour from light-skinned to black.

Therefore, just as *kufr* is a synonym for servitude in classical Muslim thought, the colour black became the most obvious sign of servitude in light-skinned Muslim thinking. In other words, to be black is to be a slave. The Arabic word *'abd* (a slave of whatever colour) went through a semantic development and came to specifically refer to 'black slave' while light-skinned slaves were referred to as *mamluks*. And further on in later developments, *'abd* in spoken Arabic, has

---

63. See al-Tabari, *History*, vol. 2, trans. W.M. Brinner (New York: State University of New York, 1987), pp. 10 ff.
64. Ibid., pp. 10–17.
65. Ibid., p. 21.
66. A. Muhammad, 'The Image of Africans in Arabic Literature: Some Unpublished Manuscripts', In Willis (ed.), *Slaves and Slavery*, vol. 1, p. 56.

130 *The Legacy of Arab-Islam in Africa*

come to mean 'black man' of whatever status.[67] This semantic evolution of the word *'abd* from a purely social to racial designation derives from the popular image of the black person in Arab history and society as a slave.

Consequently, black Muslims, having cast away the yoke of unbelief that subjected their forefathers to the servile condition, still had to battle and dislodge the notion that the colour of their skin was fettered to the condition of servitude. Responding to a contemporary controversy as to whether people from the western Sudan could ever claim to be legally free on account of their profession of Islam, Ahmad Baba (a black African Muslim) in his *Mi'raj*, insisted that the cause of slavery is the content of one's beliefs and not the colour of one's skin. Baba intimated:

> The Sudanese non-believers are like other *kāfir* whether they are Christians, Jews, Persians, Berbers, or any others who stick to non-belief and not embrace Islam ... there is no difference between all the *kāfir* in this respect. Whoever is captured in a condition of non-belief, it is legal to own him, whoever he may be, but not he who was converted to Islam voluntarily, from the beginning.[68]

Ahmad Baba went on to cite other renowned *'ulama'* to support his view that slavery in Islam is premised along creedal rather than racial lines. Baba refuted the arguments from the myth of Ham on the basis that 'the saying of Noah is in the Torah and in it there is no mention of black color. It only mentions that his [Ham's] children would be the slaves to the children of his brothers, and nothing else'.[69]

Nevertheless, having placed black Africans under a mythological curse, light-skinned Muslims justified, or rather took leave of any moral inhibitions in, the enslavement of black people. The rebuttals from black Muslim scholars such as Ahmad Baba did little to redress the trend. Blacks continued to be enslaved more on the basis of the colour of their skin and (as we now proceed to demonstrate) have since been subjected to stereotypical racial prejudice and discrimination from Arab and other light-skinned Muslim groups.

THE IMAGE OF BLACKS IN LIGHT-SKIN MUSLIM SOURCES AND SOCIETIES

In pre-Islamic Arab poetry and historical narrative, blacks – who at this stage were by and large Ethiopians – were usually referred to as Habash, the Arabic name from which the term 'Abyssinian' is derived. There is hardly any trace of

67. W.J. Sersen, 'Stereotypes and Attitudes towards Slaves in Arabic Proverbs: A Preliminary View', in Willis (ed.), *Slaves and Slavery*, vol. 1, pp. 95–7; B. Lewis, 'The African Diaspora and the Civilization of Islam', in M.L. Kilson and R.I. Rotberg (eds.), *The African Diaspora: Interpretative Essays* (Cambridge, MA: Harvard University, 1976), pp. 43–4; see also Zoghby, 'Blacks and Arabs: Past and Present', p. 12.
68. Barbour and Jacobs, 'The Mi'raj', pp. 129–30.
69. Ibid., p. 133.

Muslim Slavery and Black Africa 131

antagonism or discrimination on the basis of the skin colour in pre-Islamic and early Islamic Arabia. In line with this pre-Islamic and early Islamic period, the Qur'an, apart from one instance where the colours black and white are used in an idiomatic sense to depict evil and good respectively,[70] expresses no prejudice in matters of race or colour. Indeed, the Qur'an makes no specific reference to blacks, Africa or Abyssinia.

In social life in pre-Islamic and early Islamic Arabia there were black slaves as well as white slaves, mainly captured during war, and there is no evidence that the former suffered any specific discrimination by virtue of the colour of their skin. On the contrary, the Habash, who were active in sixth-century Arabia as allies of the Byzantines, were usually regarded as people with a higher civilization than the Arabs and respected during early Islamic times as people with a revealed religion. It was partly due to the high esteem with which the Habash were held in the early Islamic period that Muhammad advised his persecuted followers to seek asylum in Abyssinia in 615 CE.

The second caliph, 'Umar ibn al-Khattab, the conqueror of Palestine and Egypt, 'Amr ibn al-'As and several other Companions of Muhammad are known to have had black-African traits in their ancestral lines.[71] However, after the death of Muhammad and the early Muslim conquests, there developed what Bernard Lewis describes as 'an inherent and continuing contradiction between Islamic doctrine on the one hand and the social reality on the other' in the attitude of Arab and subsequently, other light-skinned Muslim societies towards blacks.[72]

The *hadiths* generally insist on the equality of all men in Islam before God. There are, however, a considerable number of *hadiths*, even though technically termed 'weak' in that doubts have been cast over their authenticity as reflecting Muhammad's or his early Companions' views, that nevertheless constitute important evidence for contemporary Muslim attitudes. A number of these *hadiths* deal with race and colour with some specifically condemning other races, especially the black race.

One such *hadith* reports Muhammad as having said of the Ethiopian: 'When he is hungry he steals, when he is sated he fornicates.' Sometimes some of these *hadiths* have an eschatological dimension, as for instance when Muhammad is quoted as having predicted that the Ka'ba would one day be destroyed by 'Black-skinned, short-shanked men', who will tear it apart and begin the destruction of the world.[73] Referring to this *hadith*, the head of the Ahmadiyya Muslim Mission in Ghana, Maulvi Wahab Adam, identifies the 'Black-skinned, short-shanked men' as Africans of Abyssinian origin and writes:

70. Sura 3: 102.
71. Lewis, 'The African Diaspora', p. 41.
72. Ibid., p. 47.
73. Cited in Lewis, *Race and Slavery*, p. 34.

132 The Legacy of Arab-Islam in Africa

The Ka'abah symbolises the unity of Allah. It is the symbol of Islam. It stands for Muslim solidarity. It represents all that is dear to all true Muslims. Attempting to destroy the Ka'abah would, therefore, mean attempting to destroy the very basis of Islam! It is only *an enemy of Islam* who would attempt to perpetrate such an ungodly act. (my emphasis)[74]

There is a possible historical antecedent for the above tradition. The Abyssinians were known, and indeed dreaded, as allies of the powerful Byzantine empire in its struggle with Persia for influence in the Arabian Peninsula. Abyssinia is known to have conquered Yemen and South Arabia in 525 CE and, in about 570 CE, an Abyssinian viceroy, Abrahah, led an expedition against Mecca to capture the city and destroy the Ka'ba, ostensibly because of its commercial importance.[75]

Even though the expedition was unsuccessful and Abrahah's army was destroyed, apparently by plague, the impact of the attempted destruction of the Ka'ba on the Meccan psyche must have been profound, to the extent that the incident is linked in traditional Muslim sources with Muhammad's birth. It is against this background that the depiction of blacks as 'enemies of Islam' in the above tradition is, perhaps, best understood.

Some other accepted *hadith*, in their very insistence on the equality between whites and blacks depict the two as occupying the extreme ends of the Best and Worst continuum respectively. One such *sahih hadith* attributed to the Prophet of Islam states: 'Obey whoever is put in authority over you, even if he be a crop-nosed Ethiopian slave.' Even though this is meant as proof of the egalitarian spirit of Islam, the 'even if' and the combination of qualities are a clear indication of ultimate improbability in physical, social and racial terms.

There are other *hadith* aimed at counteracting those that sought to foster Arab and white supremacy by insisting that true merit is found in piety and good deeds, which takes precedence over genealogy and colour. But as rightly pointed out by Bernard Lewis, these *hadith*, manufactured like those they opposed, 'clearly reflect the great struggles in the early Islamic Empire between the pure Arab conquistador aristocracy, claiming both ethnic and social superiority, and the converts among the conquered, who could claim neither ethnic nor family advantage'.[76]

In what is apparently an authentic *hadith*, cited by Fadel Abdallah in support of the interracial utopia of Islam, an Ethiopian woman is said to have come to

---

74. A. Wahab Adam, 'New Openings of Preaching in Ghana', *The Review of Religions*, vol. 81, no. 8 (August 1986), p. 6. Adam went on to outline the Ahmadiyya solution to this predicted menace of the black race to Islam in the following words: "To Hazrat Musleh Mauood, [second successor, and son of Ghulam Ahmad, founder of Ahmadiyya Movement] therefore, the answer was simple. Preaching Islam to Africans! ... Through this way they would not even think of destroying the Ka'abah. They would rather sacrifice their all, including their lives, in defence of the Ka'abah'. Ibid pp. 6–7.
75. M. Watt, *Muhammad at Mecca* (Oxford: Oxford University, 1953), pp. 11–14.
76. Lewis, *Race and Slavery*, p. 34.

Muhammad and said, 'You Arabs, excel us [Blacks] in all, in build, colour, and in the possession of the Prophet. If I believe, will I be with you in Paradise?' Muhammad replied, 'Yes, and in Paradise the whiteness of the Ethiopian will be seen over a stretch of a thousand years.' Abdallah then goes on to pose a rhetorical question: 'Does not this suggest that the issue of colour is a question that is relative to our life in this world and that it is not going to exist in the Hereafter?'[77] The answer to Abdallah's question, is, of course, No!

First of all, the very fact that the woman raised the issue of colour in her question to Muhammad is proof that colour was an issue, indeed an important issue at that time. Second, the fact that Muhammad, in his alleged attempt to console the disillusioned woman, talks about 'the whiteness of the Ethiopian' (whether taken metaphorically or literally) in paradise apparently as a 'reward' for deserving blacks, can be seen as not only implicitly confirming the superiority of white over black but as giving the issue an eschatological dimension. If anything at all, the alleged consolation implies that the colour black would not be entertained in Paradise (because it is abhorrent) and so would have to be replaced, albeit as a 'reward', with the colour white.

Blacks and people of black ancestry began to suffer various disabilities on account of the colour of their skin and racial origin in early Muslim-Arab society. Black Muslims who managed to escape the condition of servility through manumission still had a much bigger hurdle to clear in the form of persistent racial prejudice from the wider society. Celebrated black or partly black Muslim poets of early Islamic times such as 'Antara, the son of an Arab father and an Abyssinian concubine, Suhaym or 'little blackie' (d. 660), Nusayb (d. between 726 and 731), Abu Dulāma or 'father of blackness' (d. 776), Sa'id ibn Misjah (d. between 705 and 715), etc., both in their nicknames and works indicate that African blood and dark skin were marks of social inferiority and cause for insults, abuse and discrimination.

A verse attributed to 'Antara runs: 'I am a man, of whom one half ranks with the best of 'Abs. The other half I defend with my sword.' In another verse he is even more blunt: 'Enemies revile me for the blackness of my skin but the whiteness of my character effaces the blackness.'[78] As early as 671 CE, 'Ubaydallah, the son of Abu Bakra, a freed Abyssinian slave of the Prophet, was appointed governor of Sistan. But already blackness had become a reproach, and a satire against him reads as follows: 'The blacks do not earn their pay by good deeds, and are not of good repute. The children of a stinking Nubian black – God put no light in their complexions.'[79]

---

77. Abdallah, 'Islam, Slavery, and Racism', p. 42.
78. Lewis, 'The African Diaspora', pp. 39–40.
79. Cited in Ibid., p. 44.

134 The Legacy of Arab-Islam in Africa

An anecdote relating to the black poet Da'ud ibn Salm (d. 750) says that he was arrested along with an Arab called Zayd ibn Ja'far for flaunting the use of luxurious clothes. The chronicler notes that the Arab was released while Da'ud was flogged. The judge is reported to have said: 'I can stand this from Ibn Ja'far, but why should I stand it from you? Because of your base origin, or your ugly face? Flog him, boy!'

A similar anecdote preserved by early chroniclers relates to the black musician Sa'id ibn Misjah. It is reported that ibn Misjah found himself in the company of young men in Damascus, some of who accepted him while others were reluctant to be in his company. The party was served with food and ibn Misjah withdrew, saying, 'I am a black man. Some of you may find me offensive. I shall therefore sit and eat apart.' The party, relates the chronicler, were embarrassed but nevertheless arranged for ibn Misjah to dine separately.[80]

There are other anecdotes that speak of good and pious deeds by blacks, albeit in the usual fashion that simple piety is better than sophisticated wickedness, with the black used as an example of simplicity and piety. Blacks, generally, are unfavourably depicted in medieval Islamic literature and arts as savages in adventure literature, demonized in fairy tales, or commonly referred to as lazy, stupid, evil-smelling and lecherous slaves. Writing on the image of blacks in Turkish folklore, P.N. Boratav points out that 'the Negro is nothing more or less than the symbol of wickedness and barbarism'.[81]

Similarly, studies on the image of blacks in medieval Iranian writings reveal that in both Arab and Persian Muslim writings, blacks are depicted as stupid, untruthful, vicious, sexually unbridled, ugly and distorted, excessively merry, and easily affected by music and drink. Some Persian romances add to these stereotypes the image of blacks as cannibals, infidels, enemies of God and Islam, who attack and attempt to occupy Muslim lands. Jihad is portrayed as the only response to the infidel Zanj (the Persian equivalent of Negro), whom God Himself wants destroyed. The killing of a single black is penance for a lifetime of sin.[82]

Great Arab-Muslim geographers such as Ibn Hawqal of the tenth century simply did not see the need to waste ink and paper recording anything about blacks. He wrote:

I have not described the country of the African blacks and the other peoples of the torrid zone; because naturally loving wisdom, ingenuity, religion, justice and regular government, how could I notice such people as these, or magnify them by inserting an account of their countries?[83]

---

80. Cited in B. Lewis, *Race and Color in Islam* (New York: Harper & Row, 1970), p. 14.
81. P.N. Boratav, 'The Negro in Turkish Folklore', *Journal of American Folklore*, vol. 64 (1951), p. 85.
82. M. Southgate, 'The Negative Images of Blacks in Some Medieval Iranian Writings', *Iranian Studies*, vol. 17, no. 1 (1984), pp. 3–36.
83. Bovill, *The Golden Trade*, pp. 60–1.

Muslim Slavery and Black Africa 135

Other renowned medieval Muslim thinkers, such as the Spanish Sa'id al-Andalusi (1029–70), wrote that blacks 'are more like animals than men' and that 'the rule of virtue and stability of judgement' is lacking among them, with 'foolishness and ignorance general among them'. Blacks, according to al-Andalusi, 'have never made use of their minds in seeking after wisdom (*hikmah*) nor exercised themselves in the study of philosophy (*falsafa*)'.[84] Others, such as Ibn Sina (980–1037), similarly depict blacks as inherently inferior and destined to be enslaved by the rest of mankind. To Ibn Sina blacks are 'people who are by their very nature slaves'.[85]

As far as Nasir al-Din Tusi (1201–74), a famous Iranian philosopher, was concerned,

> If (various kinds of men) are taken ... and one placed after another, like the Negro from Zanzibar, in the South-most countries, the Negro does not differ from an animal in anything except the fact that his hands have been lifted from the earth, – except for what God wishes. Many have seen that the ape is more capable of being trained than the Negro, and more intelligent.[86]

Ibn Khaldun (1332–1406) on his part wrote that blacks are 'only humans who are closer to dumb animals than to rational beings'. The reason for their characteristic 'levity, excitability, and great emotionalism', according to Ibn Khaldun, is 'due to the expansion and diffusion of the animal spirit' in them. They are therefore 'remote from those of human beings and close to those of wild animals'. Blacks are 'ignorant of all religion' and 'cannot be considered human beings'. 'Therefore, the Negro nations are, as a rule, submissive to slavery because [Negroes] have little [that is essentially] human.' Ibn Khaldun disagrees with the mythological curse of Ham and its related effect on blacks and accepts another contemporary notion that the hot climatic conditions of tropical Africa are what accounts for the colour and debased characteristics of black people.[87]

Ibn Battutah (d. 1368–69), the great Arab traveller and contemporary of Ibn Khaldun, visited sub-Saharan Africa (ancient Mali) and was astonished to find that blacks, whom he had known only as slaves, were masters and rulers in their own country. Throughout his accounts, the traditional prejudices about blacks are evident. His first impression in meeting the sultan who, according to local custom, spoke to him through an interpreter, made Ibn Battutah, who was

84. Irwin, *Africans Abroad*, p. 109.
85. Lewis, *Race and Color*, p. 29. For more on Ibn Sina's comments on blacks, see E.I.J. Rosenthal, *Political Thought in Medieval Islam* (Cambridge: Cambridge University, 1958), pp. 154–5.
86. Southgate, 'The Negative Images of Blacks', p. 16.
87. Ibn Khaldun, *Muqaddimah*, pp. 119, 168–9, 174–6 and 301. Ibn Khaldun's rejection of the myth of the curse neither changed his attitude nor was it ever meant to change the attitude of his contemporaries and enhance the image of blacks. The myth was apparently too popular to be done away with by the stroke of a pen, not even the pen of Ibn Khaldun.

136 The Legacy of Arab-Islam in Africa

apparently expecting special treatment as a 'white guest', regret 'of having come to their country, because of their lack of manners'. The food that was served 'convinced' Ibn Battutah 'that there was no good to be hoped from these people'.[88] The traditional welcome meal sent to Ibn Battutah by the sultan evoked the following comment from the Arab traveller:

> I got up, thinking that it would be robes of honor and money, but behold! It was three loaves of bread and a piece of beef fried in gharty [shea butter] and a gourd containing yoghurt. When I saw it I laughed, and was long astonished at their feeble intellect and their respect for mean things.[89]

In the light of all this, it is clear that E.W. Blyden was again ill informed, to say the least, when he asserted:

> It must be evident that Negroes trained under the influence of [a Muslim] social and literary atmosphere must have a deeper self-respect and higher views of the dignity of human nature than those trained under the blighting influence of caste, and under the guidance of a [Western-Christian] literature in which it has been the fashion for more than two hundred years to caricature the African, to ridicule his personal peculiarities, and to impress him with a sense of perpetual and hopeless inferiority.[90]

An eighteenth-century African-Muslim scholar visiting Mecca, apparently on *hājj*, had this complaint about Meccan attitudes: 'In general the people of this land love no one – least of all those of our Sudanic race – unless it be for the satisfaction of some need of theirs, without any true affection or friendship.'[91] Twentieth-century Asian immigrants in East Africa (who are largely Muslim) are said to have had 'an immutable belief in their supremacy over the African', whom they exploited mainly as domestic servants.[92]

Light-skinned Muslim prejudices against blacks are reflected most in the institution of marriage. The classical Muslim teaching on marriage is that a Muslim male is allowed to marry a non-Muslim female of whatever religion. However, a non-Muslim male is not allowed under any circumstances to marry a Muslim female. Light-skinned Muslim males are permitted to have black females

---

88. Ibn Battutah, *Travels in Asia and Africa: 1325–1354*, ed. and trans. H.A.R. Gibb (London: Routledge & Kegan Paul, 1929), p. 320.

89. Rose E. Dunn, *The Adventures of Ibn Battuta: A Muslim Traveller of the 14th Century* (Berkeley: University of California, 1986), pp. 302–3. Ibn Battutah admired the just and stable government of Mali and the devotion of the local Muslims in observing their prayers and Qur'anic studies, but the above quotes nevertheless reflect the deep-seated traditional prejudice against blacks. On his departure from Mali he helped himself to a caravan of 600 female slaves.

90. Blyden, *Christianity, Islam and the Negro Race*, p. 17.

91. Cited in J.O. Hunwick, 'Black-Slaves in the Mediterranean World: Introduction to a Neglected Aspect of the African Diaspora', in Savage (ed.), *The Human Commodity*, p. 37, n. 100.

92. Yasmin Alibhai-Brown, *No Place Like Home* (London: Virago, 1995), p. 9.

Muslim Slavery and Black Africa 137

mainly as concubines and also as wives, but no black male is allowed to have any relations with light-skinned Muslim females. According to a tradition, Muhammad is alleged to have said, 'Be careful in choosing mates for your offspring, and beware of marrying the zanji, for he is a distorted creature.' Another quotes him as having said, 'Do not bring black into your pedigree.'[93]

Muslim jurists, under the legal doctrine of *kafā'ah* (loosely translated as equality of birth and social status in marriage), considered marriage between black males and Arab females a misalliance, which some jurists saw as grounds for divorce. Suhaym, a black poet of early Islamic times, in one poem laments thus: 'If my colour were pink women would love me but the Lord has marred me with blackness.'[94] In this regard, J.O. Hunwick, writing on the black diaspora in the Islamic world, notes:

> In one thing above all others the stigma of racial origin was apparent – marriage. Whereas for example, the Qaramanli sultans of Tripoli married off their daughters to European slaves to avoid dynastic rivalries, it would have been unthinkable for an Arab, or a Berber, a Turk or a Persian, [and one would add, Asian] to consent to his daughter marrying a black African, slave or freed. Marriages the other way round, between a Black girl and an Arab man, could and did take place, though due to the social obligation of at least offering marriage to a paternal cousin, few Black girls can have been the first or sole wife'.[95]

Medieval Persian collections of tales and fancy stories speak of white females being defiled and contaminated by the touch of black males with some intimating that 'only a whore prefers blacks; the good woman will welcome death rather than be touched by a black man'.[96] A medieval Muslim thinker, al-Jahiz (d. 869), said to be of partly African descent, decrying this particular attitude, reports a black man castigating Arab Muslims thus:

> It is an indication of your ignorance that you thought us fit to marry your women in the days of the jahiliyya, but when the justice of the (egalitarian) system of Islam was established you thought this reprehensible, even though we did not avoid you. The desert, on the other hand, is full of our brethren who intermarried with you, became your chiefs and lords, protected your honour and sheltered you from your enemy. You made proverbs about us and magnified our kings, in many instances preferring them to your own. This you would not have done if you had not thought us superior to you in this respect.[97]

93. See Lewis, *Race and Color*, pp. 91–2.
94. Ibid., p. 11.
95. J.O. Hunwick, 'Black Africans in the Islamic World: An Understudied Dimension of the Black Diaspora', *Tarikh*, vol. 5, no. 4 (1978), p. 35.
96. Southgate, 'The Negative Images of Blacks', pp. 24–5.
97. Al-Jahiz, 'The Boasts of the Blacks over the Whites', trans. T. Khalidi, *The Islamic Quarterly*, vol. 25, nos. 1 and 2 (1981), p. 13.

138 *The Legacy of Arab-Islam in Africa*

Two important points stand out in the above passage. First of all, it confirms the fact that in pre-Islamic Arabia blacks were held in high esteem and did marry Arab women and that the discrimination against the former on account of the colour of their skin is a development within the Islamic period. Second, it is one of the earliest confirmations that black (Muslim) men were debarred from marrying light-skinned (especially Arab) Muslim women. This situation remains largely unchanged in contemporary Middle Eastern countries, where small black communities live in ghettos and continue to marry among themselves.[98]

In our own times while examples of black men married to white blonde Europeans and Americans are a common phenomenon (with its own controversies and ramifications), such examples remain rare, if any, with Arab, Turkish, Iranian or Asian women. East African Asians, for instance, came to view the practice of their male folk taking African concubines as a social and religious anathema. Offspring from such alliances are disparagingly referred to as *chotara*.[99]

Hence J.T. Arnold's claim that 'the Arabs and all other white Muslims, whether brunettes or blondes, have always been free from colour-prejudice vis-à-vis the non-white races ... under this searching test, the white Muslims have demonstrated their freedom from race-feeling by the most convincing of all proofs: they have given their daughters to Black Muslims in marriage', and which Fadel Abdallah cites enthusiastically as proof of the egalitarian spirit of Islam is preposterous both in theory and in practice.[100]

As alluded to above, a number of notable Muslim poets and writers, mainly of black ancestry, tried in their own ways to counteract Arab Muslim chauvinism in particular and light-skinned Muslim racial prejudice in general towards blacks. One such early poet is Suhaym, who defended the colour of his skin as follows: 'My blackness does not harm my habit, for I am like musk; whoever tastes it does not forget. I am covered with a black garment, but under it there is a lustrous garment with white tails.' Nearly a century later another black poet Nusayb (d. 726), wrote:

> Blackness does not diminish me, as long as I have this tongue and this stout heart. Some are raised up by means of their lineage; the verses of my poems are my lineage! How much better a keen-minded, clear-spoken black than a mute white![101]

---

98. Lewis, *Race and Slavery*, p. 84. The situation cannot even be any different from other Muslim countries like Turkey and Pakistan. In a recent random survey on non-black attitudes towards mixed marriages with blacks in Britain televised on BBC television on 6 February 1997, Asians, mainly Pakistanis, were those who most resented it. The survey conducted by an Asian, Yasmin A. Brown, noted 'religious reasons for the resentment'.
99. Alibhai-Brown, *No Place Like Home*, p. 4.
100. J.T. Arnold, *A Study of History*, vol. 1 (London: Oxford University, 1934), p. 226. See also Abdallah, 'Islam, Slavery and Racism', p. 43.
101. Lewis, *Race and Color*, p. 12. E.W. Blyden cites some of these rebuttals as evidence of a Muslim social and literary culture free of racial prejudice against blacks. See *Christianity, Islam and the Negro Race*, pp. 16–17.

Muslim Slavery and Black Africa 139

Also al-Jahiz, mentioned above, wrote 'The Boasts of the Blacks over the Whites', citing a poem purportedly composed by a black in response to light-skinned Muslim racism in the following words: 'Although my hair is curly and my skin black as coal, I am open-handed and my honour is untarnished. My black colour is surely no cause for shame, for on the day of fearful battle I haughtily brandish my sword.'[102] Al-Jahiz went on to outline some of the virtues of blacks such as their honesty, valour, generosity, piety, oratory, etc., and the fact (or rather myth) that it was a black monarch, the Negus of Abyssinia, who was the first ruler to convert to Islam.[103]

Meanwhile, elsewhere in his writings, al-Jahiz described the Zanj as 'the least intelligent and the least discerning of mankind' and said that the Zanj 'are the worst of men and most vicious of creatures in character and temperament'.[104] Al-Jahiz no doubt admired Arab-Muslim culture and sought to identify himself with it. There is also no doubt that al-Jahiz's defence of blacks against racial prejudice was in some definite ways satirical and therefore has to be treated with caution.

Nevertheless, al-Jahiz, on the whole, was serious in his defence of blacks in the above-mentioned work. His ambivalence, though, is an indication of a man faced with a serious identity crisis. It is a wry commentary on what it was like to be educated and famous – and yet part African – in the medieval Muslim world. It has been observed in this connection that al-Jahiz 'was a ninth-century equivalent of those New World Creoles and mulattos [and, one could add, present-day Swahilis of East Africa and other mixed Arab, Moor or Berber/African offspring from North Africa] of a thousand years later who rejected the African part of their heritage in order the more enthusiastically to praise the "Christian" [and "Muslim"] and "civilised" values of those who had enslaved their ancestors' but who were, at the same time, themselves not fully accepted into those cultures.[105]

Because of their low image some blacks sought Arab pedigree to enhance their social standing. It took a ruling of Caliph al-Mahdi (775–85) to abrogate all such 'naturalizations', apparently in a bid to preserve the Arab status quo by ensuring that the colour black did not get into the Arab pedigree. Other later medieval Muslim writers such as Jamāl al-Din Abu al-Farāj ibn al-Jawzī (d. 1208) and the celebrated Egyptian jurist Jalāl al-Din al-Suyūti (d. 1505) wrote works mainly in defence of Abyssinians.[106]

---

102. Al-Jahiz, 'The Boasts of the Blacks over the Whites', p. 6.
103. Most Muslim traditions claim that the Ethiopian ruler, who accorded the early persecuted converts to Islam asylum, converted to Islam himself.
104. Lewis, *Race and Color*, p. 17.
105. Irwin, *Africans Abroad*, p. 117.
106. Lewis, 'The African Diaspora', pp. 54–5. Traces of respect and concessions for Abyssinians are not lacking in medieval Muslim writings partly because the first group of Muslim refugees were granted asylum in Abyssinia (see chapter 1 above), and partly because Arab Muslims never succeeded in conquering that part of Africa.

140 *The Legacy of Arab-Islam in Africa*

It should be emphasized, though, that light-skinned Muslim racial prejudice was not necessarily due to their religious, Islamic persuasion. On the contrary, in addition to what we have observed above on the Qur'anic position and that of pre-Islamic and early Islamic periods, the Qur'an speaks of mankind as created from a single source (a single soul and a single parentage) and regards the various differences in language, colour and race as signs of God's wonder and magnificence that has to be celebrated.[107]

Having said that, the above evidence shows that racial prejudice against blacks, pious Muslim teaching notwithstanding, if not a purely Muslim creation, surely owes its earliest and clearest ideological expression to Muslim sources. Akbar Muhammad accepts that there is racial prejudice in Muslim societies against blacks but suggests that Muslims 'echoed the external traditions of the Jews, Greeks and perhaps others'.[108] Of course to rule out completely possible influences and cultural exchanges at that or any other time in human encounter simply smacks of infantile naivety. And in this regard, it would be interesting to investigate the extent to which racial prejudice in Western Europe against blacks could have Muslim influences since the former owes much of its medieval literary and philosophical traditions to the latter.

Having said that, there is hardly any evidence to support possible Jewish and Greek influences on Muslim attitudes towards blacks. Indeed, studies on ancient Greek, Roman and rabbinical Jewish views on slavery and race contain almost no suggestion of the equation of colour to servitude or anti-black consciousness.[109] Be that as it may, that these attitudes are widely reflected in the writing of eminent and pious Muslim thinkers down the ages shows how serious the gap between teaching and practice has been in the so-called great and 'revealed' religions of the world.

The underlying reasons for the light-skin Muslim attitude towards blacks could be historical, such as the menace of Abyssinia to Arabia; the fact that Muslims down the ages encountered Africans mainly as slaves; or sociological factors as in the case of Asian attitudes towards Africans in East and Southern Africa. Whatever the case may be, it seems that by placing blacks under a mythological curse, stereotyping and stigmatizing them on account of the content of their belief and colour of their skin, Muslims of all races waged war against and raided Africans, killing millions and reducing millions of others to slavery over the last fourteen centuries. This we shall now proceed to examine.

---

107. Sura 4: 1; 30: 22.
108. Muhammad, 'The Image of Africans in Arabic Literature', pp. 69–70.
109. Irwin, *Africans Abroad*, pp. 26–31; Ephraim Isaac, 'Genesis, Judaism, and the Sons of Ham', in Willis (ed.), *Slaves and Slavery*, vol. 1, p. 77 ff; and Lewis, *Race and Slavery*, pp. 123–5.

MUSLIM SLAVERY AND THE SLAVE TRADE: THE ARAB-ORIENTAL DIMENSION

As mentioned above, hard evidence for black slaves outside tropical Africa dates back to about 200 BCE in North Africa, and especially Egypt. Similarly, the earliest documentary information about Arab traffic in black slaves from East Africa, as pointed out in the first part of this chapter, dates back to around the early second century CE. The mode of acquisition was most probably through Arab pirating, even though one cannot for certain completely rule out purchase from local agents.[110]

It is also well attested that slavery existed in pre-Islamic Arabia and, indeed, in the Mediterranean region. In these areas too there is evidence of black slaves, along with slaves from other races, who were mainly war captives. Notwithstanding the various possible meanings of the term Habash, a generally accepted term for Abyssinians in particular and blacks in general at the time, there is no disagreement over the presence of numerous black slaves in pre- and early Islamic Arabia. In fact, some scholars have argued that the power of Mecca at the time was founded on an army of black slaves.[111]

The Prophet of Islam and his Companions are known to have owned slaves through capture in war and purchase and also to have set large numbers of them free. 'Abd al-Rahmān ibn 'Awf, one of the ten closest Companions of the Prophet of Islam, is said to have freed, on his death in 652, no less than thirty thousand slaves.[112] Many of the Companions themselves are known to have had slave origins. The most well known of these was, of course, Bilal ibn Rabah, an Abyssinian slave who converted to Islam, was purchased and freed by Muhammad and became his personal attendant and the first *mu'adhdhin* (one who recites the Muslim call to prayer) in Islam.

Slavery in general and black enslavement in particular thus developed into a deeply entrenched institution, accepted in the mainline Muslim heritage by learned Muslim lawyers and pious believers as a matter of course. Right from the conquest of Egypt by Arab armies between 639 and 642 CE, the 'land of the Blacks', *bilād al-Sūdān*, became a reservoir of slaves for the Muslim world. The main sources of slaves were war (jihad), raid, tribute, purchase and kidnapping. As part of the *baqt* signed between Nubia and Muslim rulers of Egypt in the seventh century, 360 slaves were sent annually as tribute to the *emir* in Egypt and this remained in force for over seven centuries.[113]

Muslim Arabs were the chief agents of the traffic of black Africans as slaves from East and Central Africa into the Islamic heartlands virtually right from the

---

110. Beachey, *A Collection of Documents*, p. 1.
111. Watt, *Muhammad at Mecca*, pp. 154–7.
112. Petrushevsky, *Islam in Iran*, p. 158. Even though the figure may be an exaggeration, one wonders how many slaves he might have owned.
113. Y.F. Hasan, *The Arabs and the Sudan: From the Seventh to the Early Sixteenth Century* (Edinburgh: Edinburgh University, 1967), p. 134.

142 The Legacy of Arab-Islam in Africa

seventh century. The Coast of the Zanj, i.e. the coastlands of modern Kenya and Tanzania, was opened by Arabs from the Persian Gulf area from where slaves were exported to Basra and thence to Baghdad and other centres of Iraq, the sugar plantations of Khuzistan, to Bandar Abbas in southern Persia and to Al-Ahsa (Arabian Peninsula). Somalis prior to their Islamization, and later interior peoples such as the Galla, were exported as slaves from the Somali coast across into the Yemen and from there, via Mecca, to Damascus and Baghdad. From Abyssinia, Galla, Gurage, Hararis and other tribes were exported to Arabia and up the Red Sea to Egypt.[114]

In Iraq a large number of East African slaves, the Zanj, were employed in their thousands on the sugar plantations of Khuzistan and saltpetre mines of the Abbasid caliphate located on the Euphrates as early as the eighth century. Apparently due to the harsh conditions to which they were subjected, they rose in numerous revolts, and between 868 and 883 their rebellion became a real threat to the Abbasid caliphate.[115] The hunting, kidnapping, purchase and traffic of Africans into servitude went on throughout the centuries but increased greatly in the nineteenth century after Sa'īd ibn Sultan, ruler of Muscat, in 1832 moved to Zanzibar and established plantation farming.[116] Here Arab and Swahili Muslim slave traders took advantage of prevailing internecine conflicts and cashed in on the captives of war with stronger African tribes such as the Yao, Nyamwezi and Ganda acting as crucial intermediaries and accomplices.

Men like Tippu-Tib and Rumaliza organized well-armed gangs of slave raiders in the interior with the sole aim of raiding smaller indigenous communities whom they would then march, both as commodities themselves and as porters of ivory, to the coast for sale. A.J. Swann describes one of Tippu-Tib's slave caravans that he encountered during the last quarter of the nineteenth century:

> As they filed past we noticed many chained together by the neck ... The women, who were as numerous as the men, carried babies on their backs in addition to a tusk of ivory or other burden on their heads ... It is difficult to adequately describe the filthy state of their bodies; in many instances, not only scarred by the cut of a 'chikote' (a piece of hide used to enforce obedience), but feet and shoulders were a mass of open sores ... half-starved, ill-treated creatures who, weary and friendless, must have longed for death.[117]

In conversation, one of the headmen admitted that most of the slaves died during the journey of hunger and exhaustion; when asked what happens if any of the slaves became too ill or weak to continue the journey, the headman replied:

114. Hunwick, 'Black Africans in the Islamic World', p. 25.
115. Irwin, *Africans Abroad*, pp. 73 ff.
116. Beachey, *A Collection of Documents*, pp. 38–66.
117. A.J. Swann, *Fighting the Slave-hunters in Central Africa: A Record of Twenty-six Years of Travel and Adventure Round the Great Lakes and of the Overthrow of Tip-pu-Tib, Rumaliza and Other Great Slave-traders* (London: Seeley, 1910), pp. 48–9.

Muslim Slavery and Black Africa 143

'Spear them at once! For, if we did not, others would pretend they are ill in order to avoid carrying their loads. No! we never leave them alive on the road; they all know this custom.' In response to another question as to who carries the ivory when a mother carrying a baby and ivory gets too tired to carry both, the headman replied; 'She does! We cannot leave valuable ivory on the road. We spear the child and make her burden lighter. Ivory first, child afterwards'.[118]

The route from the interior of Africa through Lake Tanganyika to the coast was littered with skeletons as a result of slaves dying from exhaustion, hunger or the brutality of their couriers, sometimes still yoked together. Deaths during the journeys were so numerous that it has been estimated that for every slave who reached the coast in Zanzibar four or five lives were lost in transit. An Arab slave dealer, by name Syeb-bin-Habib, is reported in 1882 to have admitted that out of 300 slaves he acquired from the interior, only 50 reached the coast alive.[119] David Livingstone observed that if the slaughter committed during the raids is taken into account in addition to the deaths along the routes, then the price of every single slave who arrived at Zanzibar would be about ten lives.[120]

Bustling slave markets emerged in Zanzibar and along the East African coast, with eyewitness reports of young men, women and children being arrayed, inspected and sold like animals until the intervention of European colonial anti-slavery policies. Bogamogo in present day Tanzania was one such slave market. The name of the town, which means 'vomit out your heart', tells the horrors of the East African slave trade. So chilling was the experience that European eyewitnesses doubted if their sceptical countrypeople back home would ever believe their accounts. In this regard, David Livingstone deemed it extremely necessary, in his description of the horrors of the slave trade in East Africa, 'to keep far within the truth in order not to be thought guilty of exaggeration'. 'But', he added, 'in sober seriousness the subject does not admit of exaggeration. To overdraw its evils is simple impossibility'.[121]

The main areas from which slaves were drawn and exported to Egypt and other North African Muslim locations and then to the wider Islamic world were the central and western Sudan. The traffic started mainly from Nubia, from where people living to the south and east of Dongola, such as the Beja, and then tribes of the Nuba mountains much later around the fourteenth century were taken to Egypt. Slaves were exported also from Kanem-Borno via Fezzan to Cairo, Tripoli and Qayrawan. People groups living around the Lake Chad area were later exported along this route while in the eighteenth and nineteenth centuries Bagirmi slaves (especially eunuchs) formed an important part of the

118. Ibid., pp. 49 and 76.
119. Beachey, A Collection of Documents, p. 29.
120. See R. Coupland, The Exploitation of East Africa, 1856–1890: The Slave Trade and the Scramble (London: Faber & Faber, 1939), p. 140.
121. Ibid., pp. 139–40.

144 The Legacy of Arab-Islam in Africa

slave traffic along this route. Some were sent later from Tripoli to ports in modern Turkey, Greece, Albania and southern Yugoslavia which were all at the time under the Ottoman empire.[122]

Slaves from the Middle Niger and the Atlantic coast were also drawn from Gao via Warghla to Tahert (in modern Algeria) and Qayrawan and later from Timbuktu through Tuwāt to Tlemcen, Sijilmasa, Fez and other centres of the western Maghrib from where some passed into Muslim Spain and Sicily when it was under Muslim domination between the ninth and eleventh centuries. Ibn Khaldun testifies to the presence of a large black slave population in fourteenth-century North Africa when he wrote that blacks constituted 'the ordinary mass of slaves'.[123] Muslim Berber groups of North Africa like the Tuareg and Moors became the chief agents in the raiding, and in the traffic of black slaves to North Africa, Spain, Turkey and the Mediterranean world, some of whom were taken as far as India. As early as the eighth century, the Berber Ibadi community of North Africa virtually controlled the trade routes, and thus the traffic in black slaves.[124]

Indiscriminate Arab-Muslim slave raiding in the *bilād al-Sūdān* reached alarming proportions in the fourteenth century, resulting in a letter from the ruler of Bornu to the sultan of Egypt complaining about the slave-raiding attitude of some Muslim-Arabs. In the words of the ruler:

> These Arabs have devastated all our country, the whole of al-Barnu, up to this day. They have seized our free men and our relatives, who are Muslims, and sold them to the slave dealers (*jullāb*) of Egypt and Syria and others; some they have kept for their own service ... restrain the Arabs from their debauchery.[125]

The Sudan remained the main reservoir of slaves for Egypt well into the later part of the nineteenth and early part of the twentieth centuries. By the nineteenth century the slave trade had become 'a well regulated government activity' in Egypt and under the command of one Ali Khurshid Agha and one Zubair, many Sudanese tribes were raided and ravaged. Muhammad Ali spurred his troops on in this regard in a special despatch in 1823: 'You are aware that the end of all our effort and this expense is to procure negroes. Please show zeal in carrying out our wishes in this capital matter.'[126] Between 1892 and 1900 one Rabih ibn Abdallah, a ruthless slave raider, operated in the Chad region from Manifa, and later from Dikwa. He literally devastated indigenous African

---

122. Hunwick, 'Black Africans in the Islamic World', p. 25.
123. Ibn Khaldun, *Muqaddimah*, p. 118.
124. E. Savage, 'Berbers and Blacks: Ibadi Slave Traffic in the Eighth-century North Africa', *Journal of African History*, vol. 33 (1992), pp. 351–68.
125. N. Levtzion and J.F.P. Hopkins, *Corpus of Early Arabic Sources for West Africa* (Cambridge: Cambridge University, 1981), pp. 347–8.
126. Muhammad Ali to the commander-in-chief of the Sudan and Kordofan, 23 September 1823; cited in R. Hill, *Egypt in the Sudan, 1820–1883* (Oxford: Oxford University, 1959), p. 13.

Muslim Slavery and Black Africa 145

communities in the region until he was killed in battle with the French in 1900 around the area west of Lake Chad.[127]

The trans-Saharan slave trade, like its East African counterpart, increased in volume during the eighteenth and nineteenth centuries. The Ottoman rulers entered into a trading pact with Muslim Bornu, and large numbers of Bagirmi slaves were transported across the Sahara to the slave markets of Tripoli. From Kano, in modern northern Nigeria, slaves captured from non-Muslim tribes living to the south of the Hausa towns such as the Gwari and Katab and from other parts of northern Nigeria were acquired, most probably from around the sixteenth century, and taken along the 'forty-day route' to Dongola and Egypt and also via Borku and Tibesti through Kufra to Cyrenaica.[128] The jihad movements of the eighteenth and nineteenth centuries in the western Sudan degenerated into well-organized Muslim raids on 'pagan' communities for slaves meant for local use and also to supply the trans-Saharan trade route.

Many eyewitness accounts talk in very sobering terms of the loss of life along the route. One such account given by an eyewitness in 1822 talks about a well near Bir Mushuru where 'the ground around is strewed with human skeletons, the slaves who have arrived exhausted with thirst and fatigue'. At one spot there were 'more than one hundred skeletons'.[129] Gustav Nachtigal talked about littered skeletons and 'half-buried in the sand the mummified corpses of some children, still covered with the blue cotton rags' at the same well.[130] At other wells referred to as 'the wells of El Hammar', the skeletons were countless. The route itself was equally littered with skeletons accumulated at the rate of eighty and ninety a day. According to one Major Denham, 'The Arabs laughed heartily at my expression of horror, and said they are only blacks, *nam boo* (damn their fathers!), and began knocking their limbs about with the butt end of their firelocks, saying: 'This was a woman! This was a youngster!''[131] The methods of killing exhausted or sick slaves and those who attempted to escape in East Africa were also used on the trans-Saharan route. Nachtigal accompanied a caravan of hundreds of slaves from Bagirmi to the slave markets of Kuka and witnessed exhausted and sick slaves being slaughtered and their arteries cut open. After such horrid experiences, Nachtigal pointed out that 'in estimating the weight of the burden placed by the slave trade on its Pagan victims, it had to be borne in mind that for every one who arrived at Kuka there were probably three to four who died or disappeared on the way'.[132]

127. Zoghby, 'Blacks and Arabs: Past and Present', pp. 10 and 12.
128. Hunwick, 'Black Africans in the Islamic World', p. 26.
129. Major Denham, in E.W. Bovill (ed.), *Missions to the Niger*, vol. 2, part 1 (Nendeln; Kraus, 1975), pp. 200–2.
130. Nachtigal, *Sahara and Sudan*, vol. 1, p. 216.
131. Major Denham, in Bovill (ed.), *Missions to the Niger*, p. 202. See also Mahadi, 'The Aftermath of the Jihad', p. 125.
132. Nachtigal, *Sahara and Sudan*, vol. 3, p. 430.

146 *The Legacy of Arab-Islam in Africa*

A French observer estimated that the price for one slave sold in the slave markets of North Africa might represent the loss of ten others who were killed in the raids or died in transit.[133] Apart from this significantly high loss of life during the raids and the journey into servitude, conservative estimates suggest that between eleven and fourteen million Africans were transported into Muslim lands outside tropical Africa over the past fourteen centuries.[134] A highly reputable nineteenth-century Moroccan historian described the traffic and sale of blacks in North African markets as;

> The heinousness of the affliction which has beset the lands of the Maghreb since ancient times in regard to the indiscriminate enslaving of the people of the Sudan and the importation of droves of them every year to be sold in the market places in town and country where men trade in them as one would trade in beasts – nay worse than that. People have become so inured to that, generation after generation, that many common folk believe that the reason for being enslaved according to the Holy Law is merely that a man should be black in colour and come from those regions.[135]

The holiest city of Islam, Mecca, became 'the centre of the slave-trade in the world' and remained so well into the twentieth century; from there slaves captured and brought from East Africa and the Sudan were distributed to all parts of Arabia and the Muslim world.[136] It became a custom for pilgrims to take slaves for sale in Mecca or buy one or two slaves while on *hājj* as souvenirs to be kept, sold or given as gifts. High-ranking Muslims who performed the pilgrimage are known to have always taken along large contingents of slaves as porters and guards, and to tend to their master's needs. One of these needs was, as one writer puts it, cash: owners often used slaves 'as a kind of traveler's check'.[137] Mansa Mūsā of Mali during pilgrimage in 1324 CE took along a vast number of dignitaries and slaves to serve the same purposes.[138]

Slaves became a permanent feature of pilgrimage arrangements. Many unsuspecting free people were taken on pilgrimage, sold or arrested on trumped-up charges, and ultimately ended up as slaves. European colonial powers such as Holland, France and England, in a bid to protect their subjects who undertook the *hājj*, enacted laws making the head of a family or group of pilgrims accountable for each of its members.[139] The buying and selling of slaves went on in the slave markets of Saudi Arabia, Kuwait and Oman, most especially in

133. Fisher and Fisher, *Slavery and Muslim Society in Africa*, pp. 76–8.
134. M. Gordon, *Slavery in the Arab World* (New York: New Amsterdam, 1989) p. ix; See also Lewis, *Race and Slavery*, p. 135, n. 14.
135. Al-Nasiri, taken from his *Kitab al-Istiqsa*, cited from an Appendix in Hunwick, 'Black Africans in the Islamic World', p. 38.
136. G.E. Dejong, 'Slavery in Arabia', *The Muslim World*, vol. 24 (1934), p. 134.
137. Gordon, *Slavery in the Arab World*, p. 135.
138. Trimingham, *A History of Islam in West Africa*, p. 68.
139. Gordon, *Slavery in the Arab World*, p. 226.

Mecca, well into the twentieth century. As late as 1960 some Tuareg notables were reported to have sold slaves in Arabia to defray part of the expense of their pilgrimage.[140]

MUSLIM SLAVERY AND THE SLAVE TRADE: THE AFRICAN DIMENSION

Black African-Muslim involvement in enslaving traditional African believers is well known within the sub-Saharan African context. Here, the ideological and religious justification of enslavement was primarily *kufr*, non-belief in Islam. The same procedures of jihad, organized annual and sporadic raids, tribute, kidnapping and purchase were followed in acquiring slaves. In most cases these were carried out in the cruellest and most brutal forms possible.

The ruling dynasties of Islamic-inspired kingdoms that arose mainly in the western and central parts of Africa between the thirteenth and sixteenth centuries such as Songhay and Mali raided, enslaved and exported large numbers of members of neighbouring tribes. Reference has already been made to Mansa Mūsā, the most celebrated ruler of Mali, and his ostentatious pilgrimage to Mecca during which he carried along a large contingent of slaves for sale.

The famous Arab geographer, Ibn Battutah, mentioned above, during his visit to Mali in the fourteenth century observed that the inhabitants of Takedda and Walata 'live in luxury and ease, and vie with one another in regard to the number of their slaves and serving-women'.[141] The Moosi became the main target of Songhay slave raids under the Askiyas in the fifteenth century. In 1498, Askiya Muhammad I declared a jihad against the Moosi that resulted in so many slaves that a special quarter had to be built for them.[142] Some of the royals of the Askiya ruling dynasties even boasted of capturing up to ten thousand slaves in one raid. Most of these slaves were meant for local use by the Askiyas themselves, described as 'major "consumers" of slave labour', while some were either sold to the trans-Saharan slave traders or given out as pious gifts to Muslim divines.[143]

The enslavement of traditional Africans became even more intense in the eighteenth- and nineteenth-century jihad periods. While most of the jihad leaders of West Africa condemned the enslavement of fellow Muslims, their activities led to substantial raiding of non-Muslim communities. The jihad initiated by Uthman Dan Fodio in northern Nigeria, for instance, is known to have degenerated into brazen slave-raiding expeditions.

Those communities that suffered most from Fulani/Hausa slave raiding were the tribes in the Middle Belt of modern-day Nigeria and those of Adamawa

140. Ibid., p. 135.
141. Ibn Battutah, *Travels*, pp. 335, 337.
142. J.O. Hunwick, 'Notes on Slavery in the Songhay Empire', in Willis (ed.), *Slaves and Slavery*, vol. 2, p. 18.
143. Ibid., pp. 24–6.

148 The Legacy of Arab-Islam in Africa

region. Early twentieth-century observers were in no doubt that 'the slave raid, as a national habit [of the Sokoto caliphate], is still usually directed against natives of a different religion, [traditional believers] who are assumed to be of a lower order of humanity'.[144] The raids directed against mainly peasant traditional communities were always carefully planned and organized, surrounded in the general atmosphere of piety and prayer seeking the help of Allah for successful raids. The following account of a raid on the Gwari tribe taken from a novel written by a former prime minister of Nigeria, Abubakar Tafawa Balewa, gives interesting insights into the tactics employed by Muslim slave raiders against non-Muslim peasant communities:

> On their arrival in this place, they all dismounted from their horses, and lay down at the foot of some thick shady trees, where no-one could see them. At this season the rains had begun to set in, and all the farmers were about to clear their farms. Now there was no way that these pagans could sow a crop sufficient to feed them for a whole year, so they had to come out of their towns and come down to the low ground to lay out their farms in the plain. Despite this however, they were not able to tend their farms properly, for fear of raiders. When the raiders reached the village, they hid on the edge of the farms. Early in the morning, just before the time of prayer, the pagans began to come out from their villages making for their farms. The raiders crouched silently, watching everything that they were doing. They held back until all the people had come out. Then, after they had settled down to work, thinking that nothing would happen to them, the raiders fell upon them all at once, and seized men and women, and even small children. Before the pagans had realised what was happening, the raiders had already done the damage. At once other pagans began to sally forth, preparing to fight to wrest back their brothers who had been captured. Af! Before they were ready, the raiders were far away. They started to follow them, but they had no chance of catching them.[145]

The account concludes, 'they kept on going until, by God's grace, they reached home safely'. As Hiskett kept emphasizing, this is only a story, but he himself admits that these accounts nevertheless 'reflect true incidents that the author had heard of'.[146] And talking about true incidents, Umaru Nagwamatse (1859–76), emir of Kontagora and grandson of Dan Fodio, is noted as one of the most notorious slave raiders. It is said that he would normally send raiding parties into outlying hamlets, set the crops on fire and have the hamlet 'besieged and systematically starved out' of its inhabitants. According to some observers, Umaru's reign was 'the crudest, cruellest form of imperialism. To satisfy one man's ambition, families were torn asunder and flourishing communities wiped out'.[147]

---

144. Shaw, *Tropical Dependency*, p. 411.
145. Abubakar Tafawa Balewa, cited in Hiskett, 'Slavery in Hausa Islamic Literature', p. 112.
146. Ibid, p. 113.

Muslim Slavery and Black Africa 149

It has been estimated that during some eighty years of the reign of Umaru's family, a population of close to a million was reduced to hardly thirty thousand. One of Umaru's sons, Ibrahim, who ascended to the emirship in 1879, kept up the family tradition of slave raiding and was nicknamed 'the eater up of towns'. Upon hearing that the British were out for him because of his slave-raiding activities, Ibrahim is reported to have retorted, 'Can you stop a cat from mousing? When I die it will be with a slave in my mouth'.[148]

Slave raids were quite extensive in all the emirates of northern Nigeria, and in Adamawa in particular the practice continued until the 1920s. Organized raids sometimes involved the co-ordinated efforts of several political units referred to in some sources as 'polyglot raiding confederacies'. Adult men were usually killed and the women, children and younger ones carried away.[149] The Sokoto caliphate, therefore, became 'the largest slave society in Africa in the nineteenth century and one of the largest slave societies in modern history' with Adamawa as 'the major slave reservoir' of the caliphate.[150]

The situation was not dissimilar in Bornu, the domain of Shaykh Muhammad al-Amin al-Kanimi. Even though al-Kanimi opposed the jihad of the Sokoto caliphate, he shared with them the philosophy that the lot of 'pagans' in Muslim territories was enslavement. To ensure a constant reservoir of slaves to meet the insatiable demand for home and the trans-Saharan market, in Bornu, 'only the great men amongst them must become Muslim by order of the Shaykh, while the poor people are left to do as they please'.[151]

An eyewitness account of Bornu slave raiding is given by Heinrich Barth, who accompanied a slave-raiding gang against traditional believers of Musgu between 1851 and 1852. An army of over twenty thousand marched against this well-organized and industrious agricultural community, murdering, burning, and destroying crops as they went. The inhabitants fled into the forest. Only women and young people were kept. Full-grown men were massacred. Barth talks of one particular instance:

---

147. Hogben and Kirk-Greene, *The Emirates of Northern Nigeria*, p. 502.
148. P. Gervis, *Of Emirs and Pagans: A View of Northern Nigeria* (London: Cassell, 1963), p. 124.
149. A. Meyers, 'Slavery in the Hausa–Fulani Emirates', in McCall and Bennett (eds.), *Aspects of West African Islam*, pp. 177–8. Successful slave raiding in nineteenth-century Hausaland is triumphantly portrayed in Hausa Islamic literature overlaid with notions of violence and fantasy and depicted as a 'status symbol of the great captain'. See Hiskett, 'Slavery in Hausa Islamic Literature', p. 123.
150. P.E. Lovejoy, 'Murgu: The Wages of Slavery in the Sokoto Caliphate', *Slavery and Abolition*, vol. 14, no. 1 (1993), p. 168; See also Fisher and Fisher, *Slavery and Muslim Society in Africa*, p. 44.
151. Mahadi, 'The Aftermath of the Jihad', p. 115. See similar attitudes by various African Muslim communities in Fisher and Fisher, *Slavery and Muslim Society in Africa*, pp. 22–3.

150 *The Legacy of Arab-Islam in Africa*

A large number of slaves had been caught this day. Altogether they were said to have taken a thousand, and there were certainly not less than five hundred. To our utmost horror not less than one hundred and seventy full-grown men were mercilessly slaughtered in cold blood, the greater part of them being allowed to bleed to death, a leg having been severed from the body.[152]

Within the Senegambian region the pattern was no different. 'Umar al-Hajj Tal's jihad and those of several others in this region brought about a devastating effect on the acephalous traditional communities. 'Umar himself is said to have owned about four thousand slaves in 1866.[153] Samori Turè is another well-known jihadist whose slave-raiding activities brought about large-scale devastating effects on both traditional and even Muslim communities in parts of present-day Guinea, Ivory Coast, Ghana and Burkina Faso.

In the name of jihad, Muslim warriors became the principal suppliers of slaves for local use and export via the trans-Saharan and transatlantic routes. The coastal people of the Senegambian region were reduced to vassalage and raided by Muslim overlords for sale as slaves. A brother of the Muslim ruler of Futa Jallon, in response to an insinuation by a French official that Muslim wars were mainly prompted by the resultant booty of slaves, is reported to have said, 'Mahometans were no better than Christians; the one stole, the other held the bag.'[154]

Muslims were by no means the sole producers or consumers of slaves within the African context. As indicated above, powerful traditional chiefdoms such as Bambara, Dahomey and Ashanti are known for their involvement as suppliers to the transatlantic slave trade and the use of slave labour in agricultural and mining industries. However, Muslim emirates were by far the major suppliers of slaves. Indeed the trans-Saharan and transatlantic slave trades reached their peak between the late seventeenth and early nineteenth centuries when the Muslim tradition of military jihad was in the ascendancy in the western Sudan. Most of the jihad movements became the main source of slaves.[155]

Muslim merchants for their part, by virtue of their monopoly over trade at the time, also monopolized the retail part of the human commodity. The Maraka, Dyula, Yarse, Hausa, Swahili, Jabarti, Beriberi, Yao, the infamous Jallaba of Sudan, joined their Arab, Moorish and Tuareg co-religionists as the principal middlemen in the human traffic. Muslim merchants operated not only in

---

152. Barth, *Travels*, p. 412–3. Nachtigal describes similar blood-chilling scenes where crops are razed, strong adult males hacked and clubbed to death, the old left to starve and women and children carried away. See *Sahara and the Sudan*, vol. 3, pp. 340–68. Some observers noted that about two-thirds of the victims of slave raids were normally murdered: Mahadi, 'The Aftermath of the Jihad', p. 124.

153. H.J. Fisher, 'Slavery and Seclusion in Northern Nigeria: A Further Note', *Journal of African History*, vol. 32 (1991), p. 124, n. 10.

154. Cited in Sanneh, *The Crown and the Turban*, p. 50.

155. Lovejoy, *Transformations in Slavery*, pp. 184 ff; Rodney, 'African Slavery', pp. 434–5.

Muslim Slavery and Black Africa 151

Muslim-controlled areas like the emirates of West Africa or Zanzibar in East Africa, but also in areas under non-Muslim rule such as Ashanti and Christian Ethiopia.[156] This, we must intimate again, was only a matter of course because long-distance trade was virtually a Muslim monopoly at the time.

Slaves were not just acquired for sale, but were extensively employed by African-Muslim states and communities. Slave villages were created around the capitals of Muslim emirates of northern Nigeria and the Senegambian region. These settlements – always forming a ring around Muslim capitals such as Sokoto and Hamdullahi in the Senegambia and numerous others – contained between fifty and five hundred slaves. Slave labour became the economic backbone of Muslim states during this period.[157]

Muslim religious communities such as the Toronkawa of Timbuktu, those of Walata, Jenne, the Dyula diaspora and the Jakhanke clerical groups depended on slave labour for agricultural cultivation, in order to give them time to pursue their vocation of learning and trading. These groups acquired their slaves mainly through purchase from traders and raiders, as well as through pious gifts and payments for religious services. The Jakhanke and other Muslim masters came 'to measure the prestige or importance of a clerical order by the size of slave quarters existing in it'.[158]

Commenting on the difference between the attitude of Muslim Maraka and their traditional Bambara cousins in the use of slave labour, R.L. Roberts notes that 'despite changes in the economy and society during the nineteenth century, the Bambara remained peasant cultivators, and masters usually worked side by side with their slaves. In contrast, Maraka society was transformed through a progressive reliance on slave labor. Farming became a degraded occupation.'[159]

So vital was the factor of slave labour in Muslim areas that when slaves took advantage of colonial anti-slavery policies and escaped en masse from their masters, one French administrator was concerned that 'the exodus would mean ruin and maybe death by starvation for Marakas incapable of cultivating their fields'.[160] By the end of the nineteenth century, surveys conducted in Muslim parts of Africa revealed staggering proportions of slaves or people of slave origins forming part of the populations.

In 1894, thanks to the French efforts to assess the situation of slavery in the region, it was revealed that about 30 to 50 per cent of the total population of the western Sudan were slaves, with up to 80 per cent near some commercial centres. About three-quarters of the population of Senegambia were slaves. By the 1890s the slave population of the plantations surrounding Banamba, the

156. Lovejoy, *Transformations in Slavery*, pp. 90–2.
157. Ibid., pp. 190–214.
158. Sanneh, *The Jakhanke*, p. 219.
159. Roberts, *Warriors, Merchants, and Slaves*, pp. 121–2.
160. Ibid., p. 186.

152 The Legacy of Arab-Islam in Africa

commercial centre of the Maraka, outnumbered the free inhabitants by a ratio of two to one.[161]

In Touba, the Jakhanke clerical centre, the slave population of the town of about three thousand inhabitants numbered between eleven and twelve thousand. In the district of Segu, al-Hajj 'Umar's capital, the population was 53 per cent slave in 1894. The proportion of slave and people of slave origin ranged from three-quarters of the population in the Say district to 50 per cent in the districts of Djougou, Dori, Kayes, Kita, Sikasso and Timbuktu.[162]

In Kankan 57 per cent of the population were slaves while in Sikasso, the capital of Tieba, two-thirds of the population were found to be slaves in 1904. The same percentage was estimated for the slave population of Bobo-Dioulasso. In areas immediately around Kong and Bandama, however, the proportion of slaves approached 80 per cent. In northern Nigeria the same pattern of slave concentration is revealed. Kano, the largest and most prosperous province of the Sokoto caliphate, had, as a conservative estimate, slaves forming 50 per cent of the population, and more than 95 per cent in the capital.[163]

Within the Yola provincial district, population censuses taken during the colonial period reveal that there were 16,450 free Fulbe and 20,000 slaves. Within the Sokoto caliphate as a whole, during the nineteenth and early part of the twentieth centuries, slaves are said to have 'certainly numbered in many millions and perhaps as many as 10 million'.[164] On the island of Zanzibar in East Africa in 1907 there were 27,000 freed slaves, and 140,000 slaves out of an estimated population of 208,700.[165]

Muslims, with the rare and refreshing exception of al-Nasiri, a nineteenth-century Moroccan historian, generally viewed the anti-slavery measures of the European colonial powers in the nineteenth and early twentieth centuries both as a threat to their livelihood and as an attack on Islam. Al-Nasiri wrote an impassioned treatise attacking the traffic and sale of blacks in the Maghrib, castigating the slave dealers as 'men with no morals, no manly qualities and no religion'.[166] The thrust of al-Nasiri's argument was that the people of the Sudan are Muslims or at least majority Muslim which renders their enslavement illegal in Islam. Referring to what he calls the 'evils of the times', which makes it impossible to know the truth as to who is legally enslavable and who is not, al-Nasiri declared that 'anyone who enters into a transaction of this forbidden nature is imperilling his salvation'.

161. L. Sanneh, 'Slavery, Islam and the Jakhanke People of West africa', *Africa*, vol. 46, no. 2 (1976), pp. 85–6.
162. Ibid., pp. 86–7.
163. Lovejoy, *Transformations in Slavery*, pp. 184–96.
164. Lovejoy and Hogendorn, *Slow Death for Slavery*, p. 305, n. 1.
165. Gordon, *Slavery in the Arab World*, p. 218.
166. Al-Nasiri, in Hunwick, 'Black Africans in the Islamic World', pp. 38–40.

Muslim Slavery and Black Africa 153

Describing Muslim enslavement of blacks in particular as 'one of the foulest and gravest evils perpetrated upon God's religion' and the institution of slavery in general as 'an evil which is derogatory to honour and religion', al-Nasiri concludes his treatise with a prayer to God to grant success to the efforts of the abolitionists:

> For the reason in Holy Law which existed in the time of the Prophet and the pious forefathers for enslaving people does not exist today; that is, being taken prisoner in jihad which has as its object to make the word of God supreme and to bring men to His religion which he chose for His servants.[167]

The last sentence of the treatise is a plea for God's forgiveness for Muslims because 'we have wronged ourselves and if you do not pardon us and have mercy upon us we shall be among those who suffer (eternal) loss'. Refreshing as al-Nasiri's views are, his position was a rare one as far as Muslim attitudes to slavery are concerned. In response to a letter by the British consul general of Morocco in 1842 asking the sultan of that country about the measures, if any, taken to abolish the slave trade, the sultan replied in astonishment thus:

> Be it known to you, that the traffic in slaves is a matter on which all sects and nations have agreed from the time of the sons of Adam, on whom be the peace of God, up to this day – and we are not aware of its being prohibited by the laws of any sect, and no one need ask this question, the same being manifest to both high and low and requires no more demonstration than the light of day.[168]

With regard to the abolition itself, it was not until November 1962 that the government of Saudi Arabia, which was exempted from British abolitionist efforts in the nineteenth century 'on religious grounds', found 'a favourable opportunity' formally to abolish slavery on paper. The government is said to have paid £1,785,000 in compensation for the liberation of 1682 slaves. However, United Nations anti-slavery reports estimated between 100,000 and 250,000 slaves in Saudi Arabia at the time, while the then prime minister, Faisal, is reported to have revealed in an interview with a British journalist that 'the slave population numbered many thousands'.[169] There is therefore little doubt that the official number of slaves freed (as an act of propaganda) was a minuscule part of the real slave population.

On this note, Fadel Abdallah's rather fantastic claim that 'only deviation from Islam prevented elimination of slavery within the first few decades of Islam. In Arabia itself within forty years, except for temporary prisoners of war, slavery had disappeared' shows the extent to which his 'informed intellectual effort' is

167. Ibid, p. 40.
168. A translation of the letter in Lewis, *Race and Slavery*, p. 151.
169. Gordon, *Slavery in the Arab World*, pp. 232–3; John Osman, 'Slavery Lives On', *Sunday Telegraph*, March 17 and 24, 1963.

154 *The Legacy of Arab-Islam in Africa*

prepared to compromise facts and truth in order to 'defend Islam'.[170] Indeed, on the whole, as far as the Muslim world in general and the Arab world in particular is concerned:

> No moral opprobrium has clung to slavery ... The decision by Arab states to abolish slavery during this century was taken for reasons that had little to do with the moral aspects of the issue. Pressure from the Western powers, the introduction of a money economy, and the realization that maintaining slavery would forever bar Arab nations from entering the councils of international society provide a much better explanation for their announced policy. That slavery and the slave trade were inherently evil and therefore merited abolition were thoughts alien to Arab heads of state and their followers.[171]

Within sub-Saharan Africa the story is not different. The pacifist Jakhanke community strongly opposed abolition and was prepared to take up arms in defence of their age-long tradition. Tcherno Aliou, known as the Wali of Goumba, was therefore 'content to allow the repossession of slaves to be invoked as the shibboleth of a populist cause'.[172] The Sudanese, it is said, viewed abolition as interference in their way of life and the undermining of one of their major sources of livelihood that was not only unjustified but also opposed to Islam. European anti-slavery measures helped provoke the jihad of Muhammad Ahmad of Sudan (the Sudanese *mahdi*) and became the rallying cry of his uprising against the British. The fact that Europeans were the chief executors of the abolition policy reinforced the perception that the policies were 'repressive and heretical Christian laws'.[173]

Raiding and trafficking slaves were banned, but the legal status of slavery in Muslim societies and countries was generally recognized and indeed sanctioned, by the colonial powers. In Zanzibar, for example, the British, in recognition of Muslim and 'native' customary laws, ruled that non-Muslims could not legally own slaves but that a Muslim could, upon appeal to Muslim law.[174] In some instances, slaves who took advantage of colonial anti-slavery pronouncements and deserted their Muslim masters were captured and returned. Lord Lugard, the colonial high commissioner for northern Nigeria, visited Sokoto and hundreds of desperate slaves took advantage of his presence and escaped with him. But in a bizarre fashion, Lugard's response, in his own words, was as follows:

170. Abdallah, 'Islam, Slavery and Racism', p. 31.
171. Gordon, *Slavery in the Arab World*, p. x.
172. Sanneh, 'Tcherno Aliou', p. 81.
173. G.R. Warburg, 'Ideological and Practical Considerations Regarding Slavery in the Mahdist State and the Anglo-Egyptian Sudan: 1881–1918', in Lovejoy (ed.), *The Ideology of Slavery*, p. 247.
174. Fisher and Fisher, *Slavery and Muslim Society in Africa*, p. 17.

Muslim Slavery and Black Africa 155

I had promised not to interfere with existing domestic slaves ... There was nothing to be done but to send these poor wretches back, and instruct the Resident to enquire into all deserving cases ... Doubtless very many bolted to neighbouring towns, but I considered my obligations of honour and of necessity were satisfied when I turned them out of my own following, and I did not enquire too curiously what became of them.[175]

The overthrow of the ruler of Oman in 1970 revealed some 500 slaves kept by the sultan in his palace.[176] In Mauritania slavery was abolished on paper in 1981 but anti-slavery and other human-rights organizations claim that, as at 1995, about three hundred thousand black slave descendants, known as the Haratin, continue to be held in servitude. Their children are occasionally sold or given out as presents and alms.[177]

There are also claims by the United Nations Human Rights Commission and other reputable international organizations that chattel slavery persists in the Sudan. It is said that slave raiding has resurfaced in that country since the resumption of the civil war in 1985. Local Arab militia are said to raid and capture Dinka and Nuba young men, women and children, the young ones being sold or kept as personal property. In a report presented by the secretary general to the United Nations General Assembly in October 1995, the abduction and traffic of young boys and girls from southern Sudan to the northern part of the country for sale as servants and concubines is highlighted in several paragraphs.[178]

In Muslim West Africa, slave owners simply subsumed slavery from a slave–master relationship to a student–teacher relation within the Qur'an school systems. It was normal practice that when a student enrolled in a Qur'an school he was regarded as a domestic slave of the teacher. The student, for all practical

175. Lovejoy and Hogendorn, *Slow Death for Slavery*, pp. 45–6.
176. Gordon, *Slavery in the Arab World*, pp. 234–5.
177. See the article by Charles Jacobs and Mohammed Athie of AASG, *New York Times*, 13 July, 1994; and a report by Anti-Slavery International entitled *Slavery in Mauritania: A Modern Reality*, February 1995.
178. 'Human Rights Questions: Human Rights Situations and Reports of Special Rapporteurs and Representatives; A Situation of Human Rights in the Sudan', a note presented by Secretary-General to the Fiftieth Session of United Nations General Assembly on 16 October, 1995. Other documents on slavery in Sudan include: 'Evidence of Violations of Human Rights in Sudan', by Christian Solidarity International (CSI) to United Nations. Human Rights Commission (April 1996); 'Slavery in Sudan' by CSI to US Congress House Committee on International Relations (13 March, 1996); and several others in the possession of the author. Two Sudanese Muslim intellectuals, Ushari Ahmad Mahmud and Suleyman Ali Baldo, had the courage to publicize the recrudescence of slavery and slave raiding in the country only to be arrested by the police and later escape to seek political asylum in Europe. See Ushari Ahmad Mahmud and Suleyman Ali Baldo, *Human Rights Violations in the Sudan 1987: The Diein Massacre, Slavery in the Sudan* (Khartoum: n.p., 1987).

156 The Legacy of Arab-Islam in Africa

purposes, followed the same work schedule as other slaves, with the slight difference that he received a modicum of education while in residence. Upon completion parents had to redeem their wards with a slave or the price of one; failure to do so left such students in the hands of the master just as any other slave.[179] Recent studies reveal that within the northern Nigerian context, 'people can still be found who are considered slaves, although the actual number of people still technically so has declined to relative insignificance. The death of slavery, pronounced by so many observers, has been a protracted one and is still not over.'[180]

THE VARIOUS ROLES OF SLAVES IN MUSLIM LANDS

The majority of slaves in Muslim lands were destined to be domestic servants. In areas like North Africa, the Middle East and Turkey, black slaves did the meanest and hardest work. Female slaves were required as household servants and cooks and for the more specifically female tasks of wet-nurse, child-minder and, for those deemed attractive, concubine. A nineteenth-century Dar Fur song put it thus: 'If we find a girl among them [slaves], who pleases us, then she doesn't need to do any housework. I make her my wife, so that we can sleep together in bed and "eat the skin", so that we will have children. Then she becomes pregnant and has a child. If it is a boy, then everything is fine.'[181]

Slaves of different ethnic origins acquired reputations for different qualities and tasks. The Zanj and the 'Sudan' women, for instance, were regarded as good wet-nurses. They were not generally appreciated as concubines, even though in North Africa in particular they must have played the role extensively. The Nubian and Abyssinian women were highly esteemed concubines. The twelfth-century Arab geographer al-Idrisi wrote rapturously about them: 'Of all the black women they are best for the pleasures of the bed ... It is on account of these qualities of theirs that the rulers of Egypt were so desirous of them and outbid others to purchase them, afterwards fathering children from them.'[182]

Ibn Butlān wrote a dossier in the eleventh century in which he described the different qualities of slaves from various parts of the world. After warning buyers to be careful with the 'cunning tricks' of slave dealers when buying female slaves,

---

179. Sanneh, *The Crown and the Turban*, p. 57.
180. Lovejoy and Hogendorn, *Slow Death for Slavery*, p. 30.
181. Cited in R.S. O'Fahey, 'Slavery and Society in Dar Fur', in Willis (ed.), *Slaves and Slavery*, vol. 2, p. 83. Concubines, in fact like wives, were regarded purely as reproductive vessels. An Arab poet is quoted as saying: 'Do not scorn a man because his mother is of the Greeks, or black, or a Persian, because mothers of men are but vessels to which they have been entrusted for keeping; for nobility fathers are important', cited in Goldziher, *Muslim Studies*, p. 118. Malik ibn Anas is also said to have described a black concubine as 'a vessel in which honey is kept; when the honey is taken out, the vessel is cast aside and no longer bothered with', ibid., n. 6.
182. Hunwick, 'Black Africans in the Islamic World', p. 27.

he went on to outline the different qualities of slave women from the various parts of the world. Most Abyssinian women, in the words of Ibn Butlān,

> have gracious, soft, and weak bodies ... They are delicate and do not thrive in any country other than that in which they were born. They are good, obliging, tractable, and trustworthy, and distinguished by strength of body despite their slenderness and also by weakness of character and shortness of life because of their bad digestion.[183]

Similarly, the Nubian women,

> of all the black races, have ease and grace and delicacy. Their bodies are dry, while their flesh is tender... The climate of Egypt suits them, since they drink the water of the Nile ... Their characters are pure, their appearance attractive, and there is in them religion and goodness, virtue, chastity, and submissiveness to the master, as if they had a natural bent for slavery.[184]

The Zanj women, on the other hand,

> have many bad qualities. The blacker they are, the uglier their faces, the more pointed their teeth, the less use they are and the more likely to do some harm. For the most part, they are of bad character, and they frequently run away... There is no pleasure to be got from [them] because of their stench and the coarseness of their bodies.'

Even worse are the Zaghāwa. 'They are worse than the Zanj and than all the black races. Their women are useless for pleasure, and their men are useless for service.'[185]

Arab-Muslim rulers, princes and senior statesmen kept large numbers of concubines in harems while the ordinary Muslim masses had fewer concubines, who lived as part of their families. This practice ran across the Muslim world from West Africa to the Middle East and Turkey. When a concubine bore her master a child, especially a boy, then she became *umm walad* (concubine mother) who could no longer be sold or transferred and became free upon the death of the master. The child also assumed the free status of the father, if the master so recognized it. Apart from instances whereby black slaves were used as breeders to ensure the constant supply of slaves, casual intercourse and marriage between black slaves was generally prohibited.[186] Descendants of the age-old practice of concubinage in most Arab countries today regard themselves as black-Arabs, black-Moors or even outright 'white-Arabs', irrespective of their complexion.[187]

183. Ibn Butlān, *Shirā al-Raqiq*, ed. and trans. in Lewis, *Islam from the Prophet Muhammad*, p. 249.
184. Ibid., pp. 249–50.
185. Ibid., p. 249.
186. Goldziher, *Muslim Studies*, p. 118.
187. J. Mercer, *Slavery in Mauritania Today* (Edinburgh: Human Rights Groups, 1982), p. 9.

158 *The Legacy of Arab-Islam in Africa*

A good percentage of black slaves were used in plantation farming. Some of these include the indigo, sugar, and cotton plantations of eighteenth-century northern Sudan and the clove plantation of Zanzibar. The jihadist emirates of western and central Sudan also employed vast numbers of slaves in large-scale agricultural farming. As already pointed out above, large numbers of the Zanj were employed on plantation farms in Iraq as early as the eighth century. In the Persian Gulf, slaves were used in the salt-mining, fishing and pearl-diving industries.[188] Ibn Butlān had this to say about the Zanj men; 'They can endure hard work. If the Zanji has had enough to eat, you can chastise him heavily and he will not complain.'[189] The Zanj and the 'Sudan' men were regarded as best for the more physically exacting tasks while Nubian men were regarded as trustworthy and used as doormen, guards and financial assistants in Egypt and other parts of North Africa.

Male black slaves were recruited into infantry groups, a generally inferior role to that of cavalry staffed by the *mamluks* (slaves of mainly Turkish origin). Turkish military slaves became 'the best cavalry and the best cavalry were Turkish military slaves. Africans were considered inferior to Turks; they were also stereotyped as infantry, which was inferior to cavalry. Therefore, African military slaves by color and occupation were considered of less importance than Turks.'[190] It was in this stereotyped role that thousands of black slaves perished in battles, during succession-related feuds, and interracial feuds with their Berber and Turkish counterparts. Mention is made of the employment of black slaves as soldiers in considerable numbers at various times in Morocco, Tunisia, Egypt and India. The first recorded use of black slave troops is in Aghlabid Tunisia where they were used as a special corps by the ruling dynasty in the early ninth century to counterbalance the threat of Arab troops. Numerous black slave soldiers caught up in the bloody feuds of medieval Muslim North African rule were at various times slaughtered by the victorious parties.[191] It was in this role that one or two of the offspring of black concubines took over the reins of power in Muslim North Africa and Muslim India where the role of black African slaves in 'warfare and politics in the period 1400–1700 was considerable'.[192]

---

188. Z.I. Oseni, 'The Revolts of Black Slaves in Iraq under the 'Abbasid Administration in 869–883 CE', *Hamdard Islamicus*, vol. 12, no. 2 (1989), p. 58. See also B. Lewis, *Arabs in History* (London: Hutchinson University Library, 1969), p. 104.

189. Ibn Butlān, *Shirā al-Raqiq*, p. 248.

190. J.L. Bacharach, 'African Military Slaves in the Medieval Middle East: The Cases of Iraq (869–955) and Egypt (868–1171)', *International Journal of Middle East Studies*, vol. 13 (1981), p. 490. It should be added here that the military roles of blacks in the Islamic world is either simply ignored or documented with contempt by contemporary Arab-Muslim chroniclers, which reinforces the view that their role was generally seen as part of their subordination and servitude rather than as specialized tasks, as modern writers depict it.

191. Hunwick, 'black Africans in the Islamic World', pp. 30–31.

192. Ibid., p. 33.

A significant proportion of male black slaves were castrated and used in Muslim lands as eunuchs, to guard the harems and serve as attendants at holy sites such as the Ka'ba at Mecca and the Prophet's mosque at Madina. They formed a special class of highly priced slaves kept by Muslim rulers and bourgeois from the heart of the Muslim world to Muslim Africa. Ethiopia was for a very long time the main source of eunuchs for the Muslim world even though from the mid-eighteenth century Bagirmi became the main exporter.

The operation, done on boys aged between eight and ten, though prohibited under Islam, was carried out with an exceedingly high death rate. Gustav Nachtigal was told that on the whole about 30 per cent survived the operation in Bagirmi, while other estimates put the mortality rate at up to 80 per cent.[193] This barbaric act was made particularly cruel for black victims in that, in contrast to their white counterparts whose operation did not deny them the ability to perform coitus, the castration of blacks involved what was popularly referred to as 'level with the abdomen', i.e. a complete amputation of the genitalia.[194]

Some eunuchs came to hold positions of influence and it was indeed only in their capacity as eunuchs that black slaves, unlike their white counterparts, were sometimes able to play political and judicial roles of some importance in Muslim lands. Hence, in the words of J.O. Hunwick:

> It is a curious irony that while the female slave's best chance of a life of ease and respect was through the exploitation of her female sexuality as a concubine and ultimately as a mother, the male slave's surest road to prosperity and power lay in having his own sexuality sacrificed through a transformation whose physical and emotional pain can better be imagined than described.[195]

Muslim communities differed in their enthusiasm to convert their slaves to Islam. Nevertheless, a process of acculturation and conversion was almost inevitable. For as Ibn Khaldun observed, 'it is always in the nature of the conquered and captured to imitate the lifestyles of their masters in their dress, insignia, belief, and other customs and usages'.[196] There is therefore no gainsaying that Muslim slaves both without and within Africa almost invariably adopted the Islamic way of life, at least by the second or third, if not the first, generation.

Looking at the statistics of slave populations in Muslim areas in tropical Africa detailed above, there is little doubt therefore that enslavement became a major means of converting Africans to Islam both within and without the

193. Nachtigal, *Sahara and Sudan*, vol. 2, p. 217. See also Hunwick, 'Black Slaves in the Mediterranean World', p. 22 and Fisher and Fisher, *Slavery and Muslim Society in Africa*, pp. 145–6.
194. Brunschvig, "'abd', p. 33.
195. Hunwick, 'Black Slaves in the Mediterranean World', p. 24.
196. C. Issawi (trans.), *An Arab Philosophy of History: Selections from the Prolegomena of Ibn Khaldun of Tunis (1332–1406)* (London: John Murray, 1950), p. 53.

160 *The Legacy of Arab-Islam in Africa*

continent. The main means by which light-skinned Muslims introduced Islam to black Africans was through the institution of slavery. It was mainly as slaves that millions of Africans came into contact with Islam in such areas as North Africa, the Middle East, Turkey and the Indian subcontinent. However, as Bernard Lewis observes:

> All in all the cultural role of blacks in medieval Arab Islam was small and, as compared with the role of the Arabs, Persians, and Turks, of minor significance. It was primarily as slaves that they were imported to the Islamic lands, and it was as slaves of various kinds that they rendered their service to Islam.[197]

This assessment, in our view, is the most apt of the roles and general contribution of the descendants of the millions of black slaves taken into Muslim lands in the past fourteen hundred years. And this takes us to another crucial aspect of Muslim slavery, i.e. the condition of slaves in Muslim lands.

THE CONDITION OF SLAVES IN MUSLIM LANDS: THEORY VERSUS PRACTICE

Not a few leading Western travellers and scholars have been prone to expatiate on the 'mildness' and 'humanity' of Muslim slavery. The general theory has been that slaves, especially domestic slaves, were treated as well as any other family member by their Muslim masters and that they were hardly ever treated harshly or discriminated against. Hence there are those who have asserted that:

> In all fairness, the lot of slaves in Arabia must be compared to the lot of the average freeman in that country ... The slave fares almost as well as his master, and generally the conditions under which they live in bondage are better than those prevalent in their native country.[198]

Others claim that

> the status of a slave in Islam and the favourable position he occupied often worked to his advantage. The slave generally formed a part of the household as much as any member, and through a mixture of fear and respect, a feeling of security and affection, he developed a sense of loyalty which did not escape the notice of many a traveller.[199]

Some claim that 'the institution of slavery in Islam operated in such a way that the slave could advance within a given system – military, political and even economic – according to his accomplishments and merit'.[200]

197. Lewis, 'The African Diaspora', pp. 55–6.
198. Dejong, 'Slavery in Arabia', p. 139.
199. W. 'Arafat, 'The Attitude of Islam to Slavery', *The Islamic Quarterly*, vol. 10 (1966), pp. 16–18.
200. Forand, 'The Relation of the Slave and the Client', p. 66.

Muslim Slavery and Black Africa 161

There are even those who would go to the extent of lauding the values of the institution of slavery in Islam as 'a house of humanitarian correction'.[201] As we have stated above, the Qur'an counsels, but does not require, the Muslim master to be mild in his treatment of slaves. Likewise, there are numerous other Prophetic traditions that call upon Muslims to treat their slaves with kindness. One such tradition, claimed to be the last words of the Prophet, runs as follows: 'I advise you to pray and to act in a God-fearing way towards those whom your right hand possess [your slaves].'[202]

The general theory of benign Muslim slavery is based mainly on two fundamental premises, i.e. the theoretical religious and legal propositions relating to the subject and examples of a minuscule fraction of slaves who rose to positions of influence in the Muslim world. J. Comhaire, for instance, cites the accomplishments of individuals of African descent and culture (whom he refers to as 'immigrants' rather than persons with slave origins) as evidence of the interracial and benign utopia of Muslim societies.[203]

What these claims fail to mention is that in contrast to the situation of the Mamluks, 'the gelder's knife and the corps of eunuchs were virtually the only route by which a black could attain high office' of any kind within the Muslim world outside black Africa.[204] Apart from isolated and rare examples of black eunuchs like Abu al-Misk Kafur, who captured the reins of power during an interregnum in tenth-century Egypt and others like Dhu al-Nūn al-Misrī (d. 861), known as 'the head of Sufis', most if not all other persons of black descent who attained some kind of fame in the Muslim world (mainly in poetry and music) were almost always the offspring of concubines.

Looking at such rare examples against the fact that millions of blacks were taken into Muslim lands as slaves is yet another commentary on the condition of slaves in Muslim hands. Indeed, what the racial prejudice against blacks, as detailed above, suggests is that the various accomplishments of those very few people of African descent in the Muslim world were despite, not because of, a system that must have been very different from the alleged inter-racial and intercultural utopia of Muslim societies. The various accomplishments of such individuals should therefore be attributed to their own resilience and determination. Added to this is the fact that the contribution of people of black descent to Islamic civilization is either not acknowledged or is mentioned dismissively in Muslim historiography. A black Palestinian Muslim once told this writer he has never come across Bilal's name in any *isnad* of a *hadith* and wondered why this was so.

---

201. M. Hamidullah, *Le Prophète de l' Islam*, (Paris: n.p., 1959), pp. 462 ff.
202. Al-Abshīhi, *Kitâb al-Mustatraf*, ed. and trans. in B. Lewis, *Islam from the Prophet Muhammad*, p. 252.
203. J. Comhaire, 'Some Notes on Africans in Muslim History', *The Muslim World*, vol. 46 (1956), pp. 336–44.
204. Lewis, 'The African Diaspora', p. 54.

162 The Legacy of Arab-Islam in Africa

Most, if not all, proponents of the idea of idyllic Muslim slavery tend to highlight the various religious and legal stipulations on the treatment and manumission of slaves as proof of the magnanimity of Arab-Islam, more than any other system, towards slaves. It is, however, one thing having these pious religious and ethical propositions and another thing putting them into practice. Some modern Muslim apologists put together a selective collection of Qur'anic verses, *hadiths*, pious sayings and stipulations from *fiqh* on the treatment of slaves and draw wild conclusions such as:

> During the short period in which slavery was tolerated by Islam, the Muslim institutions did not leave slaves under the hard circumstances which were spread in those days and they had not deprived them of their human rights as other legislations had done. But the slaves enjoyed in Islam kind surveillance and good circumstances and gentle treatment as the outcome of the recommendations of the Prophet to his followers and according to the outlook of Islam.[205]

Talking about legislation and Prophetic recommendations on the treatment of slaves as evidence of 'good circumstances and gentle treatment' of slaves in Muslim hands is like pointing to the numerous anti-racism groups and laws in Western Europe as evidence of the absence of racism in Western society. On the contrary, one would suppose that teachings or sanctions against a given practice, rather than being proof of its absence, are strong evidence of its prevalence. It is therefore only reasonable to see the emphasis on the kind treatment of slaves in Islamic sources (with the exception of the Qur'an whose teachings on the subject can be said to be a reflection of the situation in pre-Islamic rather than Islamic Arabia) as a strong indication of their harsh, if not cruel, treatment. But let us leave the theoretical propositions for a moment and look at examples of what took place in practice.

In practice, the condition of first-generation and plantation slaves in Muslim lands was as harsh and cruel as any other such system, while successive generations of all slaves had to live under the weight and stigma of racial and social discrimination, as outlined above. As early as the ninth century, the Zanj, according to the great Arab historian al-Tabari, were employed in gangs of between 500 and 5000 in the salt marshes of southern Iraq. Al-Tabari observes that their condition was 'extremely bad' and that they were 'literally pinned down there, hopeless and homeless'. Their reward consisted of 'a few handfuls of meal'.[206] Their miserable condition led to several rebellions, the fiercest of which lasted for fifteen years from 868 to 883 CE.

---

205. A.A. Wahid Wafi, 'Human Rights in Islam', *The Islamic Quarterly*, vol. 11 (1967), p. 75, n. 1; see also 'Arafat, 'The Attitude of Islam to Slavery', pp. 14–18; Abdallah, 'Islam, Slavery, and Racism', pp. 33–40.
206. Oseni, 'The Revolts of Black Slaves in Iraq', p. 58. See also Lewis, *Arabs in History*, p. 104.

Muslim Slavery and Black Africa   163

A nineteenth-century eyewitness described the condition of slaves in the Persian Gulf regions as 'a dreadful thing'; he went on to state that 'perhaps the worst part of the whole thing is the pearl-diving'. The stronger male slaves were chosen for the task:

> And before they dive for the pearl oysters a clip is put on their nose to prevent their breathing. They then jump out of the boat, armed with a hammer and a light basket, and on coming to surface pass the oysters into the boat, and after a whiff of air are sent down again. If they don't succeed in sending up a certain number of oysters they get severely beaten. Before long their lungs begin to give way, and then it is soon all over with them.[207]

A twentieth-century eyewitness described the same situation as 'a repulsive and dreadful thing. Men and women live on the level of animals. As little is spent on them as possible, they being regarded simply as pieces of equipment for pearl diving'.[208] It has equally been pointed out that slaves in North Africa in general and Egypt in particular worked naked on starvation rations and in the unbearable climatic conditions, as a result of which they died by the hundreds, if not thousands.[209]

Within tropical Africa itself, Muslim states and communities used slaves extensively in peasant and large-scale agricultural production. The condition of slaves throughout such Muslim communities was anything but mild. In 1820, René Callié reported numerous slave-based plantations in the Senegambian region where slaves lived in several small slave villages. Callié accompanied one of his Muslim hosts to his rice plantation and described the condition of the slave workers in the following words: 'The poor slaves work entirely naked, exposed to the heat of the burning sun. The presence of the master intimidates them, and the fear of punishment expedites the work ... the women, who had little clothing, had their children tied to their backs.'[210] Reporting on massive Maraka slave desertions during the late nineteenth/early twentieth centuries, one French administrator noted: 'If the Maraka had treated their slaves with less stinginess in their food [ration] and with more humanity in their customary relations, then escapes would have been less frequent.'[211]

In Zanzibar, it is well known that slaves who advanced in age or became ill, and were of no economic value, were left to fend for themselves, and most of them ended up destitute and starved to death. Some were brutally killed by their

---

207. A letter written by a young European officer, dated 10 September, 1886, cited in Beachey, *A Collection of Documents*, p. 80.
208. P.W. Harrison, 'Slavery in Arabia', *Muslim World*, vol. 29, no. 2 (1939), p. 208.
209. Mahadi, 'The Aftermath of the Jihad', p. 125.
210. R. Callié, *Travels Through Central Africa to Timbuctoo*, vol. 1 (London: n.p., 1830), p. 211; see also Lovejoy, *Transformations in Slavery*, p. 209.
211. Roberts, *Warriors, Merchants, and Slaves*, p. 187.

164 The Legacy of Arab-Islam in Africa

masters and their bodies thrown by the seaside.[212] Among the 500 slaves discovered in the palace of the sultan of Oman after his overthrow in 1970 were those who were mute and suffered from paralysis of the neck because they were forbidden, under pain of beating, ever to speak or raise their eyes from the ground.[213]

Another indication of the harsh conditions of black slaves in the Muslim world is the high death and low birth rates alluded to in Ibn Butlān's works cited above and mentioned by many other observers. Some people attribute this to natural causes like unfamiliar weather conditions and lack of immunity. But looking at the examples given above of the conditions of slaves in Muslim lands it is not only plausible but imperative to look beyond natural causes and point to the general harsh conditions under which slaves lived, such as the inadequacy or indeed absence of coverings, and the meagre rations of food in addition to the physical, emotional and psychological torment, as the ultimate causes of the high death and low birth rates.

The numerous slave revolts in Muslim lands going back to the Zanj rebellions in eighth- and ninth-century Iraq down to nineteenth-century slave uprisings in Zanzibar and several other parts of Muslim Africa, coupled with the numerous desertions by slaves of their Muslim masters, all serve to underline the fact that, on the whole, Muslim slavery was not as idyllic as some modern Western scholars and most Muslim apologists would have us believe. Indeed, even from those who did not deny that Arab slaves were far better off than their American counterparts one hears: 'but that there was something wrong with their conditions of life is clear from the high rate of mortality and the low rate of fertility'.[214] These high death and low birth rates are further factors explaining the disproportionately small numbers of the black diaspora in the Muslim world.

Now returning to the theoretical stipulations, most of those who advance theoretical propositions on the treatment of slaves as the basis of the idyllic nature of Muslim slavery fail to mention the numerous other stipulations that in effect reduce the slave to nothing more or less than some property on the same level as animals and inanimate objects. For instance, in traditional Muslim jurisprudence the slave can be sold, given as part of a dowry or a pious gift, or as a bequest by the master. In other words they could be dispensed of as any other property. The master could put the slaves to any task, hire them out, inflict corporal as well as other punishment on his slaves and even put them to death.[215]

212. G.A. Akinola, 'Slavery and Slave Revolts in the Sultanate of Zanzibar in the Nineteenth Century', *Journal of the Historical Society of Nigeria*, vol. 6, no. 2 (June 1972), p. 222.
213. Gordon, *Slavery in Arab World*, pp. 234–5.
214. Coupland, *The Exploitation of East Africa*, p. 146.
215. For contemporary evidence of torture and killing of slaves by their Muslim masters, refer to Mercer, *Slavery in Mauritania Today*.

Muslim Slavery and Black Africa 165

The bodily harm or murder of a slave by a master carried no specific punishment. Only when the harm was deemed to be 'without cause' would atonement (*kaffara*) be required of a master. While the murder of another Muslim is punishable by death in Islamic law, a free Muslim is not liable for the murder of a Muslim slave.[216] According to classical Muslim law, slaves have no inheritance rights. In the contrary, their offspring along with their own properties are passed on as inheritance. They cannot make vows, marry or sign contracts on their own; their evidence is not admissible in court and a slave's word against that of a freeborn person is null and void.[217] As pointed out by Joseph Schacht, the counter-stipulations effectively made the protection of slaves in Muslim law 'not go beyond that of property in general'.[218] One is bound to ask, wherein then lie the 'human rights' of slaves in Islam?

The tradition recommending the manumission of Muslim slaves as an act of winning divine favour was effectively negated by the commentary of Muslim lawyers to the effect that alms-giving was preferable to freeing a slave and that a mere affirmation of the unity of God would equally earn one God's favour.[219] Hence, despite an elaborate system of manumission stipulated in traditional Muslim teaching, as we have shown above, the institution of slavery lasted longer in Muslim societies than any other society, and, indeed, persists up to the present day. Again we are faced with yet another example of practice being far off the mark of pious stipulations.

Apart from the above-mentioned counter-stipulations that in effect vitiate the spirit of the pious recommendations, popular material such as songs and proverbs, which can be said to represent a fair reflection of contemporary attitudes, is also instructive about the condition of slaves in Muslim societies. A nineteenth-century Dar Fur song entitled 'The Slave's Lot' runs as follows:

> The slaves must do the work in the house; if they are unwilling to work, they must be beaten with the whip or must be beaten with the stick. Then they begin to cry [and] be willing to work. Their language is difficult; people don't understand them.[220]

Arab-Muslim proverbs relating to slaves further throw some light on the general attitudes towards slaves. One such 'slave proverb' says: 'The slave is beaten with the stick, and advice is sufficient for the free-born'. Another says, 'Never trust a black slave; whip him well, and feed him well, and the work will be done'; 'Dear to a slave is he who overworks him' says yet another proverb. Commenting on this last proverb, al-Maydani explains that he who despises a slave 'and causes him fatigue is

216. J. Schacht, *An Introduction to Islamic Law* (Oxford: Clarendon, 1964), pp. 127–9.
217. Ibid. See also Petrushevsky, *Islam in Iran*, pp. 154–6.
218. Schacht, *Islamic Law*, p. 128.
219. Fisher and Fisher, *Slavery and Muslim Society in Africa*, p. 44.
220. O'Fahey, 'Slavery and Society', p. 83.

166 *The Legacy of Arab-Islam in Africa*

dearer to him than another, because his natural disposition is to bear humiliation.[221] Thus, W.J. Sersen points out that it 'may be a question of common attitudes and prejudice vs. religious ethic'.[222] One is even inclined to think that these could be a reflection of common practices versus religious ethic and not just common attitudes and prejudice. The following are few examples of Muslim Hausa slave proverbs:

> A slave is a slave for all that he is rich!
> A warning is for a free man, the stick for a slave.
> One man's slave is an aristocrat to another man's slave.[223]

Commenting on claims that slaves in Zanzibar were so comfortable they had no desire to be released from bondage, G.A. Akinola, writes:

> There is no denying the fact that Islam sought to liberalize the institution of slavery by restricting those who might be enslaved, by spelling out the legal rights of slaves and by recommending manumission in certain instances ... In actual practice, [however,] neither the Islamic laws on slavery nor the obligations imposed on Muslim slave-owners by their religious duties went sufficiently far to make slavery such an idyllic institution from which slaves would never be constrained to seek escape.[224]

It should be intimated, though, that there can be no doubt that some individual Muslim masters treated their slaves well, whatever that means. Similarly, we do not by any means want to suggest that cruelty and harshness on the part of Muslim slavers was due to their Islamic religious persuasion. In fact, on the contrary, on balance, the spirit of traditional Muslim teaching is geared towards ameliorating the slave's condition. The point made, nevertheless, is that conclusions should not be drawn from theoretical stipulations or examples from individual kindness to give the impression that Muslim slavery as an institution was idyllic.

This is because, just as the cruelty of Muslim slavers was by no means a Muslim or Islamic peculiarity, so should the so-called magnanimity of individual Muslim slavers or even provisions and examples of manumission of slaves not necessarily be treated as peculiarly Muslim or Islamic provisions. For 'kindness' towards slaves could and has been found in many other slave-owning societies while the principles and practices of manumitting slaves for religious motives were well known in Christian Byzantium and other slave-owning communities of antiquity.[225] In this regard, Lamin Sanneh's caution against conventional theories of benign Muslim slavery is very instructive:

---

221. Sersen, 'Stereotypes and Attitudes', pp. 97–101.
222. Ibid., p. 98.
223. Hiskett, 'Slavery in Hausa Islamic Literature', p. 123.
224. Akinola, 'Slavery and Slave Revolts', p. 221.
225. Petrushevsky, *Islam in Iran*, p. 158. For instance the Greeks are known for the very liberal manner in which they treated their slaves. See Vogt, *Ancient Slavery*, pp. 4 ff. The same is said of the Portuguese.

Muslim Slavery and Black Africa 167

Caution is necessary in thus invoking the enlightened power of the law, for the slave-dealer who suffers its reprimand for taking with left hand may offer generous ransom with the right and thus leave his critic without resources ... The whole project became water-logged with easy gain, and the bursts of humane sentiment we may get here or genuine kindness there were insufficient altogether to drain the swelling.[226]

In our view, a European missionary within the context of nineteenth-century Malindi, Tanzania, has given an apt description of the condition of slaves in Muslim lands. The missionary, Charles New, admitted that slaves were 'not so hard driven in East Africa as they were, say, in America', but that the institution was nonetheless 'heartless and cruel; it was indeed the reign of terror'. He went on to state rather succinctly that slaves were often treated 'with humanity, *upon the same principle that many men treat their horses kindly*' (my emphasis).[227] In other words, Muslim slavers took good care of their slaves more out of economic considerations than fellow human feeling. Thus good care of slaves was to the extent that it kept them performing their tasks for the slaver. The betterment of the lot of the slave under such circumstance was a by-product.

Apart from these, there remains a fundamental difficulty with the general thesis of the 'humanity' and 'magnanimity' of any institution of slavery. This difficulty was raised by David Livingstone with regard to the alleged kindness of Portuguese and Spanish masters towards their slaves. Livingstone wrote:

It is questionable whether a slave owner can be kind to those whom he robs of the first rights of humanity. There is in general no fellow feeling between the two classes. They repose no confidence in each other. The master invariably speaks disparagingly of the slaves as a class; they are blacks, beasts, etc. Particular individuals are pointed to as remarkable for having remained many years with their masters, as if it were implied that this is the exception and a conviction existed in the mind of the master that the state of bondage was far from being an enviable one.[228]

An Arabic proverb says: 'The free-born man is a free-born man, though harm befalls him. The slave is a slave, though you garb him in pearls.'[229] 'Abd al-'Azīz ibn Ahmad al-Bukhārī (d. 1330) put it even more succinctly when he wrote that 'freedom is the attribute par excellence of a living being in secular jurisdiction, whereas slaves are in the category of the dead'.[230] The very status of the slave is

226. Sanneh, *The Jakhanke*, pp. 220–1.
227. Cooper, 'The Treatment of Slaves', p. 95.
228. I. Schapera (ed.), *Livingstone's African Journal: 1853–1856*, vol. 1, (London: Chatto & Windus, 1963), p. 187.
229. Sersen, 'Stereotypes and Attitudes', p. 98.
230. Quoted in Forand, 'The Relation of the Slave and the Client', p. 61.

168 *The Legacy of Arab-Islam in Africa*

therefore cruel. It is legal, social and psychological death! Notwithstanding the conviction of past Muslim (and Christian) slavers that slavery was a blessing in disguise to the victims, the above statements indicate that even slavers were under no illusion whatsoever that slavery was a dreadful condition. No stipulation or magnanimity of individual slavers could make this hideous institution one to be lauded, more so when it is sanctioned and perpetuated in the name of God.

CONCLUSION

What we have tried to establish in this chapter is, first of all, that slavery in Africa should be understood as having three broad dimensions. First is indigenous slavery, which ancient African societies shared with other ancient human societies such as Europeans, Americans, Arabs and Asians. This form of slavery, we established, was incidental and marginal to society. The second dimension is the form of slavery inspired by the Western-Christian civilization, i.e. the large-scale transformations of the practice in eighteenth- and nineteenth-century non-Muslim African states such as Ashanti and Dahomey which were in league with European traders and slavers. Then we identified the third dimension, which constituted the primary focus of this work, in the form of Arab-Islamic-inspired forms of slavery as practised by Muslims of all races and shared by African-Muslim societies long before the European interlude.

We then outlined the traditional Muslim understanding and justification for enslavement, i.e. non-belief in Islam. In addition to the content of their beliefs, black Africans were further placed under the burden of a mythological curse, which fettered them to perpetual servitude on account of the colour of their skin. Thus we demonstrated that, contrary to conventional theories of the egalitarian spirit of Islam, light-skinned Muslims are just as colour-conscious and racist as any other modern, light-skinned society. Racial discrimination against Africans and people of African descent in medieval Muslim sources and modern, light-skinned Muslim societies are just as endemic. We then outlined how Muslims, from the pious to the nominal, within and without Africa waged jihad, raided, hunted, kidnapped and purchased tens of millions of Africans as slaves and in the process slaughtered and caused the death of tens of millions others.

We established that contrary to theories of a humane Muslim slavery, the institution and practice of slavery in Muslim societies was as cruel and harsh as any other slave system. We established that notwithstanding pious Muslim stipulations about slavery, slaves constituted a class of deprived people with the chains of servitude and caste inferiority riveted on their offspring. They were totally denied civil status, and their exclusion from responsible office was reinforced by the entire weight of Islamic law, Muslim social practice and traditional stigma. Numerous slave revolts dating as far back as the Zanj rebellion in the ninth century, high death and low birth rates amongst slaves in Muslim lands, desertions and countless attempts at desertion, all belie the theory of idyllic Muslim slavery.

5

ENCOUNTERING THE ENCOUNTERS: ARAB-ISLAM AND BLACK AFRICAN EXPERIENCE

INTRODUCTION

So far we have looked at the black African encounter with Arab-Islam through certain key themes. The first theme, examined in chapter 2 has to do with religious exchanges and conversion to Islam under the patronage of the traditional African environment before the eighteenth- and nineteenth-century jihad movements. We established that during this period the exchanges were discriminatory and mutual within an environment of mutual acceptance if not celebration of diversity. We then looked at the second theme in chapter 3, namely the jihad movements as a traditional Muslim response or reaction to the exchanges under the patronage of indigenous African environment.

The jihad movements stood and fought for the dominance of the Islamic tradition and brought in their wake an exclusivist and intolerant system that eschewed diversity. The third theme, which we examined in chapter 4 relates to the issue of Muslim slavery. The conclusions arrived at are that Arab enslavement of Africans intensified from the inception of Islam in the seventh century and persists up to the present day. The enslavement of millions of Africans by Muslims of all races (African Muslims included) down the ages was justified on account of the content of their beliefs and the colour of their skin. Muslim slavery, we have established, both in theory and practice, was as inhumane and just as cruel as any other slave system.

The question that naturally arises from the discourse so far is, what should be the response(s) to this historical legacy from both sides of the divide, i.e. the Arab-Muslim and black African worlds?[1] This is the question we seek to address

---

1. We are using 'Arab Muslim' to represent the Arab Middle East, and North Africa in

Encountering the Encounters: Arab-Islam and Black African Experience 171

in this chapter. The biggest temptation and danger for them is to react against each other, thereby perpetuating rather than dealing with the fragile and even hostile aspects of the legacy. What we are hoping to do here is explore ways and means by which the Arab-Muslim and black African worlds could react in their own ways to the dark and critical aspects of the historical past.

In this connection we shall suggest some possible ways forward for a critical and sustainable dialogue between the black African and Arab-Islamic ideological worlds in general, and Muslim and non-Muslim Africans in particular. Non-Muslim Africa here, of course includes African Christians, the overwhelming majority of whom (especially in Muslim areas such as the Sudan and the Middle Belt of Nigeria) carry their own baggage of the legacy of the encounters. First of all, in the first section of the chapter, we shall underscore the need to acknowledge historical facts and contemporary realities, hard and embarrassing as they may appear, as we have done in the preceding chapters, within the context of dialogue.

Second, we shall argue for the need of a critical rethinking of the Arab-Islamic dispensation by black Africans, not least African Muslims, in the light of the particular historical and contemporary African context, in the second section. That is to say, we shall emphasize the need for Africans to take responsibility in recasting the Arab-Islamic dispensation in the light of past and present African experience. The abiding principle here, to use the words of S.S. Nyang, is that Africans 'must assimilate the cultural values of these traditions [Arab-Islam and Western Christianity] correctly if [they] really intend to have influence on the course of world history'.[2] In this section we shall look at the whole issue of the African experience in relation to Islam and ask whether in its Arab scaffoldings Islam is any less foreign and as such any less potentially subversive to African heritage than, say, Western-Christian values.

In the third section we shall go on to address the Arab factor in Islamic 'orthodoxy' as it relates to rethinking Islam in light of the African experience. The main task here is to raise questions about the place of the Arab factor in non-Arab Muslim religious expression, on the one hand, and the appropriation of non-Arab (African) indigenous elements into Islam, on the other.

TRUTH, DIALOGUE AND CONFESSIONAL LOYALTY

Dialogue among and between communities, though not a totally new phenomenon, gained an urgency and importance unparalleled in history in the second half of the twentieth century. Dialogue is the conscious engagement

particular (as the cradle and axis of the Islamic heritage), and the Muslim world (including Muslim black Africa) in general in this context. The divide 'black African' and 'Arab-Islamic' is therefore more ideological than racial or geographical.
2. Nyang, *African Identity*, pp. 83–4.

172 *The Legacy of Arab-Islam in Africa*

and exchange of views, ideas and concerns between individuals or communities with differing, parallel, opposing or even conflicting views. The primary aim of dialogue is to eschew stereotypes and prejudices with the view of getting to know each other better and appreciating one another fully.

Dialogue, therefore, seeks to encourage tolerance and appreciation and discourage intolerance, bigotry and prejudice. Hans Küng underscores the importance of inter-religious dialogue thus: 'No peace among the people of the world without peace among the religions. No peace among the religions, without dialogue between the religions, and there is no dialogue between the religions without accurate knowledge of one another.'[3] Dialogue is, therefore, principally about gaining knowledge, which will in turn, hopefully, promote mutual trust and peaceful co-existence; knowledge of what makes the Other who they really are and not what we perceive them to be. Is dialogue therefore a mere passing of niceties? Is there a place at the round table of dialogue for the differences, contentious and controversial issues and historical excesses and wrongs to be addressed and where possible redressed? In other words, the issue we are seeking to address here briefly is the need for hard and painful historical facts and contemporary realities to be made an integral part of dialogue.

There are those who might see what has been said so far in this work, especially in the last two chapters, as raking over of the past, which is unnecessary, and as counter-productive to dialogue. How, for instance, can such painful and embarrassing accounts of slavery and racial prejudice be part of dialogue? Some might even argue that Arab-Muslim enslavement of blacks 'is past history' and as such not an important contemporary issue.[4] It is true that societies cannot afford to become prisoners of history but need to look ahead if they are to progress meaningfully into the future.

However, it is equally true that we cannot afford to look meaningfully into the future without full knowledge of the past. Hence both the past and future are two sides of the coin of the life journey. We cannot afford to focus entirely on one to the neglect of the other. Moreover, contemporary relations between communities are rooted in the historical past. And to appreciate present relations meaningfully we have to know something about past encounters. To use the words of Joseph Hajjar, 'history is very much the mistress of our lives. We must take history very seriously if we are to look to the future.'[5] This is where awkward and difficult questions cannot be avoided within the context of

---

3. H. Küng, 'Christianity and World Religions: Dialogue with Islam', in L. Swidler (ed.), *Toward a Universal Theology of Religion* (Maryknoll: Orbis Books, 1987), p. 194.
4. Ali Abu Sinn, 'Comments', in Haseeb (ed.), *The Arabs and Africa*, p. 51. As we have shown in the preceding chapter, slavery, indeed chattel slavery, still persists in Muslim countries such as Sudan and Mauritania, and most certainly in Saudi Arabia and others.
5. Joseph Hajjar, 'Comments' at a Christian–Muslim conference, Chambésy, cited in *Christian Mission and Islamic Da'wah*, p. 97.

Encountering the Encounters: Arab-Islam and Black African Experience 173

dialogue. This is particularly so when one party in the dialogue assumes a self-righteous stance and makes absolute claims for themselves and others based on myths of a glorious historical past.

At a Christian–Muslim conference in Chambésy, in 1976, Muslim participants pointed out the effects of past Christian missionary activities on contemporary Muslim societies. They argued among other things that to pave the way for dialogue, 'the wrongs of the past should be rectified as far as possible', with one calling for 'a real Christian repentance' if the consultation was to be of any avail.[6] What the Muslim participants were rightly pointing out at the conference is that dialogue has to be based on trust and trust can only be established when we frankly address, acknowledge, and where possible redress all past mishaps and mischief. Of course, the Muslim participants were reminded by Middle Eastern Christian participants that Muslims are not themselves immune from 'wrongs of the past' and that acts of repentance have to be reciprocal.[7]

Commenting on the difficulties and awkward moments associated with dialogue within the context of the above conference, David Kerr made the following submission:

> This conference has taught me much which I believe to be important in dialogue; notably, that if our commitment to 'togetherness' is persistent, this itself can contain sharp and at times angry controversies ... which may then be turned to productive result. This conference must lay once and for all the suspicion of the skeptic that dialogue is a passing of courtesies, it never has been, and after this conference it never will be.[8]

There is no doubt that the issue of Muslim slavery, for instance, constitutes one of the sharpest, if not the sharpest, cutting edge in any discussion of the encounters between Islam and Africa, not least because 'it left extreme bitterness in the Central parts of the continent against the Arab minority which lived on the [East African] coast and among its consequences was the 1964 Revolution in Zanzibar'.[9] Some ethnic groups who fell victim to Muslim Fulani slave raids, such as the Longuda of Nigeria, are also known to be scornful towards Islam and the Hausa/Fulani because of their experience.[10] Commenting on the same issue, even Peter Clarke could not help but acknowledge that the jihad of northern Nigeria,

> in so far as it was a military conquest, involved loss of autonomy and a measure of enslavement for some of the non-Muslim peoples of the region,

6. See comments by Khurshid Ahmad and Isma'il R. al-Faruqi, in ibid., pp. 95–7.
7. See Joseph Hajjar's comments, ibid., p. 97.
8. Ibid., p. 14.
9. Y. Fadl Hasan, 'The Historical Roots of Afro-Arab Relations', in Haseeb (ed.), *The Arabs and Africa*, p. 33.
10. Gilliland, *African Religion Meets Islam*, pp. 57–64.

174 *The Legacy of Arab-Islam in Africa*

thereby creating fear of and opposition to Islam which still persist to this day in many of the so-called 'pagan' areas in the north of the country, such as the Jos Plateau and most of the present-day Benue state.[11]

The same feeling of bitterness, scornfulness and resentment towards Islam in general and Arabs in particular is apparent in the Sudan and other parts of sub-Saharan Africa as a direct result of Arab-Muslim enslavement.[12] Equally, on the Muslim side any mention of Muslim slavery is generally met with knee-jerk responses. When, in 1992, President Arap Moi of Kenya publicly made references to Muslim involvement in slavery in East Africa, Kenyan Muslims were incensed, interpreting it as an affront to Islam.[13]

Reacting to some views expressed by Western writers on Muslim slavery, Abul 'Ala Mawdūdī began by highlighting Western enslavement of Africans and concluded thus: 'This is the record of the people who denounce Muslims for recognizing the institution of slavery. It is as if a criminal is pointing the finger of blame at an innocent man.'[14] It is not uncommon to hear Muslims in general and Arab Muslims in particular dismiss any mention of Muslim slavery as part of Western anti-Islamic propaganda. These reactions only demonstrate how the difficult and sensitive issue of Muslim slavery has contributed to a near imposition of taboos on this rather important historical part of Muslim and non-Muslim history.

There is no doubt that Muslim reaction to the subject of slavery has contributed to the comparatively small amount of scholarly research in the area as compared to other forms of slavery in classical, medieval and modern times. Muslim reactions have also contributed in no small way to myths that have arisen in relation to scholarly research in Islamic history in general and Muslim slavery in particular, especially in post-modern liberal Western scholarship. There is no doubt that hostile Muslim reactions to Western scholarship on Islam has driven post-modern liberal Western scholarship on Islam into another form of paternalism which operates on the unstated principle that Muslims are unable or unwilling to accept critical and tough questions relating to the Islamic past or traditions. And so one is expected, in fact required, to be critical, of, say, Christian history and traditions but not of Islamic history and Islamic traditions.

This has come about mainly because Western scholarship is itself heavily laden with a sense of inherited guilt due to its own historical legacies in the slave trade, anti-Muslim polemics, missionary and colonial enterprises. So we have a situation where culprit–victim postures are adopted in contemporary Western–Muslim

---

11. Clarke, 'Islamic Reform', pp. 519–20.
12. Referring to this general anti-Arab feeling in Africa, Abdel Malik Auda, an Arab-Muslim scholar, comments that 'slavery, I believe, is an essential issue for the Africans, who have a fixed idea of the Arabs as "racists"': 'Comments' in Haseeb (ed.), *The Arabs and Africa*, p. 52.
13. KNCC Newsletter, *JPR News Analysis and Reports*, 30 June, 1993, p. 3.
14. A. Mawdūdī, *Human Rights in Islam* (Leicester: Islamic Foundation, 1976), p. 20.

Encountering the Encounters: Arab-Islam and Black African Experience 175

dialogue at the expense of historical truth and critical academic objectivity. This situation, in our opinion, undermines the integrity of dialogue and makes it all the more vulnerable to popular mistrust. As far as the history of Muslim slavery is concerned, it is the stories and life experiences of the slavers and their descendants, but even more so the victims and those who are inheritors of that history. Muslim sensibilities alone, important as they may be, cannot and should not be allowed to impose taboos on the subject.

The question, however, remains to be answered as to why Muslims generally appear, often resentfully, to resist taking a critical view of the less glorious aspects of the Islamic past. The general knee-jerk Muslim responses to any mention of such issues as Muslim slavery have some psycho-historical underpinnings. First is the historical backlog of inter-religious polemics, especially between the Christian Occident and Muslim Orient. Under these circumstances, Muslims and Christians down the ages have tried in their own ways to discredit each other's religion in a bid to prove how 'wrong', if not demonic, the other is in essence, and how 'right' and godly their own religion is.

Related to this are European colonial and missionary factors of the eighteenth and nineteenth centuries and their physical and psychological effects on 'Third World' countries, and Muslim countries for that matter. Muslim scholars, nationalists and activists have since come to view the political, technological, economic and military domination of the 'Christian' West as a form of humiliation. Consequently, some have become understandably resentful and suspicious of anything Western, especially Western scholarship and criticism of Islam. This, to some modern Muslim scholars, constitutes 'the most patent and direct challenge' which has faced and is still facing Muslims today.[15]

The legacy of competition, polemics, mutual stereotyping, suspicion and resentment is manifold. First is the culture of reactionary apologetics in which modern Muslim scholarship in general finds itself. This culture of reaction is the tendency to adopt what has become in a large measure defensive, apologetic, vindicative and, in its extremes, vindictive approaches.[16] Under such circumstances assessment of the Muslim Self is generally pursued in contra-distinction to the Western Other. The Self is thus hardly assessed in its own right. Loyalty to the Self becomes the watchword. Self-criticism is at best done in camera and at worst resented and regarded as a form of betrayal.

While it is no doubt right and indeed imperative to respond and critically evaluate the assumptions and in some cases pretensions of Western scholarship, such an irresistible attraction seems unfortunately to have become a distraction or an excuse for avoiding a critical assessment of the Self. The point we would

15. Rahman, *Islam*, p. 212.
16. For an overview of this trend reflected in modern Muslim perspectives on Christianity and the West, see K. Zebiri, *Muslims and Christians Face to Face* (Oxford: Oneworld, 1997).

176 *The Legacy of Arab-Islam in Africa*

like to make here is that it is high time Muslim scholarship and indeed 'Third World' scholarship in general assessed historical and contemporary issues relating to the Self outside the shadows of the Western Other.

In other words, Muslim scholarship may have to graduate from the hitherto apologetic, defensive, and self-vindicating discourses which can lead (and to some extent, have led) contemporary Muslim thought into what Akbar Ahmed, a Pakistani Muslim, called 'an intellectual cul-de-sac'.[17] The tendency to adopt defensive and apologetic postures has led to a situation in which important internal issues are either ignored or only superficially addressed. Muslim enslavement is one such issue, which, as we have pointed out in the preceding chapter, has been significantly whitewashed due to irresistible comparisons with its Western counterpart. And as rightly noted by Bernard Lewis, 'the imposition of taboos on topics of historical research can only impede and delay a better and more accurate understanding'.[18]

In the case of inherited religious traditions in general and modern Muslim scholarship in particular, the apparent lack of self-criticism and resentment of any such attempts has a psycho-confessional dimension. For instance, the Islamic past, especially the *salaf*, i.e. the first three generations of Muslim history, in the words of Fazlur Rahman, has come to be regarded 'not merely as an inspiring model but literally as law to be implemented without further interpretation or adjustment'. This situation, according to Rahman, resulted in the sanctification of the early history of Islam making it 'part of faith rather than of history'.[19]

A renowned Indonesian Muslim scholar, Nurcholish Majid, puts it as follows:

> The trouble with the Muslims is that they are not very aware about the history of their religion. Also, because of the traumatic experience of Muslims in the first decades, they tend to stay away from criticising the *Sahāba* [Companions]. This ends up with the tendency to glorify and even sacralize the first generation of Muslims.[20]

To some Muslims, not just the *salaf* but the whole of the past fourteen centuries of Islamic tradition are, in the words of one scholar 'a sacred and religious history'.[21] Writing on tradition the same scholar intimates elsewhere thus:

---

17. A. Ahmed, *Postmodernism and Islam: Predicament and Promise* (London: Routledge, 1992), p. 185. The writer was specifically referring to Edward Said's *Orientalism*, calling upon his fellow Muslims 'to move beyond Said's arguments', which, he thinks have contributed to leading Muslim thinking into such a state.
18. Lewis, *Race and Slavery*, p. vi.
19. Rahman, *Islam*, p. 236.
20. Nurcholish Majid, cited in Abdullah Saeed, 'Approaches to *Ijtihad* and Neo-modernist Islam in Indonesia', *Islam and Christian–Muslim Relations*, vol. 8, no. 3 (1997), p. 287.
21. S.H. Nasr, *Traditional Islam in the Modern World* (London: Kegan Paul International, 1987), p. 76.

Encountering the Encounters: Arab-Islam and Black African Experience 177

> Tradition is inextricably related to revelation and religion, to the sacred, to the notion of orthodoxy, to authority, to the continuity and regularity of transmission of the truth ... the meaning of tradition has become related more than anything else to that perennial wisdom which lies at the heart of every religion.[22]

The Islamic past has therefore been projected by Muslim devotion as a sacred heritage requiring, as a religious duty, absolute loyalty. So history and faith have become fused in Islam to the extent that criticism of the Islamic past and its inherited traditions by non-Muslims is seen as an attack on Islam. Muslims who take a critical view of the historical past are viewed as traitors. Thus most Muslim activists and scholars tend to take an uncritical, confessional and conservative view of their historical legacy. But the question that is normally not raised is, to what extent are the past fourteen hundred years of Islam a 'sacred history'? Does this sacredness include such sordid legacies as Muslim slavery? Surely, such inward-looking conservatism implicates rather than defends Islam as a faith from human weakness and wickedness.

What is happening under such circumstances is that Islam as a faith is employed as a shield for the actions of past and present generations of Muslims. This can be seen from the fact that most Muslims find it difficult to distinguish criticism of the behaviour of Muslims (past and present) from criticism of Islam as a faith, especially when such criticism ensues from non-Muslim quarters. However, by constantly employing Islam as a shield for what is sometimes indefensible human behaviour, Muslim devotion puts the faith up as an unintended object of attacks. The point is that while it is in nobody's interest to pretend that the worst was typical of the total, it is even less so to pretend that things were ideal when they were far from so.

But then there is also another trend in modern Muslim scholarship that admits the critical parts of Muslim history such as Muslim enslavement but seeks to 'exempt' Islam from these historical circumstances. They claim that 'the problem of Islam, as has been the problem of all religions before it, is that in the course of time, its followers deviated from the pure original teachings; this deviation leads to practices that are not in harmony with the original teachings of the religion'. For this reason, Islam

> is not what some or many of its followers do and practice; rather, it is a set of teachings and beliefs that are confirmed by the deeds and practices of the Prophet Muhammad, the early true pious Muslims, and the good, virtuous Muslims of all ages.[23]

Others, while accepting that 'Africa's woes and wounds were the products of the Arabo-Berber quest for gold and slaves', have insisted that 'Islam was not really

22. S.H. Nasr, *Knowledge and the Sacred* (Edinburgh: Edinburgh University, 1982), p. 68.
23. Abdallah, 'Islam, Slavery, and Racism', p. 44.

178 The Legacy of Arab-Islam in Africa

the motivating force behind such atrocities. Like Christianity in later years, it too, was an instrument of rationalization.'[24] Apart from the obvious difficulty as to whose understanding and interpretation of Islam qualifies as 'true', 'original' and 'pure', and by whose standards we are to judge who is a 'true', 'pious' and 'virtuous' Muslim, to attempt to extricate Islam from Muslim history in such a manner and project it as a set of ideals that were only put into practice by a few saints, if not angels, is problematic in itself. In any case, if Muslim slavery is as a result of deviation or misuse of Islam, it is amazing that Muslims, from the Companions in Arabia to India, Turkey and right across to West Africa, from the seventh down to the twenty-first century, could have got it so badly wrong on this one single issue.

To some of us arguments that Muslims involvement in enslavement down the generations was as a result of 'deviation' from or misuse of Islam is not persuasive, to say the least. In fact some may see such claims on the part of modern Muslim apologists as infantile escapism and a clear demonstration of Muslim inability and/or unwillingness to face up to the Islamic past. But even granted that all these pious Muslims down the generations got it all wrong or were so selfish as to misuse Islam to satisfy their selfish human needs, what do we do with this legacy? Do we simply brush it aside because it had nothing to do with 'true', 'pure' and 'original' Islam? Surely, dismissing it as 'deviations' from true Islamic teachings is not the answer.

It is in this regard that some Muslim scholars have called for an 'enlightened conservatism' in contemporary Muslim devotion. Such conservatism neither views the whole of Islamic history as 'sacred', and therefore to be upheld and defended at all costs, nor seeks to cut off the historical legacy of whole generations of Muslims from Islamic history; but rather critically examines the whole of Muslim history as part of the Islamic legacy and then discriminately employs what suits the contemporary context 'and relevant for the erection of an Islamic future'.[25]

To take a critical view of our history or rethink the import of inherited traditions is not necessarily the same as suggesting that past generations were wrong. Emphasizing this point, another well-known and highly respected Indonesian Muslim intellectual, Abdurrahman Wahid, intimates that 'current values should not be used to judge' past generations but that the present generation has to recognize and acknowledge that 'values have changed' and new approaches have to be adopted in some cases.[26] Enlightened conservatism – for which we shall shortly proceed to argue in relation to Arab-Islam in the light of the African experience – is also an essential prerequisite of dialogue in general

24. Nyang, *African Identity*, p. 49.
25. Rahman, *Islam*, p. 250. Nurcholish comments: 'Don't idolise the time and the life of the *Sahaba*': Saeed, 'Approaches to *Ijtihad*', p. 287.
26. See Saeed, 'Approaches to *Ijtihad*', p. 289.

Encountering the Encounters: Arab-Islam and Black African Experience 179

and dialogue between Muslim and non-Muslim in Africa in particular. To quote Leonard Swidler,

> Persons entering into interreligious, interideological dialogue must be at least minimally self-critical of both themselves and their own religious or ideological traditions. A lack of such self-criticism implies that one's own tradition already has all the correct answers. Such an attitude makes dialogue not only unnecessary, but impossible, since we enter into dialogue primarily so we can learn – which obviously is impossible if our tradition has never made a misstep, if it has all the answers.[27]

As we have remarked above, there is no doubt that contemporary relations between communities in general are rooted in the historical past. The historical past, which in itself was informed by religious and ideological traditions has made some significant 'missteps' as we have shown in the preceding two chapters. It is these 'missteps' that both the Arab-Muslim and black African sides have to acknowledge, and accept so that lessons can be learnt from them, to make dialogue worthwhile and sustainable. Unless we are prepared to react to history together, we are left with no alternative but to use history to react against each other.

For while we cannot afford to return to the past, we cannot either afford to behave as if we have no past with a local and immediate potential, or think we can extract one type of the past with its structures of domination and control in our contemporary situation while ignoring or denying other aspects. Indeed, these inherited religious and ideological traditions still, directly and/or indirectly, determine our contemporary attitudes and perceptions, for better or worse. So addressing and where possible redressing the sensitive and hostile aspects of inherited traditions is essential for dialogue.

Critical assessment of one's tradition in a dialogue situation does not necessarily mean a rejection of the tradition. On the contrary, as Leonard Swidler rightly intimates, 'to be sure, in interreligious, interideological dialogue one must stand within a religious or ideological tradition with integrity and conviction, but such integrity and conviction must include, not exclude, a healthy self-criticism. Without it there can be no dialogue, and, indeed, no integrity.'[28] In other words integrity and conviction in one's inherited traditions are vital elements in dialogue, but so also is self-criticism.

This may be called *critical faithfulness*. Some Muslims have argued with much soundness that critical faithfulness to the Islamic tradition is crucial to the present generation of Muslims if they are to 'reconstruct an Islamic future on an Islamic past'.[29] Acknowledging the 'missteps' within one's inherited tradition is,

27. L. Swidler, 'The Dialogue Decalogue: Ground Rules for Interreligious Dialogue', *Journal of Ecumenical Studies*, vol. 20, no. 1 (Winter 1983), p. 3.
28. Ibid.
29. Rahman, *Islam*, pp. 235–54.

180 The Legacy of Arab-Islam in Africa

first of all, a sign of strength rather than weakness. This strength of integrity is, as Swidler has rightly pointed out above, crucial for dialogue. Second, critical faithfulness to one's tradition will, on the one hand, help bring about restorative justice to victims, and prevent the injustices associated with these aspects from repeating themselves, on the other hand. Third, being critically faithful to one's tradition will enable an intelligent appropriation and adaptation of these traditions in contemporary times.

Finally, critical faithfulness will help bring about change in old and preconceived unhelpful attitudes and perceptions so as to promote mutual respect and peaceful co-existence between and among communities. Inter-religious and inter-ideological dialogue is therefore impossible without the parties involved being prepared to be critically faithful to the various inherited traditions. It is in this light that we proceed to highlight the need for critical faithfulness to the Arab-Islamic tradition within the context of pluralistic modern sub-Saharan Africa.

THE NEED TO RETHINK ARAB-ISLAM IN LIGHT OF THE AFRICAN EXPERIENCE

Having argued for the need to acknowledge historical facts unequivocally (no matter how awkward or painful) in the interests of dialogue, we shall now proceed to argue for the need to be critically faithful to inherited traditions, which in our present context is Islam, in the light of the African experience. In view of the fact that Africans have been active parties in the encounters as the main agents of Islamization in Africa and can be said to be the principal brokers of the Arab-Islamic legacy in contemporary Africa, the responsibility of rethinking Islam in this regard is, primarily, that of Africans in general and African Muslims in particular.

For the purpose of elucidation we shall first of all highlight what is meant by the African experience in this context. We will then go on to look briefly at the course of religious (Christian and Muslim) orientations in Africa and their implications for inter-religious dialogue within the African context. Our primary working premise in this connection is that the Muslim perception of the Islamic tradition in Africa has to be critically examined in the light of past and present African experience for the sake of a sustainable Muslim–non-Muslim dialogue in Africa.

The African Experience: A Definition

With regard to the African experience, what we have in mind is the present configuration of the socio-religious and political environment of Africa evolved during the historical and continued encounters with external civilizations such as Arab-Islam and Western Christianity. It is the resultant configuration of Arab-Muslim and Western-Christian encounters with Africans and their indigenous worldviews that, collectively, make up the African experience we are talking about here. The African experience is, therefore, the socio-religious and political product of the historical encounters with these two religious civilizations through which Africans now perceive themselves (as individuals, families, communities and nations), encounter one another and others and are perceived and encountered by others.

A basic feature of the African experience, therefore, is that it is mainly tripartite, the major constituent components being the indigenous African socio-religious heritage, the Arab-Islamic tradition in its varied orientations, and the Western-Christian missionary/colonial legacies in their various denominational and political strands. Thus, the African experience or heritage within the context of our present discussion may be broadly categorized into what may be called the *basic* or *common* indigenous African heritage and the resulting *collective* African heritage/identity. The basic or common heritage here does not necessarily refer to homogeneity of features but homogeneity of status as the host or receiving traditions to such incoming traditions as Islam and Christianity.

The basic African heritage, therefore, refers to the various indigenous religious and cultural traditions and values from which Africans first encountered Islam (and Christianity), and in which many of them still live to a great extent, even as Muslims and Christians. These may include the different vernacular languages, socio-religious norms, values, ceremonies, names, and all such distinctive characteristics of Africans not shared by Europeans, Arabs or Asians. We refer to these as basic and common because they are the core of modern African identity, i.e. that which is shared by, say, Yoruba Muslims and Christians and not by their Middle Eastern or European co-religionists.

The collective African experience, on the other hand, refers to what Ali Mazrui identifies as Africa's 'triple heritage'.[30] Namely, the various indigenous traditions, the Arab-Islamic and the Western-Christian socio-religious and political legacies taken together. The collective African experience manifests itself from harmonious fusion and mutual co-existence to parallelism, competition and potential conflict, within individuals, families and nations. Throughout Africa, these traditions are not compartmentalized. At the individual level, there are those who might see themselves as Christians, Muslims or Traditionalists but continue to participate actively in certain rites and ceremonies of the other traditions.

For instance, it is common to find a Muslim going to Christian prayers for healing, a Christian using Muslim amulets and charms for the success of his/her

---

30. See Mazrui, *Triple Heritage*.

182 *The Legacy of Arab-Islam in Africa*

business and, perhaps most common of all, both Muslims and Christians actively involved in traditional African socio-religious festivals and rites. At the liturgical and organizational levels, it is equally common to find elements of traditional African religions incorporated into Muslim or Christian ceremonies and vice versa. Similarly, Muslims incorporate Christian ways of doing things into their religious and social ceremonies and vice versa.[31] This situation may be attributed to the open-ended nature of the African perception of 'religion' delineated in chapter 2.

Another related feature of the African experience is religious plurality. By religious plurality we mean the sharing of different religious traditions by the same families (immediate and extended), the same ethnic groups and nations. At the family level, it is common in Africa to find Christians, Muslims and Traditionalists living as members of the same family. It is also common to find an ethnic group (e.g. the Yoruba of Nigeria and the Boganda of Uganda) sharing the Muslim, Christian and indigenous traditions. The religious constitutions of African states bear an even more graphic testimony to the religious plurality of the continent.[32]

The different traditions, both in terms of membership and influence, constitute modern African states, and collectively hold sway throughout sub-Saharan Africa. What is, perhaps, unique about the religious plurality of Africa is that unlike, say, Western 'Christian' Europe and Muslim North Africa, the Middle East, etc. where the religious Other largely corresponds to immigrant or non-indigenous communities, in Africa the religious Other are blood relations, members of same ethnic and linguistic unit or fully fledged fellow nationals; Ghanaians, Nigerians, Kenyans, etc. Religious plurality within the African context is, therefore, a reality and not an academic theory.

Yet another feature of the African experience relates to the bonded communal nature of African societies. This bonded nature of African societies

---

31. J. Kenny, 'Religious Movements in Nigeria, Divisive or Cohesive? Some Interpretative Models', *Orita*, vol. 16, no. 2 (December 1984), pp. 122–6. The areas of incorporation include such rites as birth, marriage, death, and also names, styles of evangelism, etc. Purists on both sides would regard this as syncretism or 'mixing', but the ordinary African Muslim or Christian may not necessarily pay much concern to doctrinal controversies.

32. For instance, out of the fifty or so nation states in tropical Africa, one can confidently talk of clear Muslim majorities in ten. These are Mauritania, Senegal, Gambia, Guinea, Mali, Niger, Sudan, Somalia, Djibouti and Eritrea. In the rest Muslims are either neck-and-neck with Christians and traditional believers, as in Nigeria and Tanzania, or generally in the minority: Ghana 16 per cent; Cameroon 25 per cent; Ivory Coast 28 per cent; Ethiopia 32 per cent; Mozambique 14 per cent; South Africa 2 per cent; Zaire 2 per cent; Kenya 8 per cent; Tanzania 34 per cent; Uganda 7 per cent; Malawi 14 per cent; Zimbabwe 1 per cent; Zambia 0.5 per cent; Congo 1 per cent. See, J. Haafkens, *Islam and Christianity in Africa* (Nairobi: Procmura, 1991), pp. 2–4 and appendix.

Encountering the Encounters: Arab-Islam and Black African Experience 183

is beautifully, albeit romantically, expressed by Archbishop Desmond Tutu of South Africa. He writes:

> In our African idiom ... a person is a person through other persons. We are made for fellowship, for *koinonia*, for friendship, for togetherness because we can be human only together. We are made for inter-dependence and an absolute self-sufficient human being is that [much] less a human being. When we flout this basic law of our being, then all kinds of things go very wrong.[33]

Due to the inter-related nature of the African experience one cannot afford to talk about the course of any of the traditions in complete isolation from or opposition to the others. To do that would be courting social disharmony and bloodshed, as is happening in the Sudan and on many occasions in Nigeria. Thus, while individual Africans or communities may regard themselves as Christians, Muslims or indigenous religious practitioners, there are two fundamental realities of the African experience that none can afford to deny.

First, that Africans have something unique (such as shared historical and geographical experiences, cultural values, or languages) that collectively distinguish them from their Muslim or Christian co-religionists in the Middle East or Europe; and second, that Africa's collective heritage, i.e. the resulting socio-religious, political, ethnic and linguistic plurality of the African experience, is a state and not a phase. This means that Africans do not only have to learn to live with but find ways of celebrating this diversity. Any system, political or religious, that fails to take cognizance of the inherent diversity of the African context or seeks to treat any ethnic or religious group(s) as anything other than nationals with equal rights and responsibilities is bound to be a recipe for conflict.

Hence, the following discussion on the course of religious orientation in general and of Arab-Islam in particular within the African context will be undergirded by the historical and contemporary realities of the African experience as explained here. The underlying contention in the rest of the chapter will be that, to deal with the hostile and sensitive aspects of the past encounters, Africans cannot avoid taking their historical and contemporary fundamental realities into account in conceptualizing and actualizing their particular inherited religious and socio-political traditions.

Religious, Mainly Muslim, Orientations in Africa

As indicated in chapter 1, a near-consensus post-independent African perception of Africa's encounters with the West is that the latter has exploited both the human and material resources, undermined and subverted Africa's collective

---

33. Archbishop Desmond Tutu, 'The Religious Understanding of Peace', in Gerrie Lubbe (ed.), *A Decade of Interfaith Dialogue, Desmond Tutu Peace Lectures* (Johannesburg: South African Chapter of the World Conference on Religion and Peace, 1994), p. 13.

184 *The Legacy of Arab-Islam in Africa*

dignity and cultural identity through the slave trade, missionary activities and colonialism. In other words, Africa's encounter with the West has, in some important respects, brought about material and cultural poverty. The generality of African Muslims share this general, if rather elitist, perception towards Western imperial and missionary enterprise in Africa. Ali Mazrui is only one of many African-Muslim scholars who have written on the impact of Western-Christian civilization on the black African.

Mazrui argues, among other things, that the Christian West accomplished 'the dis-Africanisation of the collective pride' of Africans through various processes of cultural imperialism. These Mazrui identifies as the imposition of Anglo-Saxon and Hebraic names upon imported black slaves; 'a ruthless negative indoctrination' whereby slaves were taught to accept their condition; a religious disenfranchisement whereby African slaves were deprived of their traditional religious heritage; and linguistic dis-Africanization through the imposition of the masters' languages. As a result, Mazrui further expounds, modern Africans both in Africa and the West in their responses have embarked upon a process of 're-Africanisation' or 'cultural revivalism',[34] geared towards an African self-assertion and self-definition.

We are not going to concern ourselves with the details of the various aspects of Mazrui's claims. What interests us within the context of our present discussion is, first of all, the underlying thesis that Africans in their encounter with Western-Christian civilization have gone (and are still going) through a process of cultural imperialism and the subversion of their collective dignity and identity. The second issue of interest is the thesis that as a result of the 'dis-Africanization' processes, Africans, both on the continent and in the diaspora, in their own ways have embarked upon a wave of cultural revivalism or 're-Africanization'. This cultural revivalism and 're-Africanization' entails a challenge to and rejection of Western cultural and racial chauvinism.

African Christians, as we have pointed out in chapter 1, in line with this trend have, since independence, taken a critical, and in some cases hostile, view of Christianity in its Western trappings, on the one hand, and, on the other hand, have grown in their affirmation and appropriation of indigenous elements in their expression of Christianity. Speaking on dialogue with traditional African religions, Pope John Paul II intimated that 'a serene and prudent dialogue will be able ... to foster the assimilation of positive values'. The Holy Father continues: 'adherents of African traditional religion should therefore be treated with great respect and esteem, and all inaccurate and disrespectful language should be avoided'.[35]

---

34. Mazrui, *Triple Heritage*, pp. 109–11.
35. Pope John Paul II, in the Post-synodal Apostolic Exhortation, Ecclesia in Africa, released on 14 September, 1995. Cited from *World Mission*, August 1997, p. 26. The

Encountering the Encounters: Arab-Islam and Black African Experience   185

While the Pope was no doubt talking on behalf of the Roman Catholic Church, his remarks, generally speaking – with the exception of Neo-Pentecostal Churches (largely urban-based American-inspired ministries) who remain hostile to indigenous traditions – are representative of the Christian churches' position on dialogue with indigenous Africa. The study of African traditional religion(s) has since been made an essential part of theological training in Catholic and mainline Protestant seminaries across the continent.

Affirming this trend in Christian religious orientation in Africa, S.S. Nyang writes:

> Christian missionaries working in African lands are now more tolerant and accommodating [of indigenous African elements], and their new spirit of evangelism has opened doors of co-operation which were effectually closed when their more intolerant brethren tried to run down the African's throat an undigested Christianity which is more European than Christian.[36]

Hence, it can be said that the Christian tradition in Africa is at least at what Leonard Swidler calls 'the first phase of dialogue'[37] with indigenous African traditions, namely the unlearning of misinformation and prejudices about indigenous traditions with attempts to affirm and appropriate their values.

AFRICAN-ORIENTED MUSLIM REFORM TENDENCIES

As we have pointed out above, African Muslims take part, and rightly so, in the critical assessment of the effects of the Western-Christian legacy on Africa. The Islamic tradition has its own examples, albeit controversial and generally unpopular, of African Muslims attempting to de-emphasize the Arab factor in Islam. These trends include what Ali Mazrui describes as 'the phenomenon of indigenisation through prophetic intervention and purposeful religious reform' aimed at 'giving greater native meaning to the imported religions or seeking to close a cultural and psychological gap which Islam and Christianity have sometimes created in Africa'.[38]

An example of this within the Islamic tradition in Africa is, first of all, manifested in the claims and teachings of one Seydina Mouhamoudou Limamou Laye (1845-1909).[39] Limamou, a native of Yoff, a small village north of Dakar, capital of modern-day Senegal, claimed in 1884 that he was a reincarnation of

weakness, though, of the churches' position on dialogue with African religions is that such 'dialogue' is seen 'as a preparation for the Gospel ... in fulfilment of [the churches'] evangelizing mission'. Ibid.

36. Nyang, *African Identity*, pp. 68–9.
37. Swidler, 'Dialogue Decalogue', p. 4.
38. Mazrui, *Triple Heritage*, p. 150.
39. M. Singleton, 'Seydina Mouhamoudou Limamou Laye (1845–1909) – The Black Mahdi of Senegal', *CSIC Papers*, no. 2, August 1990. The information on Limamou is largely derived from this article.

186 The Legacy of Arab-Islam in Africa

the Prophet of Islam. This was in the wake of a succession of mahdist claims by numerous Muslim divines, and a corresponding zeal to 'reform' Islam within the central and western Sudan region.

Limamou founded a religious confraternity, the Layennes but, unlike most mahdist claimants in the region, preached not a military jihad but the fear of God, respect for the lawful authority of rulers and parents, purity and conjugal fidelity. Limamou encouraged the use of Wolof instead of Arabic in chanting, a practice still common among Layennes in modern-day Senegal. Biographers, who are mainly Layennes themselves, depict Limamou variously as a hero, an inspired leader, a sage and a very good patriot for the Wolof, Senegalese and the black race.

He is reported to have castigated those who doubted his claim as *mahdi* thus: 'Is it the colour of my skin which prevents you from believing? You would not have hesitated had I been white.' While at one stage he told those he felt were too impressed with the prestige of the Arabic language that 'on the day of the resurrection I will speak to you in Wolof'.[40] One biographer maintains that Limamou,

> consciously or unconsciously, accomplished a genuine spiritual revolution. In fact, at that time, Senegalese, indeed Africans as such, especially the Wolof and Lebou were convinced of the inferiority of the black race. In their eyes the negro would not be a divine envoy, was not even worthy to be one, as it seemed to them he was not much more than one of the damned of this earth. Limamou showed the opposite and proved that the black race was as worthy if not more so than any other, that God created men differently and did not privilege some races more than others. One can ask oneself today if the apostle of God, Limamou Laye, was not also one of the first pioneers of negritude, albeit a misunderstood one.[41]

To his followers, therefore, Limamou was someone who held high the flag of Wolof, Senegalese and black African dignity and identity within the context of racial and religious chauvinism. Hence some of them, like the biographer quoted above, called for Limamou's mission to be recognized and placed within the wider context of African self-assertion and self-determination.

Within the same trend of asserting an African image from within the Islamic tradition in Africa, is the controversial Maitatsine movement of northern Nigeria.[42] This is a sect founded by one Mohammadu Marwa (d. 1980), a Cameroonian national who lived for a long time in northern Nigeria, established

40. Ibid., pp. 5, 8.
41. Ibid., pp. 8–9.
42. Allan Christelow, 'Religious Protest and Dissent in Northern Nigeria: From Mahdism to Qur'ānic Integralism', *Journal of the Institute of Muslim Minority Affairs*, vol. 6, no. 2 (July 1985), pp. 375–88; M. Adeleye Ojo, 'The Maitatsine Revolution in Nigeria', *American Journal of Islamic Social Sciences*, vol. 2, no. 2 (1985), pp. 297–306.

Encountering the Encounters: Arab-Islam and Black African Experience 187

himself as a renowned Muslim scholar, patronized by politicians and business-men and widely respected by the masses of Kano state. Marwa went on *hājj* in 1971, and proclaimed himself a prophet in 1980 with the mission of cleansing and purifying Islam. He decried materialism, the possession of bicycles and wristwatches, the use of tobacco, all traits of the affluent Muslim elite of Kano.

Marwa is said to have prohibited his followers from mentioning the name of the Prophet of Islam, calling him an Arab, rejected the Sunna as a source for Muslim faith and behaviour, insisting that the Qur'an was the only valid guide for Muslims. He reportedly ordered his followers to pray three times a day instead of the traditional five times; prohibited them from facing Mecca during prayers (a practice he insisted arose from the custom of Muhammad) on the basis of a Qur'anic text which says, 'And unto Allah belongs East and West, so whatever way you turn, there is the Face of God' (Sura 2: 115).[43]

Marwa's teaching was understandably seen as a threat not only to 'orthodox' Islam but the status quo. This resulted in bloody conflicts in Kano and other parts of northern Nigeria in the early 1980s during which he apparently died from injuries sustained from one such riot. Marwa was subsequently depicted as a lunatic in the press, a wild heretic by the religious authorities and a threat to political stability by the political leadership.

Mervyn Hiskett characteristically joined the bandwagon of the establishment, casting aspersions on Marwa and his movement, calling him a 'cenobitic leader', 'the Kano heresiarch', 'flagrantly unIslamic', and concludes from unsubstantiated allegations against the group that they were 'animists or at any rate only faint Muslims, still strongly imbued with animist culture'.[44] Hiskett, nevertheless, acknowledges the 'remarkable appeal' of Marwa's preaching and attributes it to the fact that

> he angled his interpretations to accommodate a largely non-literate congregation for whom the classical exegesis, based on classical Arabic, and on a Middle Eastern environmental frame of reference, was a closed book. Instead, the Maitatsine related his tafsir to the local West African scene with which the perceptions of such a congregation could readily cope.[45]

In other words the focus of Marwa's teaching was the local West African context with which his followers could readily identify rather than the classical exegesis based on an Arab Middle Eastern frame of reference. Notwithstanding the actual

43. M. Hiskett, 'The Maitatsine Riots in Kano, 1980: An Assessment', *Journal of Religion in Africa*, vol. 17, no. 3 (1987), p. 219.
44. Ibid., 217. Hiskett, however, arrived at this conclusion by merely implying that no 'good' Muslim can do some of the things Marwa and his followers were alleged to have been involved in, i.e. dealings in human parts. And so they must have been 'animists', even though Hiskett provides no evidence whatsoever of such practices among the so-called 'animists' themselves.
45. Ibid., p. 218.

188 *The Legacy of Arab-Islam in Africa*

content of his reform programme, which has come down largely from antagonists whose aims have been to discredit the movement, amongst the inspirations that may be deduced to explain Marwa's anti-Arab stance, is an African self-assertion and self-determination.

Ali Mazrui observes that 'the most distinctive yearning within his [Maitatsine] sect was a burning desire for the Africanisation of Islam, which later became a burning desire for an African prophet'.[46] Indeed, newspaper reports during the riots at Kaduna in 1980 suggested that his followers regarded him as a prophet for Africans.[47] Hence, even though Marwa was killed and his corpse burnt in flagrant disregard of Islamic teaching, the appeal of his teaching did not necessarily die with him and, as observed by Allan Christelow, might have gone into 'a sort of hijra underground'.[48]

In a less dramatic way but still within the trend of de-emphasizing the Arabicity of Islam in Africa is a controversy involving Shaykh Muhammad Ramiya, son and successor of Shaykh Ramiya, former slave and founder of the Qadariyya order in East Africa. Shaykh Muhammad was engaged in a controversy over the ethnicity of Muhammad in the late 1930s. A letter written in 1938 by the acting district commissioner reporting the controversy to his provincial superior spoke of

> an unfortunate internal dissension ... that has sprung up in Bagamoyo township among the local Moslem leaders. A short time ago Sheikh Mohamed Ramia (son of a former liwali, and a Manyema by tribe) pronounced twice in a local Mosque that the Prophet was not an Arab. Other Sheikhs and local Arabs were incensed at this heretical statement, while many adherents of the religion took a keen interest in the matter.[49]

Shaykh Muhammad, who himself described the incident as 'an enormous controversy', contended that even though Muhammad was physically born of Arab parentage, he was man of all races: 'He was a personage of Arabs, Swahilis and other peoples.'[50] In the shaykh's opinion, the universal nature of Muhammad's prophethood overrides his ethnic affiliation though the former does not completely deny the latter.

Although the shaykh did not declare himself *mahdi* or prophet, as did Limamou and Marwa respectively, his stance was seen as heretical. But even

---

46. Mazrui, *Triple Heritage*, p. 36.
47. P.M. Lubeck, 'Structural Determinants of Urban Islamic Protest in Northern Nigeria: A Note on Method, Mediation and Materialist Explanation', in W.R. Roff (ed.), *Islam and the Political Economy of Meaning: Comparative Studies of Muslim Discourse* (Berkeley and Los Angeles: University of California, 1987), p. 105.
48. Christelow, 'Religious Protest and Dissent', p. 389.
49. Cited in A.H. Nimtz, *Islam and Politics in East Africa: The Sufi Order in Tanzania* (Minneapolis: University of Minnesota, 1980), pp. 138–9.
50. Ibid., p. 139.

Encountering the Encounters: Arab-Islam and Black African Experience 189

more importantly his statement on Muhammad's ethnicity have been described by one '*alim* as a reflection of 'a long-standing dislike Shaykh Muhammad had for the Arabs, which was based largely on their former role as slave traders and owners, particularly as it involved his father'.[51]

Added to this was the growing perception of Arabs, Asians and Europeans as racial chauvinists amongst people of African descent in the region in general and Bagamoyo in particular. Hence, the dispute about Muhammad's ethnicity 'resulted from the effort of former slaves, in the person of Shaykh Muhammad, to undermine the influence of the Arabs, the former slave owners, in the religious sphere'.[52] Sentiments of African self-assertion and self-determination within the Islamic religious tradition in the East African context remain pronounced.

However, it must be made clear that these trends remain on the periphery of Islamic religious orientation in Africa. As we have seen, they are spurned by the religious establishment as untenable. Indeed, some contemporary African-Muslim scholars regard such African-oriented reform tendencies as part of the mischief of the European legacy. For 'the identity crisis' faced by African-Muslims as expressed through the above-mentioned tendencies came about 'precisely because Europeans had dis-Africanised Muhammad by making Africa end at the Red Sea' instead of the Persian Gulf.[53]

As far as such Muslim scholars are concerned, the answer is geographical, i.e. a redefinition of Africa's boundaries to make the Arabian Peninsula part of Africa. Meanwhile some Arab-Muslim nationalists contemptuously dismiss attempts by non-Arab Muslims to contest the Arab factor in Islam as 'naïve provincialism ... doomed never to behold the universally moral, the ethically final, but wallow in particularism and utility until a stream of being with destiny and conscious of its mission – be it the Arab or some other stream – sweeps them off to oblivion'.[54] Thus, reform towards the orient appears to have an upper hand. This we now proceed to examine.

CONSERVATIVE MUSLIM REVIVALIST TRENDS

The trend that appears most confident within the range of Muslim religious orientations in Africa is that which is commonly referred to in contemporary discourse as 'Muslim fundamentalist' or 'Islamist'. Because of the controversial connotations these terms have come to acquire, we shall refer to this trend in its

51. Ibid. Indeed, Shaykh Muhammad's radical and self-assertive disposition is reflected in his rejection of anything that would perpetuate his subservient status before the former masters of his father such as availing himself of help from them in times of need. Ibid., p. 100.
52. Ibid., p. 140.
53. Mazrui, *Triple Heritage*, p. 36.
54. Al-Faruqi, '*Urubah*, p. 199.

190 *The Legacy of Arab-Islam in Africa*

diverse manifestations as 'conservative Muslim revivalist trends'. Revival rather than reform because the former as far as the agents of this trend are concerned means a return to the 'true' or 'original' expression of Islam and a corresponding denial of virtue in non-Islam.

Within this broad category can be located such movements and governments as the Wahhābiyya Movement, founded by Muhammad Ibn 'Abd al-Wahhāb (d. 1787) of Saudi Arabia; the *Ikhwān al-Muslimūn* or Muslim Brotherhood, founded by Hasan al-Banna (d. 1949) of Egypt; the Islamic government of the Sudan; to some extent the *Jamā'at-i Islāmi*, literally the 'Islamic Party', founded by Sayyid Abul 'Ala Mawdūdī (d. 1979) of Pakistan; the Islamic Revolution of Iran ushered in by Ayatollah Khomeini in 1979; and a host of others. Between and within the above-mentioned groups, details of the 'true' or 'original' Islam are, of course, fraught with controversies.[55]

Within the tropical African context, the eighteenth- and nineteenth-century jihad movements discussed in chapter 3 historically represent the conservative revivalist tradition. In the present-day African context, the trend, localized and fragmented, is continued mainly by individuals and groups who overtly or covertly draw inspiration from the jihad tradition and/or the groups and governments mentioned above. In this regard Wahhābiyya-inspired revivalist trends, in their various local designations, appear to be the most active in contemporary Africa.[56]

Some of the basic features of the conservative revivalist trends include the inclination to be self-righteous, rigid, exclusivist and doctrinaire, in addition to a monolithic reading of the Islamic past in general and the inherited Islamic tradition in Africa in particular; a hankering for Islam in its Arab cultural trappings and the jihad models of eighteenth- and nineteenth-century Africa with a corresponding longing for their revival; a denial of any virtue in indigenous African traditions and Western democracies; and within the Muslim community itself, an avowed anti-Sufi stance.

In line with the jihadists, Muslim radicals such as Ibraheem Sulaiman, whose views are very influential in northern Nigeria, use terms like *kufr* (unbelief) to refer to everything that is non-Islamic; non-Muslims are 'unbelievers' and 'enemies' of God and any associations with them abhorred as un-Islamic. Sulaiman writes:

> A Muslim is not a person who merely believes, but rather a person who practises Islam and, in addition, hates unbelief, its symbols and men ...
> A person who, in spite of being a Muslim, fraternizes with unbelievers and

---

55. For a critical analysis of the internal dynamics of the 'fundamentalists' programmes and thought, see O. Roy, *The Failure of Political Islam*, trans. C. Volk (London: I.B. Tauris, 1994).
56. Hunwick, 'Sub-Saharan Africa'; L. Kaba, *The Wahhabiyya: Islamic Reform and Politics in West Africa* (Evanston: Northwestern University, 1974).

Encountering the Encounters: Arab-Islam and Black African Experience 191

innovators and [seeks] worldly benefit from them is, to all intents and purposes, a hypocrite. The people of the Sunna have to keep their distance from those who are the declared enemies of Allah: how can anyone claim to be a lover of Allah if he fraternizes with His enemies?[57]

Jihad, according to Sulaiman, is 'an ideological war between a believer and an unbeliever, or between a Muslim nation and an unbelieving power, with the sole purpose, from the Muslim's perspective, of either preserving the order of Islam or establishing it'. He then goes on to write:

> This struggle should, however, not merely seek to sweep the polytheists from power but should establish the rule of Islam ... The ideal here is a situation in which 'all religions will have perished except Islam'. In addition, Muslims are obliged to continue putting pressure on unbelievers until their false life is weakened beyond recovery.[58]

Jihad therefore remains a religious duty incumbent upon Muslims as long as 'unbelief' and 'unbelievers' remain on the face of earth. Umar Abdullahi approvingly quotes a Companion of Muhammad 'as saying, while holding a sword by his right hand and a Qu'ran by his left hand and pointing at the two: "We are directed by the Messenger of Allah to hit with this [the sword] who deviates from this [the Qur'an]"'.[59] Ironically Sulaiman insists that 'yet jihad is not inhumane: despite its necessary violence and bloodshed, its ultimate desire is peace, which is protected and enhanced by the rule of law'.[60] Peace and rule of law indeed! Muslims cannot accept modern-day secular and democratic systems of governance because these are the products of Christianity and therefore constitute 'unbelief'.

Like the eighteenth- and nineteenth-century jihadists who renounced the socio-political institutions of the time, contemporary Muslim revivalists regard Western-inspired democratic pluralism, which essentially involves choice, as *kufr.* Sulaiman writes:

> To the extent that secularism was imposed on the people by the same power that imposed Christianity, the two approaches to life can logically be construed as representing the two faces of the same coin: Western Imperialism. Muslims have therefore no reason to accept secular values, or to have any faith in secularism.[61]

57. I. Sulaiman, *The Islamic State and the Challenge of History: Ideals, Policies and Operations of the Sokoto Caliphate* (London: Mansell, 1987), p. 3.
58. Sulaiman, *Revolution in History*, p. 120.
59. Abdullahi, *Political Thought*, pp. 69–70.
60. Sulaiman, *Revolution in History*, p. 131.
61. I. Sulaiman, 'Islam and Secularism in Nigeria: An Encounter of Two Civilisations', *Impact International* (10–23 October, 1986), p. 8.

192 The Legacy of Arab-Islam in Africa

Sulaiman goes on to insist that Muslims 'want the full restoration of Islam, as a religion, as a polity, as a civilisation' because 'Islam by its integrative and all-embracing nature renders Secularism even in its best form irrelevant'. The only acceptable framework for Muslims, as far as he is concerned, is the model established by Muhammad in seventh-century Madina:

> This is the eternal, unalterable model the Sunnah laid down by the blessed Prophet for all times, and for mankind. It is, moreover, the only acceptable framework for Muslims. Muslims have, therefore, an eternal obligation not merely to live as a religious community, but to set up for themselves a state which will safeguard the interests of all people and enhance their moral integrity; a state where Islamic ideals can be given concrete manifestation.[62]

On Muslims living under non-Muslim authority or rule, Abubakar Mahmud Gumi, one time grand mufti (supreme Islamic judge) of Nigeria, in line with the nineteenth-century jihadist views, thinks it is incompatible with Islam to have a non-Muslim in leadership position over Muslims. Gumi thinks it is not acceptable to have a non-Muslim as leader of a political party to which Muslims belong or for Muslims to live under a non-Muslim head of state. Gumi declared: 'I don't think a Moslem can join a party where a non-Moslem is leading', and if Christians refuse to join a party led by Muslims then 'there will appear a two party system' and 'the two party system ... will not be south against north but Islam against Christianity'.[63]

Even in South Africa, where Muslims constitute less than 2 per cent of the population, during the 1994 elections some Muslim groups found it unthinkable to vote for non-Muslim candidates because Muslims 'will not be ruled by kaffirs, meaning blacks'.[64] This is because, as far as the conservative reformists are concerned, it is simply 'absurd to have a pagan at the head of a country that is largely Muslim'.[65] Gumi insists elsewhere that 'Nigerian unity is to try to convert Christians and non-Muslims ... until the other religions become minorities and do not affect our society'.[66]

So crucial is Muslim political supremacy over non-Muslims that Gumi is prepared to compromise on *ikhtilat* (the mixing of men and women in public places), strongly condemned by Dan Fodio and prohibited in Islamic states such as Saudi Arabia. Gumi compromised on *ikhtilat* in order to allow Muslim women to take part in election procedures so as to enhance the chances of

---

62. Ibid, p. 9.
63. Abubakar Mahmud Gumi, interview in *Quality* (Lagos), October 1987, cited in Clarke, 'Islamic Reform', p. 530.
64. F. Esack, *Qur'an, Liberation and Pluralism: An Islamic Perspective of Interreligious Solidarity against Oppression* (Oxford: Oneworld, 1997), pp. 219–21.
65. Sulaiman, *Revolution in History*, p. 124.
66. S.A. Gumi, cited in F.O. Nwaiwu, 'Interreligious Dialogue in an African Context' (Ph.D. thesis, Pontificia Universitas Urbaniana, 1989), p. 75, n. 61.

Encountering the Encounters: Arab-Islam and Black African Experience 193

Muslim candidates over their non-Muslim opponents.[67] It is interesting that Gumi is bending the rules here not so as to give back to women their inalienable political right but to ensure that non-Muslims don't gain political authority over Muslims. As far as Gumi is concerned 'this religion [Islam], if you do not protect it, it will not protect you', and the only way to protect Islam is for Muslims to gain political dominance over their non-Muslim fellow nationals. For, according to Gumi, 'politics is more important than prayer'.[68]

Mervyn Hiskett came to the painful realization that such an inflexible attitude on the part of present-day Muslims is 'perhaps the greatest problem facing a would-be democratic and pluralist Nigeria; and, indeed, at the global level, it may be among the most intractable problems that face the non-Muslim world today'.[69] Some people may, as usual, dismiss such observations as alarmist and accuse us of exaggeration. But we need to bear in mind that most if not all the most dastardly human acts in history, be it the Holocaust, Rwandan genocide or the ethnic cleansing in the former Yugoslavia, almost always grew out of and fed upon xenophobic rhetoric. When such rhetoric is allowed to go on unchallenged, it is only a matter of time for a Hitler to emerge and turn it into an attractive ideology to be pursued and implemented as official policy.

On attitudes towards traditional African culture and ways of life, African Muslims in general regard the traditional African worldview as 'a *period of ignorance*' (*jahiliyyh*) with Islam ushering in a period of '*enlightenment*'.[70] Even among Yoruba Muslims where there has been a great deal of acceptance of traditional customs, there have been sermons against and condemnation of Muslim acceptance of traditional Yoruba practices such as the use of indigenous Yoruba names and deference and humility shown before traditional rulers.[71] Others such as Ibraheem Sulaiman, have written approvingly of the jihadist destruction of traditional African ways of life, lamenting European intervention that halted such mayhem, and in fact blame Europeans for interrupting and preventing Islam from accomplishing a noble task.[72]

Still some regard trends of reviving indigenous African culture as 'a threat to Islam' comparable to secularism, albeit a lesser threat.[73] Others, such as Ibraheem Sulaiman are more radical and forthright in referring to African

---

67. Interview with Gumi quoted in Allan Christelow, 'Three Islamic Voices in Contemporary Nigeria', in Roff (ed.), *Islam and the Political Economy of Meaning*, p. 233.
68. Ibid.
69. M. Hiskett, 'Preface', p. xii.
70. E.D. Adelowo, 'Islamic Monotheism and the Muslim Reaction to Christian and Traditional African Concepts of the Godhead', *The Islamic Quarterly*, vol. 24, nos. 1 and 2 (1980), p. 127.
71. Clarke, 'Islamic Reform', p. 523.
72. Nyang, *African Identity*, p. 40.
73. Mazrui, *Triple Heritage*, p. 19.

194 *The Legacy of Arab-Islam in Africa*

customs and ways of life as 'reprehensible and evil customs'.[74] The same writer declares that 'Islam does not accept that people should have customs or traditions other than religious ones; for if Allah's ways is a comprehensive way of life, what is there for custom and tradition?'[75] In fact it is rare to read of an African Muslim writing in appreciation of traditional African customs and ways of life. Even those who indulge in practices that clearly manifest traditional elements would deny their indigenous roots and justify and defend them on the grounds that they are essentially Islamic.

On the issue of the *shari'a* Nigerian-Muslim activists are only publicly articulating the private opinions of the vast majority of African Muslims. In fact at a conference in Abuja in 1989 African-Muslim scholars and activists from across the continent and the Western world resolved to 'struggle to re-instate the application of the Shari'a' in Africa.[76] This is because, as Sulaiman puts it 'it should have been clear to every conscious mind ... that all efforts to solve Nigeria's problems without reference to Allah, without reference to the sacred sharia and to Islam have failed'. The writer goes on to dare historians to name any successful and disciplined governments in the history of Africa other than the nineteenth-century jihadists' *shari'a*-based governments![77]

The recent clamour and unilateral declarations and implementation of *shari'a* in a number of northern Nigerian states started by Zamfara in October 1999, despite having been part of Nigerian politics since the late 1970s, are concrete evidence of conservative revivalism in modern sub-Saharan Africa. Launches of the *shari'a* in the states of Zamfara, Niger, Sokoto, Kano, etc. against directives from the federal government were attended by ambassadors and other diplomatic officials, mainly from Arab diplomatic missions. In attendance also at the launching of the *shari'a* in Kano on 21 June 2000 were delegates from neighbouring republics of Niger, Cameroon and other African countries.[78]

The fact that these developments are taking place barely five months after the inauguration of the first democratically elected Christian head of state, President Olusegun Obasanjo, has brought about conspiracy theories. Some of these theories have it that the rush to implement *shari'a* after the election of a non-Muslim head of state shows how Nigerian Muslims are determined not to live under a government headed by a non-Muslim. Now that the federal government is not headed by a Muslim, Nigeria has become an un-Islamic state. For, to use the well-known maxim of Uthman Dan Fodio, 'the status of a town is the status of its ruler: if he be Muslim, the town is Muslim, the town belongs to Islam; but

---

74. Sulaiman, *Revolution in History*, p. 49.
75. Ibid., pp. 49 and 58.
76. Alkali et al. (eds.), *Islam in Africa*, pp. 432–3.
77. Sulaiman, 'The "Moment of Truth"', p. 10.
78. Farooq A. Kperogi and Aliyu M. Sulaiman, 'Sharia: Triumph of Kano Masses', *Weekly Trust*, vol. 3, no. 20 (30 June–6 July, 2000), p. 7.

Encountering the Encounters: Arab-Islam and Black African Experience 195

if he be heathen the town is a town of heathendom from which flight is obligatory'.[79]

Hence the retreat by predominantly Muslim states into *shari'a* rule. In fact after the governor of Zamfara state, Alhaji Sani Ahmed Yerima Bakura, set the *shari'a* bandwagon rolling the clamour for *shari'a* from Muslim masses in most of the other northern states was almost spontaneous. In some cases the governors and state assemblies were reluctant but had to succumb to public demands whipped up by groups of Muslim scholars. Kano state is a clear example. The headline of the newspaper report referred to above says it all 'Sharia: Triumph of Kano masses'! After talking about how the state governor had to keep away from public functions for fear of his life, the report ended: 'Meanwhile, in all this, the Kano state governor seemed to have learnt a lesson: in Kano, the love of the Sharia or at any rate a pretence to that effect is the beginning of wisdom.'[80]

There are examples of other less militant but nevertheless Arab-oriented tendencies in Muslim religious expression in Africa. A typical example has been illuminatingly discussed within a rural Mende Muslim community in Sierra Leone.[81] It started, as it has in most cases, with a rural *imam* who went on pilgrimage to Mecca. Fascinated not only by the travel but by 'what he saw' during the pilgrimage, he came back with enthusiasm for reform. 'Alhaji Airplane', as he became known, returned home and wanted to 'make religious and ritual practices in Kpuawala [his native village] conform to his ideal of "good" Muslim behaviour in the larger Islamic world, and particularly in what he saw as its conceptual and spatial centre – "Mecca"'.[82]

Alhaji's reform was specifically targeted at a Mende initiation rite known as Sande, which marked the transition of young girls into adult marriageable womanhood. Alhaji's reform brought about what became known as the 'Muslim Sande' in contradistinction to actual traditional Sande. The 'Muslim Sande', however, only succeeded in driving the indigenous elements of the rite underground, as the women continued with some of the practices in secret. Eventually, Alhaji's 'reform' project was frustrated by the female Sande leadership who, after a few years of going underground with some of the practices, won the day with open defiance.

The failure of Alhaji to get rid of the indigenous elements is by no means unique. On the contrary, it is typical of both moderate and radical, past and present conservative Muslim revivalism in Africa. For such projects, situated

---

79. Bivar, 'The Wathiqat ahl al-Sudan', p. 239.
80. Kperogi and Sulaiman, 'Sharia: Triumph of Kano Masses', p. 7.
81. M. Ferme, 'What "Alhaji Airplane" saw in Mecca, and what Happened when he came Home: Ritual Transformation in a Mende Community (Sierra Leone)', in Stewart and Shaw (eds.), *Syncretism/anti-Syncretism*, pp. 27–42.
82. Ibid., p. 28.

196 *The Legacy of Arab-Islam in Africa*

locally but oriented towards an encompassing, international Islamic community, are not always successful, and either lapse over time, as in the case of the nineteenth-century jihadist programmes, or are actively resisted in a variety of ways from within the local Muslim community itself. Writing on conservative revivalism in the Ivory Coast, Robert Launay observed that its influence is limited because when faced with such radical choice between loyalty to their locally anchored Islamic traditions and the externally or internationally oriented values of Wahhābism, 'the vast majority are unwilling to renounce their membership' of the former.[83]

IMPLICATIONS FOR THE AFRICAN EXPERIENCE

Tensions related to conservative revivalist trends in contemporary Africa, such as the eighteenth- and nineteenth-century jihad movements, have a sharp intra-Muslim dimension.[84] While these intra-Muslim controversies, tensions and, sometimes, bloody confrontations can seriously threaten and indeed undermine the pluralistic heritage of modern Africa, it is the Muslim–non-Muslim tensions and conflicts generated by conservative revivalism that is our concern here. The aims of contemporary conservative revivalists in Africa include the reformulation of local Muslim religious orientations towards antagonism to, and final domination of Islam over, other religions and Muslims over non-Muslims.

Some may see the above analysis as an alarmist and pessimistic non-Muslim interpretation of the trends. Peter Clarke, for instance, is of the opinion that, 'rumour, rhetoric and misinformation apart, there is nothing in the Muslim demands to support the more alarmist non-Muslim interpretation'.[85] Indeed, as far as the revivalists' programmes are concerned, the vast majority and most influential of ordinary African Muslims are as suspicious and, as pointed out above, can be just as hostile in opposing them when such programmes are seen as a direct or even indirect threat to the status quo. Umar Abdullahi admits that the content of the jihadists' programme, which he sees as the panacea for Nigeria's problems, 'is too revolutionary to the taste of the [contemporary] Hausaland 'Ulamā'.[86]

In fact, the interesting thing about the *shari'a* controversy in modern Nigeria is that both the Muslim masses who clamour for its introduction and the non-Muslim population who strongly oppose it have little if any idea as to what the *shari'a* actually entails. In other words, no one knows the fine details of that

---

83. Launay, *Beyond the Stream*, p. 100.
84. For details of the tensions, confrontations and all-too-often open hostilities within the Muslim community involving conservative Muslim reforms in Africa, see Kaba, *The Wahhabiyya*, pp. 195 ff; A. Christelow, 'Three Islamic Voices'; and other relevant chapters in Brenner (ed.), *Muslim Identity and Social Change*.
85. Clarke, 'Islamic Reform', pp. 535–6.
86. Abdullahi, *Political Thought*, pp. 44 ff.

Encountering the Encounters: Arab-Islam and Black African Experience 197

which constitutes the *shari'a* not even the chief architect, Governor Sani of Zamfara state. It would have been interesting to see what the results would have been if the whole *shari'a* issue were subjected to a truly democratic process whereby Nigerian *'ulama* were tasked to produce a common *shari'a* document containing all the fine details that would then be discussed and approved by the various state assemblies and put to the public in a referendum.

But having said that, while the non-Muslim interpretation of these trends may be deemed cynical, what is more cynical is the apparent lack or indeed muzzling of unequivocal public Muslim criticism and disapproval of the conservative revivalists' exclusivist and xenophobic rhetoric and programmes against non-Muslims. This disturbing scenario is further exacerbated by a fact Peter Clarke himself admits, namely, that so-called 'moderate Muslim reformers' aspire, without stating in detail, to that which 'the fundamentalists' expend most of their energies in pursuit, i.e. Muslim governance, or more appropriately Muslim dominance over non-Muslims.[87] Commenting on the extremist rhetoric of African-Muslim revivalists on relations with non-Muslims, Mervyn Hiskett points out that 'Shehu Umar Abdullahi and Ibraheem Sulaiman certainly represent radical rhetoric at its fiercest. Yet it is not clear that many northern Muslims seriously dissent from the content of what they have to say, though some might deplore the tone in which they say it.'[88]

This is borne out in an observation made by a BBC reporter on the introduction of *shari'a* in northern Nigeria that 'I didn't meet any Muslim men in Zamfara who were not in favour of it'. The reporter, however, went on to point out that some leading Muslims in other parts of northern Nigeria oppose the introduction of the *shari'a* and condemn it privately. Some of these leading Muslim figures point out that the introduction of the *shari'a* in a multireligious and multicultural modern Nigeria is ill thought out and reckless, not least with regard to Muslim relations with non-Muslims. The reporter however pointed out that those Muslims who so disapprove the introduction of the *shari'a* could only say so in private and that one leading Muslim politician told him that to oppose it publicly 'would be to leave yourself open to the accusation that you are un-Islamic'.[89]

This takes us to a key difficulty in Islam as far as relations between Muslims and non-Muslims are concerned: namely that even though some Muslims may genuinely be interested in seeking and promoting peaceful co-existence on equal terms with non-Muslims, they seem to have a difficult task in finding a credible rationale and validation for such an enterprise from within received Islamic traditions. One wonders if this partly explains the fear of being labelled

87. Clarke, 'Islamic Reform', p. 522.
88. Hiskett, 'Preface', p. xiv.
89. Barnaby Phillips, 'Laying Down the Islamic Law', in *BBC Focus on Africa Magazine* (January–March 2000), p. 19.

198 The Legacy of Arab-Islam in Africa

un-Islamic and the disturbing silence of 'moderate' Muslims in the face of xenophobic claims by their conservative co-religionists. The conservative revivalists, on the other hand, seem to have no problem in finding genuine Islamic validation for their position of Muslim domination of, antagonism towards and, at best, contemptuous toleration of non-Muslims as *dhimmis* under Muslim rule.

Traditional Muslim thought and attitudes towards non-Muslims, like most other aspects of mainstream Islamic thought, are firmly grounded in Qur'anic texts, *hadiths* and juristic opinions formulated under the environment of Muslim political dominance over non-Muslims beginning from the *hijra* through to the first three generations of Muslim history, the *salaf*. In what is generally known as the Madinan verses, the Qur'an repeatedly warns Muslims against taking 'unbelievers' as friends (Suras 3: 28; 4: 144; 9: 23; 60: 1; etc.), and approves of antagonism towards them (Suras 9: 5, 29, 36, 73 and 123, among others). The more conciliatory pasages in the Meccan texts, such as the oft-cited 'there is no compulsion in religion' (Sura 2: 256), are regarded in mainstream Muslim thinking as abrogated by the domineering and antagonistic ones.[90]

Right after the death of Muhammad in 632 and Muslim conquest of vast non-Muslim territories that followed, the *hadiths* and authoritative Muslim legal opinions formulated, and in effect, canonized, during this period with regards to Muslim relations with non-Muslims generally incline towards the position of contemptuous toleration of the weak by the strong. The preoccupation of Muslim jurists at the time was to work out appropriate arrangements for the vast colonized non-Muslim populations, the *dhimmis*. The resultant literature, as rightly pointed out by Bernard Lewis, clearly reflects the belief that the process of Islamic domination over non-Islam would continue until, in a not-too-distant future, the whole world either accepted the Islamic faith or submitted to Muslim rule.[91]

The question of Muslims living on equal terms with non-Muslims or as subjects under non-Muslim rule hardly arose and, where it did, received only minor and fleeting attention. This is the legacy bequeathed to contemporary Muslims who have come to view it not as history but, to use the words of Fazlur Rahman, 'para-history' and therefore part of faith requiring unquestioning adherence and re-enactment at all times and all places.[92] As long as this received tradition maintains the para-history status that disallows critical re-examination, Muslim relations with non-Muslims within the contemporary multireligious and multicultural context will remain frosty, to say the least.

90. See the first section of Chapter 3 above.
91. B. Lewis, 'Legal and Historical Reflections on the Position of Muslim Populations under Non-Muslim Rule', in B. Lewis and D. Schnapper (eds.), *Muslims in Europe* (London: Pinter, 1994), p. 6.
92. Rahman, *Islam*, pp. 236–7.

Encountering the Encounters: Arab-Islam and Black African Experience 199

It is in this connection that the late Mahmud M. Taha of Sudan attempted his controversial and fatal rethinking of Islamic traditions within the Sudanese context. Taha started by acknowledging that no amount of ingenious interpretation or reinterpretation of traditional Muslim sources will satisfactorily deal with the problem. In Taha's view, any honest approach to received Islamic traditions in our modern pluralistic context has to be radical. Taha therefore proposed what he called 'the evolution of Islamic interpretation' by which he sought, through the doctrine of *naskh*, abrogation, to invoke texts and related traditions espoused during the earlier period of Islam in Mecca in place of their opposites of the later Madinan period.

In other words, Taha held the view that 'the evolutionary principle of interpretation is nothing more than reversing the process of *naskh* or abrogation so that those texts which were abrogated in the past can be enacted into law now, with the consequent abrogation of texts that used to be enacted as *Shari'a*.'[93] What Taha sought to accomplish in his radical approach was to reverse the doctrine of abrogation so that instead of Madinan verses overriding Meccan ones it should be the other way round. He maintained that 'the earlier message of Mecca is in fact the eternal and fundamental message of Islam, emphasizing the inherent dignity of all human beings, regardless of gender, religious belief, race, and so forth'. These Meccan texts, Taha believed, are those most suitable for the modern pluralistic context.[94]

Farid Esack, a South African Muslim and one of the few courageous African-Muslim scholars of our time, has in this regard also made some groundbreaking exegesis on what he calls the terms of 'exclusion' and 'inclusion', using *iman*, *Islam* and *kufr* as hermeneutical keys 'to deal with the ideological connotations acquired by these terms and to present a conscious preference for a new meaning, which seeks the liberation of all people'.[95] Esack's exegetical concerns arose from his involvement in the anti-apartheid movement in South Africa, within which he had a positive experience of working with non-Muslims, especially Christians. His approach to the Qur'an is therefore unashamedly contextual.

Esack admits that limiting inter-religious solidarity to Muslims, Jews and Christians 'could be construed as an alliance of the powerful' and cautions that 'a qur'anic hermeneutic concerned with interreligious solidarity against injustice would seek to avoid such alliances and would rather opt for more inclusive categories which would, for example, embrace the dispossessed of the Fourth World', i.e. marginalized and oppressed indigenous communities.[96] Nevertheless,

---

93. A.A. An-Na'im, *Toward an Islamic Reformation: Civil Liberties, Human Rights and International Law* (New York: Syracuse University, 1990), p. 56.
94. Ibid., pp. 52–3.
95. Esack, *Liberation and Pluralism*, p. 116.
96. Ibid., p. 153.

200 *The Legacy of Arab-Islam in Africa*

Esack's religious Other remains Jews and Christians, i.e. People of the Book. Apart from general statements like 'liberation of all people', 'justice for the oppressed', etc. that can be taken to mean an inclusion of indigenous African believers, Esack makes no direct reference to this group in connection with his inter-religious solidarity.

Esack's reticence, despite his undoubtedly genuine and rare attempt to evaluate the Islamic tradition in relation to non-Muslims, may be attributed to various factors. These may include the rather categorical nature of Muslim scriptures on relations with 'idol-worshippers' and indeed Christians or 'People of the Book'. If this is the case, as we are inclined to think it is, Esack's struggle is yet another commentary on the difficulty facing Muslims with his conviction who are trying with great difficulty to find genuine Islamic validation for their conciliatory approaches towards non-Muslims. And it should be added here that both Taha and Esack's positions are rejected by the vast majority of modern African-Muslim scholars. Taha's views were adjudged heretical and he was accordingly executed by the Numeri Military government in 1985.

Esack's reticence on the issue of traditional African believers could also be due to the general, albeit mistaken, assumption that traditional African believers are trapped in an irrecoverable decline – even though within the South African context they constitute about fourteen per cent of the population, as opposed to under two per cent Muslims – and the related widely held misconception that indigenous socio-religious belief system is on its way out if not already overthrown by Islam and Christianity. In this connection, the indigenous African and his/her socio-religious traditions may be perceived as a phase or spent force rather than a group that has to be taken notice of in any project of inter-religious dialogue. But as is now being increasingly acknowledged, the indigenous religion of Africa

> exists nowhere, but is everywhere, in the consciousness, in the attitudes, gestures, thoughts, images, symbols, stories, proverbs, legends, myths, etc. It is everywhere, in the countrysides and cities, in the judiciary processes and conventions. It is in the behaviour of Christians, Muslims, atheists and agnostics. Indeed it is latent in every aspect of African ways of life.[97]

The indigenous African factor is therefore not an issue that one can conveniently evade. Contemporary tropical Africa is made up of countless numbers of families and ethnic groups still involved at various levels with indigenous religious practices either as part of their faith or cultural identity. Related to the purveyance of indigenous religions there is the long-standing blending between the host indigenous African traditions and values with the incoming traditions of Arab-Islam and Western Christianity. A positive appreciation of indigenous values by all sides in such a situation could be a possible bridge for intra- and

---

97. T.K.M. Buakassa, cited in Nwaiwu, 'Dialogue in an African Context', p. 126, n. 76.

Encountering the Encounters: Arab-Islam and Black African Experience 201

inter-religious dialogue. Conversely, a hostile view of indigenous traditions in that context such as that of the jihadists and contemporary conservative Muslim activists, could be a real stumbling block for intra- and inter-religious dialogue, if not a direct source of conflict.

Some Muslims have always tried to reassure non-Muslims that as *dhimmis* under an Islamic system, they have nothing to fear. However, leaving aside the obvious debilitating and discriminatory aspects of the *shari'a* regarding the *dhimmis*,[98] the meaning of the term itself, 'protected persons', is not only condescending and patronizing but also implies hostility and therefore arouses suspicion. As one observer rightly queried: 'One must ask: "protected against whom?" When this "stranger" lives in Islamic countries, the answer can only be: against Muslims themselves.' The so-called contract, i.e. the *dhimma*, which is derived from the *shari'a* is itself 'an unequal contract', it is not a contract negotiated between two equal parties. On the contrary, 'it is quite arbitrary. The person who grants the treaty is the only one who decides what he is prepared to concede' and also retains the right to revoke it.[99]

Indeed, as a non-Muslim, it is bemusing, to put it mildly, to hear repeated claims by Muslims that the *shari'a* has nothing to do with non-Muslims and that it would only be applied to Muslims, or that it is in fact a just system. First of all, these claims give the false impression that under a *shari'a* system Muslims and non-Muslims live in compartmentalized ghettos with little or no relations whatsoever with one another. Or, second, that disputes under a *shari'a* system are to be purely within the various religious communities and between members of the same faith communities. An obvious question that one cannot help but ask is: what happens in a case, civil or criminal, involving a Muslim and a non-Muslim?

But even more importantly, if those who make these claims are honest with themselves, then one could only grant them the benefit of the doubt on the grounds that they do not know what the *shari'a* entails with regards to the place of non-Muslims. For instance, under *shari'a* rule:

> Non-Muslims do not enjoy full political participation or equality before the law, and are disqualified from holding any public office which involves exercising authority over Muslims. Those who are accepted as believers by *sharia* criteria (mainly Christians and Jews) are [subject to certain restrictions] allowed freedom to practise their faith and a degree of communal autonomy in conducting their personal or family affairs. But

---

98. A.A. An-Na'im, a Sudanese-Muslim scholar, delineates the discriminatory prescriptions of the *shari'a* towards non-Muslims and women, and rejects them as 'serious and unacceptable discrimination on grounds of gender and religion'. See *Islamic Reformation*, pp. 88–9, 129–31 and 176.
99. Jacques Ellul, in his preface to Bat Ye'or, *The Dhimmi: Jews and Christians under Islam*, (London and Toronto, Associated University Presses, 1985), p. 30.

202 The Legacy of Arab-Islam in Africa

these limited rights are denied to, for example, the adherents of Traditional African Religions, because they are deemed by *sharia* to be non-believers.[100]

In fact, despite the repeated claims that the *shari'a* in northern Nigerian states has nothing to do with non-Muslims, there are already clear signs that like the nineteenth-century jihadist system the *shari'a* institutionalizes and sanctions not only discrimination along religious lines but that it is set to impose Islamic value systems and legal codes on non-Muslims. For instance, after insisting the *shari'a* would not affect non-Muslims, the governor of Zamfara state in an interview declared that 'only men with beards will be awarded government contracts' under his *shari'a* rule.[101] In Kano, after giving assurances that the application of the *shari'a* would not be extended to non-Muslim settlements, a few days before launching the *shari'a*, Sheikh Umar Ibrahim Kabo, chairman of the Council of Ulama in Kano, declared at a press conference that 'the government of Kano State does not reserve any area where the commission of crime is allowed'.[102]

Hence, there is no way in which one can honestly say the *shari'a* system will promote peaceful co-existence between Muslims and non-Muslims on equal terms in our modern nation-state systems of Africa. For as Abdullahi Ahmed An-Na'im points out:

> There is a fundamental tension, for example, between sharia notions of the Muslim umma (the exclusive community of Muslims) and national unity among Muslim and non-Muslim citizens of the modern nation state. At the international level, the sharia legitimation of the use of force in jihad and direct action in furtherance of 'Islamic' objectives can hardly be reconciled with the modern principles of equal sovereignty of non-Muslim states and the rule of law in international relations.[103]

One can only attribute the spontaneous clamour for the *shari'a* as a panacea for Nigeria and Africa's socio-political, economic and moral malaise to the myth of glorious past *shari'a* governments and the drive by African Muslims to follow the footsteps of their Arab co-religionists in every way possible. The governor of Zamfara sent people to Saudi Arabia for training as judges for *shari'a* courts and did not hide the fact that he intended 'to replicate the Sharia code used in Saudi Arabia'. He went on to ask the reporter: 'Have you been to Saudi Arabia? There is no crime there at all, you can leave your possessions outside your house, and they will never be stolen.'[104]

Commenting on the concept of *dhimma* within the Indonesian context, Abdurrahman Wahid states:

100. An-Na'im, 'Islam and Human Rights', p. 88.
101. See Phillips, 'Islamic Law', p. 18.
102. Kperogi and Sulaiman, 'Sharia: Triumph of Kano Masses', p. 7.
103. An-Na'im, 'Islam and Human Rights', p. 89.
104. Phillips, 'Islamic Law', p. 18.

Encountering the Encounters: Arab-Islam and Black African Experience 203

My belief and the very core of my own existence reject *dhimmism* because, as an Indonesian and because of our national priorities, my main thinking is that I have to reject it. All citizens are equal. That is the problem. That is why I do not know what to do with it. It is there [in Islamic thought] but I reject it. So that means plurality should be there in the sense of let everybody live according to their own respective ways ... So in the last analysis if I have to choose between the constitution and the concept of Islamic *Shari'a* on this point I will follow the constitution.[105]

Among the many reasons why non-Muslims cannot accept any arrangement under a *shari'a* system in a modern pluralistic context is the very basis and motivation for the application of the *shari'a*. In Muslim understanding, the practice of Islam means a whole way of life, prescribed in detail by the holy texts and treatises based on them. It is not just a way of life, but *the* way of life, the 'straight path'. To lead this way of life, it is not enough for a Muslim to do good and refrain from evil. The primary duty of Muslims is to 'command good and forbid evil'. Muslims are therefore required to command and forbid – that is, to exercise authority. That same principle applies in general to the *shari'a*, which must not only be obeyed but also enforced.[106]

Consequently, in the view of many jurists, a Muslim must not only worship One God; he must call upon others, if necessary by dint of arms, to worship the One God. A Muslim is not only to abstain from drinking alcohol and eating pork; he must also destroy strong drink and ban the sale of pork. Non-Muslims are expected, indeed required, to convert to Islam, but Muslims are prohibited, on the pain of death, to convert to any other religion. A Muslim man can marry a non-Muslim woman, but a non-Muslim man cannot, on pain of death, marry a Muslim woman, because, it is believed, in marriage the man is the dominant partner. In this connection, Mawdūdī declared

Non-Muslims have been granted the freedom to stay outside the Islamic fold and to cling to their false, man-made ways if they so wish. They have, however, absolutely no right to seize the reins of power in any part of God's earth nor to direct the collective affairs of human beings according to their own misconceived doctrines.[107]

Power or authority 'in any part of God's earth' must be exercised by Muslims. In any encounter between Muslims and non-Muslims, therefore, Muslims must dominate, i.e. exercise power over non-Muslims. This is to enable Muslims to effectively command good and forbid evil. For

105. Abdurrahman Wahid, cited in Saeed, 'Approaches to *Ijtihad*', pp. 291–2.
106. Lewis, 'Muslim Populations under Non-Muslim Rule', pp. 12–13.
107. A.A. Mawdūdī, *Towards Understanding the Qur'an*, ed. and trans Z.I. Ansari (Leicester: Islamic Foundation, 1988) (commentary on Sura 9: 29).

204 The Legacy of Arab-Islam in Africa

whoever really wants to root out mischief and chaos from God's earth ... it is useless for him to work as a mere preacher. He should stand up and finish the government run on wrong principles, snatch power from wrongdoers and establish a government based on correct principles and following a proper system.[108]

While Muslims have the right under a democratic system to demand their religious and other rights, such demands can only be put forward with the understanding that Islam is one among many equals. But the moment demands are put with the understanding that Islam is the 'truth' and Muslims cannot live on equal terms with or under 'false' non-Muslim systems, as is often the case, then it is surely bound to be a problem in our contemporary multifaith and multicultural African context. Apart from the inalienable right of non-Muslims to hold on to their '*kufr*' and all their 'falsehood', what Muslims forget when they make absolute claims like those made by Mawdūdī, Sulaiman, Abdullahi and Gumi is

that such Islamic certainties exclude the right of the non-Muslim to disagree: to insist, for instance, that the Islamic Sharī'a is in many respects neither just nor fair, or to retort that for those whose recent forefathers were enslaved by the Muslims, such grandiloquent claims are sawdust in the mouth.[109]

The difficulty is not *what* constitutes Islam per se, but *how* Muslims should practice Islam. For instance, it is perfectly fine, in our pluralistic world, for a Muslim to hold and express his/her belief in one God freely both in private and in public; or abstain from taking alcohol as a religious duty. But the problem is when the Muslim goes beyond that to restrict or prevent others outside the faith community from holding and expressing their belief in multiple gods on the grounds that the belief in multiple gods is an affront to his/her belief in one God. It is this traditional Muslim understanding of the practice of Islam that Sulaiman re-echoes in declaring that 'a Muslim is not a person who merely believes, but rather a person who practises Islam and, in addition, hates unbelief, its symbols and men'.[110] The imposition and institution of Islamic sanctions on non-Muslims is also self-evident from the remarks made by the chairman of the Council of Ulama of Kano state that the government does not reserve any area where the commission of 'crime' is allowed.

These are not mere rhetoric but real issues. The millions of traditional African believers who were slaughtered by Muslim jihadists in eighteenth and nineteenth-century tropical Africa, as detailed in chapter 3, suffered this fate for no other reason than the fact that they believed and expressed what the jihadists

---

108. Cited in C. Troll, 'Two Conceptions of da'wa in India: Jama'at-i Islami and Tablighi Jama'at', *Archives de Sciences Sociales des Religions* (July–September 1994), p. 130.
109. Hiskett, *The Course of Islam in Africa*, p. 195.
110. Sulaiman, *The Islamic State*, p. 3.

Encountering the Encounters: Arab-Islam and Black African Experience 205

saw as *kufr.* In 1992 in northern Ghana, where this writer comes from, a Christian gathering was attacked by a group of Muslims on the grounds that the preacher repeatedly used the designation 'Son of God' in reference to Jesus, which is blasphemy in Islam. When the Christians insisted it is their belief and they are required as such to refer to Jesus as the Son of God, the Muslims retorted that it is blasphemous to impute a son to God! This was a small skirmish in a small town, but the potential for such a position having far-reaching consequences in a multifaith environment is clear. Another clear example is the Roman Catholic bishop who was publicly flogged in the Sudan for the possession of alcohol.

As a non-Muslim, I think this is the main underlying difficulty with Islam in a pluralistic world. It is in this vein that a few Muslims whom we have referred to above are calling for radical reinterpretation of received Islamic tradition. But as we have pointed out with regard to Esack, there is a limit to which they themselves can go. The same can be said of Fazlur Rahman. Rahman for instance is very insistent that

> The task of rethinking and reformulating Islam at the present juncture is much more acute and radical than has faced the Muslims since the 3rd/9th century, and the requisite performance is equivalent to the performance of the first two centuries and a half. In other words, *the thinking Muslim has to go right behind the early post-Prophetic formative period itself and to reconstruct it all over again.* (my emphasis)[111]

But there still remain two fundamental difficulties with Rahman's thesis. First of all, Rahman argues for the need to reformulate the political dogma of Islam (among other issues) but sees the end result of this reformulation in terms of a government by the Muslims, of the Muslims and for the Muslims. Thus, after talking about keeping the reformulation process free from what he calls 'external propaganda' and describing any adoption of secular form of government by Muslims as 'tantamount to changing the very nature of Islam', Rahman declares: 'As for political life its foundation is the Muslim Community itself. This Community is constituted by its acceptance of the Shari'a or Islamic imperative, as its goal: i.e. it agrees that it shall realize the Shari'a gradually in its individual and collective life.'[112] So in effect if there is going to be a place for any form of non-Muslim involvement in Rahman's proposed Islamic political dogma at all, this can only be within the parameters of *shari'a* prescriptions and concessions.

Hence we are back to where we started. No doubt Rahman in much of his work is preoccupied with contemporary political dictatorship and tyranny in his native Pakistan and other Muslim countries. On this count, one is inclined to grant him the benefit of the doubt and attribute the inward-looking nature of his

111. Rahman, *Islam*, p. 251.
112. Ibid. pp. 240, 249 and 260.

206 *The Legacy of Arab-Islam in Africa*

thesis to oversight, and a serious one at that. Having said that, the above categorical statements coupled with the fact that a man of Rahman's academic stature, well informed and acquainted with international law and human-rights issues, makes it difficult to put his insistence that the community that qualifies to participate in his proposed Islamic political system must accept the 'Islamic imperative' and agree to realize the *shari'a* in its life down to a simple matter of oversight. This brings us to the second difficulty with Rahman's thesis, i.e. his suggestion that modern Muslims can only reconstruct a meaningful Islamic future by going 'right behind the early post-Prophetic formative period'.

The conservative Muslim views of Islamic dogmas which Rahman rightly regards as constituting one of two basic and, in his own words, 'grave' problems and challenges (alongside modern materialism) facing the contemporary world, are as much products of the Prophetic formative period itself as they are of the early post-Prophetic formative period. For Muslim thought conceives Islam as having undergone a definite progression from the Meccan preacher, warner, minority and powerless paradigm into the definitive Madinan paradigm of statesmanship, armed struggle, majority and power. This transition, Rahman (in line with traditional Muslim thought) insists, was not accidental but rather is the '*élan*' of the Qur'anic message 'for it is part of the Qur'anic doctrine that simply to deliver the Message, to suffer frustration and not to succeed, is immature spirituality'.[113]

In this transition from the Meccan to Madinan paradigm, Muhammad and the community he founded in Madina become not just vehicles through which God communicates His will to humanity, but more importantly they are the means through which divine wrath is expressed towards those who refuse to heed the warnings. The armed struggles and victories of Muhammad over his Meccan adversaries and spectacular success of early Muslim conquest helped not just in entrenching but in making the Madinan paradigm of power and success the Islamic *norm*. Muhammad's treatment of and relations with non-Muslims such as Jews, Christians and traditional believers becomes the standard Muslim treatment and relations with these communities wherever and whenever Muslims come into contact with them. Muslims who find themselves in minority positions under non-Muslim rule, analogous to the Meccan paradigm, must seek to re-enact the transition first enacted by Muhammad in order to attain the ideal Madinan paradigm.[114]

So simply going back to the formative Prophetic period still does not solve the problem as far as Muslim conceptions of Islam in a pluralistic context is concerned. Perhaps this is the actual reason why, despite his refreshing analysis

113. Ibid., p. 16.
114. For a well-argued analysis of this Mecca to Madina transition within the context of Muslim relations with non-Muslims, see Marshall, *God, Muhammad and the Unbelievers*, pp. 191 ff.

of the Islamic legacy and the need for modern Muslims to rethink it, Rahman ended up with the same exclusivist models of Islam as his arch-protagonists, the conservatives. Of course we couldn't agree more with Rahman that Muslims have to go right behind the early post-Prophetic formative period for any meaningful task of reformulating Islamic thought. However, it is our considered opinion that simply going back to the Prophetic formative period to re-enact it all over again, as Rahman appears to have done, will not yield any different result on the issue of Islamic practice in contemporary multifaith and multicultural contexts.

In our view three fundamental questions have to be addressed with regards to the Prophetic formative period itself as far as Islamic practice in a pluralistic context is concerned. The first question is whether it can be objectively and satisfactorily established that the so-called progression of Islam from the Meccan to the Madinan paradigm constitutes the *élan* of the Qur'anic message or whether the *élan* is read into the Qur'an through the lenses of *received tradition* which Rahman and other modern Muslim thinkers regard as the main stumbling block to contemporary rethinking of Islam. Surely, received tradition and the lust for power apart, it appears to us that it would be difficult satisfactorily to dismiss the Meccan paradigm purely on the grounds of an inner logic of the Qur'an. So far it seems arguments that have been advanced to absolutize the Madinan paradigm ensue either largely from *received tradition* or in defence of Muhammad's Madinan experience against non-Muslim Western criticism.

The second question worth raising with regards to the formative Prophetic period is to what extent can Muslim devotion view the role of Prophets in general and that of Muhammad in particular beyond being the spokesperson of God, i.e. a warner, and to what extent, fallible as they are, can prophets move beyond the warner role into indicting, prosecuting, convicting, passing sentences and carrying out those sentences on behalf of God without infringing upon divine prerogatives? I am aware of, and indeed share to some extent in, Rahman's concern that

> a God to whom it is, in the final analysis, indifferent whether He is effective in history or not is certainly not the God of Muhammad and the Qur'an. If history is the proper field for Divine activity, historical forces must, by definition, be employed for the moral end as judiciously as possible.[115]

We agree that God must be seen to be active in history and we also agree that divine activity cannot be outside the historical field. The difficulty, though, is that by insisting it is not enough for Prophets and their followers to be 'simple' preachers and spokespersons on behalf of God and their faith, Muslim thought

115. Rahman, *Islam*, p. 21.

208 *The Legacy of Arab-Islam in Africa*

risks reducing God to that very role of a 'simple preacher' or nominal head of state with the Prophet retaining the role of prime minister, i.e. executive head of government. And let me add straight away that this has nothing to do with an addiction 'to pathetic tales of sorrow, failure, frustration and crucifixion' which are incapable of conceiving success.[116] Of course, it depends on what we mean by 'success', but the main point at issue here is not 'success' and 'failure'. It is about the fact that while we cannot have a God who is indifferent to historical events, equally we cannot have a God who has become a prisoner of 'historical forces', in fact, a single historical force.

Having said that, granted that it can be argued that a Prophet by virtue of his calling can perform all the above duties on behalf of or upon the instruction of God, the third related question that is worth raising in relation to the formative Prophetic period is the extent to which that Prophetic experience can be absolutized as the definite exemplar model for the faithful to seek to re-enact. For instance the all-too-familiar Muslim maxim 'In Islam there is no separation between religion and politics' is based upon Muhammad's example as religious, military, political and judicial leader in Madina. But one wonders whether it can be argued that Muhammad was able successfully and effectively to fuse all these different roles together precisely because of his unique Prophetic authority in Islam.

The emergence of rulers in Sunni Islam who claimed to be 'God's Representatives on Earth' and the Ayatollah (Sign of God on Earth) in Shi'a Islam may be regarded by many as serious deviations. These are, however, extreme examples of the fact that in order to run an effective political system that is a re-enactment of a Prophetic model like that in Islam rulers would have to be invested with, at least, quasi-metaphysical authority that sets them apart from the ruled, giving them absolute power accountable only to God and not man. As is all too familiar, such scenarios are recipes for dictatorship, despotism, tyranny and naked abuse of power. With or without some amount of divine aura surrounding the ruler, governance under such a religio-political system is bound to be riddled with competing, divergent and conflicting claims and interpretations.

The argument by Fazlur Rahman and many other Muslim intellectuals who, for political reasons, have fled their home countries and sought asylum in the West from their home 'Islamic' governments that the 'abuses' of power in those countries are as a result of misreading and misapplication of the Islamic political dogma is not persuasive. In fact the claims and counter-claims of these modern Muslim scholars and their conservative protagonists are yet another illustration of the scenario we have just described above. For what else can you expect from a political system that is based on eternal absolute claims derived from nebulous

116. Ibid., p. 19.

Encountering the Encounters: Arab-Islam and Black African Experience 209

texts such as scripture. It is in this connection that we regard the reformulation attempts by modern Muslim scholars such as Rahman as cosmetic and as a recycling of ideas that is unlikely to yield any different results.

A subsidiary but very important question is, granted that Muhammad's religio-political experience of seventh-century Arabia has to be re-enacted by Muslims for Muslims, to what extent can Muhammad's encounter and relations with non-Muslims be seen as applicable in our contemporary pluralistic twenty-first century? I am raising this question bearing in mind that Muslims conceive Muhammad's armed struggle with the non-Muslims of Mecca and the eventual conquest of Mecca as standard for Muslim relations with traditional believers for all time. Similarly, Muhammad's rather frosty and hostile encounters with the Jews especially, and also Christian communities, in seventh-century Arabia is regarded not only by the conservatives but, in fact, by modern Muslim intellectuals like Rahman as 'the standard Muslim treatment of Jews and Christians'.[117] Meanwhile, in discussing the *sunna*, Rahman, unlike his conservative co-religionists, talks about 'the *ad hoc* character of Prophetic decisions and precepts', which was 'usually occasioned by particular situations'.[118]

Surely there is need for some clarification here. For if we admit that Muhammad's actions and declarations which constitute the *sunna*, were occasioned by *particular situations* (and hard-line conservatives cannot run away from this fact, even if they refuse to accept it), then there must be a very good reason as to why his treatment of the Meccan polytheists, Jews and Christians should be absolutized, enshrined and taught as 'the standard Muslim treatment' of these communities for all times and all places. We know not of any good reason yet provided by Muslims for this stand beyond the acritical appeal to received tradition. In fact it is because of the lack of good reasons that a few Muslim thinkers like Abdurrahman Wahid of Indonesia, quoted above, totally reject the *dhimmī* concept as incompatible with modern realities.

Whatever one's opinion may be with regard to the questions raised above (and we are not oblivious to the fact that the vast majority of Muslim intellectuals would reject them, not least because a non-Muslim is raising them), they do highlight the need for a critical reappraisal of the inherited Islamic traditions if Muslim relations with non-Muslims in the twenty-first century are to have better prospects. So long as Muslims continue to cling to the traditional view that the way Muhammad dealt with non-Muslims in the seventh century is the standard norm for all Muslim generations, then there is virtually no hope for peaceful Muslim relations with non-Muslims in a pluralistic modern context.

117. Ibid., p. 28.
118. Ibid., p. 53.

210 The Legacy of Arab-Islam in Africa

This is particularly so within the sub-Saharan African context where the traditional Islamic political dogma invoked by the eighteenth- and nineteenth-century jihadists with such devastating consequences on non-Muslims 'is latent and potentially revivable'.[119]

It is in order to avoid a repeat of this scenario that we have called upon Muslims not only to enter intellectually into dialogue with indigenous African heritage but even more so to re-examine critically their inherited traditions in the light of the African experience. It is within this context that we have insisted throughout that critical faithfulness to the Islamic (and Christian) tradition is crucial in Africa. For, as rightly observed by an African-Muslim scholar, ironically after writing approvingly of and lauding the jihadists' activities,

> African man must assimilate the cultural values of these traditions [Islam and Christianity] correctly if he really intends to have influence on the course of world history. Without being thoroughly digested these elements of the Abrahamic tradition will be terribly distorted and the unifying character of their ecumenical doctrines will be lost. This is especially true now that the African wishes to impress upon the world both his right to be different and his determination to be a celebrated participant at the banquet of civilizations.[120]

Apart from the existential imperatives outlined in the foregoing to underline the need to digest critically the inherited traditions, there is an equally important ideological imperative for a critical rethinking of Arab-Islam in the light of the African experience. This we now proceed to highlight.

ARAB-ISLAM AND BLACK AFRICAN IDENTITY

As we have pointed out in chapter 1, there is a strong perception that Western Christianity has been employed to impoverish and undermine African cultural identity and dignity, and therefore either has to be rejected outright by Africans or adapted to suit their particular historical and cultural context. This perception is the main contributory factor to the African quest to retrieve and affirm their cultural dignity and identity. The question we are seeking to raise here is whether a similar case can be made for a revival and retrieval of African identity within the Islamic context.

With regard to the Islamic dispensation some people have (implicitly and explicitly) argued that any quest for an African identity against the backdrop of the Arab-Islamic interlude is either uncalled for, because the Arab-Islamic civilization has done nothing to undermine African culture, or mistaken, because Islam and Arab culture are in essence *African*. In other words, there is no question of 're-Africanization' within the Islamic tradition in Africa because

119. Mazrui, *Triple Heritage*, p. 135.
120. Nyang, *African Identity*, pp. 83–4.

Encountering the Encounters: Arab-Islam and Black African Experience 211

there has been and can be no 'dis-Africanization' in Africa's encounters with Arab-Islam.

Regarding the suggestion that Islam has not undermined African culture, Ali Mazrui points out that Africans were the main agents of Islamization in tropical Africa, and because Islam has over the years blended well with various indigenous African customs, the Islamic dispensation in Africa is already 'Africanized' enough. In the words of Mazrui: 'One explanation for the vigour of Islam in West Africa could be its greater degree of indigenisation and Africanisation. Islam had ceased to be led by the Arabs and had acquired an independent dynamism in western Africa'.[121] Mazrui then goes on, rather ironically, to cite Dan Fodio amongst 'the great leaders and religious [African] preachers' of Islam in Africa. Similarly, Ahmadou Hampâté Bâ wrote that 'the empire of Islam in Africa established itself, I shall not say upon the ruins of animism, for it survives still … but upon the foundations of animism'.[122] Writing on Islamization in tropical Africa, Nehemiah Levtzion observed that 'the Islamization of Africa became more successful because of the Africanization of Islam'.[123] As we have intimated in chapters 1, 2 and 3, there is no doubt that Islam has blended with indigenous African elements, indeed more than its Western-Christian rival.[124]

The issue, therefore, is not whether traditional African elements have been blended with Islamic practice in Africa. The point at issue is the 'surprising hiatus' of the lack of Muslim appreciation of and dialogue with indigenous values 'given the long history of borrowing between Islam and local religious elements' in Africa.[125] Also, African-Muslim preachers such as Uthman Dan Fodio, seen by African Muslims and key Western observers as the rightful carriers of the banner of Islam in Africa, have been decidedly hostile to indigenous customs, as demonstrated in chapter 3. This means that one cannot simply justify the African identity of Islam on the basis that African elements are found in Islam or Africans were its agents.

The perception that Islam is an African religion, indeed, the 'original' African religion, seems to have emerged or rather gained currency among a certain

121. Mazrui, *Triple Heritage*, pp. 136–7. This thesis, however, does not include the African diaspora in the Muslim world; they, just like their counterparts in the West, have been Islamized and to all intents and purposes 'dis-Africanized'.
122. G. Asfar, 'Amadou Hampâté Bâ and the Islamic Dimension of West African Oral Literature', in Harrow (ed.), *Islam in African Literature*, p. 149.
123. Levtzion, 'Islamization in West Africa', p. 208.
124. However, as we have argued in chapter 2, it wasn't so much the question of Islam showing a great degree of indigenization (the very excuse for the jihad movements) as the indigenous traditions showing a great degree of flexibility and discretion in accommodating Arab-Islamic values. In areas with a jihad tradition, the persistence of indigenous elements owes more to the intrinsic appeal and resilience of such elements than the benevolence of jihad Islam.
125. Sanneh, *The Crown and the Turban*, p. 21.

212 The Legacy of Arab-Islam in Africa

section of the African diaspora in the United States of America.[126] A certain Timothy Drew Ali, founder of the Moorish Science Temple cult, conceived the idea in 1913 in New Jersey. Ali claimed that 'the true religion of black people was Islam' and saw himself as commissioned by Allah to restore to African Americans the knowledge of their 'true self and identity which had been stolen from them by Christians'.[127]

Ali's teachings had a strong influence upon Wallace Fard Muhammad who in 1930 founded the Nation of Islam. Fard declared that Mecca was his original hometown and that he was descended from the royal dynasty of the Hashemite clan of Muhammad. Fard taught that blacks were in reality Arabs and Muslim Asiatics who were enslaved by the 'blue-eyed devils', i.e. whites. Fard was later deified as God incarnate, and succeeded by Elijah Muhammad in 1934 who saw himself as the Messenger of Allah, i.e. the Messenger of Fard.[128]

Since then, both activists and converts of the Nation of Islam largely regard the conversion of blacks to Islam as a form of rediscovering their 'African identity'. A letter copied and sent by potential converts to Elijah Muhammad attests to this. It reads in part, 'I desire to reclaim my Own. Please give me my Original Name. My slave name is as follows: – ' (i.e. Western or 'Christian' names).[129] Christianity is projected as the religion of former slave masters, i.e. the religion used to exploit, degrade, oppress and dehumanize the African.

With regard to the position of the Nation of Islam, the main thrust of their claims about African identity is aimed at boosting the self-esteem of converts in the face of white supremacy and racial discrimination. In doing this they 'sought to combine black identity with the culture of Islam to form the myth of black supremacy'.[130]

---

126. Although the Nation of Islam is primarily an American, and to some extent, British phenomenon, its views on this issue are crucial for various reasons. First of all, as we have stated, our use of the term 'black Africa' is as geographical as it is ideological. Hence Africans in the diaspora are included and their views are not only relevant but crucial. Second, the Nation of Islam claims for itself the role of calling Africans back to their 'origins' and 'true' identities. And third, quite recently the current leader, Louis Farrakhan, has being going round certain parts of black Africa, such as Ghana and South Africa, trying to sell the message of the Nation.

127. N. Tinaz, 'The Nation of Islam: Historical Evolution and Transformation of the Movement', *Journal of Muslim Minority Affairs*, vol. 16, no. 2 (1996), pp. 193–4.

128. Ibid., pp. 194–5.

129. Martha F. Lee, *The Nation of Islam: An American Millenarian Movement* (New York: Syracuse University, 1996), p. 37. The 'Original Name' given to converts was most often an 'X' (such as Malcolm X), interpreted as symbolizing not only the fact that the convert was 'ex' his/her pre-conversion self, but also the fact that African Americans could not know their real names. This was abandoned and converts given Arabic names. For example Malcolm X, after pilgrimage, became known as El Hajj Malik El-Shabazz while Cassius Clay, the renowned World Heavyweight Champion, upon conversion became Muhammad Ali.

130. Tinaz, 'The Nation of Islam', p. 206.

Encountering the Encounters: Arab-Islam and Black African Experience 213

While one can sympathize with the Nation of Islam's analysis of the historical experiences of African Americans, there are some basic difficulties with some of its ideological and religious claims. For instance, to claim Arab origins for Africans, conversion to Islam and the adoption of Arab names as a form of 're-Africanization' or liberation from the servile past, in the light of the Arab/Muslim enslavement of blacks down the centuries as detailed in the preceding chapter, makes such an ideology naive, to say the least.

But before we rush to such conclusions, it is worth pointing out that the Nation of Islam's appeal is to mythology rather than history, which makes these particular aspects of their claims, at best, articles of faith than historical facts. Nevertheless, while the myth of Arab-Islamic origins might appeal to a certain section of the African diaspora in the West, it is nothing short of an identity suicide to, at least, the southern Sudanese whose war with successive Arab-Islamic governments is basically to remain non-Arab.[131] This has nothing to do with Arab culture per se, but resistance to real or imagined cultural imperialism irrespective of its origins.

Within the multilingual, multicultural and multiethnic African context, it is not only ethnic and cultural imperialism that are resisted, but any marginalization or inadequate acknowledgement and appreciation (real or imagined) of any one specific cultural group. These, among other factors, underlie the tensions and bloody conflicts in parts of the continent such as Rwanda, Burundi, Liberia, Sierra Leone, etc. Such conflicts also underline the sensitivity and passion Africans have for their cultural heritages.

But, perhaps even more significantly, renowned African scholars such as Ali Mazrui equally express the view that Islam is an African religion in essence. Mazrui opines that Africa acted as a safe haven for the early converts to Islam; that the Amhara of Ethiopia and Somalia share some cultural similarities with the Arabs; that Greater Yemen is separated from Djibouti 'by only a stone's throw'; and that the whole of North Africa has been Islamized and Arabized.

On this basis, Islam, according to Mazrui, is 'eligible for consideration as originally African, as well as Asian'. According to Mazrui, it is European geographers who, by declaring the Red Sea rather than the Persian Gulf as Africa's north-eastern boundary, 'dis-Africanised the Prophet Muhammad' and as such Islam. Mazrui then continues to speculate, 'would the desire for the Africanisation of Islam have been politically diffused if it was demonstrable that Islam itself was an African religion?'[132] The essence of all the foregoing claims,

---

131. See *Facing Genocide*. Relating the Nuba people's pride in their distinctive traditions of music, dance, body art and wrestling, and to Northern Arab Sudanese contempt of these practices, the report observes that 'in an important sense, the war is a struggle for who has the right to define Nuba identity': Ibid., p. 5.
132. Mazrui, *Triple Heritage*, p. 36. Mazrui argues, on the other hand, that Christianity can only be considered African in so far as its Semitic origins can be proven to have

214 The Legacy of Arab-Islam in Africa

implicitly and explicitly, is that African identity should not or cannot be distinguished from Arab-Islamic identity.

Mazrui appears to accept the principle of an African identity that requires affirmation, and as such endeavours towards the 're-Africanization' of the Arabian Peninsula and Islam by redrawing Africa's boundaries. Mazrui himself, however, acknowledges the wistfulness of this thesis when he concedes that 'the re-Africanisation of the Arabian Peninsula is only an idea in the head of a scholar. It may never become a course in the hearts of men.' The wistfulness of Africanizing the Arabian Peninsula is even more so, in Mazrui's own words, because:

> The most difficult people to convince of a greater territorial Africa may well turn out to be the inhabitants of the Arabian peninsula. They have grown to be proud of being the 'Arabs of Asia' rather than the 'Arabs of Africa'. They are not eager to be members of the Organisation of African Unity, however helpful such a move would be for the OAU's budgetary problems.[133]

In fact it is not only the inhabitants of the Arabian Peninsula who would resist being identified as or with black Africa but those within the continent. In reference to lip-service paid to African unity by North African leaders, an African-Muslim head of state described Arab attitudes to black Africa as a 'manipulation ... which has just become like a game of chess for certain ends that are difficult for those outside the Arab political problems to understand'.[134]

The fact of the matter is that Arabs, whether within or without the African continent, are not only acutely aware of their racial, cultural, historical and regional specificity and therefore Arab identity, but are quite understandably proud of it. Commenting on the suggestion that Arabs and Africans have one and the same identity, an Arab scholar rightly intimated that

> It would be more appropriate to admit that the Arabs have a separate identity from the Africans than to rule out any such distinction ... It is true that there

> African roots. In reality, however, 'Christianity is a religion of Europe' because it 'has basically been rejected by its founders': Ibid., p. 37. Some Arab-Muslim scholars have also expressed the view that there can be no distinction between Arab identity and African identity. In a paper presented at a seminar of Arab-Muslim scholars organized in 1983 in Amman, Jordan, Izzu-din Amar Musa argued that to hold Arab identity as distinct from African identity is not only erroneous but mischievous. According to Amar Musa, the term 'Afro-Arab relations' 'is used by scholars, politicians, Arabs and Africans alike, as if they are dealing with two different entities and as if there are Arabs without Africa, or Africans without Arabs'. In other words, despite the mistake, or rather mischief, of European geographers, both the Messenger and message of Islam are African. Izzu-din Amar Musa, 'Islam and Africa', in Haseeb (ed.), *The Arabs and Africa*, p. 58.

133. Mazrui, *Triple Heritage*, p. 38.
134. Seyni Kountche of Niger, at an Islamic conference in Taif, Saudi Arabia, in 1981. Cited in O.H. Kokole, 'Religion in Afro-Arab Relations: Islam and Cultural Changes in Modern Africa', in Alkali et al. (eds.), *Islam in Africa*, p. 245.

Encountering the Encounters: Arab-Islam and Black African Experience 215

is no Africa without Arabs ... But it is not accurate to consider African cultures, or the cultural development of African peoples, as being identical with Arab culture ... There are certain well-known differences in race, language and culture, which do not damage Afro-Arab relations, so long as the African identity is recognised and given due respect.[135]

Having said that, assuming for the sake of argument that Arab culture, and as such Arab-Islam, are essentially African, there are two crucial queries that can still be raised. First, within the context of multicultural and multireligious Africa, should Arab-Islamic culture be seen as *the* African heritage or an aspect of it? Mazrui seems to be suggesting that the Arab-Islamic heritage is the ultimate African heritage.

This can be deduced from Mazrui's tacit approval and prediction that through the twin processes of Arabization and Islamization the destiny of non-Arab and non-Muslim Africans such as the southern Sudanese 'appears to be a slow but definite assimilation into the Arab fold'.[136] Leaving aside the brutal policies of the Arab-Islamic-led Sudanese government towards African groups like the Nuba,[137] any programme of assimilating non-Arab and non-Muslim Africans (and even non-Arab Muslims) into the Arab fold is no less culturally and ideologically imperialistic and subversive than the infamous French colonial policy of assimilation.

We would like to suggest with regard to Arab-Islam and African identity that, first and foremost, it is wishful thinking and escapist to conceive of Africanizing Islam by redrawing Africa's geographical boundaries to include the Arabian Peninsula in Africa. Indeed, the geographical or cultural origin of Islam is not the point at issue. The issue is whether the Islamic dispensation has been employed to dehumanize and degrade Africans, as demonstrated in chapters 3 and 4, or not. If it has, then a more realistic approach is to evaluate the past critically and take steps towards adapting the Islamic tradition in the light of contemporary African experience as African Christians are doing with their inherited traditions.

Second, whether Arabs and Islam are part of Africa or not is not an issue. The fact is that Africans and Arabs have different and most often mutually exclusive cultural identities and historical experiences that cannot simply be glossed over even with the best of intentions. It is up to Africans, like Arabs, to be true to themselves and acknowledge the differences. Different identities are not necessarily stumbling blocks for co-operation. On the contrary, a genuine

---

135. Abdelkader Zebadia, 'Comments', in Haseeb (ed.), *The Arabs and Africa*, p. 81.
136. Mazrui, *Triple Heritage*, p. 92.
137. For graphic and sombre accounts of how the Islamist government of Sudan is systematically destroying villages of the Nuba mountains and abducting inhabitants to 'peace camps' where the Arab-Islamic culture is enforced upon the victims, see *Facing Genocide*.

216 *The Legacy of Arab-Islam in Africa*

Afro-Arab co-operation has to involve the affirmation, appreciation and celebration of the inalienable differences inherent on either side.

One cannot deny that Africans have chosen Islam and that such legitimate choices make Islam an African heritage. Thanks to their longstanding historical encounters with Arab-Islam in all its socio-religious, economic and political guises, the Arab-Islamic dispensation has made indelible imprints on the cultural identities of African groups, Muslim and non-Muslim. To such African groups as the Fulani, the Mandingo, the Hausa, the Yao, etc. Islam is inextricably tied up with their various local histories and cultures, making it an integral part of the collective African heritage and identity.

Indeed, black African Muslims, both in Africa and the diaspora, have in the last few decades become increasingly assertive of their Islamic identity.[138] The point at issue, therefore, is not whether Islam has become an intrinsic part of contemporary African heritage and identity. On the contrary, it is because Islam is an intrinsic aspect of the collective African heritage that there is a need to celebrate it within the African rather than any other context. In other words, the African colouring of Islam should be unequivocally acknowledged and unashamedly celebrated by African Muslims. But can this be a realistic option in light of Arab-Islamic orthodoxy?

THE ARAB FACTOR IN SUNNI ISLAMIC ORTHODOXY

In the light of some of the things said above it may be wondered whether Muslim religious orientation could be divorced from the Arab factor. After all, unlike Christianity whose umbilical cord with its cultural cradle is all but severed, 'Islam is the spiritual base of Arab culture'.[139] To use the words of al-Faruqi:

> Islam did not come into existential being *ex nihilo*; nor did it ever create for itself a consciousness or spirit that was not Arab. Its original Arab spirit was never dislodged or even contested by the particular spirit of the ethnic groups that embraced Islam, as was to happen to Christianity after the Reformation.[140]

In other words, there is an inextricable link between Islam, on the one hand, and the Arabic language and Arab cultural values, on the other. The question we are seeking to address here is whether non-Arabs in general and Africans in particular can afford to take a critical look at the Arab cultural trappings of Islam

138. L. Brenner, 'Muslim Representations of Unity and Difference in the African Discourse', in Brenner (ed.), *Muslim Identity and Social Change*, pp. 1 ff. All the essays in the book underscore the fact that African Muslims, in line with global developments in the Muslim world, are taking their Islamic identity seriously.

139. Y.F. Hasan, 'Comments', in Haseeb (ed.), *The Arabs and Africa*, p. 56.

140. Al-Faruqi, '*Urubah*, p. 202.

Encountering the Encounters: Arab-Islam and Black African Experience 217

without tripping over the hurdle of 'orthodoxy'. The Arab factor, we believe, is a fundamental issue that cannot be avoided when talking about the need to rethink Islam within the pluralistic African context and affirming and celebrating the African factor in Islam.

Many people will agree that Islam was historically conceptualized within the Arab cultural context and inevitably took that context as its medium of expression. For instance, the Qur'an was revealed in the Arabic language using such familiar Arab mediums as poetical prose, socio-religious expressions, symbolism and rituals.[141] Now, of course, questions regarding pre-Islamic Arab elements in Islam are, at best, devoid of significance for conservative Muslims, and, at worst, blasphemous. This is primarily due to the traditional Muslim belief that the pre-Islamic Arab rituals appropriated into Islam were part of the religion of Abraham, the ancestral father of the Arabs, which was corrupted by later generations and purified by Muhammad.

Nevertheless, this belief does not negate the fact that there was as much Islamization of the Arabs as there was Arabization of historical Islam. Al-Faruqi makes this point very poignantly when he talks about the fact that 'Islam, being the transcendental ideal values themselves, could acquire real existence only by determining the consciousness and will, the soul of a real-existent people – in this case, of the Arab stream of being'.[142] The question, however, is: where does this place the Arab factor in the non-Arab-Muslim expression of Islam?

As far as al-Faruqi, and indeed traditional Muslim devotion, is concerned it means Islam is 'solely given in terms of Arab consciousness, necessarily informed in the Arabic tongue, necessarily figurized in Arab ethic and culture and necessarily embodied in the Arab stream of being'.[143] The emphasis on the 'solely' and 'necessarily' suggests that the Arab factor is absolute and non-negotiable as far as Islam is concerned. Thus in effect, the Arabic language and culture cannot be divorced from Islam.

Al-Faruqi spells out the full implications of the Arab factor in Islam for non-Arab converts in the following words:

> Converts to Islam [have] to learn an Arabic Qur'an; that is, ethically and religiously think in Arabic, and to think in terms of ideas of Arab consciousness. They [have] to emulate Arab conduct; that is to realize values whose ought-to-be's and ought-to-do's have been constructed as particulars of Arab personal and social life.[144]

141. Mohamed El-Awa, 'The Place of Custom ('Urf) in Islamic Legal Theory', *The Islamic Quarterly*, vol. 17, nos. 3 and 4 (July–December 1973), pp. 177–80; Watt, *Muhammad at Mecca*, pp. 47 ff; C. Wendell, 'Pre-Islamic Period of Sīrat'l-Nabī', *Muslim World*, vol. 62 (1972), pp. 12–41.
142. Al-Faruqi, *'Urubah*, p. 204.
143. Ibid., pp. 203–4.
144. Ibid., p. 204.

218 *The Legacy of Arab-Islam in Africa*

In effect, the indispensability of the Arab factor in Islam is justified on the basis that historical Islam was originally conceptualized and mediated through Arab channels. Some would further argue that this is due to the fact that Arabs are a divinely favoured people 'and there can be no doubt that no people can match the Arabs in their provision of spiritual guidance and their earnest solicitude for the faith'.[145]

Others take the Qur'anic verse 'ye are the best of people brought forth unto mankind' (3: 110) as asserting 'a historical fact that is eternally true', that Arabs are 'doubly qualified for ethical excellence, first as humans, and secondly, as Arabs'. And they talk explicitly of the 'divinely favoured position of the Arab stream of being, that is, favoured in comparison to the Faustian, Hellenic, Chinese or Hindu streams of being'.[146] There is therefore no way, some have explicitly argued, in which Islam can be separated from the Arab factor because 'Arab history is inseparable from the history of Islam and Arabic was the vehicle by which Islam was initially conveyed to different parts of the world'.[147]

To separate Islam from the Arab factor, some have insisted, would only lead in one direction: decline and degeneration, if not dissolution. To quote al-Faruqi once again:

> a Pakistani, a Nigerian or Croatian may possess [Islam] in a degree as high or higher than any Meccan, Syrian or Egyptian. But commitment to [Islam] of the many communities within this stream on the whole varies in one direction only: It becomes progressively weaker, just as the stream water becomes progressively shallower, the further it is removed from the principal bed of the stream.[148]

Thus, Islam, in effect, can only be found in its purest or fullest form in its original Arab cultural garb.

All non-Arab cultures are potential sources of dilution and have to be relegated to the realm of hopeless *kufr*, standing in need not just of Islamization but also Arabization. That is why

> the Prophet's requirement was that the non-Arab converts ought to be Arabicized and the divine dispensation that the Qur'an – the main fount of Islam – is divine in its Arabic and hence untranslatable, thus establishing once

---

145. Al-Kawākibī, quoted in A.A Duri, *The Historical Formation of the Arab Nation: A Study in Identity and Consciousness*, trans. L.I. Conrad (London: Croom Helm, 1987), p. 191.
146. Al-Faruqi, *'Urubah*, pp. 6, 204. About a quarter of a century later, al-Faruqi seems to have realized the insobriety of his views even though he never directly retracted any of his earlier claims. See *The Cultural Atlas of Islam* (New York: Macmillan, 1986), pp. 188 ff.
147. Mohamed El-Mili, 'Comments', in Haseeb (ed.), *The Arabs and Africa*, p. 49.
148. Al-Faruqi, *'Urubah*, p. 199. Al-Faruqi thinks that by virtue of being the original recipients of the Islamic revelation, Arab Muslims are 'at an advantage over those who have to struggle to appropriate this revelation': Ibid., p. 6.

Encountering the Encounters: Arab-Islam and Black African Experience 219

and for all that the ideal values can be reached only through the medium of Arab consciousness.[149]

The strength and weakness of the superiority and non-negotiability of the Arab factor, of course, depends entirely on the claim that its case is made in heaven, a claim that can neither be proven nor rationally and empirically disproved. If, however, a non-Arab assessment of claims of Arab cultural and racial superiority were to be made with the same passion as al-Faruqi does in his *'Urubah*, it would no doubt reject such claims with equal if not more contempt than al-Faruqi does concerning non-Arab factors. Such a non-Arab assessment would view any such claims as an Arab cultural imperialism gone crazy.

Indeed, a few people will disagree that the chief underlying cause for the mainly Persian protest movement culminating in the emergence of Shi'i Islam as early as 661 CE was a resistance to and rejection of Arab cultural and racial chauvinism in the name of Islam. Similarly, Turkish nationalism under Mustafa Kemal Ataturk (1881–1938) and his ideology of 'Turkification' received impetus against the background of perceived Arab imperialism under the guise of Islam. The same is true of other sparks including those of sub-Saharan Africa as briefly detailed above and contemporary Berber cultural revivalism in North Africa.

The questions that a non-Arab may want answered in relation to claims of Arab superiority may not necessarily be why the latter is 'divinely favoured', but why non-Arab factors are less favoured by God. Why, for instance, is the Arab patriarchal system accepted as part of Muslim family laws while the matriarchal systems of African groups such as the Beja, the Yao and the Akan not acceptable? Why are non-Arab names, languages, legal codes and socio-political systems at best accorded an inferior status to their Arab parallels and at worst labelled *kufr*?

In a controversy regarding the invocation of ancestors in Kilwa, East Africa, indigenous Muslims queried why they should be denied the right to invoke their ancestors when Arab ancestors are invoked in Muslim prayers, *du'ā*.[150] Indeed, al-Faruqi came to admit (about a quarter of a century later) that to 'divide humanity ... into castes and assign "spirituality" and "talent" to some and deny others' is mediocre and irrational.

> Partiality may be a characteristic of a tribal, ethnocentric God. It is certainly not one of Islam. The tribalist God can escape the charge of arbitrariness no more than He can escape the charges of irrationality. Racism, election, parochialism, or favouritism do not become stronger when they attribute their judgement to God.[151]

149. Ibid., pp. 204–5.
150. P. Lienhardt, 'A Controversy over Islamic Custom in Kilwa Kivinje, Tanzania', in Lewis (ed.) *Islam in Tropical Africa*, p. 298.
151. Al-Faruqi, *Cultural Atlas*, p. 189.

220 The Legacy of Arab-Islam in Africa

In other words, al-Faruqi is in a sense admitting here that claims of favouritism, election, and therefore superiority anchored in divine decrees on the part of any one particular tribe or culture are not just ridiculous but scandalous. There is therefore no doubt that modest Arabs and most non-Arabic-speaking Muslims would find any suggestion of Arab racial and cultural superiority over others uncomfortable, patronizing, and, indeed, unacceptable.

However, in Africa as in other parts of the non-Arab Muslim world, there remains a latent and sometimes explicit suggestion that the degree of one's Islam depends on the level of one's knowledge of the Arabic language. Hence, by implication, an intriguing situation arises in which the prestigious and revered status of Arabic, in effect, acts to relegate non-Arabic-speaking Muslims to the anomalous position of second-class Muslims.

Within the African context, one of al-Maghīlī's central charges against the Muslim scholars of fifteenth-century Timbuktu was that

> they are non-Arabs, understanding nothing of the Arabic language save a little of the speech of the Arabs of their land, in so distorted, corrupted, and barbarous a fashion that they do not understand the arguments of the scholars nor yet are they aware of the distortion and corruption.[152]

On the basis of their being non-Arabs, among other 'handicaps', al-Maghīlī ruled that jihad against such scholars was more worthy than that against outright 'unbelievers'.

Similarly, the jihadists of eighteenth- and nineteenth-century Africa, as we indicated in chapter 3, saw the promotion of the Arabic language and cultural values as a central part of their mission. To use the words of Lamin Sanneh, 'the central task of the reformers [i.e. jihadists] was to achieve in black Africa the sacralization of the Arabic cultural milieu with which Islamic mission is properly identified'.[153] It is this tendency, not only of patronizing but of invoking the sword in the struggle to assert the primacy of Arabic in scripture, law and devotion, on the part of the Muslim zealots that is particularly worrying.

Nevertheless, very few would disagree with the basic fact that Islam is inextricably linked to Arabic language and culture. In the African-Muslim mind, just as other non-Arab Muslim minds, the Arabic language is part and parcel of the Islamic faith, indeed a revealed language rather than a language of revelation. Arabic is, to use the words of Ali Mazrui, 'the language of God'.[154] African Muslims and non-Arab Muslims in general, ordinary and sophisticated, traditional and modern, are therefore united in acknowledging 'the mesmerizing powers of the Arabic language'.[155]

152. Hunwick, Shari'a in Songhay, pp. 60–1.
153. Sanneh, Translating the Message, p. 225.
154. Mazrui, Triple Heritage, p. 141.
155. Nyang, African Identity, p. 85.

Encountering the Encounters: Arab-Islam and Black African Experience 221

As a result of this understanding, there are instances where Muslims who themselves have only a nodding acquaintance with Arabic have resisted non-Muslims taking responsibility for it in any capacity. For instance, in 1923 Geoffrey Dale, a Christian missionary, undertook the first complete translation of the Qur'an into Swahili and Muslims in East Africa resented it mainly on the grounds that Dale was a non-Muslim. They alleged he had no knowledge of Arabic, even though Dale had five Arabic professorships at British universities.[156]

In tropical Africa, as in other parts of the non-Arab Muslim world, Muslim liturgical prayers are preceded by the *adhan*, the call to prayer, in Arabic, Qur'anic verses recited during the prayer have to be in Arabic, and in most cases even the sermon is entirely in Arabic, irrespective of the fact that the overwhelming majority of worshippers do not comprehend Arabic. Similarly, although the whole Qur'an, or parts of it, have been 'translated' into some vernacular African languages such as Swahili, Hausa, Wolof, etc. these have no status whatsoever in the Islamic dispensation.

This stems from the traditional Muslim belief that the Arabic Qur'an cannot be translated into any other language. The art of reciting the Qur'an has to be learnt in Arabic. Thus, 'strictly from the issue of the language of worship, Islam has been less compromising than Christianity. It is as if the God of Islam understood only one language, Arabic'.[157] Writing on the Jakhanke, Sanneh notes that even though, due to their peaceful dissemination of Islam, Jakhanke Islam inevitably has a high degree of tolerance for appropriating local elements,

> yet both in the traditions concerning the founder of the clerical tradition as well as in the detailed work of the clerical center ... Mecca remains the unwavering point of religious orientation, reinforced by observance of the *salāt*, the standing reminder of the *hājj* obligation, and the use of Arabic in study, teaching, and counselling.[158]

The Jakhanke therefore appear to have strong commitments to the Arab factor and the appropriation of indigenous elements. This is borne out by the fact that there is little if any suggestion of nagging or pressure in Jakhanke traditions for an either/or approach towards the Arab and indigenous factors. In their commitment towards the Arab factor the Jakhanke, unlike the jihadists and contemporary revivalists, do not give any indication that they are driven by ideological considerations.

156. See J. Lacunza-Balda, 'Translations of the Quran into Swahili, and Contemporary Islamic Revival in East Africa', in Westerlund and Rosander (eds.), *African Islam*, pp. 96–105. Conversely, non-Muslims also see Arabic as an obvious sign of the Islamic religion, and in some cases, like the southern Sudan and some parts of Africa, resist its introduction in schools for fear of conversion.
157. Mazrui, *Triple Heritage*, p. 141.
158. Sanneh, *Translating the Message*, p. 228.

222 The Legacy of Arab-Islam in Africa

Similarly, in appropriating local elements into their expression of Islam the Jakhanke, unlike, say, Marwa and Limamou, do not appear to be doing it with an 'African agenda'. This suggests that their attitude to both the Arab and indigenous factors is functional. The non-ideological Jakhanke attitude towards both Arab and indigenous factors is typical of the vast majority of African Muslims in particular, and one may even say non-Arab Muslims in general.

Nevertheless, the question that naturally arises from this situation is why the Arab factor continues to appeal to African Muslims long and far removed from the Arab context and without a 'Vatican'? Lamin Sanneh suggests that the strength of both the jihadists' and revivalists' case in invoking Islam in its Arab garb as a model for their own time and place lies in the non-translatability of Muslim scriptures. He writes: 'In the sphere of its monotheist tradition, to take one example, Islam is able to act with effective authority because its judgement is enshrined in the material of a nontranslatable Qur'ān, which itself fosters a devotion and veneration bordering on the magical.'[159] Other factors, according to Sanneh, may include 'the limited literacy of the Muslim educational elite, the pressures of a foreign community, the impact of trading contracts, and the larger world of dealing with other nations and their nationals'.[160]

While all these factors may be important, not least the non-translatability of Muslim scriptures, neither the desire to be faithful to tradition nor external (and internal) pressures in themselves satisfactorily explain the strong appeal of Arabic to non-Arab Muslims in general. The appeal of Arabic must have some underlying functional basis. As far as the jihadists and revivalists are concerned, the appeal of Arabic is in their conviction and concern for the 'purity' of Islam in its Arab form with a corresponding conviction of an inherent corruption in indigenous traditions.

The non-ideological commitment to the Arab factor on the part of the vast majority of African and other non-Arab Muslims, as suggested above, is not necessarily in order to preserve the 'purity' of Islam in its Arab garb. We want to suggest that the underlying purpose for the appeal of Arabic in the religious expression of the majority of African Muslims appears to be functional and utilitarian. In other words, there may be a more fundamental spiritual purpose for the use of Arabic to non-Arab African Muslims.

We want further to suggest that a tentative explanation for the spiritual purpose of the Arab factor may be found in the non-translatability of Muslim scriptures. This explanation is not necessarily anchored either in claims of the superiority of the Arab factor as Arab-Muslim nationalists claim or the alleged impossibility of translating the Arabic Qur'an as in traditional sources. The clue to understanding the functional purpose of the appeal of Arabic in non-Arab

159. Sanneh, 'Translatability in Islam and Christianity', pp. 31–2.
160. Ibid., p. 33.

Muslim religious expression may be found in a particular perception of translation in religious matters.

Translation in religious matters may imply recasting esoteric material from strange and unfamiliar mediums to popular and familiar ones. Any successful translation in this regard may involve 'divulging', 'unveiling' and 'exposing' of hitherto hidden or 'secret' phenomena. These 'secrets', i.e. the strangeness of the phenomena, are, however, essential as far as spirituality to African cultures, and one may say most cultures (with the possible exception of post-enlightenment Western society and its culture of rationalism), are concerned. In other words there is an inherent element of not just the unknown but also the unknowable in religion, the 'unveiling' of which threatens its effectiveness and, therefore, appeal.

Writing on the controversies in East Africa surrounding Geoffrey Dale's first translation of the Qur'an into Swahili, Justo Lacunza-Balda notes that 'the Arabic language veiled and covered, so to speak, the text of the Quran for those without knowledge of Arabic, who were opposed to any uncovering or translation'. Also, 'the Sufi-inspired brotherhoods had underlined the mystical and esoteric dimension of the Quran. Translation into Swahili, or into any other language, took away the mystery attached to the Quranic text.'[161]

That is to say, the strangeness of the Arabic adds to the Qur'an its religious authority and appeal thereby making it more attractive to non-Arab African Muslims. To 'uncover' or 'expose' that strangeness, i.e. to translate it into comprehensible languages, is seen as a possible threat to its effectiveness and therefore appeal. To put it differently the unfamiliarity of the Arabic breeds faith in the Qur'anic message within a non-Arab milieu.

There are, of course, advantages and disadvantages in translation and non-translation. On the one hand, translation may bring about informed adherence to a religion, and, on the other hand, can lead to divisive, rationalizing and nominal tendencies as can be said in relation to the Christian tradition. Conversely, non-translation may foster unity and simplicity but is more likely to breed blind adherence and ignorance of belief on the part of those who are non-literate in the original languages as it may be said of the Islamic tradition to some extent.

Expressing this concern, Shaykh al-Amin bin Ali al-Mazrui, one of the most celebrated Muslim thinkers of East Africa, writes: 'What kind of [religious] ignorance is this for a Muslim to pray without knowing the meaning of what he reads in his prayer, or to recite the Quran like a parrot?'[162] It is generally argued within the context of translation in Christianity, though, that 'familiarity breeds faith'.[163] That is to say, translation of the Christian scriptures into various

161. Lacunza-Balda, 'Translations of the Quran into Swahili', pp. 100, 114.
162. Cited in ibid., p. 97.
163. Sanneh, *Translating the Message*, pp. 192 ff.

224 *The Legacy of Arab-Islam in Africa*

vernacular languages around the world has fostered rather than hindered the appeal of the Christian message. This may be due to two factors. First, translation does not necessarily involve divesting a religious tradition of its mystery or strangeness, and second, mystery or strangeness does not necessarily mean 'foreignness'.

Translation in religious matters, more often than not, may therefore involve reinterpreting and reinvesting local mysteries with imported vocabulary, concepts and value preferences, or indeed vice versa. This is particularly so within the indigenous initiated churches where local religious titles, rites and elements are infused with Christian meanings.[164] Thus, what takes place in translation is a blending or recasting of local and imported elements resulting in what may be called 'home made mysteries'.

The same can be said of the Islamic tradition in Africa. The 'indigenization' of Islam in Africa 'through blind social forces'[165] has not undermined the mysterious element and therefore appeal of the Islamic tradition. Like the Christian tradition in the indigenous initiated churches, within the Arab-Islamic tradition, local material has been reinterpreted and reinvested with Islamic terminology, concepts and value preferences. Commenting on the 'syncretizing reality' of Islam in Africa, C.F. Molla writes: 'Sacrifices are made in the name of Allah, but one is surprised to note that the former gestures have undergone no change whatsoever. Circumcisions are performed but other rites lead up to them and follow them. The new taboos join ranks with old ones.'[166] For instance, in addition to the Arabic Qur'an, the Islamic tradition has been rendered through indigenous religious figures, rites, shrines, etc. In most cases these religious figures and shrines are a more immediate focus of devotion of ordinary believers than the Prophet of Islam or the Hijaz respectively. For example, within Mouride Islam in Senegal, followers, according to one writer, 'have a reputation for revering their *shaykh* as if he were God himself'.[167] Similarly, the *magal* (the annual pilgrimage to the Mourides' holiest city, Touba), in the minds of ordinary followers parallels the annual *hājj* to Mecca.

The Arab factor, in the devotion of the vast majority of non-Arab African Muslims therefore, serves a functional purpose in the same way as does the indigenous African factor. In either case the approach seems to be pragmatic and both/and rather than ideological and either/or. In other words, both the Arab and non-Arab indigenous factors, in the devotion of ordinary African Muslims, are not in competition and confrontation as nationalists on both sides and religious 'puritans' suggest. Rather, they are seen as complementing each other.

---

164. Peel, *Aladura*, pp. 36 ff.
165. Mazrui, *Triple Heritage*, p. 150.
166. Molla, 'Islam in Africa – South of the Sahara', p. 467.
167. R. Lake, 'The Making of a Mouride Mahdi: Serigne Abdoulaye Yakhine Diop of Thies', in Westerlund and Rosander (eds.), *African Islam*, p. 217.

Encountering the Encounters: Arab-Islam and Black African Experience 225

This approach calls for critical appropriation of both factors rather than a total promotion of one and total rejection of the other. Indeed, it may be suggested that the pragmatic approach of ordinary African Muslims to Arab and non-Arab indigenous factors is more in tune with the history of the Islamic tradition than the ideological approach of the nationalists and religious puritans. For instance those who advance the absolute and non-negotiable adoption of the Arab factor base their argument on the fact that the Islamic dispensation was originally conceptualized within the Arab cultural context.

Al-Faruqi, for instance, refers to the repeated Qur'anic insistence that it was revealed in the Arabic language and asserts that 'these divine statements are not tautologies; they are not analytical, but synthetic propositions, affirming of the Qur'an, and of Islam in consequence, the fact that they are given solely in terms of Arab consciousness'. This, al-Faruqi insists, is a 'divinely favoured position of the Arab stream of being', and not 'something anybody's thinking could alter'.[168]

The original conception of historical Islam within the Arab cultural context therefore means that the Arab factor supersedes all other factors. Thus, the superiority and non-negotiability of the Arab factor within the Islamic tradition seem to be 'a lyrical gloss on the fact that the final revelation had to be in Arabic' or a simple 'turn on the fact that Arabs, through the Qur'an, were the people who, thanks to the Arab Muhammad, "enjoin the good and forbid the evil"'.[169]

There are, however, a few other Muslim scholars who, referring to Sura 14: 4, see the basis of Islamic prophetology and revelation differently. This verse states: 'And We have never sent a messenger save with the language of his folk, that he might make (the message) clear for them.' This text is, first of all, affirming a Muslim belief that Prophets, numbering 124,000 according to tradition, have been raised from among every people at one time or another.

Nurcholish Majid is of the view that if prophets have been raised at one time or another among all people, belief in all the prophets and their missions as traditional Muslim teaching requires 'implies that truth is everywhere and every time'.[170] In other words, the basis of the traditional Muslim understanding of prophethood and revelation does not favour the monopoly of truth and goodness in one culture. On the contrary, it implicitly acknowledges the possibility of truth and some good in every culture.

On that basis, there is no justification in any implicit or explicit assumption that all other cultures, apart from the Arab one, are nothing but *jahl* or *kufr* and therefore totally baneful. Thus, even at the heart of a core traditional Muslim belief, room could be found for translation, which presupposes that there might and indeed should be some truth or something good in every culture.

---

168. Al-Faruqi, *'Urubah*, p. 203.
169. Cragg, *Troubled by Truth*, p. 134.
170. Nurcholish Majid, in Saeed, 'Approaches to Ijtihad', p. 291.

226 *The Legacy of Arab-Islam in Africa*

The African factor seems to be denied this benefit of the doubt by both Muslim revivalists and most Western scholars, as indicated earlier in this chapter and in chapter 1. Revivalist Muslim activists and most Western scholars of Islam in Africa have been unequivocal in explicitly and implicitly regarding the appropriation of indigenous African elements into Islam as a sign of 'contamination' and 'pollution' of 'pure' Islam.

To some the socio-political role of Muslims is also a basis for the grading of Islam in Africa. David Robinson, for instance, speaks of a 'theocratic sub-culture' in West Africa where 'Islam is pervasive and the pre-eminent socio-political authorities are what we might call Muslim professionals', and the 'syncretic sub-culture' where 'Islamic authorities take their place alongside blacksmiths, village chiefs and other authorities'.[171] To most of these activists and scholars, therefore, the 'orthodoxy' or otherwise of Islam in Africa depends on its degree of Africanness.

As rightly observed by Kenneth Cragg in relation to al-Faruqi's romantic universalization of the Arab factor, though, 'beneath the assurance and verve of his pen there lay a deep concern for the vulnerability of Islam itself'.[172] In other words, the Arab factor is invoked with the view of protecting Islam. The same concern underlies the views of Muslim revivalists in Africa and those Western scholars they have carried along. The concern for vulnerability, legitimate as it is, however, should be balanced against quarantining the Islamic dispensation in an Arab cultural fortress. As we have demonstrated above, there is a need for pragmatic and discriminatory approaches towards the Arab factor, on the one hand, and dialogue with the common or basic African heritage, on the other, within the African context.

This approach seems to be the norm rather than exception throughout the history of Muslim religious expression. As we have alluded to above, it is well attested to in Muslim and non-Muslim sources that the Prophet of Islam was never puritanical or idealistic in his attitude towards indigenous Arab elements. Giving many stories to demonstrate the non-idealistic spirit of the Prophet of Islam, Hasan al-Karmi writes that 'this spirit of compromise pervaded many of the teachings of Islam. Think of the rules of marriage, the prohibition of wine, slavery, and others: they were all examples of compromise.' This spirit of compromise, the writer goes on to insist, 'was a source of strength rather than weakness'.[173]

Similarly, Mohamed El-Awa, pointing out that 'Islam was not a legislative revolution directed against all that was known and practised by the Arabs before its emergence', goes on to state that 'the Prophet, in his capacity as Islam's

171. Robinson, 'An Approach to Islam', pp. 124–5.
172. Cragg, *Troubled by Truth*, p. 129.
173. Hasan al-Karmi, 'The Prophet Muhammad and the Spirit of Compromise', *The Islamic Quarterly*, vol. 8, nos. 3 and 4 (1964), p. 94.

Encountering the Encounters: Arab-Islam and Black African Experience 227

legislator, made innumerable rulings legalizing Arabian customary law'.[174] Examples given by El-Awa include the laws on marriage and divorce, retaliation and the payment of blood-money, and the concept of *shūrā*, consultation. Thus, far from being idealistic, puritanical and uncompromising, the Prophet of Islam was a realist and a pragmatist on the issue of appropriating indigenous elements.

The same spirit of realism is known to have been exhibited by the early companions of Muhammad, not only towards pre-Islamic Arab cultural values, but also non-Arab values. 'Umar ibn al-Khattāb, the longest serving 'rightly guided' calif, is known to have drawn very much upon Byzantine legal and political culture.[175] Within Islamic law there has been extensive discussion on the place of *'urf*, local custom, as a source of legislation.[176] Thus, very few people will dispute the fact that during the early period 'in certain respects the formation of Islamic societies was a recapitulation of earlier processes of Middle Eastern historical development and a redefinition of pre-Islamic institutional forms in Muslim cultural terms.'[177] In actual practice, non-Arab Muslim pragmatic approaches to the Arab factor, on the one hand, and non-Arab factors, on the other, in the Islamic faith have been in existence and commonly employed right from the time Islam expanded beyond its Arabian confines into Asia and Africa. It is well known that early Muslims engaged in deep and extensive cultural exchanges with such non-Arab cultures as Jewish, Byzantine, Persian, Hellenistic, Indian, etc.

Writing on the cultural transformation during the Abbasid period (from 750 CE), I.M. Lapidus notes that 'Persian culture not only became the characteristic style of Iran, but had an important influence upon the development of Muslim culture in Inner Asia, India, and Indonesia'.[178] In the same vein, it has been demonstrated that in North Africa Berber and Roman pre-Islamic elements have been extensively appropriated into Muslim practices and festivals such as the Muslim new year, the Prophet of Islam's birthday and the Muharram of Shi'a Muslims.[179]

Thus, to the Muslim puritans of contemporary Africa, we can only echo the words of Muhammad al-Amin al-Kanimi to his contemporary Sokoto puritans. He wrote:

174. El-Awa, 'Custom in Islamic Legal Theory', p. 177.
175. Ibid., pp. 178–9.
176. M.H. Kamali, *Principles of Islamic Jurisprudence* (Cambridge: Islamic Text Society, 1991), pp. 283 ff.
177. I.M. Lapidus, *A History of Islamic Societies* (Cambridge: Cambridge University Press, 1988), p. 121.
178. Ibid. pp. 154.
179. E. Westermarck, *Pagan Survivals in Mohammedan Civilisation* (London: Macmillan, 1933), pp. 145–75.

228 *The Legacy of Arab-Islam in Africa*

Egypt is like Bornu, or even worse. So also is Syria and all the cities of Islam ... No age and no country is free from its share of heresy and sin. If, thereby, they all become pagan, then surely their books (which you admire and quote from) are useless. So how then can you construct arguments based on what those who (by your own standards) are infidels?[180]

Indeed, both Muslim and non-Muslim scholars have described the cultural dynamism and exchanges in Muslim religious expression as enriching. Ali Mazrui, for instance, talks about the Persian contribution to Islam as 'inestimable' and goes on to point out that 'the Moghul empire of India has also been a major enriching experience in Islamic history, architecture and art'.[181]

Writing on early Muslim cultural exchanges with such cultures as Jewish, Christian, Persian and Hellenistic, Western writers insist, and rightly so, that 'no matter how deliberate the appropriation' was in literature, law, theology, mysticism, philosophy, etc., 'the resulting configuration was original and unmistakably Islamic'.[182] Hence, these historical precedents are used, and rightly so, as proof of the tolerance and dynamism of Islam.

The irony, though, is that when it comes to the question of 'orthodoxy', Muslim and non-Muslim scholars, on the whole, are at best ambivalent and at worst pessimistic and even hostile to the appropriation of such non-Arab cultural values. This is more so with African elements as indicated above. Hence one is inclined to suggest that the pessimistic and chauvinistic attitudes towards African values constitute 'an explicitly or implicitly racist evolutionary discourse'.[183] And this is something African Muslims might want to consider as all the more reason why the Islamic tradition has to be recast in light of past and present African experience.

CONCLUSION

Our primary aim in this chapter has been, in the light of what has been said in the preceding three chapters, to explore the possible way(s) forward for dialogue between the black African and Arab-Muslim ideological worlds, on the one hand, and the Muslim–non-Muslim African divides, on the other. The first point we made in this direction is that there is the need to confront rather than avoid the hostile and critical aspects of the historical past. This is crucial, we have argued, because present relations are consciously and/or unconsciously prefigured upon past encounters. On this note, we called for some amount of self-criticism on the part of Muslims if there is to be sustainable inter-religious dialogue between Muslims and non-Muslims in Africa.

180. Cited by Muhammad Bello in his *Infaq al-Maysur*, trans. T.L. Hodgkin, in *Nigerian Perspectives*, 2nd edn., (Oxford: Oxford University Press, 1975), p. 263.
181. Mazrui, *Triple Heritage*, p. 146.
182. Lapidus, *A History of Islamic Societies*, p. 121.
183. Launay, *Beyond the Stream*, p. 7.

Encountering the Encounters: Arab-Islam and Black African Experience 229

We also argued in the same vein that the prospect of sustainable dialogue is directly linked to the need for critical faithfulness to inherited traditions. In this connection we argued, basically, that in the light of the African experience, there are two fundamental reasons for a critical rethinking of the Arab-Islamic tradition in the pluralistic modern African context: first, for the sake of peaceful co-existence between Muslims and non-Muslims on equal terms, and second, for an affirmation and celebration of African identity within the context of the Islamic dispensation. In either case, we argued that there is the need for a critical appropriation of the African and Arab factors.

6

CONCLUSION

The main aim in this work has been to undertake a thematic assessment of the black African encounter with the Arab-Islamic dispensation from an African perspective. The themes include that of religious change or conversion, and Muslim ideologies and practices of jihad and slavery. The purpose has been to address and where possible redress some prevailing post-colonial impressions about the encounters and its legacies. In chapter 2 the fact that Islam was introduced into tropical Africa not by an invading army of Muslim conquerors but by dispersed Muslim professionals, i.e. traders and religious divines, is highlighted.

It has been intimated that neither of these groups were 'missionaries' and that conversion associated with their activities was, in the main, indirect. We also highlighted the non-kin or 'stranger' identities of Muslims who were accommodated by non-Muslim host communities. The main point made in this regard is that under the patronage of the non-Muslim indigenous communities, non-kin Muslim minorities were hosted, protected and freely held on to their beliefs and practices. Pragmatism and compromises on both the host indigenous and non-kin Muslim communities fostered and safeguarded ethnic, linguistic and religious pluralism.

The accommodation of minority Muslim communities is underscored in this work in order to point out the tolerant and open nature of the traditional environment, while the non-kin and stranger status of Muslim communities is examined to show, among other issues, the dynamics and complexities involved in religious exchanges and conversion. On the part of migrant Muslim groups and indigenous communities, propagating Islam and conversion to Islam were respectively seen as a risk which could compromise one's identity.

Conclusion 231

The impression created by some observers therefore that because Africans were the main propagators of Islam it facilitated the adoption of Islam by other African groups is shown to be rather too simplistic.

In addition to the non-kin identities of Muslim groups, we highlighted the traditional African understanding of 'religion' in order to bring out the dynamics of religious change or African conversion to Islam. In the main, the aim has been to assess suggestions that the indigenous host traditions were weak and passive objects of religious change. We questioned this suggestion by making the point that the traditional African understands 'religion' as having no boundaries and therefore no definition. It has been intimated that 'religion' in the traditional African understanding is functional rather than epistemological, doctrinal or argumentative. It is also non-missionary. One African writer put it bluntly as follows: 'If religion consists of deifying one character and crusading around the world to make him acceptable to all mankind, then the African has no religion. But if religion means doing, rather than talking then the African has a religion.'[1] The open view of 'religion', on the one hand, fostered the accommodation of various religious traditions and participation in certain aspects of its rituals, and on the other hand, hampered 'conversions' to missionary religions such as Islam (and Christianity). In this regard, while the open and tolerant disposition of the traditional understanding of 'religion' was vital in accommodating Muslim groups and the Arab-Islamic tradition in Africa, and therefore fostered diversity and pluralism, the same mechanism fostered a critical borrowing of certain aspects of Islam. Thus most rulers, for instance, admired and utilized Muslim charms, amulets, prayers, etc. while at the same time remaining wary of its socio-political and legal content.

Some Muslim groups saw the very nature and role of the indigenous world-view as incompatible with their understanding of the mission of Islam. As far as these Muslims were concerned, nothing but the complete overthrow and overhaul of the indigenous environment was a fulfilment of Islamic mission. In this mission they saw military jihad as the legitimate Muslim religious response. This theme is developed in chapter 3 focusing mainly on the eighteenth- and nineteenth-century jihad movements of the western Sudan.

The jihadists had a twin programme of 'de-traditionalization', i.e. over-throwing and overhauling the indigenous African and his/her heritage, and Islamization, an enforcement of the legal and political content of Islam, aspects that most rulers in Africa regarded as incompatible with the traditional world view. There was no room for pluralism and diversity of beliefs in the jihadists' programme. Both in their writings and actions, the jihadists anathematized and demonized the indigenous African and his/her traditions as representatives and elements of *kufr*, whose lot was total surrender, death or enslavement.

1. M. Ojike, *My Africa* (New York: John Day, 1946), p. 181.

232 The Legacy of Arab-Islam in Africa

The central goal of the jihadists was to establish the primacy of the Arab factor in scripture, devotion and law in black Africa. They espoused a prescriptive adherence to Islam that had no room for indigenous traditions and customs. Nevertheless, despite the untold suffering meted out to practitioners of indigenous African traditions, symbols and socio-political institutions, the jihadists did not succeed in destroying their intrinsic appeal. The jihadists, however, succeeded in moving Islam from the periphery to the centre stage of the African experience in some parts of sub-Saharan Africa, but had little success in putting their ideals into practice.

Even though the jihad movements were mainly successful in the western Sudan and cannot therefore be spoken of as a continental phenomenon, the course of the jihadists and their attitudes towards indigenous Africa is deeply rooted in the Islamic tradition. Indeed, if the words of Muhammad al-Ghamba quoted in chapter 3 and the calls for jihad by some Muslim figures of East Africa[2] are anything to go by, it means that but for stronger traditional kingdoms, the intervention of the 'Christian' kingdom of Ethiopia and the colonial authorities, the jihad tradition would have possibly been a widespread continental phenomenon.

In the fourth chapter, the third theme, i.e. Muslim slavery, is examined. We pointed out that slavery in Africa has three dimensions. First, indigenous slavery which ancient African societies shared with other ancient human societies in Europe, America the Middle East and Asia. Second, the Western-Christian-inspired form of slavery, i.e. the large-scale transformations of slavery in eighteenth- and nineteenth-century non-Muslim African kingdoms such as Ashanti and Dahomey which became the main trading partners with Europeans. Then, third, Arab-Islamic-inspired slavery in African-Muslim societies.

We intimated that the fact that Africans enslaved fellow Africans (just as other races once upon a time did to their own kind) is no explanation, excuse or justification for their mass and systematic enslavement by light-skinned Muslim and Western-Christian societies. Indeed, allusions to African–African enslavement within the context of Western European or Muslim enslavement of blacks are the equivalent of, say, making references to intra-Jewish feuds within the context of the Holocaust in a bid to explain, if not excuse or justify, the latter.

We went on to demonstrate that the institutionalized and systematic enslavement of Africans by Muslim societies is better explained by the religious, racial and ideological frameworks within which the African, either by virtue of his/her beliefs, colour of skin or both, was stereotyped as destined to be enslaved. We also pointed out that the socio-economic and religious transformation of slavery in Muslim Africa was not a mere development of a pre-Islamic 'pagan' practice independent of an Islamic stimulus.

---

2. For Muhammad Baba's statement, see chapter 3 for the calls for jihad in East Africa see Ahmed, *Clerics, Traders and Chiefs*, pp. 135–7.

Conclusion 233

The fact that Muslims across racial, sectarian and geographical boundaries justified enslavement mainly on religious grounds is highlighted. Non-belief in Islam, *kufr*, is seen as the *casus belli* for enslavement. African-Muslim societies shared this ideology and justified the enslavement of fellow Africans mainly on account of their non-belief in Islam. In addition to *kufr*, light-skinned Muslims placed black Africans under a mythological curse which fettered them to servitude. This developed to such an extent that 'slave and black (*'abd*) became synonymous',[3] in light-skinned Muslim sources and societies in general and Arab sources and society in particular.

A related observation pointed out in the work is that contrary to possible impressions of colour-blind Muslim societies, light-skinned Muslims are as colour-conscious as European societies and harbour racial prejudice against blacks. Blacks are stereotyped and demonized in Muslim sources as sub-human, at best, and non-human at worst. Light-skin Muslim racial prejudice against Africans is reflected most in the institution of marriage. Since medieval times, Arabs, Berbers, Moors, Asians, Persians, Turks, etc. have regarded any relationship between their female folk and African males as a socio-religious anathema.

In this regard, claims made by E.W. Blyden and other modern Western and Muslim observers to the effect that 'the Mohammedan Negro has felt nothing of the withering power of caste' or that 'there is nothing in Mohammedan literature corresponding to the Negro – or "nigger"' of the Western world, are ill-informed, to say the least.[4] Bernard Lewis is right in describing these perceptions as myths created, partly by people like Blyden and mainly by the West, 'to serve a Western purpose'. That is, to invent a stick with which to chastise Western failings, and a 'nostalgia for the white man's burden ... this time as a burden not of power but of guilt, an insistence on responsibility for the world and its ills that is as arrogant and as unjustified as the claims of our imperial predecessors'.[5]

The systematic and mass Muslim enslavement of Africans is then detailed. First, the light-skinned (mainly Arabs, Turks and Persians) Muslim dimension and, second, the Muslim-African involvement. The main point made in this regard is that contrary to conventional theories of a humane Muslim slavery, the institution and practice of slavery in Muslim societies was as cruel and harsh as any other slave system. We demonstrated that on the whole practice was far removed from pious theories. By pointing out several cases of harsh and inhumane treatment of slaves, we illustrated that despite pious and legal stipulations that sought to ameliorate the condition of the slave, in Muslim lands slaves constituted a class of deprived and despised people.

---

3. Zoghby, 'Blacks and Arabs: Past and Present', p. 12.
4. Blyden, *Christianity, Islam and the Negro Race*, pp. 15 and 17.
5. Lewis, *Race and Slavery*, p. 102.

234 *The Legacy of Arab-Islam in Africa*

I am aware some people might accuse the work as lacking in balance in some of the issues I have highlighted in, especially chapters 3 and 4. Even though I do not think that an objective reading of the work will produce any such accusation, I should like to reiterate here a point made in chapter 1: the aim of the work is to highlight certain issues with the view of addressing and redressing some claims and myths created in post-colonial discourse on the Islamic past in Africa. It is to meet this specific aim that certain themes and issues had to be singled out for special emphasis. The important underlying aim of the work, however, is a call for dialogue and an aversion for all forms of discrimination and intolerance.

We also appreciate claims by modern Muslim apologists that 'true' and 'pure' Islam 'is not what some or many of its followers do and practice; rather, it is a set of teachings and beliefs that are confirmed by the deeds and practices of the Prophet Muhammad, the early true pious Muslims, and the good, virtuous Muslims of all ages'.[6] This may well be a legitimate intra-Muslim debate. From the non-Muslim perspective, this faceless set of 'true', 'pure' and 'original' teaching and beliefs of Islam is not an issue. The issue that concerns non-Muslims is 'Islam' as it is understood and lived by their Muslim relations and neighbours. It is this Islam, and not the so-called 'true' and 'original' Islam in textbooks, that affects non-Muslims.

It has been suggested, in relation to the issue of slavery for instance, that 'today's Arabs [and Muslims in general] should not be held responsible for what was done in the past' and that 'the best approach is to say that it was also done by others in Europe and America'.[7] However, it is one thing to address an issue in its historical perspective and quite another thing to attempt to justify or excuse it on account of others. In talking about Muslim slavery, it is not suggested, for instance, that Muslims are the only culprits in this obnoxious practice, neither are we holding the present generation of Muslims responsible for the actions of past generations.

To use a contemporary well-known analogy, the purpose of this work may be compared to that of the South African Truth and Reconciliation Commission, whose aim is to establish the bitter and hard facts of the apartheid period not for conviction and condemnation but for possible healing and reconciliation.[8] The issue of slavery is therefore treated here not as a peculiarly 'Muslim' phenomenon, but as a specific manifestation of a wider historical phenomenon that has to be acknowledged and treated within its specific cultural and historical context. Thus, rather than being an attack on 'Islam', as some might see it, it is an attempt to rake up the thorny and potentially hostile bits of the past as a kind of therapy for dialogue and reconciliation.

6. Abdallah, 'Islam, Slavery and Racism', p. 44.
7. Abdel Malik Auda, 'Comments', in Haseeb (ed.), *The Arabs and Africa*, p. 52.
8. Archbishop Desmond Tutu, chairman of the South African Truth and Reconciliation Commission, in an interview with Channel Four News, 25 September, 1997, said that what the Commission seeks to establish is not 'retributive' but 'restorative' justice.

Conclusion 235

Consequently, in chapter 5, the primary aim has been, in the light of what has been said in the preceding three chapters, to explore ways and means by which the Arab-Muslim and black African worlds could react in their own ways to the critical and hostile aspects of the historical past. The underlying purpose is to find a way forward for critical and sustainable dialogue between the black African and Arab-Islamic ideological worlds, on the one hand, and Muslim and non-Muslim Africans on the other. The hope here is to deal with the legacy of resentment, fear and sometimes hatred that some aspects of the history has engendered within some African communities.

The point stressed throughout the chapter, therefore, is that the present generation of Muslims should accept and unequivocally acknowledge the critical sides of the historical past as part of their heritage. There is no doubt that answers cannot be found to all the questions related to some of the critical aspects of the past. But then, under such circumstances, it is better to retain difficult and awkward questions than to give easy answers. In the same vein, Muslims have to take a critical view of their inherited traditions with the view of adapting them to meet contemporary pluralistic African realities without necessarily losing their essence. For 'without a critical patriotism, historiography becomes hagiography and patriotism becomes the glorification of everything, including that which should be criticised in the name of the ancestors'.[9]

This general argument is then taken further and applied to the Islamic tradition within the African context. Here I suggested, basically, that in light of the African experience there are very crucial existential and ideological considerations for rethinking Islam within the context of past and present African experience. To demonstrate this point, key trends and perceptions in Muslim religious orientation in Africa have been highlighted. I identified what I called African-oriented trends, which seek to de-emphasize the Arab factor in Islam, and then conservative revivalist trends, which seek the reverse.

It is argued that in the light of the African experience, it is neither in the interest of intra-Muslim nor inter-religious dialogue for Islam to be transported and transplanted entirely in its conservative medieval Arab cultural garb. In this connection African Muslims are called upon, first of all, to take a critical assessment of the African encounters with the Arab-Islamic dispensation and, second, to enter into dialogue with the indigenous African heritage by way of affirming and celebrating Africa's cultural and historical distinctiveness. It is suggested that such an approach would serve as a possible bridge for an African inter-religious dialogue.

Some existential and ideological considerations are then highlighted to underline the need to rethink Islam in the light of the African experience.

---

9. W.J. Hollenweger, 'Foreword', in Olupona and Nyang (eds.), *Religious Plurality*, pp. xii–xiii.

236 The Legacy of Arab-Islam in Africa

Among the existential considerations is the fact that sub-Saharan African societies, unlike, say, Saudi Arabia, are basically heterogeneous in nature. Religious pluralism in Africa is a reality and particularly unique because not only are, say, Muslims and Christians nationals and full-fledged citizens, but countless family units right across the continent comprise traditionalists, Muslims and Christians, if not more.

In this pluralistic context, Muslims live, relate and closely interact with relatives, friends and neighbours of different religious persuasions either as majorities or minorities. To espouse a thorough-going Islamic conservatism which has no room for tolerating let alone celebrating diversity and difference can (and has proven to be) potentially bloody. While taking a critical view of such legacies as the jihad tradition and the history of Muslim slavery will not only reassure non-Muslim Africans who see themselves as victims and create an atmosphere for dialogue, but would also help Africans to learn lessons from their past.

As far as the ideological considerations are concerned, they basically have to do with the appreciation and affirmation of the historical and cultural Otherness of Africa. An Arab Muslim lamented that 'it is a real pity that Asians and Africans should yearn after the kind of state which was born out of the intellectual and spiritual movements in Europe beginning with the Reformation and finishing in the nineteenth century Romanticism'.[10] The issue, though, is that quite apart from its blatantly discriminatory prescriptions against women and non-Muslims, non-Muslim Africans will equally see any adoption or imposition of the *shari'a*, which resulted from the intellectual and spiritual movement of the seventh-century Arab cultural milieu, as no less of a pity! An African self-appreciation and affirmation in the light of the Islamic tradition is therefore just as important as it is with the Christian West.

S.S. Nyang's comments on cultural chauvinism and imperialism within the context of Christianity in Africa are therefore very illuminating in this regard. Nyang observes that 'Christianity's future [in Africa] will be a bleak one if African man is not allowed to weave a form of Christianity that is not destructive of the African personality'. Nyang goes on to state that 'Christian missions will continue to play a useful role in African societies so long as African pride and dignity are not violated in the name of a bogus Christianity that is based on the cultural superiority of its alien promoters'.[11]

Applying these instructive observations to Arab-Islam and Arab cultural and racial superiority towards Africans and in Africa, Africans are called upon to take responsibility in working out a form of Islam that eschews all forms of Arab racial and cultural supremacy and affirms an African identity by engaging the indigenous African environment in dialogue.

10. Al-Faruqi, in *Christian Mission and Islamic Da'wah*, p. 87.
11. Nyang, *African Identity*, pp. 68–9.

Conclusion 237

And when we talk of engaging African heritage in dialogue, it does not necessarily have to involve making 'space for the righteous and just Other in a theology of pluralism for liberation'[12] i.e. a doctrinal and ideological 'acquittal' or 'inclusion' of the hitherto indicted and excluded. For instance, on whose terms of 'righteousness' and 'justice' is that procedure going to be based? Any such 'acquittal' and 'inclusion', in my view, is no less presumptuous than the earlier indictment and exclusion.

The first step of dialogue with indigenous Africa should be to unlearn acquired misinformation and stereotypes and to begin to appreciate the Other through their own lenses. In other words, Muslims may want to divest inherited Islamic traditions of acquired religious and ideological prejudices, and of the stereotyping, stigmatizing and demonizing of the indigenous believer and the common or basic African heritage, and, of course, vice versa where such parallels are found within the indigenous and other traditions.

African-Muslim dialogue with indigenous Africa should, therefore, first of all, be geared towards bringing about a change of perception and attitude in the Self. In this regard, the Self needs as much liberation as the Other. For, as Leonard Swidler has observed, there must be a possibility for change within the Self, and a disturbing one at that, in dialogue 'if we would act with integrity'.[13] This change or liberation will in turn produce the climate for the second phase Swidler identifies, namely to 'begin to discern values in the partner's tradition and wish to appropriate them into my own tradition'.[14]

In the case of the Islamic tradition in Africa, it may even be said that the second phase is not so much appropriation – for as I have indicated in many instances throughout this work, appropriation has already taken place – but rather a critical affirmation of appropriated local values. The lack of an affirmation of the common African heritage on the part of well-meaning Muslims is what revivalist 'puritans' exploit in declaring local customs *kufr* and by extension declaring the vast majority of ordinary and traditional Muslims *kuffār* for retaining indigenous customs.

Second, engaging in dialogue with indigenous Africa can provide possible bridges for an African inter-religious dialogue and solidarity. As indicated in the work, Africans, both on the continent and in the diaspora, have been very critical, to say the least, of European Christianity, mainly because of the perception – largely supported by the historical encounters – that it has been used to humiliate and dehumanize the African and his/her cultural values. Concomitantly, post-independent African socio-religious and political thought has been geared towards a retrieval, affirmation and reassertion of the common or basic African heritage.

---

12. Esack, *Liberation and Pluralism*, p. 14.
13. Swidler, 'Dialogue Decalogue', p. 1.
14. Ibid., p. 4.

238 *The Legacy of Arab-Islam in Africa*

A specifically African-Muslim contribution to this post-colonial African intellectual environment in the form of an intellectual attempt to affirm the common African heritage within the Islamic tradition would no doubt bring some unique insights into the discussions. Such a Muslim endeavour will also strike a chord with non-Muslim Africans engaged in this exercise on the Christian side, thereby offering Africans not only a concerted front against all forms of externally anchored cultural and racial chauvinism but, even more so, a possible bridge for inter-religious dialogue between Africans.

As demonstrated in chapter 2, until the jihad periods there were longstanding harmonious inter-religious exchanges and relations between Muslims and non-Muslims, which is still the case in most parts of Africa. Most observers attribute this peaceful relationship to mechanisms inherent in the indigenous heritage. Ali Mazrui calls it 'the basic compassion of indigenous African cultures'.[15]

S.S. Nyang on his part talks about 'the secret language ... of tolerance and social harmony' evolved by the African over 'several thousand years of experimentation with the old religion'. This is the 'language', as Nyang rightly points out, that Islam (and Christianity) 'must cultivate ... if they are to fulfil their mission both in Africa and the modern world'.[16] This 'basic compassion' or 'secret language of tolerance' is manifested in the principles of accommodation within African cultures as delineated in chapter 2.

We suggested that room could be found in Muslim belief in prophethood and revelation, prophetic and historical precedent for a pragmatic rather than an ideological approach towards Arab cultural values, on the one hand, and non-Arab indigenous values, on the other. To those who are concerned with 'purity', 'orthodoxy' and 'normativeness' of the Islamic dispensation, the following observation from I.M. Lewis may serve as timely food for thought:

> It is not just oral, pre-Islamic culture that dilutes the unswerving eternal truths conserved in literate mainstream Islam. Elements in literate main-stream Islam also introduce and perpetuate alternative renderings of the Prophet's message. Islam is thus not the 'religion of the book' but, rather, the 'religion of the books', a package of written compendia that in their catholic profusion facilitate the diffusion and rediffusion of so-called pre-Islamic survivals.[17]

The call for a critical attitude towards the Arab factor in Islam does not mean that African Muslims should not aspire for values of their choice. It is their

15. A. Mazrui, 'African Islam and Comprehensive Religion: Between Revivalism and Expansion', in Alkali et al. (eds.), *Islam in Africa*, p. 251.
16. Nyang, *African Identity*, pp. 86–7. Ironically, this statement was made after the writer approvingly wrote about the jihadist programme of 'de-traditionalisation', calling the European intervention, which halted it as 'a tragic experience' and a 'blunder'. Ibid., p. 40.
17. Lewis, *Religion in Context*, p. 107.

Conclusion 239

democratic right to make such choices so far as they recognize the rights of other Muslims and non-Muslims to make and hold on to their choices. The assertions made by some Muslims that theirs is 'the eternal, unalterable model ... for all times and for mankind' is certainly not conducive to peaceful relations in a pluralistic context.[18]

Also, by suggesting a critical approach to Islam fashioned either from earlier or contemporary Arab and other non-African contexts, we are by no means decrying Islam in the garbs of non-African cultures. In other words, by suggesting that Islam in its Arab cultural trappings is not conducive to the African context we are not implying that Arab forms of Islam are bad or wrong. On the contrary, it is our considered opinion that the adaptation of Islam into any culture, including the African one, has been and remains not only inescapable but also desirable.

It is on this basis that we have been critical of the universalization of the Arab factor in Islam as 'orthodox' and therefore the only vehicle of expressing 'true' and 'pure' Islam. It is in this vein that we have been critical of the apparent double standards, whereby indigenous Persian, Indian and North African elements appropriated in Muslim practice are regarded as 'original and unmistakably Islamic'[19] whilst African elements are indiscriminately branded as 'pagan survivals'. In short, the question raised in the work is not whether Islam in an Arab cultural garb is right or wrong but why in African cultural trappings it is at best inferior and at worst *kufr*.

Some have virtually argued that one cannot talk of African Muslims affirming and celebrating their cultural and historical otherness because 'there exists the *umma*, the global, undivided moral community of Muslims'.[20] Of course, we are not oblivious of the Muslim belief in and indeed spontaneous sense of the *umma*. But this *umma*, as demonstrated in chapter 5, has never meant uniformity in beliefs and practices in every detail. For, as rightly pointed out by R.R. Williams, 'People are not "religious-in-general", but "religious-in-particular". They follow specific traditions, with texts, history, rituals and leaders specific to a group. These are transmitted in a language, with music, persons, and gestures joined in rituals that have meaning in a specific social location'.[21]

Many people will therefore agree that the concept of the *umma* in Islam has always meant 'unity in diversity'. African Muslims do not therefore necessarily have to sacrifice their roots in order to reach out to their fellow co-religionists. Hampâté Bâ apparently expressed this view by pointing out the different cultural colouring of Islam and at the same time insisting that there is nothing like

18. Sulaiman, 'Islam and Secularism in Nigeria', p. 9.
19. Lapidus, *A History of Islamic Societies*, p. 121.
20. Launay, *Beyond the Stream*, p. 229.
21. R.R. Williams, *Religions of Immigrants from India and Pakistan: New Threads in the American Tapestry* (Cambridge: Cambridge University Press, 1992), p. 280.

240 The Legacy of Arab-Islam in Africa

'un Islam noir, pas plus qu'un Christianisme noir ou un Judaisme noir. C'est qu'il ya, avant tout, c'est l'Islam principiel, le seul qu'il convienne d'étudier'.[22]

Bâ went on to recall what his teacher told him, 'qu'il peut arriver, il arrivera très fréquemment, qu'en s'islamisant, un pays adopte une des couleurs multicolores que le gigantesque prisme triangulaire islamique peut offrir'.[23] The implication of this to Hampâté Bâ, and one would say the vast majority of African Muslims, is that real and profound as the regional and cultural particularities of Islam might be, they are nevertheless an integral part of 'le gigantesque prisme triangulaire islamique' rather than fracturing Islam and therefore the *umma*.

It should nevertheless be underlined that African Muslims need to have a sense of belonging to the global Muslim *umma*. In that regard there can be no denying the fact that African Muslims would have to exchange ideas with other Muslim groups in other parts of the Muslim world, especially the Arab-speaking countries. All that is suggested here is that these exchanges should be both mutual and critical. A wholesale importation of values, whether from the West or from the East, will only serve to perpetuate Africa's longstanding predicament of being 'the dumping ground of cultural and ideological ideas', which African Muslims rightly decried in Abuja in 1989.[24]

One way of enhancing this mutuality is for African Muslims to make a specifically African contribution to Islamic thought by claiming a place for the African factor within the Islamic tradition. I shall therefore conclude by echoing the following wish of W.J. Hollenweger:

> I am looking forward to a time when African theology and history of religion will no longer be the sole domain of Africanologists and missionlogists but takes its rightful place in the worldwide ecumenical debate. Then it will also take its rightful place in Systematic and Practical Theology, exegesis of the Bible and the Qur'an, the discussion of history and medicine.[25]

In the final analysis, it is to claim the rightful place for an African contribution in the worldwide ecumenical debate that this work has called upon African Muslims intellectually to engage the basic African heritage in dialogue. For it is only by going into the ecumenical debate fully affirming our Otherness and those of others that Africans of all religious persuasions can make their unique, and, hopefully, invaluable contribution.

---

22. Monteil, *L'Islam noir*, p. 44.
23. Ibid.
24. Alkali (ed.), *Islam in Africa*, p. 432 (in appendix).
25. Hollenweger, 'Foreword', p. viii.

BIBLIOGRAPHY

MONOGRAPHS

Abdullahi, Shehu U., *On the Search for a Viable Political Culture: Reflections on the Political Thought of Shaikh 'Abdullāhi Dan-Fodio* (Kaduna: Commercial Printing Department, 1984)

Ahmed, A., *Postmodernism and Islam: Predicament and Promise* (London: Routledge, 1992)

Ahmed, H., 'Clerics, Traders and Chiefs: A Historical study of Islam in Wallo (Ethiopia) with Special Reference to the Nineteenth Century (Ph.D. thesis, University of Birmingham, 1985)

Ali, M.C., *A Critical Exposition of the Popular 'Jihad', Showing that all Wars of Muhammad were Defensive; and that Aggressive War, or Compulsory Conversion, is Not Allowed in the Koran* (Delhi: Idarah-I Adabiyat-I Delli, 1884)

Alibhai-Brown, Y., *No Place Like Home* (London: Virago, 1995)

Alkali, N. et al. (eds.), *Islam in Africa: Proceedings of the Islam in Africa Conference* (Ibadan: Spectrum, 1993)

Anderson, J.N.D., *Islamic Law in Africa*, 2nd edn (London: Frank Cass, 1978)

An-Na'im, A.A., *Toward an Islamic Reformation: Civil Liberties, Human Rights and International Law* (New York: Syracuse University, 1990)

Anwar-ul-Haqq, *Abrogation in the Koran*, 1st edn (Bihar: n.p., 1926)

Arnold, J.T., *A Study of History*, vol. 1 (London: Oxford University, 1934)

Atta-Wenchie, A.K., 'Ahmadiyya Movement in Ghana', (BA dissertation, University of Cape Coast, 1986)

Atterbury, A.P., *Islam in Africa* (New York: G.P. Putnam's Son, 1899)

Balogun, I.A.B., (ed. and trans.), *The Life and Works of 'Uthmān Dan Fodio* (Lagos: Islamic Publication Bureau, 1975)

242 *The Legacy of Arab-Islam in Africa*

Barth, H., *Travels and Discoveries in North and Central Africa*, vol. 2, 2nd edn (London: Longmans, Green, 1857)

Beachey, R.W., *A Collection of Documents on the Slave Trade of Eastern Africa* (London: Rex Collings, 1976)

Bediako, K., *Christianity in Africa: The Renewal of a Non-Western Religion* (Edinburgh: Edinburgh University, 1995)

Bello, A., *My Life* (Cambridge: Cambridge University, 1962)

—— *Infaq al-Maysur*, trans. T.L. Hodgkin, in *Nigerian Perspectives*, 2nd edn (Oxford: Oxford University, 1975)

p'Bitek, O., *African Religions in Western Scholarship* (Kampala: East African Literature Bureau, 1970)

Blakely, T.D. et al. (eds.), *Religion in Africa: Experience and Expression* (London: James Currey, 1994)

Blyden, E.W., *Christianity, Islam and the Negro Race* (Edinburgh: Edinburgh University, 1967)

Boer, J.H., *Christianity and Islam under Colonialism in Northern Nigeria* (Jos: Institute of Church and Society, 1988)

Bolaji-Idowu, E., *Oludumare: God in Yoruba Belief* (London: Longman, 1962)

Bovill, E.W., *The Golden Trade of the Moors* (New York: Oxford University, 1958)

Bovill, E.W. (ed.), *Missions to the Niger* vol., 2, part 1 (Nendeln: Kraus, 1975; repr.)

Brenner, L. (ed.), *Muslim Identity and Social Change in Sub-Saharan Africa* (London: Hurst, 1993)

Busia, K.A., *The Position of the Chief in the Modern Political System of Ashanti* (London: Oxford University, 1951)

Callié, R., *Travels through Central Africa to Timbuctoo*, vol. 1 (London: n.p., 1830)

—— *Christian Mission and Islamic Da'wah: Proceedings of the Chambésy Dialogue Consultation* (Leicester: Islamic Foundation, 1982)

Clarke, P.B., *West Africa and Christianity* (London: Edward Arnold, 1986)

—— *West Africa and Islam: A Study of Religious Development from the 8th to 20th Century* (London: Edward Arnold, 1982)

Cohen, E. et al. (eds.), *Comparative Social Dynamics: Essays in Honour of S.N. Eisenstadt* (Boulder: Westview, 1985)

Cooley, J.K., *Baal, Christ, and Muhammad: Religion and Revolution in North Africa* (New York: Holt, Rinehart & Winston, 1965)

Coupland, R., *The Exploitation of East Africa, 1856–1890: The Slave Trade and the Scramble* (London: Faber & Faber, 1939)

Cragg, K., *Troubled by Truth: Life Studies in Inter-faith Concern* (Edinburgh: Pentland, 1992)

Dia, M., *Islam et civilisation Negro-Africaines* (Dakar: Les Nouvelles Editions Africaines, 1980)

Dunn, R.E., *The Adventures of Ibn Battuta: A Muslim Traveller of the 14th Century* (Berkeley: University of California, 1986)

Duri, A.A., *The Historical Formation of the Arab Nation: A Study in Identity and Consciousness*, trans. L.I. Conrad (London: Croom Helm, 1987)

Bibliography 243

Echerne, M., *Victorian Lagos* (London, n.p., 1977)
Encyclopaedia of Islam (Leiden: E.J. Brill, 1936; new edn, Leiden: E.J. Brill, 1960)
Esack, F., *Qur'an, Liberation and Pluralism: An Islamic Perspective of Interreligious Solidarity against Oppression* (Oxford: Oneworld, 1997)
Esposito, J.L. (ed.), *Voices of Resurgent Islam* (New York: Oxford University, 1983)
Facing Genocide: The Nuba of Sudan (London: African Rights, 1995)
al-Faruqi, I., *On Arabism: 'Urubah and Religion: A Study of the Fundamental Ideas of Arabism and Islam as its Highest Moment of Consciousness* (Amsterdam: Djambatan NV, 1962)
—— *The Cultural Atlas of Islam* (New York: Macmillan 1986)
Finley, M.I. (ed.), *Slavery in Classical Antiquity: Views and Controversies* (Cambridge and New York: Heffer/Barnes & Noble, 1968)
Fisher, A.G.B. and Fisher H.J., *Slavery and Muslim Society in Africa: The Institution in Saharan and Sudanic Africa and the Trans-Saharan Trade* (London: Hurst, 1970)
Fortes, M. and Evans-Pritchard, E.E., *African Political Systems* (London: Oxford University, 1940)
Fūdī, 'Abdallāh B., *Tazyīn al-Waraqāt*, ed. and trans. M. Hiskett (Ibadan: Ibadan University, 1963)
Gervis, P., *Of Emirs and Pagans: A View of Northern Nigeria* (London: Cassell, 1963)
Gilliland, D.S., *African Religion Meets Islam: Religious Change in Northern Nigeria* (New York: University Press of America, 1986)
Goldziher, I., *Introduction to Islamic Theology and Law*, trans. A. and R. Hamori (Princeton: Princeton University, 1981)
—— *Muslim Studies*, vol. 1 (*Muhammedanische Studien*), ed. S.M. Stern (London: George Allen & Unwin, 1967)
Goody, J. (ed.), *Literacy in Traditional Societies* (Cambridge: Cambridge University, 1968)
Gordon, M., *Slavery in the Arab World* (New York: New Amsterdam, 1989)
Greenidge C.W.W., *Memorandum on Slavery* (London: Anti-Slavery Society, 1953)
Guillaume, A., *The Life of Muhammad: A Translation of Ibn Ishāq's Sirat Rasul Allāh* (London: Oxford University, 1955)
Gwarzo, H.I., 'The Life and Teachings of al-Maghīlī, with Particular Reference to the Saharan Jewish Community (Ph.D. thesis, University of London, 1972)
Haafkens, J., *Islam and Christianity in Africa* (Nairobi: Procmura, 1992)
Hamidullah, M., *Le Prophète de l'Islam*, (Paris: n.p., 1959)
Harrow, K.W. (ed.), *Faces of Islam in African Literature* (Portsmouth: Heinemann Educational Books, 1991)
Hasan, Y.F., *The Arabs and the Sudan: From the Seventh to the Early Sixteenth Century* (Edinburgh: Edinburgh University, 1967)
Haseeb, K. El-Din (ed.), *The Arabs and Africa* (London: Croom Helm, 1985)
Hill, R., *Egypt in the Sudan, 1820–1883* (Oxford: Oxford University, 1959)
Hiskett, M., *The Course of Islam in Africa* (Edinburgh: Edinburgh University, 1994)
—— *The Development of Islam in West Africa* (London: Longman, 1984)

244 The Legacy of Arab-Islam in Africa

—— The Sword of Truth: The Life and Times of the Shehu Usuman Dan Fodio, (Evanston: Northwestern University, 1973; 2nd edn, Evanston: Northwestern University, 1994)

Hodge, C.T. (ed.), Papers on the Manding (Bloomington: Indiana University, 1971)

Hogben, S.J. and Kirk-Greene A.H.M., The Emirates of Northern Nigeria: A Preliminary Survey of their Historical Traditions (London: Oxford University, 1966)

Hunwick, J.O. (ed. and trans.), Shari'a in Songhay: The Replies of al-Maghīlī to the Questions of Askia Al-Hājj Muhammad (New York: Oxford University, 1985)

Ibn Battutah, Travels in Asia and Africa: 1325–1354, ed. and trans. H.A.R. Gibb (London: Routledge & Kegan Paul, 1929)

Ibn Fudi, Uthman, Bayān Wujūb al-Hijrah 'Ala 'l-'Ibad , ed. and trans. F.H. El Masri, (Oxford: Oxford University, 1978)

Ibn Khaldun, The Muqaddimah: An Introduction to History, vol. 1, trans. F. Rosenthal (London: Routledge & Kegan Paul, 1958)

Irwin, G.W., Africans Abroad: A Documentary History of the Black Diaspora in Asia, Latin America, and the Caribbean during the Age of Slavery (New York: Columbia University, 1977)

Issawi, C. (trans.), An Arab Philosophy of History: Selections from the Prolegomena of Ibn Khaldun of Tunis (1332–1406) (London: John Murray, 1950)

Johnson, H.A.S., The Fulani Empire of Sokoto (London: Oxford University, 1967)

Kaba, L., The Wahhabiyya: Islamic Reform and Politics in West Africa (Evanston: Northwestern University, 1974)

Kamali, M.H., Principles of Islamic Jurisprudence (Cambridge: Islamic Text Society, 1991)

Kato, B.H., Theological Pitfalls in Africa (Nairobi: Evangel, 1975)

Kelsay, J. and Turner, J. J., Just War and Jihad: Historical and Theoretical Perspectives on War and Peace in Western and Islamic Traditions (New York: Greenwood Press, 1991)

Khadduri, M., War and Peace in the Law of Islam (London: Johns Hopkins Press, 1955)

Kilson, M.L. and Rotberg, R.I. (eds.), The African Diaspora: Interpretative Essays (Cambridge: Harvard University, 1976)

Lane, E.W., An Arabic–English Lexicon, part 2 (London: Williams & Norgate, 1865)

Lapidus, I.M., A History of Islamic Societies (Cambridge: Cambridge University, 1988)

Last, M., The Sokoto Caliphate (London: Longmans, Green, 1967)

Launay, R., Beyond the Stream: Islam and Society in a West African Town (Berkeley: University of California, 1992)

Lawson, J., 'Nigerian Historiography and the Sokoto Jihads', (MA dissertation, School of Oriental and African Studies, University of London, 1989)

Lee, M.F., The Nation of Islam: An American Millenarian Movement (New York: Syracuse University, 1996)

Levtzion, N., Muslims and Chiefs in West Africa: A Study of Islam in the Middle Volta Basin in the Pre-Colonial Period (Oxford: Clarendon, 1968)

Levtzion, N. (ed.), *Conversion to Islam* (New York and London: Holmes & Meier, 1979)

Levtzion, N. and Fisher, H.J. (eds.), *Rural and Urban Islam in West Africa* (Boulder: Lynne Rienner, 1987)

Levtzion, N. and Hopkins, J.F.P., *Corpus of Early Arabic Sources for West Africa* (Cambridge: Cambridge University, 1981)

Levtzion, N. and Voll, J.O. (eds.), *Eighteenth-Century Renewal and Reform in Islam* (New York: Syracuse University, 1987)

Lewis, B., *Arabs in History* (London: Hutchinson University Library, 1969)

—— *Islam from the Prophet Muhammad to the Capture of Constantinople*, vol. 2, *Religion and Society* (New York: Macmillan 1974)

—— *Race and Color in Islam* (New York: Harper & Row, 1970)

—— *Islam and the West* (New York: Oxford University, 1993)

—— *Race and Slavery in the Middle East: An Historical Enquiry* (New York: Oxford University, 1990)

Lewis, B. and Schnapper, D. (eds.), *Muslims in Europe* (London: Pinter, 1994)

Lewis, I.M., *People of the Horn of Africa. Somali, Afar and Saho* (London: International African Institute, 1955)

—— *Religion in Context: Cults and Charisma* (Cambridge: Cambridge University, 1986)

Lewis, I.M. (ed.), *Islam in Tropical Africa*, 2nd edn (London: Hutchinson University Library, 1980)

Lovejoy, P.E., *Transformations in Slavery: A History of Slavery in Africa* (Cambridge: Cambridge University, 1983)

Lovejoy, P.E. (ed.), *The Ideology of Slavery in Africa* (London: Sage, 1981)

Lovejoy, P.E. and Hogendorn, J.S., *Slow Death for Slavery: The Course of Abolition in Northern Nigeria, 1897–1936* (Cambridge: Cambridge University, 1993)

Lubbe, G. (ed.), *A Decade of Interfaith Dialogue, Desmond Tutu Peace Lectures* (Johannesburg: World Conference on Religion and Peace, 1994)

Lucas, J.O., *The Religion of the Yorubas* (Lagos: CMS Bookshop, 1948)

Mahmud, U.A. and Baldo, S.A., *Human Rights Violations in the Sudan 1987: The Diein Massacre, Slavery in the Sudan* (Khartoum: n.p., 1987)

Marshall, D., *God, Muhammad and the Unbelievers: A Qur'anic Study* (London: Curzon, 1999)

Mawdūdī, S.A.A., *Human Rights in Islam* (Leicester: Islamic Foundation, 1976)

—— *Jihad in Islam*, 3rd edn (Lahore: Islamic Publications, 1980)

—— *Towards Understanding the Qur'an*, ed. and trans. Z.I. Ansari (Leicester: Islamic Foundation, 1988)

Mazrui, A.A., *The African Condition: A Political Diagnosis* (London: Heinemann, 1980)

—— *The Africans: A Triple Heritage* (London: BBC, 1986)

Mbiti, J.S., *African Religions and Philosophy*, 2nd edn (Oxford: Heinemann, 1989)

—— *Concepts of God in Africa* (London: SPCK, 1982)

McCall, D.F. and Bennett, N.R. (eds.), *Aspects of West African Islam* (Boston: African Studies Center, 1971)

246 *The Legacy of Arab-Islam in Africa*

McManners, J. (ed.), *The Oxford History of Christianity* (Oxford: Oxford University, 1993)

Mercer, J., *Slavery in Mauritania Today* (Edinburgh: Human Rights Group, 1982)

Miers, S. and Kopytoff, I. (eds), *Slavery in Africa: Historical and Anthropological Perspectives* (London: University of Wisconsin, 1977)

Monteil, V., *L'Islam noir* (Paris: Éditions de Seuil, 1964)

Nachtigal, G., *Sahara and Sudan*, 4 vols., trans. A.G.B. Fisher and H.J. Fisher (London: Hurst, 1987)

Nasr, S.H., *Knowledge and the Sacred* (Edinburgh: Edinburgh University, 1982)

—— *Traditional Islam in the Modern World* (London: Kegan Paul International, 1987)

Nimtz, A.H., *Islam and Politics in East Africa: The Sufi Order in Tanzania* (Minneapolis: University of Minnesota, 1980)

Nwaiwu, F.O., 'Inter-religious Dialogue in an African Context' (Ph.D. Thesis, Pontificia Universitas Urbaniana (Rome), 1989)

Nyang, S.S., *Islam, Christianity, and African Identity* (Brattleboro: Amana, 1990)

O'Brien, D.B.C. and Coulon, C. (eds.), *Charisma and Brotherhood in African Islam* (Oxford: Clarendon, 1988)

Ojike, M., *My Africa* (New York: John Day, 1946)

Olupona, J.K. (ed.), *African Traditional Religions in Contemporary Society* (New York: International Religious Foundation, 1991)

Olupona, J.K. and Nyang, S.S. (eds.), *Religious Plurality in Africa* (Berlin: Mouton de Gruyter, 1993)

Peel, J.D.Y., *Aladura: A Religious Movement among the Yoruba* (London: Oxford University, 1968)

Peters, R. (ed. and trans), *Islam and Colonialism – The Doctrine of Jihad in Modern History* (Paris and New York: Mouton, 1979)

—— *Jihad in Medieval and Modern Islam* (Leiden: E.J. Brill, 1977)

Petersen, K.H. (ed.), *Religion, Development and African Identity* (Uppsala: Scandinavian Institute of African Studies, 1987)

Petrushevsky, I., *Islam in Iran*, trans. H. Evans (London: Athlone, 1985)

Pickthall, M.M., *The Meaning of the Glorious Qur'ān: An Explanatory Translation* (London: Ta-Ha, 1930)

Quinn, C.A., *Mandingo Kingdoms of the Senegambia: Traditionalism, Islam, and European Expansion* (London: Longman, 1972)

Rahman, F., *Islam*, 2nd edn (Chicago: University of Chicago, 1979)

Rasmussen, L., *Religion and Property in Northern Nigeria: Socio-economic Development and Islamic and Christian Influence in Northern Nigeria, with Special Reference to the Rights and Views of Property among the Birom and Kilba* (Copenhagen: Academic, 1990)

Roberts, R.L., *Warriors, Merchants, and Slaves: The State and the Economy in the Middle Niger Valley, 1700–1914* (Stanford: Stanford University, 1987)

Robinson, D., *The Holy War of Umar Tal. The Western Sudan in the Mid-nineteenth Century* (London: Oxford University, 1985)

Bibliography 247

Roff, W.R. (ed.), *Islam and the Political Economy of Meaning: Comparative Studies of Muslim Discourse* (Berkeley and Los Angeles: University of California, 1987)

Rosenthal, E.I.J., *Political Thought in Medieval Islam* (Cambridge: Cambridge University, 1958)

Roy, O., *The Failure of Political Islam*, trans. C. Volk (London: I.B. Tauris, 1994)

Ryan, P.J., *Imale: Yoruba Participation in the Muslim Tradition: A Study of Clerical Piety* (Missoula: Scholars Press, 1978)

Saad, E.N., *Social History of Timbuktu: The Role of Muslim Scholars and Notables* (Cambridge: Cambridge University, 1983)

Said, E., *Orientalism* (New York: Vintage, 1979)

Sanneh, L., *The Crown and the Turban: Muslims and West African Pluralism* (Boulder and Oxford: Westview, 1997)

—— *The Jakhanke: The History of an Islamic Clerical People of the Senegambia* (London: International African Institute, 1979)

—— *Translating the Message: The Missionary Impact on Culture* (Maryknoll: Orbis, 1989)

Savage, E. (ed.), *The Human Commodity: Perspectives on the Trans-Saharan Slave Trade* (London: Frank Cass, 1992)

Schacht, J., *An Introduction to Islamic Law* (Oxford: Clarendon, 1964)

Schapera, I. (ed.), *Livingstone's African Journal: 1853–1856*, vol. I (London: Chatto & Windus, 1963)

Searing, J.F., *West African Slavery and Atlantic Commerce: The Senegal River Valley, 1700–1860* (Cambridge: Cambridge University, 1993)

Shaw, F.L. (Lady Lugard), *A Tropical Dependency: An Outline of the Ancient History of the Western Soudan with an Account of the Modern Settlement of Northern Nigeria* (London: James Nisbet, 1905)

Smith, E.W. (ed.), *African Ideas of God: A Symposium* (London: Edinburgh House, 1950)

Smith, M.F., *Baba of Karo: A Woman of the Muslim Hausa* (London: Faber & Faber, 1954)

Stewart, C. and Shaw, R. (eds.), *Syncretism/Anti-syncretism: The Politics of Religious Synthesis* (London: Routledge, 1994)

Sulaiman, I., *The Islamic State and the Challenge of History: Ideals, Policies and Operations of the Sokoto Caliphate* (London: Mansell, 1987)

—— *A Revolution in History: The Jihad of Usman Dan Fodio* (London and New York: G. Mansell, 1986)

Swann, A.J., *Fighting the Slave-hunters in Central Africa: A Record of Twenty-six Years of Travel and Adventure Round the Great Lakes and of the Overthrow of Tip-pu-Tib, Rumaliza and Other Great Slave-traders* (London: Seeley, 1910)

Swidler, L. (ed.), *Toward a Universal Theology of Religion* (Maryknoll: Orbis, 1987)

al-Tabari, *History*, vol. 2, trans. W.M. Brinner (New York: University of New York, 1987)

Taha, M.M., *The Second Message of Islam*, trans. A.A. an-Na'im (New York: Syracuse University, 1987)

248 *The Legacy of Arab-Islam in Africa*

Thomas, H., *The Slave Trade; The History of the Atlantic Slave Trade: 1440–1870* (New York: Simon & Schuster, 1997)

Trimingham, J.S., *A History of Islam in West Africa* (Oxford: Oxford University, 1962)

—— *The Influence of Islam upon Africa* (London: Longmans, Green, 1968)

—— *Islam in Ethiopia* (London: Oxford University, 1962)

—— *Islam in East Africa* (Oxford: Clarendon, 1964)

—— *Islam in West Africa: A Report of a Survey Undertaken in 1952* (London: Wyman & Sons, 1953)

Turkson, P. and Wijsen, F. (eds.), *Inculturation: Abide by the Otherness of Africa and the Africans* (Kampen: Uitgeversmaatschappij J.H. Kok, 1994)

Usman, Y.B. (ed.), *Studies in the History of the Sokoto Caliphate: The Sokoto Seminar Papers* (Zaria, Nigeria: Ahmadu Bello University, 1979)

Vaughan, J.H. and Kirk-Greene A.H.M., *The Diary of Hamman Yaji: A Chronicle of a West African Muslim Ruler* (Bloomington: Indiana University, 1995)

Vogt, J., *Ancient Slavery and the Ideal of Man*, trans. T. Wiedemann (Oxford: Basil Blackwell, 1974)

Watson, J.L. (ed.), *Asian and African Systems of Slavery* (Oxford: Basil Blackwell, 1980)

Watt, M., *Muhammad at Mecca* (Oxford: Oxford University Press, 1953)

Wensinck, A.J., *The Muslim Creed: Its Genesis and Historical Development* (London: Frank Cass, 1965)

Westerlund, D. and Rosander, E.E. (eds.), *African Islam and Islam in Africa: Encounters between Sufis and Islamists* (London: Hurst, 1997)

Westermarck, E., *Pagan Survivals in Mohammedan Civilisation* (London: Macmillan, 1933)

Wilks, I., *Asante in the Nineteenth Century: The Structure and Evolution of a Political Order* (London: Cambridge University, 1975)

Williams, R.R., *Religions of Immigrants from India and Pakistan: New Threads in the American Tapestry* (Cambridge: Cambridge University, 1992)

Willis, J.R., *In the Path of Allah: The Passion of Al-Hajj 'Umar: An Essay into the Nature of Charisma in Islam* (London: Frank Cass, 1989)

Willis, J.R. (ed.), *Slaves and Slavery in Muslim Africa*, vols. 1 and 2 (London: Frank Cass, 1985)

—— *Studies in West African Islamic History*, vol. 1 (London: Frank Cass, 1971)

Zebiri, K., *Muslims and Christians Face to Face* (Oxford: Oneworld, 1997)

ARTICLES

Abba, Y., 'The 1804 Jihad in Hausaland as a Revolution', in Usman (ed.), *History of the Sokoto Caliphate*

Abdallah, F., 'Islam, Slavery, and Racism: The Use of Strategy in the Pursuit of Human Rights', *The American Journal of Islamic Social Sciences*, vol. 4, no. 1 (1987), pp. 31–50

Adam, W., 'New Openings of Preaching in Ghana', *The Review of Religions*, vol. 81, no. 8 (August 1986), pp. 5–18

Bibliography 249

Adeleye Ojo, M., 'The Maitatsine Revolution in Nigeria', *The American Journal of Islamic Social Sciences*, vol. 2, no. 2 (1985), pp. 297–306

Adelowo, E.D., 'Islamic Monotheism and the Muslim Reaction to Christian and Traditional African Concepts of the Godhead', *The Islamic Quarterly*, vol. 24, nos. 1 and 2 (1980), pp. 118–34

Akinola, G.A., 'The Mazrui of Mombasa', *Tarikh*, vol. 2, no. 3 (1968), pp. 26–40

—— 'Slavery and Slave Revolts in the Sultanate of Zanzibar in the Nineteenth Century', *Journal of the Historical Society of Nigeria*, vol. 6, no. 2 (June 1972), pp. 215–28

Amar Musa, I., 'Islam and Africa', in Haseeb (ed.), *The Arabs and Africa*

An-Na'im, A.A., 'Islam and Human Rights in Sahelian Africa' in Westerlund and Rosander (eds.), *African Islam*

'Arafat, W., 'The Attitude of Islam to Slavery', *The Islamic Quarterly*, vol. 10 (1966), pp. 12–18

Asfar, G., 'Amadou Hampâté Bâ and the Islamic Dimension of West African Oral Literature', in Harrow (ed.), *Islam in African Literature*

Babatunde, A., 'Slavery in Yoruba Society in the 19th Century', in Lovejoy (ed.), *The Ideology of Slavery*

Bacharach, J.L., 'African Military Slaves in the Medieval Middle East: The Cases of Iraq (869–955) and Egypt (868–1171)', *International Journal of Middle East Studies*, vol. 13 (1981), pp. 471–95

Baer, G., 'Slavery in Nineteenth Century Egypt', *Journal of African History*, vol. 8, no. 3 (1967), pp. 417–41

Barbour, B. and Jacobs, M., 'The Mi'raj: A Legal Treatise on Slavery by Ahmad Baba', in Willis (ed.), *Slaves and Slavery*, vol. 1

Battran, A.A., 'The Kunta, Sidi al-Mukhtar al-Kunti, and the Office of Shaykh al-Tariqa al-Qadiriyya', in Willis, (ed.), *The Cultivation of Islam*

Bennett, N.R., 'Christian and Negro Slavery in Eighteenth Century North Africa', *Journal of African History*, vol. 1, no. 1 (1960), pp. 65–82

Berinyuu, A.A., 'The Encounter of Western Christianity and Civilization, and Islam on Ghanaian Culture: Implications for the Ministry of Pastoral Care and Counseling', *Africa Theological Journal*, vol. 17, no. 2 (1988), pp. 140–9

Biobaku, S. and al-Hajj, M. 'The Sudanese Mahdiyya and the Niger–Chad Region', in Lewis (ed.), *Islam in Tropical Africa*

Bivar, A.D.H., 'The Wathiqat ahl al-Sudan: A Manifesto of the Fulani Jihad', *Journal of African History*, vol. 2, no. 2 (1961), pp. 235–43

Boratav, P.N., ' The Negro in Turkish Folklore', *Journal of American Folklore*, vol. 64 (1951), pp. 83–8

Brenner, L., 'Muhammad al-Amin al-Kanimi and Religion and Politics in Bornu', in Willis (ed.), *The Cultivators of Islam*

—— 'Muslim Representations of Unity and Difference in the African Discourse', in Brenner (ed.), *Muslim Identity and Social Change*

—— 'Muslim Thought in Eighteenth-century West Africa: The Case of Shaykh Uthman b. Fudi', in Levtzion and Voll (eds.), *Eighteenth-century Renewal and Reform*

250 *The Legacy of Arab-Islam in Africa*

Brown, L.C., 'Color in Northern Africa', *DŒDALUS: Journal of the American Academy of Arts and Sciences,* vol. 96 (1967), pp. 464–82

Brunschvig, R., "Abd', in *Encyclopaedia of Islam,* new edn, vol. 1

Christelow, A., 'Religious Protest and Dissent in Northern Nigeria: From Mahdism to Qur'ānic Integralism', *Journal of the Institute of Muslim Minority Affairs,* vol. 6, no. 2 (July 1985), pp. 375–89

—— 'Three Islamic Voices in Contemporary Nigeria', in Roff (ed.), *Islam and the Political Economy of Meaning*

Clarke, P. B., 'Islam, Development and African Identity: The Case of West Africa', in Petersen (ed.), *Religion, Development and African Identity*

—— 'Islamic Reform in Contemporary Nigeria: Methods and Aims', *Third World Quarterly,* vol. 10, no. 2 (1988), pp. 519–38

Collins, R.O., 'The Nilotic Slave Trade: Past and Present', in Savage (ed.), *The Human Commodity*

Colvin, L.G., 'Islam and the State of Kajoor: A Case of Successful Resistance to Jihad', *Journal of African History,* vol. 15, no. 4 (1974), pp. 587–606

—— 'The Shaykh's Men: Religion and Power in Senegambian Islam', in Levtzion and Fisher (eds.), *Rural and Urban Islam*

Comhaire, J., 'Some Notes on Africans in Muslim History', *The Muslim World,* vol. 46 (1956), pp. 336–44

Constantin, F., 'Charisma and the Crisis of Power in East Africa', in O'Brien and Coulon, *Charisma in African Islam*

—— 'Leadership, Muslim Identities and East African Politics: Tradition, Bureaucratization and Communication', in Brenner (ed.), *Muslim Identity and Social Change*

Cooper, F., 'Islam and Cultural Hegemony: The Ideology of Slaveowners on the East African Coast', in P. Lovejoy (ed.), *The Ideology of Slavery*

—— 'The Treatment of Slaves on the Kenya Coast in the 19th Century', *Kenyan Historical Review,* vol. 1, part 1 (1973), pp. 87–108

Cornevin, R., 'Fulbe', in *Encyclopaedia of Islam,* new edn, vol. 2

Curtin, P., 'Jihad in West Africa: Early Phases and Inter-relations in Mauritania and Senegal', *Journal of African History,* vol. 12, no. 1 (1971), pp. 11–24

Dahiru, Y., 'Colonialism in Africa and the Impact of European Concepts and Values: Nationalism and Muslims in Nigeria', in Alkali et al. (eds.), *Islam in Africa*

Dejong, G.E., 'Slavery in Arabia', *The Muslim World,* vol. 24, (1934), pp. 126–44

Della Vida, G.L., 'Kharidjites', in *Encyclopaedia of Islam,* new edn, vol. 4

Dilley, R.M., 'Spirits, Islam and Ideology: A Study of a Tukulor Weavers' Song (DILLERE)', *Journal of Religion in Africa,* vol. 17, no. 3 (1987), pp. 245–60

El-Awa, M., 'The Place of Custom ('Urf) in Islamic Legal Theory', *The Islamic Quarterly,* vol. 17, nos. 3 and 4 (July–December 1973), pp. 177–82

Ellul, J., 'Preface' in Bat Ye'or, *The Dhimmi: Jews and Christians under Islam* (London and Toronto: Associated University, 1985)

Fage, J.D., 'Slavery and the Slave Trade in the Context of West African History', *Journal of African History,* vol. 10 (1969), pp. 393–404

Ferme, M., 'What "Alhaji Airplane" saw in Mecca, and what Happened when he Came Home: Ritual Transformation in a Mende Community (Sierra Leone)', in Stewart and Shaw (eds.), *Syncretism/Anti-syncretism*

Fisher, H.J., 'Conversion Reconsidered: Some Historical Aspects of Religious Conversion in Black Africa', *Africa*, vol. 43, no. 2 (1973), pp. 27–40

—— 'Early Arabic Sources and the Almoravid conquest of Ghana', *Journal of African History*, vol. 23, no. 4 (1982), pp. 549–60

—— 'The Juggernaut's Apologia: Conversion to Islam in Black Africa', *Africa*, vol. 55, no. 2 (1985), pp. 153–70

—— 'Many Deep Baptisms: Reflections on Religious, Chiefly Muslim, Conversion in Black Africa', *Bulletin of the School of Oriental and African Studies*, vol. 57, part I (1994), pp. 68–81

—— 'Slavery and Seclusion in Northern Nigeria: A Further Note', *Journal of African History*, vol. 32 (1991), pp. 123–35

Forand, P.G., 'The Relation of the Slave and the Client to the Master or Patron in Medieval Islam', *International Journal of Middle East Studies*, vol. 2 (1971), pp. 59–66

Ghoraba, H., 'Islam and Slavery', *The Islamic Quarterly*, vol. 2, no. 3 (1955), pp. 153–9

Glassman, J., 'The Bondsman's New Clothes: The Contradictory Consciousness of Slave Resistance on the Swahili Coast', *Journal of African History*, vol. 32 (1991), pp. 277–312

Goody, J., 'Restricted Literacy in Northern Ghana', in Goody (ed.), *Literacy in Traditional Societies*

—— 'Slavery in Time and Space', in Watson (ed.), *Asian and African Slavery*

Green, K.L., 'Dyula and Sonongui Roles in the Islamization of the Region of Kong', in Levtzion and Fisher (eds.), *Rural and Urban Islam*

Grégoire, E., 'Islam and the Identity of Merchants in Maradi (Niger)', in Brenner (ed.), *Muslim Identity and Social Change*

Harrison, P.W., 'Slavery in Arabia', *Muslim World*, vol. 29, no. 2 (1939), pp. 207–9

Hasan, Y.F., 'The Historical Roots of Afro-Arab Relations', in Haseeb (ed.), *The Arabs and Africa*

—— 'The Penetration of Islam in the Eastern Sudan', in Lewis (ed.), *Islam in Tropical Africa*

Hiskett, M., 'Enslavement, Slavery and Attitudes Towards the Legally Enslavable in Hausa Islamic Literature', in Willis (ed.), *Slaves and Slavery*

—— 'An Islamic Tradition of Reform in the Western Sudan from the Sixteenth to the Eighteenth Century', *Bulletin of the School of Oriental and African Studies*, vol. 25 (1962), pp. 577–96

—— 'Kitab al-Farq: A Work on the Habe Kingdoms Attributed to 'Uthman Dan Fodio', *Bulletin of the School of Oriental and African Studies*, vol. 23 (1960), pp. 558–79

—— 'The Maitatsine Riots in Kano, 1980: An Assessment', *Journal of Religion in Africa*, vol. 17, no. 3 (1987), pp. 209–22

—— 'Preface', in Hiskett, *The Sword of Truth*, 2nd edn

Horton, R., 'African Conversion', *Africa*, vol. 41, no. 2 (1971), pp. 85–107

252 The Legacy of Arab-Islam in Africa

—— 'On the Rationality of Conversion', part I, *Africa*, vol. 45, no. 3 (1975), pp. 219–34; Part II, *Africa*, vol. 45, no. 4 (1975), pp. 373–97

Hunwick, J.O., 'Black Africans in the Islamic World: An Understudied Dimension of the Black Diaspora', *Tarikh*, vol. 5, no. 4 (1978), pp. 20–40

—— 'Black-Slaves in the Mediterranean World: Introduction to a Neglected Aspect of the African Diaspora', in Savage (ed.), *The Human Commodity*

—— 'Notes on Slavery in the Songhay Empire', in Willis (ed.), *Slaves and Slavery*, vol. 2

—— 'Religion and State in the Songhay Empire, 1464–1591', in Lewis (ed.), *Islam in Tropical Africa*

—— 'Sub-Saharan Africa and the Wider World of Islam: Historical and Contemporary Perspectives', in Westerlund and Rosander (eds.), *African Islam*

Isaac, E., 'Genesis, Judaism, and the Sons of Ham', in Willis (ed.), *Slaves and Slavery*, vol. 1

Isichei, E., 'The Maitatsine Risings in Nigeria 1980–85: A Revolt of the Disinherited', *Journal of Religion in Africa*, vol. 17, no. 3 (1987), pp. 194–206

Jah, O., 'The Impact of Jihad on the Senegambian Society', in Alkali et al. (eds.), *Islam in Africa*

al-Jahiz, 'The Boasts of the Blacks over the Whites', trans. T. Khalidi *The Islamic Quarterly*, vol. 25, nos. 1 and 2 (1981), pp. 3–26

Jennings, R.C., 'Black Slaves and Free Blacks in Ottoman Cyprus, 1590–1640', *Journal of the Economic and Social History of the Orient*, vol. 30 (1987), pp. 287–302

Jones, H.M., 'Slavery in the Ancient World', in Finley (ed.), *Slavery in Classical Antiquity*

al-Karmi, H., 'The Prophet Muhammad and the Spirit of Compromise', *The Islamic Quarterly*, vol. 8, nos. 3 and 4 (1964), pp. 89–94

Kateregga, B., 'The Islamic Da'wah: How to Carry it to Christians', *Al-Islam*, vol. 7, no. 2 (June 1983) pp. 18–20

Kenny, J., 'Religious Movements in Nigeria, Divisive or Cohesive? Some Interpretative Models', *Orita*, vol. 16, no. 2 (1984), pp. 111–27

Klein, M.A., 'The Slave Trade in the Western Sudan During the Nineteenth Century', in Savage (ed.), *The Human Commodity*

Kokole, O.H., 'Religion in Afro-Arab Relations: Islam and Cultural Changes in Modern Africa', in Alkali et al. (eds.), *Islam in Africa*

Kperogi, F.A. and Sulaiman A.M., 'Sharia: Triumph of Kano Masses', *Weekly Trust*, vol. 3, no. 20 (30 June–6 July, 2000)

Küng, H., 'Christianity and World Religions: Dialogue with Islam', in Swidler (ed.), *Toward a Universal Theology*

Lacroix, P.F., 'Islam among the Fulbe of Adamawa', in Lewis (ed.), *Islam in Tropical Africa*

Lacunza-Balda, J., 'Translations of the Quran into Swahili, and Contemporary Islamic Revival in East Africa', in Westerlund and Rosander (eds.), *African Islam*

Lake, R., 'The Making of a Mouride Mali: Seringe Aboulaye Yakhine Diop of Thies', in Westerlund and Rosander (eds.), *African Islam*

Bibliography 253

Last, M., 'Some Economic Aspects of Conversion in Hausaland (Nigeria)', in Levtzion (ed.), *Conversion to Islam*

Law, R.C.C., 'The Garamantes and Trans-Saharan Enterprise in Classical Times', *Journal of African History*, vol. 8, no. 2 (1967), pp. 181–200

Levtzion, N., 'Abd Allah b. Yasin and the Almoravids', in Willis (ed.), *The Cultivators of Islam*

—— 'Merchants vs. Scholars and Clerics in West Africa: Differential and Complementary roles', in Levtzion and Fisher (eds.), *Rural and Urban Islam*

—— 'Patterns of Islamization in West Africa', in Levtzion (ed.), *Conversion to Islam*

—— 'Slavery and Islamization in Africa: A Comparative Study', in Willis (ed.), *Slaves and Slavery*, vol. 1

—— 'Sociopolitical Roles of Muslim Clerics and Scholars in West Africa', in Cohen et al. (eds.), *Comparative Social Dynamics*

Lewis, B., 'The African Diaspora and the Civilization of Islam', in Kilson and Rotberg (eds.), *The African Diaspora*

—— 'Legal and Historical Reflections on the Position of Muslim Populations under Non-Muslim Rule', in Lewis and Schnapper (eds.), *Muslims in Europe*

Lewis, I.M., 'Introduction', in Lewis (ed.), *Islam in Tropical Africa*

Lienhardt, P., 'A Controversy over Islamic Custom in Kilwa Kivinje, Tanzania', in Lewis (ed.), *Islam in Tropical Africa*

Lovejoy, P.E., 'Concubinage and the Status of Women Slaves in Early Colonial Northern Nigeria', *Journal of African History*, vol. 29 (1988), pp. 245–66

—— '*Murgu*: The Wages of Slavery in the Sokoto Caliphate', *Slavery and Abolition*, vol. 14, no. 1 (1993), pp. 168–82

Lubeck, P.M., 'Structural Determinants of Urban Islamic Protest in Northern Nigeria: A Note on Method, Mediation and Materialist Explanation', in Roff (ed.), *Islam and the Political Economy of Meaning*

Macdonald, D.D., 'al-Mahdi', in *Encyclopaedia of Islam*, new edn, vol. 3

Mahadi, A., ' The Aftermath of the Jihad in the Central Sudan as a Major Factor in the Volume of the Trans-Saharan Slave Trade in the Nineteenth Century', in Savage (ed.), *The Human Commodity*

Makar, T., 'The Relationship between the Sokoto Caliphate and the Non-Muslim Peoples of the Middle Benue Region', in Usman (ed.), *History of the Sokoto Caliphate*

Mazrui, A., 'African Islam and Comprehensive Religion: Between Revivalism and Expansion', in Alkali et al. (eds.), *Islam in Africa*

McDougall, A.E., 'Salt, Saharans, and the Trans-Saharan Slave Trade: Nineteenth Century Developments', in Savage (ed.), *The Human Commodity*

Meyers, A., 'Slavery in the Hausa–Fulani Emirates', in McCall and Bennett (eds.), *Aspects of West African Islam*

Miers, S. and Kopytoff, I., 'Introduction', in Miers and Kopytoff (eds.), *Slavery in Africa*

Mohammed, A.R., 'The Influence of the Niass Tijaniyya in the Niger–Benue Confluence Area of Nigeria', in Brenner (ed.), *Muslim Identity and Social Change*

254 *The Legacy of Arab-Islam in Africa*

Molla, C.F., 'Some Aspects of Islam in Africa – South of the Sahara', *International Review of Missions*, vol. 56 (1967), pp. 459–68

Muhammad, A., 'The Image of Africans in Arabic Literature: Some Unpublished Manuscripts', in Willis (ed.), *Slaves and Slavery*, vol. 1

Musa, I.A., 'Islam and Africa', in Haseeb (ed.), *The Arabs and Africa*

Norris, T.H., 'Znaga Islam during the Seventeenth and Eighteenth Century', *Bulletin of the School of Oriental and African Studies*, vol. 32 (1969), pp. 496–526

O'Fahey, R.S., 'Slavery and Society in Dar Fur', in Willis (ed.), *Slaves and Slavery*, vol. 2

Omari, C.K., 'Christian–Muslim Relations in Tanzania: The Socio-political Dimension', *Bulletin on Islam and Christian–Muslim Relations in Africa*, vol. 2, no. 2 (April 1984) pp. 5–14

Oosthuizen, G.C., 'Traditional Religion in Contemporary South Africa', in Olupona (ed.), *African Traditional Religions*

Opoku, K.A., 'African Traditional Religion: An Enduring Heritage', in Olupona and Nyang (eds.), *Religious Plurality*

Oseni, Z.I., 'The Revolts of Black Slaves in Iraq under the 'Abbasid Administration in 869–883 C.E.', *Hamdard Islamicus*, vol. 12, no. 2 (1989), pp. 57–64

Osman, J., 'Slavery Lives On', *Sunday Telegraph*, 17 and 24 March 1963

Owusu-Ansah, D., 'Islamization Reconsidered: An Examination of Asante Responses to Muslim Influence in the Nineteenth Century', *Asian and African Studies*, vol. 21 (1987), pp. 145–63

—— 'The State and Islamization in 19th Century Africa: Buganda Absolutism versus Asante Constitutionalism', *Journal of Muslim Minority Affairs*, vol. 8, no. 1 (1987), pp. 132–41

Palmer, H.R., 'An Early Fulani Conception of Islam', *Journal of the African Society*, vol. 13 (1913–14), pp. 407–14; vol. 14 (1914–15), pp. 185–92

Pardo, A.W., 'The Songhay Empire under Sonni Ali and Askia Muhammad', in McCall and Bennett (eds.), *Aspects of West African Islam*

Person, Y., 'Samori and Islam', in Willis (ed.), *The Cultivators of Islam*

Phillips, B., 'Laying Down the Islamic Law', *BBC Focus on Africa Magazine* (January–March 2000)

Porter, G., 'A Note on Slavery, Seclusion and Agrarian Change in Northern Nigeria', *Journal of African History*, vol. 30 (1989), pp. 487–91

Quinn, C.A., 'Mandingo States in the 19th Century', in Hodge (ed.), *The Manding*
—— 'A Nineteenth Century Fulbe State', *Journal of African History*, vol. 12, no. 3 (1971), pp. 427–40

Rigby, P.J.A., 'Sociological Factors in the Contact of the Gogo of Central Tanzania with Islam', in Lewis (ed.), *Islam in Tropical Africa*

Robinson, D., 'An Approach to Islam in West African History', in Harrow (ed.), *Islam in African Literature*

Rodney, W., 'African Slavery and Other Forms of Social Oppression on the Upper Guinea Coast in the Context of the Atlantic Slave-Trade', *Journal of African History*, vol. 7, no. 3 (1966), pp. 431–43

Ryan, P.J., 'Islam and Politics in West Africa: Minority and Majority Models', *Muslim World*, vol. 77, no. 1 (1987), pp. 1–15
—— 'Ariadne auf Naxos: Islam and Politics in a Religiously Pluralistic African Society', *Journal of Religion in Africa*, vol. 16, no. 3 (1996), pp. 308–27
Saeed, A., 'Approaches to *Ijtihad* and Neo-Modernist Islam in Indonesia', *Islam and Christian–Muslim Relations*, vol. 8, no. 3 (1997), pp. 279–94
Sanneh, L., 'The Domestication of Islam and Christianity in African Societies', *Journal of Religion in Africa*, vol. 11, no. 1 (1980), pp. 1–11
—— 'The Origins of Clericalism in West African Islam', *Journal of African History*, vol. 17, no. 1 (1976), pp. 49–72
—— 'Slavery, Islam and the Jakhanke People of West Africa', *Africa*, vol. 46, no. 2 (1976), pp. 80–92
—— 'Tcherno Aliou, the Walī of Goumba: Islam, Colonialism and the Rural Factor in Futa Jallon, 1867–1912', in Levtzion and Fisher (eds.), *Rural and Urban Islam*
—— 'Translatability in Islam and Christianity in Africa: A Thematic Approach', in Blakely et al. (eds.), *Religion in Africa*
Savage, E., 'Berbers and Blacks: Ibadi Slave Traffic in the Eighth-century North Africa', *Journal of African History* vol. 33 (1992), pp. 351–68
Sersen, W.J., 'Stereotypes and Attitudes towards Slaves in Arabic Proverbs: A Preliminary View', in Willis (ed.), *Slaves and Slavery*, vol. 1
Shaltut, Shaykh M., 'The Koran and Fighting', in Peters (ed.), *Jihad in Islam*
Shroeter, D.J., 'Slave Markets and Slavery in Moroccan Urban Society', in Savage (ed.), *The Human Commodity*
Singleton, M., 'Seydina Mouhamoudou Limamou Laye (1845–1909) – The Black Mahdi of Senegal', *CSIC Papers*, no. 2 (August 1990)
Skinner, E.P., 'Islam in Mossi Society', in Lewis (ed.), *Islam in Tropical Africa*
Smith, M.G., 'The Jihad of Shehu Dan Fodio: Some Problems', in Lewis (ed.), *Islam in Tropical Africa*
Southgate, M., 'The Negative Images of Blacks in Some Medieval Iranian Writings', *Iranian Studies*, vol. 17, no. 1 (1984), pp. 3–36
Sulaiman, I., 'Islam and Secularism in Nigeria: An Encounter of Two Civilisations', *Impact International* (10–23 October, 1986), pp. 8–9
—— 'The "Moment of Truth" in Nigeria: Truth is that you can Build Nothing on "the debris of Western Imperialism"', *Impact International* (13–26 April, 1984), pp. 8–10
Swidler, L., 'The Dialogue Decalogue: Ground Rules for Interreligious Dialogue', *Journal of Ecumenical Studies*, vol. 20, no. 1 (Winter 1983), pp. 1–4
Talhami, G.H., 'The Zanj Rebellion Reconsidered', *International Journal of African Historical Studies*, vol. 10, no. 3 (1977), pp. 443–61
Tanner, R.E.S., 'African Traditional Religions and their Reactions to other Faiths', *Studia Missionalia*, vol. 42 (1993) pp. 375–84
Tinaz, N., 'The Nation of Islam: Historical Evolution and Transformation of the Movement', *Journal of Muslim Minority Affairs*, vol. 16, no. 2 (1996), pp. 193–206
Troll, C., 'Two Conceptions of Da'wa in India: Jama'at-i Islami and Tablighi Jama'at', *Archives de Sciences Sociales des Religions* (July–September 1994) pp. 122–38

256 *The Legacy of Arab-Islam in Africa*

al-Turabi, H., 'The Islamic State', in Esposito (ed.), *Voices of Resurgent Islam*

Tutu D., 'The Religious Understanding of Peace', in Gerrie Lubbe (ed.), *A Decade of Interfaith Dialogue*

Tyan, E., 'Djihad', in *Encyclopaedia of Islam*, new edn, vol. 2

Ubah, C.N., 'Colonial Administration and the Spread of Islam in Northern Nigeria', *Muslim Word*, vol. 81, no. 2 (1991), pp. 133–48

Uchendu, V.C., 'Slaves and Slavery in Igboland, Nigeria', in Miers and Kopytoff (eds.), *Slavery in Africa*

der Veer, P., 'Syncretism, Multiculturalism and the Discourse of Tolerance', in Stewart and Shaw (eds.), *Syncretism/Anti-syncretism*

Wafi, A.A.W., 'Human Rights in Islam', *The Islamic Quarterly*, vol. 11 (1967), pp. 64–75

Warburg, G.R., 'Ideological and Practical Considerations Regarding Slavery in the Mahdist State and the Anglo-Egyptian Sudan: 1881–1918', in Lovejoy (ed.), *The Ideology of Slavery*

Watt, W.M., 'Some Problems before West African Islam', *The Islamic Quarterly*, vol. 4, no. 1 (1957), pp. 43–51

Wendell, C., 'Pre-Islamic Period of Sīrat Al-Nabī', *Muslim World*, vol. 62 (1972), pp. 12–41

Wilks, I., 'The Position of Muslims in Metropolitan Ashanti in the Early Nineteenth Century', in Lewis (ed.), *Islam in Tropical Africa*

—— 'The Transmission of Islamic Learning in the Western Sudan', in Goody (ed.), *Literacy in Traditional Societies*

Willis, J.R., 'Jihād Fī Sabīl Allāh – Its Doctrinal Basis in Islam and Some Aspects of its Evolution in 19th Century West Africa', *Journal of African History*, vol. 8, no. 3 (1967), pp. 395–415

—— 'Jihad and the Ideology of Enslavement in Islam', in Willis (ed.), *Slaves and Slavery*, vol. 1

Zoghby, S.M., 'Blacks and Arabs: Past and Present', *Current Bibliography on African Affairs*, vol. 3, no. 5 (May 1970), pp. 5–19

OTHER DOCUMENTS

Drumbeats from Kampala, AACC Document (1963)

Engagement: The Second AACC Assembly – 'Abidjan 69' (Nairobi: All-Africa Conference of Churches, 1970)

'Evidence of Violations of Human Rights in Sudan', Christian Solidarity International (CSI) to United Nations, Human Rights Commission (April 1996)

'*Slavery in Sudan*' by CSI to US Congress House Committee on International Relations (13 March, 1996)

'Human Rights Questions: Human Rights Situations and Reports of Special Rapporteurs and Representatives; A Situation of Human Rights in the Sudan', a note presented by Secretary-General to the Fiftieth Session of United Nations General Assembly on 16 October, 1995

KNCC Newsletter, *JPR News Analysis and Reports*, 30 June, 1993

INDEX

'abd 129–30, 233
'Abd al-'Aziz ibn Ahmad al-Bukhāri 125,
   167–8
'Abd al-Qadir al-Jilani 27, 75
Abdallah, F. 111–12, 118, 132–3, 138,
   153–4
Abdullahi, S.U. 5, 82, 96, 98, 100, 105–6,
   191, 196, 197
Abdullahi dan Fodio 64, 76, 91, 98, 99,
   105
Abrahah 132
accommodation 61, 238
Adam, M.W. 131–2
Adama, Modibbe 91
Africa
   heralds of Arab-Islam 26–33
   introduction of Islam to 24–6
   Western Christian legacy 2, 3, 6, 7,
   181–2, 184
African experience
   definition of 180–3
   conservative revivalism and 196–210,
   226
African heritage 235, 236–7
   African Muslim dialogue with 236–7
   basic and collective 181–2, 216
   need for affirmation 237, 238
   see also traditional culture

African identity, Islam and 3, 33, 181,
   210–16
African Independent Churches 3
Africans, traditional
   conversions of 47–55, 103
   as enemies of Islam 95, 97, 99
   as kufr 93, 95
   jihads against 91–4, 95–6, 102
Ahmad al-Bakka'i al-Kunti 47, 79, 86, 87,
   93–4
Ahmad Baba 127, 130
Ahmad Bamba 29
Ahmad Lobbo 78–9
Ahmad Mirza Nasir 46
Ahmadiyya Movement 46–7
Akinola, G.A. 166
Alhaji Sani 195
Ali, M.C. 125
Ali, T.D. 212
All Africa Conference of Churches 3, 5, 8
Almoravid movement 25
An-Na'im, A.A. 202
al-Andalusi, Sa'id 135
'Antara 133
appropriation 237
Arab culture 26
   Islam and 216–28, 238–9
   non-Arabs and 218–19, 222, 224–5, 228

258 *The Legacy of Arab-Islam in Africa*

Arab identity 214–15
Arab penal code 98
Arab superiority 46, 218–19, 220
Arab world, black slaves in 141–2,
    143–4
Arabian Peninsula, re-Africanization of
    189, 213, 214, 215
Arabic language 6, 28, 220–1
    Qur'an and 222–3
Arabization 98–9, 218, 219
Arnold, J.T. 138
Ashantis 31, 44, 60, 61
Askiya Muhammad 69–70, 73–4,
    147
    al-Maghīlī and 71–2
assimiliation 62

Balewa, Abubakar Tafawa 148
Bambara 43, 89, 120, 151
Barth, H. 90, 91, 149
Beidelman, T.O. 41
Berbers 25, 26, 144
black Africans, images of in Muslim
    sources 130–40
Blyden, E.W. 4, 33, 127, 136, 233
Bolaji-Idowu, E. 35
bonded society 182–3
Boratov, P.N. 134
Bornu 76, 90
    slave raids in 144, 149–50
Brunschvig, R. 123
Burkina Faso 52, 59
Busia, K.A. 56, 57

Callie, R. 163
castration of slaves 159
Chad 144–5
chiefs 56, 57
    Islamization and 60, 61, 63
    Muslims as 59–60
Christianity 33–4, 37, 55, 210, 236
    and African identity 2–3, 4
    and African religiosity 51, 52
    and colonialism xv, 2–3, 6
    conversion to 55
    de-Westernization of 3
    in Ethiopia 39–40
    impact of 5, 184–5, 237

Muslims and 175
    and slavery 2, 16, 212, 232
    translation of scriptures 223–4
Clarke, P. 13, 16, 173, 196, 197
colonialist interpretation of jihad 81
colour 130, 133
    in Muslim ideology of slavery 128–30,
    131–2, 232
    prejudice on account of 133–40, 168,
    233
Comhaire, J. 161
compromise 226
concubines, slaves as 156, 157
conservative revivalism 189–96
    African experience and 196–210, 226
conversion to Islam 8–9, 103, 230
    illness and 52, 53
    indigenous environment and 33–8,
    47–55
    Muslims under indigenous patronage
    38–44
    of slaves 159–60
    socio-political dimension 55–61
    unborn children and 52, 53
Cragg, K. 226
critical faithfulness 179–80, 210, 229
cultural imperialism 213, 236
Curtin, P. 58

Dale, G. 221
Dar al-Harb 67, 68, 72, 77
Dar al-Islam 67, 72, 77
Dar al-Sulkh 67
Da'ud ibn Salm 134
de-colonialist interpretation of jihad 81,
    82, 88
dhimmīs (protected minorities) 2, 198,
    201, 202–3
dialogue 171–3, 237
    with indigenous religion 184–5,
    200–1
    inter-religious xi, xv–xvi, 2, 18, 172,
    179, 184, 210
    self-criticism and 179–80
domestic servants, slaves as 156
dress, Muslim 30, 75, 98
Dupuis, J. 43
Dyula 29, 30, 31, 43, 45–6, 47, 49

Index 259

East Africa 41, 45
  slavery in 117
Egypt
  Arab Muslim invasion 25
  black slaves in 141, 144
El-Awa, M. 226–7
El-Masri, F.H. 107
Elijah Muhammad 212
enclavement 34–5, 38, 39–44, 61
enlightened conservatism 178–9
enslavement *see* Muslim slavery; slavery
Esack, F. 199–200
Ethiopia 25, 30, 39
  Christianity in 39–40
eunuchs, slaves as 159, 161

faith, history as part of 176–7
Fard, Wallace 212
al-Faruqi, Ismail 19, 217, 218, 219–20,
  225
Fisher, A.G.B. 17, 111–12, 118, 119
Fisher, H.J. 8–9, 17, 36–7, 111–12, 118,
  119
flexibility of Islam 7, 9–10, 35, 36
Fulani 14, 47
  jihad 76, 82, 83–4, 88, 90
fundamentalism 12, 13, 189–96

generosity of Islam 9–10
al-Ghamba, Muhammad 63
al-Ghani, Muhammad Abu Talib 78
Ghoraba, H. 125
Ghana 41, 58, 59, 101, 205
  Ahmaddiya Movement 46–7
  Kusasi people 52, 53–4
Gilliland, D.S. 14
Giriama people 52
Guinea 79
Gumi, Mahmud 100, 192–3

Habash 130, 131, 132, 141
al-Hajj Salim Suware 28, 58
Ham, myth of 127–8, 130
Hamman Yajgi 92
Hampâté Bâ, Ahmadou 5, 211, 239–40
Hasan al-Karmi 226
Hausa 26, 77, 82, 90
  conversion to Islam 50

Dan Fodio and 75, 76, 77, 90, 97, 104,
  106
Hausaland, jihad in 75–7, 90, 92, 97
Hiskett, M. 32, 81, 97, 104, 148, 187, 193,
  197
  and jihad 105, 106
  and land ownership 56–7
  and al-Maghīlī 73, 86
  The Sword of Truth 11–12, 13, 15
  history 172–3, 179, 228
  Muslims and 177–8, 204, 206–7
Hollenweger, W.J. 240
Horton, R. 5, 35–6
Hunwick, J.O. 70, 72, 73, 137, 159

Ibadiyya 66
Ibn Abdullah, Rabih 144–5
Ibn Battutah 135–6, 147
Ibn Butlān 156–7, 158
Ibn Hawqal 134
Ibn Khaldun 135, 144, 159
Ibn Misjah, Sa'id 134
Ibn Sina 135
ikhtilat 192–3
inclusive religiosity 51, 53
indigenous environment 8–9, 231, 232
  and conversion to Islam 33–8, 47–55
indigenous slavery 110, 111–14, 116, 121,
  123, 168, 232
institutions, Arabs and 4
intra-Muslim conflict 67, 78–9, 88–91,
  93–4
Iraq, black slaves in 142
Islam 6, 67
  as African religion 4, 34, 211–16
  and African traditions 4, 5, 7, 8, 34–5,
  61, 193–4
  and Arab culture 216–28, 238–9
  contrasted with western Christianity
  7–8, 19
  deviations from 178
  indigenization of 185–9, 211, 224,
  226
  and Muslim history 177–8, 204, 206–7
  non-belief as justification for slavery
  125–8
  pluralistic context 204–7
  Prophetic period 206–8

260 The Legacy of Arab-Islam in Africa

reformulation 205–7, 209
'spread by sword' 68
Islam in Africa Organization 7, 12
Islamization 8, 50, 101, 108
  Africans and 60, 61, 63, 211
  of Arabs 217–18
  jihadist policies 9, 92, 96, 97, 99, 108,
    231
  militant 68–70, 74–80
Ivory Coast 45, 79

al-Jahiz 137, 139
Jakhanke tradition 28–9, 58, 221–2
  slavery and 151, 152, 154
jama'at (religious communities) 27, 28
Jews, campaigns against 70–1
jihad movement xv, 9, 10, 63–4, 65, 231–2
  concept of in Africa 70–4
  conservative revivalism and 190–1
  detraditionalization of 8, 92, 96, 97, 99,
    108, 231
  European intervention 85
  evaluation of 100–7
  interpretation of 10, 11–14, 80–94
  intra-Muslim dimension 67, 78–9,
    88–91, 93–4
  policies towards traditional Africa
    94–100, 220
  reformist tradition 72–3, 86–8, 92–3,
    94, 103
  slavery and 102, 125, 126, 147–9, 150
  Sunni Muslim doctrine of 64–8
  theories and campaigns in Africa
    68–70, 74–80
John Paul II, Pope 184

Kano 194, 195, 202
Kerr, D. 173
Kenya 52, 53
al-Khattab, 'Umar ibn 131, 227
khawarij (seceders) 66, 73
Khilāfah 66
kinship 49
Kopytoff, I. 17, 110, 111, 113–14
kufr (non-belief) 190, 191, 218, 219
  jihad and 73, 95, 96, 125, 231
  as justification for slavery 117, 125,
    126, 233

  see also unbelievers
Küng, H. 172
Kunta 27
Kusasi people 52, 53–4

Lacunza-Balda, J. 223
land 40, 55–7
Lane, E.W. 64–5
Lapidus, I.M. 227
Last, M. 29–30, 81, 100
Launay, R. 196
Lawson, J. 81, 86
leadership
  African 29
  immigrant Muslims and 46
  non-Muslim 192, 194
  see also chiefs; rulers
Levtzion, N. 87, 211
Lewis, B. xii, 131, 132, 160, 176, 198,
  233
Lewis, I.M. 5, 238
liberation theology 3
Limamou Laye, S.M. 185–6
literacy 28, 31, 37, 43, 62
Livingstone, David 143, 167
Longuda 173
Lovejoy, P.E. 114, 116, 119
Ludwig, E. 35
Lugard, Lord 154–5

al-Maghīlī, Abd al-Karim 70–4, 77, 86–7,
  126, 220
Maitatsine movement 186–8
Majid, N. 176, 225
Makar, T. 91
Mali 26, 69, 147
Mande people 26, 28–9
Maraka 120, 151, 163
marriage, colour and rules on 136–8,
  233
Marwa, Mohammadu 186–8
Mauritania 74, 155
Mawdūdī, A.A. 203
Mazrui, Ali 5, 8, 16, 34, 238
Mbiti, J.S. 35, 49–50, 51
Mecca, as centre of slave trade 146
Miers, S. 17, 110, 111, 113–14
Molla, C.F. 224

Monteil, V. 8
Moole-Dagbane people 52, 53
Moosi people 44, 48, 73
  target of slave raids 147
Mouridiyya 29
Muhammad (the Prophet) 131, 188, 192,
  206–7, 208, 226–7
  advised followers to seek asylum in
    Ethiopia 39, 131
  and colour 133
  encounter with non-Muslims 209
  and slaves 141
Muhammad, Akbar 140
Muhammad al-Amin al-Kanimi 76, 77–8,
  93, 149, 227–8
Muhammad Ali 144
Muhammad Bello 76, 89, 103, 104
mujaddid (reformers) 71, 75
Murabitun movement 69
Mūsā, Mansa 69, 146, 147
Muslim itinerant communities see non-
  kin Muslim communities
Muslim divinations 31, 72
Muslim–non-Muslim distinction, in
  pre-European Africa 30, 45
Muslim–non-Muslim relations 94–5,
  96–8, 102, 197–8, 206, 209–10
  antagonism in 196
  Muhammad and 209
  shari'a law and 201–2, 203
  see also non-Muslims
Muslim religious communities, use of
  slave labour 151
Muslim scholarship
  Islam and 177–8
  lack of self-criticism 176–7, 228
Muslim scriptures, non-translatability of
  222–4
Muslim slavery 104, 170, 173–4, 234
  African dimension 147–56
  Arab-Oriental dimension 141–7
  condition of slaves 160–8, 168–9, 233
  and conversion to Islam 159–60
  'humane nature' of 160–1, 162, 166,
    167, 168–9
  ideological basis 118, 121, 122, 124
  institutionalization of 114, 118–19,
    141, 232

interpretations of 10–11, 14–18
  jihad and 102, 147–9, 150
  justifications for 117–18, 124–8, 232,
    233
  roles of slaves 156–60
Muslim traders 26–7, 29–30, 32
  patronage of 41, 43
  and slave trade 150–1

Nachtigal, G. 17, 119, 145
Nafata 50, 75
Nana Osei Kwame 44
Nasir al-Din 74
Nasir al-Din Tusi 135
al-Nasiri 152–3
Nation of Islam 212–13
nationalism 84–5·
Native Authority Ordinance 106
New, C. 167
Niass, Ibrahim 29
Nigeria 7, 41–2, 50, 192, 193
  anti-Islam feeling in 103
  British in 106
  Christians in 13
  fundamental and moderate Muslims in
    13
  jihad in 75–7, 90, 91–2, 97, 103
  patronage on 41–2
  riots in 187, 188
  shari'a law in 12–13, 106, 194–5,
    196–7, 202
  slave population 152
  slaves from 116, 145, 147–9
non-Arab culture 218, 227–8
non-kin Muslim communities 38–9,
  58–9, 61–2, 230
  enclavement 40–4
  hospitality shown to 43–4
  jihad against non-Muslim indigenous
    communities 82–3, 85–6, 89, 91–4
  patronage to 40–1, 42
non-Muslims 87, 190–1
  options after declaration of jihad 66
  political domination of 197–8
  as second-class citizens 98
  shari'a law and 201–2, 203, 236
  see also unbelievers
Nubia 25, 143

262 The Legacy of Arab-Islam in Africa

Nusayb 138
Nyang, S.S. 6, 8, 34, 44, 92, 185, 236, 238

Oosthuizen, G.C. 37
Opoku, K.A. 38
orthodoxy 9, 52, 86, 87, 88, 228, 238, 239
Owusu-Ansah, D. 55, 60–1

past
    critical view of 235, 236
    knowledge of 172–3, 179, 228
    self-justifying myths in post-colonial
        discourses 10–18, 19
patronage 40–2, 43, 75
pilgrimage, slaves and 146
plantation farming, slaves and 158, 163
poetry, images of black people in 130,
    133–4, 138–9
political power 58, 60, 61, 96
politics, religion and 58, 208–9
post-jihad apologia 76–7, 81, 86
prayers 31
prophetic tradition 67, 206–7

Qadiriyya Sufi order 27, 47
Qur'an 124, 187
    in Arabic 217, 218, 221, 222, 225
    and colour 131, 140
    and jihad 65, 68
    on relations with unbelievers 198–9,
        207
    on slavery 124, 125, 161, 162

racial prejudice 16, 128–30, 140, 168, 233
Rahman, F. 176, 198, 205–7, 209
Ramiya 29
Ramiya, Muhammad 188–9
Rasmussen, L. 40, 56
reactionary apologetics 175, 176
realism 227
received tradition xv, 207
reform, African-oriented 185–9
'refusers' 47–8
religion
    African understanding of 35–6, 37–8,
        48–52, 231
    indigenous 51–2, 53, 103, 200–1, 204
    see also Christianity; Islam

religious experts, and introduction of
    Islam to Africa 27–9, 30–2
religious imperialism 99
religious orientation 183–5
religious pluralism 182, 231, 236
Rigby, P.J.A. 41
Roberts, R.L. 151
Robinson, D. xiv, 89, 226
rulers
    indigenous 40–1, 56, 57, 60
    Muslim 92–3, 96–7, 98, 122
    status of land dependent on 77, 96, 194

Samori, Turè 79–80, 84, 150
Sande 195
Sanhaja 25, 69
Sanneh, L. 58, 69, 101, 167, 220, 221, 222
    and conversion 54–5
    and enclavement 34–5, 38
Saudi Arabia, slave population 153
secularism 191–2
Segu 89–90, 152
Senegambia 26, 29, 56–7, 74, 84
    slavery in 120–1, 150, 151–2, 163
Sersen, W.J. 166
Shaltut, M. 68
shari'a 100, 105–6, 108, 194–5
    jihad to enforce 72, 87, 98
    non-Muslims and 201–2, 203, 236
Shaw, F.L. 106, 120
Sierra Leone 101, 195
slave labour 151
slave raids 94, 114, 119, 121, 122, 142,
    144, 148–9
slave trade 115–16, 119, 142–3, 145–6
slavery 14, 16, 113, 174–5
    abolition of 120, 152, 153–4
    as blessing in disguise 127–8
    domestic 15, 113
    in non-Muslim Africa 110–11, 112–13,
        118, 119, 121–2, 153–4
    transformation of 110, 111, 115–17,
        121–3
    see also Muslim slavery; slaves
slaves
    birth/death rates of 164
    concentration of 119, 120–1, 151–2
    condition of 160–8, 168–9, 233

Index 263

manumission of 165, 166
revolts of 164
roles of in Muslim lands 156–60
women 156–7
Smith, H.F.C. 81
Smith, M.G. 80
Sokoto caliphate 76, 89, 91, 96, 103, 106
slave society 15, 16, 147–9, 152
soldiers, slaves as 158
Songhay 69
Sonni Ali 69, 72
Sonninke people 26
South Africa 192
Christians converting to Islam 6
Sudan 31, 70, 76, 89–90, 215
Arab invasion 25, 26
jihad in 82, 232
patronage in 41
resentment towards Islam 174
slave population 151, 155
slaves from 143–4
Sufism 29, 47, 65
Suhaym 137, 138
Sulaiman, Ibraheem 16, 82, 100, 191–2, 197
and African customs 8, 193–4
and unbelievers 190–1, 204
Sunni Muslim 208, 209
and jihad 64–8, 86, 87
Supreme Being 35–6, 37
Swann, A.J. 142
Swidler, L. 179, 237

al-Tabari 162
Taha, M.M. 199, 200
tajdid 72–3, 87
Tanner, R.E.S. 48
Tanzania 46
tariffs 57
taxation 72, 103–4
Tcherno Aliou 154
Thomas, H. 110
Tijaniyya 29, 47
Timbuktu 69–70
Tippu-Tib 142
tolerance 34, 39–40, 228, 238
trading networks 29–30
see also Muslim traders; slave trade

tradition 176–7, 179
critical assessment of 178–80
traditional culture, Islam and 4, 5, 7, 8, 34–5, 61, 193–4
translation 222–4, 225
Trimingham, J.S. 14–15, 43, 47, 55, 60, 62, 83
triple heritage 181
trust 173
Tutu, Desmond 183

Uchendu, V.C. 116
Umar Ibrahim Kabo 202
Umar Tal, al-Hajj 78–9, 84, 89, 96, 150
Umaru Nagwamatse 148
umma (community) 239–40
unbelievers 78, 86, 94, 107
categories of 72
jihad against 92–3, 95, 96
al-Maghīlī and 71, 73, 87
non-Muslims as 87, 190–1
see also kufr
Uthman dan Fodio 11, 50, 87, 98, 103, 106–7, 211
and Hausa rulers 75, 76, 77, 90, 97, 104
influence of 12, 75
jihad of 75, 76, 92–3
al-Maghīlī's influence on 77, 86
and unbelievers 86, 92–3, 95, 96

violence 103

Wahhābiyyah Movement 190
Wahid, A. 178, 202–3, 209
Wallace, William 120
washenzi (savages) 46
Western scholarship 94
Muslim reactions to 174–6
Williams, R.R. 239
Willis, J.R. 126
Wolof 50, 186
women 192–3
slaves 156–7

Yandoto 76, 83
Yarse 48
Yoruba 26, 193
Yunfa 75, 76

Zamfara 194, 202
Zanj 139, 142
   treatment of, as slaves 162–3
Zanzibar, slaves in 120, 143, 152, 154, 164

Zimbabwe 27
Zoghby, S.M. 18
zongos (strangers' quarters) 41, 48